UNDERSTANDING THE *FRENCH REVOLUTION*

UNDERSTANDING THE *FRENCH REVOLUTION*

by Albert Soboul

INTERNATIONAL PUBLISHERS, New York

Translation by April Ane Knutson

1st printing, 1988
Manufactured in the United States of America

Library of Congress Cataloging-in-Publication Data

Soboul, Albert.
Understanding the French Revolution.

Translation of: Comprendre la Révolution.
Bibliography: p.
1. France—History—Revolution, 1789-1797.
I. Title.
DC143.S713 1988 944.04 88-1215
ISBN-0-7178-0658-8 (pbk.)

CONTENTS

Foreword

This compilation of writings of Albert Soboul, published in the year before his death, is a fascinating, masterful presentation of various aspects of the great French Revolution, which began when the people of Paris stormed the hated Bastille prison on July 14, 1789. It ended more than ten years later with Napoleon's coup d'état on November 9, 1799 (18th brumaire).

Soboul does not give us a chronological, blow-by-blow account of the Revolution that marked the end of the *ancien regime* and the beginning of modern European history. Rather, Soboul probes a series of political and social problems, stimulating us to consider, or reconsider, the enormous complexity of the dialectical movement of the French Revolution—and of all revolutionary change.

These essays encourage us to re-think much of what we thought we knew about the French Revolution. By presenting much new data and illuminating many paths of inquiry, Soboul argues persuasively that the Revolution was a very complex process, joined by many social categories with vastly different goals and needs. Amateur historians, students—all lovers of a good tale—will enjoy Soboul's handling of the revolutionary process and his moving sketches of its key participants. Professional historians will be further inspired to research economic and social issues on the plane that Soboul so deftly delineates.

All readers will gain a new understanding of the conditions leading to the Revolution and of the various attempts by different factions of the rising bourgeoisie to forge a society that would allow capitalism to fully develop, yet placate and contain the just grievances of the angry multitudes—the artisan-workers and peasants.

Each chapter focuses on a single aspect or question; readers are encouraged to explore, perhaps reading first the chapters of most immediate personal interest.

Chapter one is a quite condensed philosophical summary that assumes some knowledge of the Enlightenment philosophers. Chapter two is especially rich in background information for the selections that follow. Here and in succeeding chapters we are immersed in developing class struggles and popular democracy, and the problems of the revolutionary state. Soboul captures the ferocity of the struggles in the streets and the radical nature of the democratic procedures instituted in the neighborhood assemblies.

Chapters six and seven are a detailed look at the questions around work and wages during the revolutionary period.

Soboul provides copious notes with each chapter. Notes that refer to archives in the National Library in Paris are of little immediate use to most American readers. But others refer to standard works on the French revolution and to the classics of Marx, Engels and Lenin, readily available in English. Still other notes enrich the content of this work on the forces that moved the revolution forward and those that braked its egalitarian thrust. Some notes pose additional questions about the revolutionary process or ideology.

Chapter eight has the most extensive notes. Here Soboul gives data on the occupations of all subscribers to Babeuf's *Tribun du peuple* and of all those arrested with Babeuf in the spring of 1796, as well as in the attempted takeover of the Grenelle Camp in the early summer of the same year. Soboul is interested not only in the jobs of the Babouvists but in discovering how many of them had been active in community politics (particularly in the sectional assemblies) in the most democratic year of the Revolution, year II (Sept. 22, 1793 to September 21, 1794). He concludes that the overlap is not as large as might have been expected, and suggests that the Conspiracy for Equality led by Babeuf had some weaknesses in its methods of forging essential links with the popular masses.

François-Noël Babeuf was born and educated in rural France, in the Picardy region. His first job was as clerk for a land commissioner, an expert hired by a feudal lord to research all the ancient and current economic rights that the lord held over the peasants, in order to reclaim the old aristocratic rights lost to the central state during the reign of Louis XIV. Babeuf would later write in his newspaper, *Le Tribun du peuple*, that it was "in the dust of the feudal archives that I discovered the mysteries of the usurpations of the noble caste." Babeuf's revolutionary program called for an end to inheritance of property and an absolutely equal distribution of the land. After leading numerous struggles for peasants' rights in Picardy, Babeuf was imprisoned in Paris in 1790, but won release through the efforts of Marat, among others. Appointed administrator of the Montdidier district by the Directory, he was again threatened with imprisonment after attempting to distribute national lands to poor peasants. Returning to Paris, he worked in the food distribution administration and foresaw the possibility of mass starvation in Paris. He began to formulate a program linking the interests of the peasants with those of the urban poor. In the autumn of 1794, he launched the *Tribun du peuple*, outlining his program for equality and calling for insurrection.

The struggles of Babeuf and "the Equals" is significant as the last act of the popular movement during the French Revolution, and as the harbinger of the Paris Commune, and the later struggles for socialism in the 20th century.

*

Soboul chronicles the extraordinary behavior of the people of Paris and those in various French provinces as they conducted the revolution. The chapter, "Patriot Saints and Martyrs of Liberty," describes the bizarre rituals developed by peasant rebels and Parisian sans-culottes to honor slain heroes and heroines of the revolution. Soboul asks his readers to consider the possibility that these cults replaced what he calls the "traditional cult" (i.e., Catholicism) in the hearts of a fundamentally religious people who had thrown themselves into a revolutionary upheaval.

Chapter 11 is the only one in this book that had not been published previously in a French historical or philosophical journal. We are reminded that women participated in both direct action in the streets and in electoral politics in the assemblies. Women claimed and exercised these "rights" in years I and II. After the thermidorian reaction (July 1794), women were forced back to their "natural sphere"—home and children. French women did not vote again until after World War II.

In chapters 12 and 13 Soboul examines the question of regional identities and the process of creating a modern *nation.* Early in chapter 13, he paints for us the famous tableau of the 1792 battle of Valmy where the French rallied to the cry, "Vive la Nation!" and turned back the Prussian advance on Paris. Soboul recounts that Goethe witnessed the historic rally and proclaimed, "On this day and at this place begins a new era in world history."

*

While associating the American Revolution with earlier upheavals in Europe that ended in compromise to maintain the dominance of private wealth, Soboul singles out our revolution for special comment:

> ...it was in the name of the theory of free contract that they [the American colonies] justified their secession, and their Declarations proclaimed the rights of man, not just those of Americans—universalism of natural right appeared in public law. It is not possible, however, to conceal the flagrant contradictions that marked the application of the principles so solemnly proclaimed. The Blacks remained slaves. And, if equality of rights was admitted between whites, the social hierarchy founded on wealth did not suffer any blows.

Herbert Aptheker, a foremost American Marxist historian, has similarly characterized our American Revolution. He and Soboul also agree in their affirmation that a *majority* of the people participate in revolutionary upheaval. On the American Revolution, Aptheker asserts:

> ...we deny the proposition—assertedly "the rule of history"... that revolutions are minority efforts. On the contrary, we think there is nothing more democratic than a revolutionary movement and we believe that the success of such a movement can be explained to a decisive degree on the basis of its representing the desires of the overwhelming majority of the inhabitants of the society being revolutionized. We say this because of the immense power ordinarily held by the vested interests against whom the revolutionary movement is directed, as well as because of the normal inertia afflicting people in terms of acting outside of the ordinary routine—and certainly revolutionary conduct is extraordinary behavior, involving enormous risks and burdens.*

Soboul frequently cites Alexis de Tocqueville, known to many American readers for his study, *Democracy in America.* In a note to chapter 16, Soboul quotes the rhetorical questions asked by de Tocqueville in the introduction to that work, written in 1836: "Would it be wise to believe that a social movement that has come so far will be suspended by the efforts of a generation? Do people think that after having destroyed feudalism and kings, democracy will retreat before the bourgeois and the rich?"

These questions echo over the past 150 years of battles waged and victories won; over the struggles in our own time, and those yet to come.

April Ane Knutson

---

*Herbert Aptheker, *The American Revolution, 1763-1783* (New York: International Publishers, 1960), p. 55

UNDERSTANDING THE *FRENCH REVOLUTION*

1

Reform or Revolution? On the historical function of enlightened absolutism[1]

In the second half of the century of Enlightenment, absolutism reigned over most of Europe with diverse nuances from one country to another, and the philosophers celebrated the merits of the enlightened monarchs. "Philosopher kings" or "enlightened monarchs": these expressions recognize the ascendancy of philosophy over power. As for the expression "enlightened despotism," no one in that epoch used it. An invention of German historians of the middle of the 19th century and for a long time in current usage in historiography, it is today being replaced by the preferred term "enlightened absolutism." Enlightened despotism: the coupling of these two words would have horrified the philosophers who would have, without a doubt, rejected the expression because of its contradiction and incompatibility with the spirit of Enlightenment. Despotism: the word, which appeared in 1699 in *Télémaque* by Fenelon, is applied particularly, according to Montesquieu, to Asiatic monarchies. Let us recall however that the physiocrat Mercier de La Rivière, in *L'Ordre naturel et essentiel des sociétés politiques* (1767), contrasts legal despotism founded on knowledge of natural law with necessarily arbitrary despotism, such as the "ministerial despotism" so often denounced in France at the end of the *Ancien Régime* [the old order: feudal, monarchic France before the Revolution].

In fact, and despite the bitterness of the struggles between the monarch and the nobility, the State of the Ancien Régime remained that of an aristocracy. Divine right traditionally associating the throne and the altar, the Church propped up the State. Would the monarchs have yielded to the cultural ambiance of the century? Would they have ceded to the optimism of the philosophers, to the belief in progress and the perfectibility of human societies? Here it is necessary to go beyond the traditional concept of the history of ideas, which envisages ideas in themselves and in their relations to each other, without worrying about researching their connections with the general history of the time, including economic and social facts. The ideology of enlightened absolutism could not be developed, except in the general ideological field, and also in relation to social structures that supported it and were reflected in it. Its motor: the monarchs and philosophers, concrete individuals, and real history reflecting itself in them, following the complex ties of the individual to history.

I

Enlightened absolutism: in the thought of the philosophers and the physiocrats, the expression did not assume the same sense as in the practice of the sovereigns; the concept still remains obscure today.

The philosophers, stretching the conquests of modern rationalism of which Descartes had been the initiator in the preceding century, began to think that economy, society and politics were comprised, like nature, of rules that it was important to know in order to bring about reform. Let us recall here L'*Esprit des lois*: "I do not treat laws," writes Montesquieu, "but the spirit of laws ... This spirit consists of the various connections that laws may have with various things." (I,3.) The laws brought to light by the philosophers will permit the monarch to correct human laws; political science runs into the work of the legislator. "Law in general is human reason, inasmuch as it governs all the peoples of the earth; and the political and civil laws of each nation must be only particular cases where this human reason is applied." (I,3.) Montesquieu is intending to disengage the real laws of human societies from the apparent laws which they give themselves, in order to denounce their vices and correct them. The fundamental maxim of Cartesian rationalism—"Know the world in order to be in a position to change it"—here took on its full meaning.

It follows that the freedom of research and criticism are necessary. The philosopher "does not dazzle people with words," one reads in the *Encyclopédie*; and, in the article "Eclectisme": "the eclectic is a philosopher who, trampling underfoot prejudices, tradition, ancientness, universal accord, authority, in a word all that subjugates the crowd of minds, dares to think for himself." The object of the critical reflection of the philosopher is man and society; he devotes himself to economy, law, politics, posing the foundations of a new science. This general questioning was going in the direction of the interests of the new bourgeoisie who, in the name of social utility, was criticizing mercantilism as well as monarchical arbitrariness. The philosophy of the Enlightenment finally provided the bourgeoisie with a system of thought which, contributing to the awakening of its class consciousness, led to an efficient social praxis. Tolerance and respect for the person, abolition of privilege; civil equality, upward mobility in society and the State for everyone on the basis of talent alone; abolition of serfdom and mobility of the land; "laissez faire, laissez passer": individual initiative and the taste for profit could only multiply wealth and bring civilization to its highest point.

And now the means to these reforms. The English revolutions of the 17th century presented a model. No one among the philosophers, however, not even Montesquieu who nevertheless praised them, dreamed of recommending the adoption of political institutions and a constitutional regime following the English model. Nor did anyone, until Rousseau, dream of invoking natural law and the social contract to reform society and the State. It was enough to appeal to the authority of the monarch, alone capable of imposing desirable reforms on his ignorant and routine-minded subjects, because he alone held the necessary authority. Yet if he listened to the philosophers, he must necessarily adapt himself to the natural laws that they had discovered and to the conclusions that conformed to reason. It was necessary, in a word, that absolutism be *enlightened.* "We must agree that some very wise men, perhaps very worthy of governing, have written on the administration of the States, either in France, Spain, or England. Their books," according to Voltaire in the article "États, Gouvernements" of the *Dictionnaire philosophique*, "have done much good .... These good books form young men destined for high places; they form princes."

These lines evoke the image of the philosopher king sketched by Plato in *The Republic* and which, from Voltaire to Rousseau, inspired the political thought of the century.[2] Already in *Télémaque*, Fenelon had insisted on the necessary education of kings for the progress of the society and the State. This idea traversed the whole century, from the *Lettres philosophiques* of Voltaire to the *Discours sur les sciences et les arts* of Rousseau, to the *Essai sur la société des gens de lettres* of d'Alembert, to the article "Luxe" of the *Encyclopédie* attributed to Diderot. In Voltaire, this Platonic idea that philosophers should be the instructors of princes led to the concept of the enlightened despot: aided by the enlightenment of philosophy, the absolute monarch is alone capable of realizing the necessary reforms. In *A.B.C.* written at the end of his life, the patriarch of Ferney had an Englishman say: "Do you take so little account of the fact that there are today philosophers on the throne, in Berlin, in Sweden, in Poland, in Russia?"

Subordinated to social utility, submitted to the law, the monarch would no longer be the proprietor of his kingdom, but the first servant of the national community. The 1798 edition of the *Dictionnaire* of the Academy, which essentially represents the text elaborated between 1762 and 1792, specifies in the article "Peuple" that in speaking to a prince the formula *vos peuples* signifies not "that the people are his property, but that they are the object of his care." This notion responded to the situation of the States of continental Europe where, with the exception of the United Provinces, the bourgeoisie, excluded from power and most often confined to a subordinate position, was becoming aware of its power, without yet having the audacity to use it to emancipate itself.

As for the monarchs, the enlightened absolutism of the philosophers allowed them new means to increase the wealth and the power of their States. Concerned also with effectiveness, the "enlightened despots" strove for a rationalization of the State which would have reinforced their power. Royal power, although theoretically absolute, was limited by aristocratic privilege, provincial and municipal autonomy, and an imperfect centralization still incapable of organizing a complex administration created without an overall plan, under the weight of historical circumstances. In this sense, enlightened absolutism is inscribed in the line of the monarchic absolutism of the preceding century: reinforcement of the State in a national territorial framework; economic expansion under the protection of the State itself which thus found the means of developing its administrative structure and its military power; development of commercial capitalism in the hands of a bourgeoisie who in turn furnished administrators and financiers to the monarchic authority.

All these traits already characterized the absolute monarchy of Louis XIV. It is toward that reign that the enlightened monarchs lifted their eyes, while appearing to listen to the advice of the philosophers; it is that reign that they retained for a model, like Versailles for their castles, in order to arrive at the summit of power. They drew inspiration from a past that had proven itself, rather than imitating a society and a State for which the philosophers were sketching an ideal model. Frederick II was very little concerned with Montesquieu or Voltaire when he was working to amass resources and to assemble under his authority all the forces necessary for his political ambitions. Everywhere these sovereigns played Louis XIV's [1643-1715]* game: consolidate the State by putting at its service all the economic resources—a good portion of which were destined for war—an old instrument of monarchic prestige. In order to succeed, they stimulated economic progress pushed ahead by their reforms. They pretended that the fate of their subjects was their principal concern, while they were dreaming only of increasing their power.

Is this to say that the Sun King would have been the first of the "enlightened despots"? No, doubtless the arbitrary power of the monarch often

*Soboul's added comments or explanations have been placed in parentheses throughout. The translator's are in brackets.

served his personal aims rather than the interest of the State. If Voltaire glorified *Le siècle de Louis XIV*, if he went so far as to affirm in his introduction that this century was "the most enlightened that ever was," the wastefulness of the court, the magnificent constructions, the wars of prestige, the disastrous consequences of the revocation of the Edict of Nantes gave rise to critical reflection: this was not the image of the ideal king of Salente that Fenelon had sketched in *Télémaque*.

If on the whole the governmental practice of the century of Enlightenment did not thus differ essentially from that of the century of Louis XIV, it nevertheless adapted itself to new concepts advanced by social and economic evolution. In Prussia, at mid-century, the *Aufklarung* became the philosophy of civil servants, pastors and professors. But taught by Lutheranism to obey temporal powers, paid by the prince, deprived of the support of a vigorous bourgeoisie, they adjusted rationalism to the policies that the natural conditions and the historical circumstances had imposed on the Hohenzollern: it was less a matter of reforming society than of improving and strengthening the State. In the Russia of the Romanovs, it was still necessary to form the State. This situation is affirmed in the reforms of Catherine II, which perfected the administration and accentuated political centralization. In her Instruction to the commission charged with drawing up a plan for a new code of laws (the famous *Nakaz*), Catherine II developed the concept of an absolute monarchy founded on fundamental laws and protected from personal arbitrariness. But she was interpreting these principles borrowed from Montesquieu in a strictly bureaucratic spirit: intermediate bodies and authorities, barriers against despotism, would be created by the monarch himself and would remain subordinate to him. By "enlightening" itself, absolutism tried its best, with some success, to reinforce the power of the State without changing the social foundations. The question was not to bring legislation in accordance with natural law, even if that was referred to. The sovereigns' efforts to constrain the aristocracy were not meant to equate that class to the Third Estate.

The enlightened monarchs thus endeavored to set up a centralized administration and an effective bureaucracy, they practiced a strict mercantilism, they hastened the formation of modern armies. They reached their goal: fill their treasuries, reinforce their military power, acquire territories.

It is appropriate to add that the work of the enlightened sovereigns also contributed to the diffusion of other elements of the civilization that had been developed in Western Europe, to the constitution of an aristocratic cosmopolitanism where the language, letters, arts and fashions of France were generally assured preference. The enlightened monarchs were proof of a refined taste for matters of the mind, without worrying about getting these through to the masses. Most often reduced to utilitarian precepts by the *Aufklarung*, the *Lumières* served as a justification in the eyes of public opinion, as the enlightened monarchs were praised unreservedly by the philosophers. Concerned above all about intellectual liberty, the latter appreciated the religious tolerance, the relative freedom accorded to philosophic reflection and scientific research. In *La Princesse de Babylone* (1768), Voltaire wrote this commendation of Catherine II: "The first of her laws has been the tolerance of all religions ... Her powerful genius knew that if cults are different, morality is everywhere the same."

In fact, enlightened declarations and good intentions were for the sovereigns mere games of wit and propaganda, as the growth of their power was their essential preoccupation. The praise of the philosophers and the favor of public opinion served their interests. Endeavoring with a mediocre success to indoctrinate the sovereigns and to tear to pieces the Catholic clergy, the philosophers did not realize that for Frederick II and Catherine II, who headed national churches separated from Catholicism, tolerance was a more comfortable policy. Historical tradition and desire for power regulated the conduct of the "enlightened" sovereigns, more than the doctrine of the philosophers and a concern for humanity.

In d'Holbach's *Examen sur l' "Essai sur les préjugés"* (1770), Frederick II underlines the dangers that must be avoided by anyone who aspires to the title of philosopher. "His voice will not serve as a trumpet to sedition, as a rallying signal to the malcontents, as a pretext to rebellion; he will respect the usages established and authorized by the nation, the government, those who comprise it and those who depend on it." Thus were fixed the limits that the interests of absolutism imposed on the alliance with philosophy. In a letter of October 27, 1772, this same Frederick II mocked philosophers, theoreticians and encyclopedic legislators who, never having governed, amused themselves by constructing States where they placed men of fantasy. Again in 1779, in his *Lettres sur l'amour de la patrie*, Frederick II is annoyed with the Encyclopedists whose ideas "lead to the dissolution of the social union, by unfeelingly uprooting from the minds of the citizens the zeal and attachment they owe to their country."

One can see the contradictions in the relations between monarchs and philosophers, between the mind and political power. Frederick II had granted asylum to the persecuted La Mettrie, yet he instructed the governor charged to receive Rousseau in Prussian territory to "prevent him as much as possible from writing." Rousseau, for his part, could not admire "a man without principles, who began his Machiavellianism by refuting Machiavelli." Rousseau refused, with justification, to distinguish between "the king of Prussia and the philosopher of Sans-Souci."

Beyond the contradictory conceptions, however, that philosophers and sovereigns derived from the enlightened policies of monarchic power, it is appropriate to specify the historical function of enlightened absolutism. This system has often been opposed to the French Revolution in order to conclude that the abrupt mutation brought about by the latter was not necessary, the former having obtained the same results. Would the reformism of the enlightened monarchs really have made the economy of a revolution? Once again it is appropriate to examine the social foundations of the one and the other.

II

The theory of absolutism, as it was outlined in the 16th century, affirmed in the 17th and inscribed in the policy of sovereigns in the 18th, in no way corresponded—whatever may have been said—to a state of equilibrium between bourgeoisie and aristocracy. Doubtless the policy of enlightened absolutism favored in a certain sense the growth of the bourgeoisie by the protection accorded to nascent capitalism, as by the creation of frameworks necessary for the administration of the State. One could say of the enlightened monarchs that they were in the process of incorporating the bourgeoisie and elements of capitalism into the old order (embourgeoisaient l'Ancien Régime) Yet at the same time, they braked the rapid expansion of the bourgeoisie by the maintenance of traditional social structures and control of productive activities. In fact, in considering the classical period of monarchic absolutism, that of Frederick II or Catherine II, it is necessary to state that behind the facade of a theoretically absolute authority, the privileges of the nobility were safeguarded, seigniorial exploitation maintained, and aristocratic society stabilized for a time. Such guarantees no doubt contributed, as much as did fear, to the new docility of the European nobility: docility toward a conservative authority incarnate in the person of the sovereign. The monarchies of central and western Europe in fact abandoned the peasantry to the advances of aristocratic social reaction. A century later, the government of Catherine II, like that of Louis XIV, showed the same severity toward peasant insurrections; both favored a seigniorial reorganization which gravely damaged peasant interests.

Enlightened despotism finally found its chosen domain in the monarchies of central and eastern Europe, among scattered populations of peasants in bondage, small-scale artisans, bourgeoisies concentrated in ports or in several towns noted for their fairs, dominant aristocracies whose social authority remained intact when it was not strengthened. The social policies of a Frederick II or a Catherine II proved to be even more conservative and aristocratic than those of the sovereigns of western Europe.

Throughout Europe the aristocracy was thus maintained in a state of juridic superiority relative to the bourgeois categories. But in western Europe, if the aristocracy was privileged, the peasants were not unconditionally abandoned. In Prussia and Russia the landed property remained as a rule the monopoly of the nobility; it was about the same for all the high administrative and military offices. Conceiving of the social structure in the same way as the sovereigns of western Europe, the enlightened monarchs judged the nobility likely to furnish the best auxiliaries to the absolutist monarchy. Peter the Great, by the *tchin*, had forced the aristocracy into the service of the State. Frederick II thought that his officers should as a matter of course belong to the nobility; he left it a certain degree of administrative autonomy; nobility reigned over the provincial States. Catherine II handled the nobility even more carefully, ending by giving it, in 1785, a charter which established it as a body in each government, with elected assemblies and officers and special courts.

Looking more closely at the policies of Catherine II,[3] they appear characteristic of an aristocratic state capable of a certain modernization, imposed by the imperatives of the epoch, in the domains of administration, justice, education and culture, partially in the economic and social domain, to the degree that this modernization did not affect the foundations of the system but instead contributed to its adaptation to new historical conditions. It is in the framework of a still-feudal Russia that the enlightened absolutism of Catherine II encouraged the development of capitalism and a certain bourgeoisie. But if this policy was sometimes affirmed counter to the claims of powerful factions of the nobility, it nevertheless kept in view the general interests of the nobility as a whole and the political and economic consolidation of the nobiliary State.

The bourgeoisie remained in a strictly subordinate condition. While in western and southern Europe the bourgeoisie could acquire some lands, seigniories and fiefs, and even in France some posts leading to ennoblement, in Prussia as in Russia, the bourgeoisie could not buy lands without authorization; ennoblement, while not impossible, rarely occurred; the venality of charges did not exist. The most important grievances were without a doubt economic. If the capitalist entrepreneur felt favored by protectionism, the spirit of initiative was braked, and not only by regulations. In Prussia, to make the perception of the *accise* [excise tax] more favorable, the king forbade the manufacture and trade of taxed products outside the towns. In Russia, the peasants being serfs of the crown or the lords, the bourgeois could not employ them without authorization. Now in western Europe, it was through the exploitation of the rural worker, paid less and exempt from corporative control, that scattered manufacturing and commercial capitalism were developed. By shackling the expansion of rural industry, the enlightened monarchs, doubtless unconsciously, compromised the success of their policy of economic development and slowed down the rise of the bourgeoisie.

The most characteristic trait of the collusion of enlightened monarchs and the aristocracy was nevertheless the increased enslavement of the peasantry. Whatever the reforms may have been, enlightened absolutism did not eliminate the foundations of the second serfdom in central and eastern Europe. In Russia, it consolidated them. In Prussia, if Frederick II abolished the *Leibeigenschaft*—serfdom, properly speaking—and authorized the fixing of the forced labor, the *corvée,* and even its repurchase, and regulated taxes, he was careful not to interfere in the economy of the seigniorial domain. The peasant remained a subject under seigniorial jurisdiction; the lord had the right at his discretion to inflict corporal punishment; the king collected taxes through the nobility. In Russia, the discretionary power of the lord was even worse than in Prussia; he could detach the serf from the land, deport him, sell him; the serf had no access to the state tribunals. To her favorites Catherine II distributed numbers of peasants coming from the nationalized lands of the clergy or taken from the crown's estates, where they supposedly received better treatment; she introduced serfdom in the Ukraine. It is during her reign that the system of serfdom was established in its most severe form.

That compromise with the aristocracy was for enlightened absolutism the very condition of its existence is shown by the endeavor of Joseph II in his hereditary States and even more in Hungary.[4] The Hapsburg monarchy participated in the Germanic culture; the *Aufklarung* enlightened its officials, who were also affected by the teaching of the physiocrats and the English economists. Joseph II and Leopold II remained good Catholics and distrusted the philosophers, particularly Voltaire, whom Joseph II did not want to see during his trip to France. Yet they were doubtless the only monarchs of the period who truly merited the term *enlightened*: in their innovative boldness, they did not hesitate to attack the very structures of the aristocratic society of the Ancien Régime. Sketched from the period of Maria-Theresa, in particular in the program elaborated in 1761 by Chancelor Kaunitz, the system which carries the name of Joseph II was inspired by the German natural law and reflected the French and Italian experiences: it was liable to break apart the framework of persistent feudal structures. With implacable obstinacy, Joseph II was not content with suppressing nobiliary autonomy by eliminating the provincial States and especially, in Hungary, the cooperation of the *comitats* and the aristocratic Tables. He abolished serfdom in the domains of the nobility, as well as in his own; he ordered the fixing of the *corvée* and fees; authorized, then made obligatory, their commutation to legal tender. Finally in 1789, he reorganized the land tax and dared to fix the tenant's percentage of net revenue that the seigniorial fees could not surpass: 70% to the tenant, 12.33% to the State, 17.67% to the lord. This was too much. The feudal lords took the lead in the resistance. A general coalition joined together against Joseph II, principally in Hungary, owing to the war against the Turks begun in 1787; the coalition provoked the failure of the monarchy. The financial reform was abandoned. In the course of the reaction that followed the death of Joseph II, the reestablishment of the seigniory with all its prerogatives marked the failure of enlightened absolutism and the triumph of the aristocracy.

In considering the Spain of Charles III, Pierre Vilar has qualified his enlightened despotism as a homeopathic precaution against bourgeois revolution; instinctive mediation, he specifies, not conscious, except perhaps for the Count Aranda, "a sharp political genius more than a simple disciple of the philosophers."[5] But nobiliary privileges and prejudices persisted in Spain, profiting diverse nobilities; the feudal system, in all its social and regional complexity persisted all the more. As for the nascent, but purely local bourgeoisie, the exceptional prosperity brought by the colonies during the years 1750-1792 assured too many satisfactions for it to feel revolutionary. If the Spain of Charles III was indeed the time of reforms, it was also the time of resistance of threatened traditions. The forces of conservation finally carried the day.

It went the same way in Italy[6] where enlightened sovereigns and ministers, however, had favored an undeniable economic expansion and the development of social classes involved in this movement, and who from that time exerted pressure to obtain the suppresssion of the constraints of the old system of privileges, of monopolies and of the regulating interference of the State. But it remained no less a regime that was still for the most part feudal. If there was, in the Tuscany of Leopold in particular, agreement between the principal defenders of enlightened reformism and the reformist will of the prince, this understanding and this will collided with the basic structures of a society where the aristocracy dominated: they could not be overwhelmed by enlightened princes consubstantially tied to these structures and this aristocracy. Landed property, the foundation of the system, still remained aristocratic for the most part, and anyway was conditioned by the nobiliary preponderance and the feudal relics. Thus the limited character, as if halted in midstream, of the most characteristic economic reforms of the Italian enlightened absolutism, of the mortmain in the seigniorial jurisdictions, of the trust in the rural areas, and this even in the States most advanced in innovative policies, like Tuscany.

These limits that the structure of the society and the state imposed on enlightened absolutism were affirmed again in the consequences of the resounding work of Beccaria, *Des délits et des peines* (1764). If it was welcomed in Italy, as in all of Europe, with enthusiasm, it had from the beginning no practical consequence, even in the Lombardy of the Hapsburgs where it had been conceived and where philosophic ardor was going to be used up in a shortsighted bureaucratic reformism. In 1786, only, "criminal reform" decreed in Tuscany by Leopold effected the principles of Beccaria. But, if this enlightened prince was able to promulgate a code of an astonishing modernity, he had to renounce the elaboration of a constitution which foresaw the election of a national representation. Enlightened absolutism, as advanced as it was, could not negate its absolutist nature and overturn, in the name of the *Lumières*, the foundations and structures of power.

A proof to the contrary is the atypical case of Denmark.[7] Twice in the second half of the 18th century, the Danish government assumed the reforming role that enlightened absolutism assigned to the ideal government: at the time of Struensee's aborted endeavor, and even more during the years following the coup d'état of 1784. Imposed by enlightened ministers, the agrarian reforms, by radically transforming the conditions of property, of persons and production, constituted a juridicial, social and economic revolution from above. In comparison with the Prussian reforms and the attempts of Joseph II on one hand, with the French Revolution of the other, the Danish case goes up in value as an example: enlightened absolutism here knew how to respond to essential social exigencies by initiating a policy of a radical change in structure which profoundly affected the position and the interests of the landed aristocracy, to the benefit of the peasantry and the urban bourgeoisie. Danish absolutism, tempered by the consultative assemblies in the 1830's, lasted until the Constitution of 1849. The reforms imposed from above in the course of the period from 1784 to 1800 nonetheless marked the Danish way of passage from feudalism to capitalism.

At the end of this sketch, we should attempt a typology that would account for all the nuances flowing from the social structures at the different stages of historical evolution, essentially the more or less great force of resistance of late feudalism and the more or less advanced degree of decomposition of the feudal system under the impact of new economic and social forces. It would also be appropriate to distinguish the different conditions of development of enlightened absolutism for the great powers (Prussia, Russia, Austria) and for the less important states. The latter had two variants: one, a royal government like the Spain of Charles II, or following a bid for power, the Sweden of Gustave III; the other, a government by prime minister like that of Pombal in Portugal or of Struensee and Bernstorff in Denmark.

But whatever the variants of enlightened absolutism across Europe in the second half of the 18th century may have been, we cannot doubt the nature of the system: the enlightened monarchs could not, without undermining the very foundations of their absolutism, attack the bases of the society of the Ancien Régime, aristocratic privilege and feudal structures. The case of Denmark proves it, where the destruction of the Ancien Régime was imposed from above, even more than that of France, where it occurred from below.

III

The course of the French Revolution was completely different from that of enlightened absolutism. If one stresses the rationalization of the state to define enlightened absolutism as H. Pirenne does, then the Revolution only completed the work of the monarchy and its enlightened ministers. Let us note, however, that the great monarchic achievement, national unity, remained incomplete. Challenging the structure of a society founded on aristocratic privilege was the very negation of national unity.

Some have insisted on the importance of the reforms undertaken by the enlightened ministers and have been astonished by their failure. The "disgrace" of Turgot (May 12, 1776) would be due essentially to the weakness of Louis XVI [1774-1792], to the monarch's inability to arbitrate.[8] But how could the liberal reforms, thus undertaken, have succeeded, as long as the feudal structures and aristocratic privilege persisted? However enlightened, this minister, just like the monarchs of central and eastern Europe, never intended to touch those structures. As for the capacity of the king of France for arbitration and reform, this was limited by the very nature of the monarchic State, the state of the aristocracy. This is illustrated by the declaration of Louis XVI at the time of the royal session of June 23, 1789: "The King wishes that the ancient distinction of the three orders of the State be conserved in its entirety, as essentially tied to the constitution of his kingdom" (first article). Aristocratic privilege was thus maintained. "All property without exception will be constantly respected and His Majesty expressly includes under the names of property the feudal and seigniorial tithes, quota of taxes, rents, rights and duties and generally all the rights and prerogatives, useful or honorific, attached to the lands or the fiefs, or belonging to persons" (article 12 of the *Déclaration des intentions du Roi*). Feudalism was thus maintained.[9] We know what came of that. Enlightened reformism could only fail because it did not touch, no more than enlightened absolutism, the basic structures of the traditional economy and society.

Following the enlightened ministers of the monarchy, the French Revolution certainly perfected national unity, regularized the administrative organization, finally reinforced central power and the state structures. This had also been the ambition of the enlightened monarchs. Emperor Leopold and the Prussian minister Herzberg appreciated in this regard the decrees of the Constituent Assembly.

But the French Revolution also meant a constitutional monarchy, royal power subordinated to an elected national representation. For monarchs, even enlightened ones, the blow was mortal; it is not astonishing that upon reflection, they condemned and fought the revolutionary nation. Even more, the French Revolution meant the abolition of privilege, and the equality of rights sanctioned by the consecutive decrees of the night of August 4. This was the liberation of the peasant and his land by the destruction of all that survived of serfdom and feudalism, by the definitive abolition of the feudal rights, without repurchase or compensation, by the law of July 17, 1793. As with monarchic absolutism, the aristocracy was definitively hit in its economic foundations and its social preponderance.

The French Revolution finally meant the arrival of the bourgeoisie, which enlightened absolutism, through a contradiction inherent in its very nature, could not accept. The alliance of sovereigns and their nobility was thereby reinforced, the counterrevolution being even more aristocratic than absolutist. Enlightened absolutism established itself in advance as the exact negation of the Revolution, deliberately contrary as a social and political choice.

In drawing up a balance sheet of enlightened absolutism, it is impossible to mask certain positive aspects: the reinforcement of the State as a counter to social egoisms and local particularisms; a step forward toward the secularization of society, if not the state, to the detriment of the trusteeship of the churches; a certain progress in the diffusion of education and culture; the awakening of a certain national consciousness even among the peasant masses. The episode of enlightened absolutism did not fail to leave traces in the minds and consciousness of those who had cooperated with conviction and competence. The case of Hungary is significant in this respect. The noble or intellectual officials of Joseph II, although they became adversaries of his system, gave rise to the conception of the Hungarian State, a nobiliary one, certainly, but already open to bourgeois tendencies.

Nevertheless, in taking a global view of enlightened absolutism, it must be stated that like the French model of enlightened reformism, it ended in failure. In Portugal, at the death of José I in 1777, Pombal was dismissed, his work interrupted. In Spain, the installation of Charles IV in 1788 was the signal for reaction, and the death of Joseph II in 1790 had the same results in the Hapsburg domains. In those of the Hohenzollern, Frederick-William, the successor to Frederick II, was incapable of consolidating the fragile reforms; the Prussian State was headed for the collapse of Iena. In Russia, Catherine II, consolidating old foundations, bequeathed to the 19th century a heavy heritage of autocracy, orthodoxy and aristocracy. Attached by too many ties to *their* clergy, to *their* nobility, these so-called enlightened monarchs belonged, every one of them, to the Ancien Régime, an edifice too old to restore. The Revolution, followed by the Napoleonic conquest, dragged the whole system down to ruin.

*

By a remarkable reversal of history, would not the last of the enlightened despots have been Napoleon, as certain historians have suggested? ... The last, or more precisely the only one, as he was a true man of enlightenment, but also a son of the Revolution. Whatever may have been his evolution toward despotism, the emperor could not efface the indelible mark of the origin of his power, nor the revolutionary filiation of his regime. He was indeed the soldier of the Revolution, for which the monarchs of the Ancien Régime never ceased reproaching him. For if the emperor governed despotically, he nevertheless maintained the abolition of privilege and feudalism, the liberation of the peasant and the land, civil equality, the secularization of the state: in sum the essential gains of the Revolution, the very negation of the whole system of enlightened absolutism. But at the same time, Napoleon taught the monarchs how to govern despotically under the guise of popular sovereignty and a Constitution, how to turn the work of unification and rationalization of the Revolution to the profit of despotism. He showed the aristocracy that equality of rights, henceforth an untouchable principle, was not incompatible with the social authority of the *notables*, notability defining itself now as much by money as by birth. This lesson in true enlightened absolutism was not lost, as the further course of history has attested.

2

Classes and class struggles during the Revolution[1]

The French Revolution, along with the English revolutions of the 17th century, constitutes the crowning achievement of a long economic and social evolution that made the bourgeoisie the master of the world.

This truth, which today is commonplace, has been proclaimed from the 19th century on by the most conscious doctrinarians of the bourgeoisie. Using history to justify the Charter,* Guizot demonstrated that the originality of French society consisted essentially in the existence, between the people and the aristocracy, of a strong bourgeois class which had slowly specified its ideology, then created the framework of a new society, of which 1789 was the consecration.[2] After Guizot, Tocqueville, then Taine, sustained the same opinion. Tocqueville spoke with "a kind of religious terror of this irresistible revolution that has marched for so many centuries over all obstacles, and which is still seen today advancing in the middle of the ruins that it made."[3] Taine sketched the slow ascension of the bourgeoisie up the social ladder, at the end of which inequality became intolerable.[4] But, confident though they were that the birth and the progress of the bourgeoisie had as first cause the appearance and development of personal wealth, commercial and industrial enterprises, these historians were quite indifferent to producing a precise study of the economic origins of the Revolution or of the social classes that conducted it.

Above all, whatever the clairvoyance of the historians of the bourgeoisie at its apogee may have been, they could not have shed light on the essential: that the Revolution is explained in the final analysis by a contradiction between the relations of production and the character of the productive forces. Marx and Engels strongly underscored in *The Communist Manifesto* that the means of production, on whose base is erected the power of the bourgeoisie, were created and developed within feudal society itself. At the end of the 18th century, the feudal regime of property, the feudal organ-

*[The fundamental law; that is, the limited concessions granted by the bourgeois monarchy (1830-1848). Guizot was prime minister in its last year.]

ization of agriculture and manufacturing, no longer corresponded to productive forces that were developing and in fact constituted shackles to these forces. "It was necessary to break these chains," wrote the authors of the *Manifesto.* "They were broken."[5]

Jaurès was inspired to a certain degree by historical materialism— only to a certain degree—doesn't he in fact write, in his general introduction, that his interpretation of history will be "at once materialist with Marx and mystical with Michelet"? In his *Histoire Socialiste*, Jaurès restored to the history of the Revolution its economic and social substructure in a vast fresco eloquently executed and which still remains a valuable monument.[6] "We know," he writes, "that economic conditions, the mode of production and property are the basis of history."[7] To the extent that he was able to advance the historiography of the Revolution, Jaurès owes a debt to the development of the organized labor movement at the beginning of the 20th century. This debt was sensed, if not clearly expressed, by Albert Mathiez in his 1922 preface to a new edition of *Histoire Socialiste*, when he wrote that Jaurès brought to the study of the documents of the past "the same sharpened sense, the same flair" that guided him in political struggles. "Mingling in the feverish life of assemblies and parties, he was more able than a professor or a cabinet minister to revive the emotions, the clear or obscure thoughts of the revolutionaries."[8] Perhaps the work of Jaurès is marred, however, by schematism. The development of the Revolution is quite plain: its cause resides in the economic and intellectual power of the mature bourgeoisie; its result was the consecration of that power in law.

Sagnac and Mathiez, going farther, studied the aristocratic reaction of the 18th century (culminating in 1787-1788). Mathiez characterized this reaction by the ambiguous expression, *révolte nobiliaire*[9]: that frantic opposition of the nobility to all attempts at reform, even more this hoarding of all the offices of the State by a privileged minority, this obstinate refusal to share preeminence with the upper bourgeoisie. Thus the violent nature of the Revolution was explained and the fact that the advent of the bourgeoisie resulted not from a progressive evolution but from a sudden mutation.

But the Revolution was not the work of the bourgeoisie alone, even though that class profited most from it. Mathiez, after Jaurès, insisting on the rapid dissociation of the Third Estate and on the antagonisms which were not slow to manifest themselves among the diverse factions of the bourgeoisie and the popular classes, recognized the complexity of revolutionary history and of the progression of its successive stages. Turning his eyes from the Parisian stage and the cities, which up to that point had monopolized the attention of historians, Georges Lefebvre devoted himself to the study of the peasantry (for France at the end of the 18th century was after all essentially rural). Until his work, peasant action had been regarded as a repercussion of urban movements, directed essentially in accord with the bourgeoisie, against feudalism and royal power. Thus the homogenous aspect and the majesty of the course of the Revolution were preserved. Georges Lefebvre, starting from precise social analyses, demonstrated that within the framework of the bourgeois Revolution, a peasant stream developed possessing its own autonomy as to its origin, its methods, its crises and its tendencies. It is necessary, however, to stress that the fundamental objective of the peasant movement coincided with the goals of the bourgeois Revolution: the destruction of feudal relations of production. The Revolution broke the feudal regime of property in the countryside; it ruined the feudal organization of agriculture.

We value the work of Georges Lefebvre for its clear demonstrations and precise examples. If we set aside the ground he has cleared, the social history of the Revolution has yet to be written. Only such a work will permit knowledge to advance. It is only by starting from detailed analyses of landed and personal wealth, of the economic power of diverse social classes and of the groups within them that we will account for the play of antagonisms and class struggles, that we will define the vicissitudes and the progress of the revolutionary movement, that we will finally draw up the exact balance sheet of the Revolution.

Significantly, whereas the bourgeoisie have reigned uncontested for 150 years, we possess no history of the French bourgeoisie during the Revolution. Putting aside several attempts that are more a study of mentality than of economic power, several monographs dedicated to a region or a city, to a family or a category (valuable monographs in that they stick to documentary research and show the path to follow), we are compelled to point out the slow progress in this area of revolutionary studies. Doubtless we are not lacking descriptions of "society" (read "good society"), that of the dominant classes; but these (following memoirs and correspondence) accomplish little besides painting customs or sketching ideas, whereas it is necessary to specify the relations of production, revenues and credit. We have no more a history of the nobility throughout the course of the Revolution than we do of the bourgeoisie. Even less, it goes without saying, do we have a history of the mass classes. The first goal of serious historical research is the institution of local and regional monographs, based on verifiable statistical data provided by economic and fiscal documents. It would then be possible to produce comprehensive works on various classes and social categories, the only works that would enable us to delineate antagonisms and trace social struggles in the complexity of their dialectical movement. If, for example, the exploitation of the sugar islands and the dependent maritime commerce have often been described, we do not have at our disposal a thorough work on the bourgeoisie of Bordeaux: all the studies of the Gironde will be in vain as long as the power of the class it represented has not been measured nor its limits outlined. It is easy to multiply the examples: we maintain that an immense field remains to be cleared and that many episodes of the Revolution remain in the shadows due to a lack of an exact understanding of the social forces present.

The pages that follow do not pretend to tackle, even in a limited sector, this indispensable study. But simply to sketch, beyond the fundamental antagonism of the society of the Ancien Régime, the complexity of complementary social antagonisms which throw a light on the evolution of social struggles. The Revolution destroyed feudal relations of production, liberated productive forces developing in the heart of feudal society; in a word, the Revolution assured the economic expansion and the political preponderance of the bourgeoisie. To say nothing of the aristocrat whose economic base was in part destroyed along with the feudal relations of production, the Revolution also precipitated the ruin of certain categories of the Third Estate which had profited from the feudal system of property and agriculture. Again, it is necessary to account for all these assertions.

I

The social structure at the end of the 18th century always remained strongly marked by the preeminence of the aristocracy, vestige of an age when the land, being the only wealth, conferred on its proprietors all rights over those who worked it. A long evolution had, however, increased the power of personal wealth, thus of the bourgeoisie who held it. Thus in direct correlation with these relations of production, two classes confronted each other. But history had introduced into each of these classes nuances and differentiations that took all homogeneity away from them: when it was necessary to choose sides, interests diversified attitudes.

The power of the aristocracy was founded on landed property and on the perception of feudal and seigniorial rights attached to the land. Traditional prejudice kept this class from lending itself to any productive activity: that would have been demeaning. Colbert had permitted himself to get involved in the great maritime commerce: few did likewise. The economic evolution that brought personal wealth to the fore, the rise in prices, and the corresponding drop in rents (which had been controlled for a long time), had introduced in the ranks of the aristocracy—otherwise solid—an extreme inequality of fortune and a great variation in their conditions of living. Notably, and this is the most important element of differentiation, a significant fraction of the landed aristocracy no longer disdained the revenues that capitalist enterprise procured, whether agricultural or industrial. Several redecorated their coats of arms, allying themselves with finance; others, touched by agromania, renovated their lands; still others became interested in industrial enterprises, particularly in metallurgy. Thus they drew closer to the bourgeoisie.

That the French bourgeoisie led the Revolution is today an obvious truth. Still, it is necessary to specify what factions of the bourgeoisie led and which ones profited from it. The bourgeoisie did not, in the society of the 18th century, constitute a homogenous class. Certain factions were integrated into the economic and social structures of the Ancien Régime while others, unable to expand under the old order, originated new forms of production whose development was constrained by the feudal structure of the society. These innovators took the lead in the Revolution, in order to finally profit from it.

At the end of the 18th century, various factions of the bourgeoisie participated in varying degrees in the privileges of the dominant class, either through landed wealth and rights as much feudal as seigniorial, or through membership in the apparatus of the state, or through administration of the traditional forms of finance and economy.

At the outer limits of the aristocracy, certain commoners lived like nobility: their fortunes permitted them to subsist on their wealth, exempting them from all work. As for the aristocracy, this wealth was essentially of the land: hereditary rents and seigniorial rights, much more than personal, transportable wealth. All ties having disappeared between the social hierarchy and the judicial status of the land, some bourgeois held fiefs and exercised privileges from seigniorial authority, or what was left of it at the end of the 18th century: police and justice of the village, honorific rights, especially personal taxes and forced labor [*corvées*]; charges on the peasants justified by the eminent ownership of the land, economic monopolies like the obligatory use of seigniorial property [*banalités*] and the hunt.

With the development of the apparatus of the State and the progressive centralization of the monarchy, especially since the 16th century, a new social category was formed in the heart of the bourgeoisie, that of the "*officiers*." Proprietors of their offices through the system of venality, grouped according to their work, later forming corps to protect their prerogatives and privileges, they peopled tribunals, and various offices of finance, elections and administration. One section of these "*officiers*" being noble, this category opened onto the *noblesse de robe*. In order to augment its resources, the royalty sold offices in magistracy, finances, army and administration; in return, and in order to increase their value, nobility was conferred on certain offices. If this new oligarchy, strongly unified by class solidarity and professional interests, quickly espoused the cause of the aristocracy, sharing its customs and haughtiness, it was no less a center of attraction for the bourgeoisie of the offices.

Equally integrated into the traditional economic and social structure was the great bourgeoisie of finance. Very early, investments in the funds of the State had been one of the first means to capitalist development for the bourgeoisie. At the end of the 18th century, finance held an eminent place in the State, which could not survive without the help of *fermiers généraux*—providers to armies, principal boosters of the actions of privileged financial companies, *Compagnie des Indes* or the national bank. The fermier généraux, necessary intermediaries between the monarchy and the taxable masses, were deeply involved in the system of the Ancien Régime.

These factions of the bourgeoisie showed solidarity with the aristocracy by playing their parts in the traditional economy—landed or financial. Does this mean they embraced the cause of the aristocracy without hesitation or reservation? History is not so simple.

The finance bourgeoisie of the Ancien Régime formed, to use an expression of Jaurès, "a hybrid social force at the crossroads of the Ancien Régime and the new capitalism."[10] The fermier généraux in particular had an interest in maintaining the traditional State; they cannot be classified among the new forces, even if certain ones, like Lavoisier, were sons of the Enlightenment who contributed to progress in the sciences. But a not insignificant fraction of the capital of the fermier généraux was invested in industrial enterprises: for example, the factories created by the son of Dupin de Francueil at Chateauroux. As they could only hope for the survival of a system whose fruitful monopolies assured their preponderance, these men of finance suffered elsewhere in their activity from the defects of an irresponsible bureaucracy and from the arbitrariness of an absolute power. The national bank, suppressed several times and then reestablished, constituted for the royal Treasury in moments of national crisis a reserve from which the Controller-general withdrew as he pleased. Thus was revealed, even for the financiers of the Ancien Régime, the incompatibility between the disorder of the monarchic administration and the guarantees and rules of accountability inherent in the working of capitalist enterprises.

Likewise, the bourgeoisie of the "*officiers*" and the numerous men of law (prosecutors, notaries, bailiffs who also bought their offices, and the lawyers who, like them, formed a corps)—to say nothing of the other bourgeois of liberal professions—adhered to the principles of the philosophy of the Enlightenment which was undermining the foundations of the traditional social structure to which they were tied. The critical examination of the economic, social and political institutions of the Ancien Régime, like the practice of public functions, prepared these men to conduct the Revolution: some of them launched it.

Opposed to these factions of the bourgeoisie who were integrated, to various degrees, in the traditional economic and social structure and who thus suffered in various degrees from the Revolution, were the commercial and industrial bourgeoisie who were smothering in the old frameworks of the economy. The latter factions intended to break these frameworks and they in fact broke them. Initiators of new forms of production and exchange—shipowners, merchants, manufacturers—they tolerated with a growing impatience the shackles that the regime of property and the organization of production placed on their capitalist enterprises. Doubtless we must not exaggerate their importance at the end of the 18th century. Following tradition, commerce held the first place, and especially the great maritime commerce. Capitalism was still essentially commercial. It dominated an important sector of production, whether in cities like Lyon since the 16th century, or in the countryside with the expanded development of the 18th century: the "*fabricant*" was really a merchant who furnished the raw materials to the artisans working at home. The 17th century had seen the development of manufacturing; in the second half of the 18th century appeared the great industrial enterprises in the modern meaning: metallurgy, the textile and chemical industries were partly renovated by capitalism.

It is significant that the sight of this economic activity gave the bourgeoisie a consciousness of their class and made them understand that it was irremediably opposed to the feudal aristocracy. Sieyes, in his famous brochure, defined the Third Estate by its *private* works and its *public* functions: the Third Estate was the whole nation. The nobility could not take part, it did not enter into the social organization: it remained immobile in the midst of general movement, it devoured "the best part of the product, without having cooperated in anything to bring it about. Such a class is assuredly estranged from the nation by its *idleness*."[11]

Even more penetrating is the analysis of Barnave. It is true that he had been raised in the middle of this economic activity which, if we believe Roland—inspector of manufacturing—writing in 1785, made the Dauphiné the first province of the realm due to the variety and density of its enterprises and the importance of production. In his *Introduction to the French Revolution*, written after the separation of the Constituent Assembly,[12] Barnave, having posed the principle that property "influenced" institutions, states that those institutions created by the landed aristocracy opposed and retarded the coming of the industrial era. "Once the arts and commerce had penetrated the people and created a new means of wealth with the help of the laboring class, they prepared a revolution in the political laws; a new distribution of wealth produces a new distribution of power. In the same way that the possession of lands raised the aristocracy, industrial property raised the power of the people" (let us emphasize in passing how the bourgeoisie of the 18th century, like every authentic revolutionary class, identified itself with the nation: Barnave writes *people* where we understand *bourgeoisie*). The industrial property or, more broadly, personal wealth, brought about the political advent of the class which held it. Barnave affirmed clearly the antagonism between landed property and personal wealth and between the classes founded on them.

Tightly bound to the revolutionary bourgeoisie by hatred of the aristocracy who exploited them and hatred of the Ancien Régime whose full weight they bore, the popular urban classes were nonetheless divided into diverse categories whose behavior was not uniform in the course of the Revolution. If all rose up against the aristocracy and the Ancien Régime, attitudes varied regarding the successive factions of the bourgeoisie that led the revolutionary movement.

The masses who work with their hands and who produce are designated by the aristocratic or bourgeois owners, at the end of the 18th century, by the somewhat disdainful term of "people." In fact, from those who constituted the middle bourgeoisie—to use current terminology—to the proletariat, the nuances were numerous, as were the antagonisms. One often quotes the opinion of the wife of Lebas—a member of the Convention—the daughter of the "menuisier" Duplay (read an entrepreneur in carpentry, not a carpenter himself), the host of Robespierre, according to whom her father, mindful of his bourgeois dignity, had never admitted one of his "serviteurs," that is to say, workers, to his table: one thus measures the distance separating Jacobins and sans culottes, petty or middle bourgeoisie from the popular class, properly speaking.

Where did the limits of one and the other end? It is difficult, if not impossible to specify. In this society of aristocratic preponderance, the social categories included under the general term of Third Estate were not clearly carved out; capitalist evolution took it upon itself to specify the antagonisms. The dominant artisan production and the boutique system of exchange brought about imperceptible transitions from the people to the bourgeoisie. The journeyman worked and lived with the small artisan whose mentality and material conditions of existence he shared. From the small artisan to the entrepreneur (who always conserved his professional qualification and called himself "menuisier" or "charpentier," even when he employed several dozen journeymen), the nuances were multiple and advancement occurred slowly, in small steps. At the top of the ladder, these almost imperceptible changes led to a brusque mutation: certain professionals—booksellers, printers, apothecaries, postmasters—found themselves isolated in the first rank of the middle class and already at the frontier of the true bourgeoisie due to the importance of the enterprise, a certain closeness to the liberal professions, as well as particular privileges and a special regimentation. They looked down on shopkeepers, journeymen and workers, yet were irritated to see the bourgeois—properly speaking—treating them in the same way.

On these still poorly defined social categories weighed the contradictions of an ambiguous situation. Falling under the province of the popular classes through their conditions of existence and often their poverty, the artisans nonetheless possessed their workshops, their little sets of tools and were looked upon as independent producers. Having journeymen and apprentices under them and under their discipline accentuated their bourgeois mentality. But the attachment to the system of small production and direct sale opposed them irremediably to the bourgeoisie. Thus, among these artisans and shopkeepers who formed the bulk of the sans-culotte movement and with whom the bourgeois Revolution must end, arose a social ideal in contradiction with economic necessities. Could they stand up against the concentration of property in the hands of the large manufacturers? They were themselves proprietors, and when the most advanced demanded the "maximum" [upper limit] of wealth in the year II, they were not conscious of the contradiction between their social position and their demands. Could they demand that their work be protected, their wages guaranteed? That would mean loosening the bridle on their journeymen. The demands of this class of artisans and shopkeepers were sublimated in passionate complaints, in spurts of revolt, without ever specifying a coherent program of reforms.

With the journeymen and the proletariat (in the still narrow degree where the great capitalist industry existed), class spirit was missing. Scattered in numerous modest workshops, unspecialized as a consequence of the still restrained technical development, not concentrated in either great enterprises or in industrial quarters, often little differentiated from the peasantry, the workers, no more than the artisans, were incapable of conceiving of effective remedies for their misery. The weakness of the guilds attested to this: narrowly corporative, often rivals, the various *devoirs* competed jealously with one another to the point of becoming bloody brawls. The hatred of the aristocracy, the irreducible opposition to the "fat" and to the rich were the only fermenting agents for unity of the working masses. When a bad harvest and the industrial crisis that necessarily resulted had set them in motion, they launched themselves with a sure instinct in the wake of the bourgeoisie: thus were born the most effective blows against the Ancien Régime. But the victory that the working masses thus carried off was, in the phrase of Marx and Engels, "a bourgeois victory."

Only the bourgeoisie, through its economic position and its intellectual power, brought a coherent program: it alone was ready to direct the revolutionary action.

The same unity and the same contradictions brought the peasant world together and at the same time tore them apart.

The feudal relations of production dominated in the countryside. The regime of property remained feudal; and feudal the organization of agriculture. On the peasantry in its entirety weighed the heavy burden of seigniorial rights, of the ecclesiastical tithe [*dîme*] and the royal taxes: this alone sufficed to unify the peasantry against the landed aristocracy.

The capitalist movement that renovated industrial production also tended to transform the countryside, introducing elements of differentiation and antagonism. From the middle of the 18th century, and the development of the physiocratic school had been its obvious sign, the application of capital and its own methods to agricultural production, with a scientific and intensive culture in mind, brought evident repercussions on the peasant condition in the lands of great cultivation. A new class of big farmers, capitalists of agricultural exploitation, developed widely at the end of the Ancien Régime; in their hands concentration—if not of landed property, at least of exploitation—was implemented while an accrued mass of production transformed the conditions of the traditional marketing of foodstuffs, essentially of cereals. In the "cahiers de doléance" [lists of grievances brought to the convocation of the Estates-General] from Ile-de-France, Picardy, Flanders, the most advanced agricultural regions, the peasants complained that the land had been "fixed up" by the proprietors, and little farms replaced by huge acreages. Thus to the traditional antagonism between the peasantry and the aristocracy was now added, in the lands of large cultivation, the antagonism of a capitalist agriculture and a more or less proletarianized peasantry. Lacking land, stripped of their collective rights to the degree that private property and expanded exploitation fortified itself, the poor peasants swelled the ranks of a miserable and unstable rural proletariat, ready to rise up against the great farms as well as against the castles.

Doubtless we must not generalize these traits and extend them to the whole of France. On the eve of the Revolution, the largest part of the country remained the domain of small traditional cultivation. But even there elements of dissociation were in play, sources of future antagonisms. Inequality was introduced into the heart of the rural community. Collective property and exploitation of common goods, the collective constraints on private property (interdiction of closed fields, obligatory crop rotation), the usage rights on the fields (rights of pasturing and gleaning) and in the woods constituted solid economic foundations of the rural community and welded a social unity until the middle of the 18th century; even when diverse levels of life coexisted there, the fundamental antagonism of rural France of the Ancien Régime—the rural community against the seigniory—flowed from the feudal rights of the seigniorial regime. In the second half of the 18th century, in these lands of small cultivation, the economic evolution brought to the front ranks the class of laboureurs—"coqs de village"—on whom unskilled workers and small peasants depended for work: an affluent peasantry, a rural bourgeoisie, different essentially from the category of capitalist farmers, but who, already producing more or less for the market, adapted to the agricultural renovation. To the antagonism of rural communité/seigniory was added, in the very heart of the community, the antagonism "laboureurs"/unskilled workers.

This proprietary peasantry (its property was still of a feudal type), almost as much as the aristocracy who burdened the land with their seigniorial rights, was truly hostile to the rural community which constrained it with their collective rights: it aspired to liberate the property from all these limitations and restrictions. The poor peasantry, on the other hand, to the degree that its conditions of existence were aggravated with the progress of the new agriculture, became even more attached to its collective rights and traditional modes of existence, which it felt were slipping away.[13]

Thus the game of social antagonism was being complicated and diversified in the countryside. Already there was the perception that to the fundamental antagonism of peasantry/aristocracy was being added an underlying antagonism of proprietary peasant/poor peasant, which alone would remain once the feudal regime of property had been destroyed.

II

The real complexity (under an apparent simplicity) of the social structure of the society of the Ancien Régime acknowledges the turns taken by the class struggles during the Revolution.

The Revolution had as its essential cause the power of a mature bourgeoisie cramped by the privileges of a decadent aristocracy; the result was the legal consecration of that power. In this sense the French Revolution, an episode in the general ascension of the bourgeoisie, but the most resounding episode, was one and indivisible: we cannot follow Mathiez who, after the "révolte nobiliaire" of 1787-1788 and the bourgeois revolution of 1789, distinguishes a third revolution, that of August 10, 1792, democratic and republican, then a fourth, that of May 31—June 2, 1793, which ended with an outline of social democracy. That the 10th of August and the 2nd of June constituted crucial stages in the Revolution, we agree; but it was a question of an aggravation, of a deepening of the struggles of the bourgeoisie against the aristocracy, marked by the entrance on the scene—in the wake of the bourgeoisie—of the middle class and the popular classes, not of a change in the nature of the class struggle. The goal in the year II was the same as in 1789: to knock down the aristocracy. In this sense, it is not possible to speak of a "change in the front" of the bourgeoisie after the fall of Robespierre: before and after the 9 Thermidor, the essential enemy remained the aristocracy, which would not disarm. The Thermidorians thought that they could do without the popular alliance in this struggle. That calculation was proven false: the Brumairians, always dreading the sans-culotte masses, but dreading the aristocratic peril just as much, finally had to turn to the dictatorship: Bonaparte was indeed the soldier of the bourgeois Revolution.

But underneath this essential unity, the Revolution is a complex fact; its unfolding is neither linear nor schematic. It is composed of various stages that convey the fluctuations of the struggle against the aristocracy, the progress and the set backs: the Third Estate disintegrated rapidly, the diverse factions of the bourgeoisie split up as the conflict increased. The Revolution is also composed of various currents that complemented the principal current: without the peasantry and the sans-culotterie, the bourgeoisie would not have knocked down the aristocracy; the sans-culotterie and the peasantry were also seeking, beyond the destruction of the aristocracy, goals which were not those of the bourgeoisie.

The fierce resistance of the aristocracy in defense of its class interests explains why the bourgeoisie had to turn to the popular masses in order to conquer. The appeal to foreign countries by the counterrevolution made even more necessary the alliance with the sans-culotterie—an alliance which did not appear without danger to the most wealthy factions of the bourgeoisie and which brought about the splitting of various factions of the ruling class. Thus the stages of the Revolution were marked in step with the aggravations and complications of the class struggle. It is not a question of retracing them here, but simply of posing several problems, otherwise organically linked: that of the failure of the politics of compromise, that of the Girondist "weakness" facing the necessities of the war, that of the Jacobin dictatorship.

The ruling factions of the French bourgeoisie would have accepted the compromise which—in the image of the English Revolution of 1688—would have installed the domination of the upper bourgeoisie and the aristocracy, the *notables* of money above the enslaved popular classes. The aristocracy did not want any of this, thus making the bourgeois appeal to the popular masses inevitable in order to break aristocratic resistance. Only a minority, that the name of La Fayette symbolized, understood that the aristocracy would lose nothing with this compromise: the example of England proved that. But the French aristocracy of the 18th century exhibited traits completely different from those of the English aristocracy of the previous century. In England, the fiscal privilege did not exist: the nobles paid taxes. The military character of the nobility was, moreover, attenuated, if it had not disappeared. The nobility did not degrade itself by engaging in business: the maritime and colonial boom had associated the nobility and the capitalist bourgeoisie. The aristocracy thus participated in the rush of new productive forces. Most importantly, the feudal relations of production had been destroyed, property and production liberated. These conditions, particular to England and a more advanced evolution, were thus acknowledged in the compromise of 1688.

In France, the nobility still maintained an essentially feudal character. Devoted to military careers and, with a few exceptions, excluded from fruitful commercial and industrial enterprises by the social convention that such activity was humiliating to their class, the nobles remained even more attached to old structures which assured their existence and preponderance. Was the aristocracy going to accept without resistance the destruction of its old structures, the ruin of the feudal regime of property in particular, for the profit of new forces? Its obstinate attachment to its economic and social privileges, its extreme exclusiveness, its feudal mentality impervious to bourgeois principles, froze the French nobility in an attitude of refusal.

Some asked themselves if compromise was possible in the spring of 1789. It would still have been necessary for the monarchy to boldly take the initiative: its attitude showed (if there was any need) that it was no longer the instrument of domination of one class. The appeal to the soldier, which Louis XVI decided upon in the first days of July, appeared to signify the end of the bourgeois Revolution whose outlines were being sketched. The popular force saved it. Was compromise still possible, after the 14th of July and the days of October? Some thought so—in the ranks of the bourgeoisie as well as in those of the aristocracy—La Fayette as well as Mounier.

Mounier thought it possible to obtain in 1789, as in 1788 in Vizille during the "revolution of the notables" of the Dauphine, the agreement of the three orders to a limited revolution. His design, as he wrote later, was "to follow the lessons of experience, to oppose reckless innovations and to propose in the already existing forms of government only those modifications necessary to guarantee liberty."[14] The majority of the nobility and the aristocratic high clergy refused this plan, accepting neither the voluntary meeting of the three orders nor the Declaration of the Rights of Man, nor the decisions of the night of the 4th of August; that is to say, the partial destruction of feudalism. Mounier left Versailles on the 10th of October: his politics of compromise having failed, he rejoined the camp of the aristocracy and counterrevolution. On May 22, 1790, he emigrated.

Either political incomprehension or ambition made La Fayette persist longer. A great lord, the "hero of two worlds," he had what it took to seduce the upper bourgeoisie. His politics tended toward conciliation—in the framework of a constitutional monarchy like England's—of a landed aristocracy and an industrial and commercial bourgeoisie. The hope of a compromise caressed by La Fayette was revealed to be an illusion: the aristocracy persisted in its resistance. Even more, the troubles due to the food crisis and in many regions the agrarian revolts motivated by the obligation of the repurchase of feudal rights, confirmed by the law of March 15, 1790, hardened the resistance of an aristocracy more and more threatened. From the summer of 1790, the politics of compromise were ruined.

In fact, the search for a compromise between the aristocracy and the upper bourgeoisie was fanciful as long as the Ancien Régime had not been irremediably destroyed. As long as any hope remained of seeing its interests maintained, the aristocracy offered the most lively resistance to the triumph of the bourgeoisie; that is to say, to a triumph of new structures which brought an end to its interests. In order to defeat this resistance, the bourgeoisie had to turn to an alliance with the popular urban masses and the peasantry; finally, it was later to accept the Napoleonic dictatorship. When it was obvious that feudalism was destroyed forever, the aristocracy finally accepted the compromise which, under the July monarchy, awarded it power shared with the upper bourgeoisie.

La Fayette having been eliminated and precedence given to the Feuillants, the great bourgeoisie in power (under the cover of triumvirate Du Port, Lameth and Barnave) were alarmed by the progress of the democrats and the popular agitation. They intended to stop the Revolution: citizens who did not have the right to vote were excluded from the national guard, and collective petitions were prohibited; on June 14, 1791, the Le Chapelier law prohibited coalitions and strikes. However, the resistance of the aristocracy made this policy impossible. The appeal to foreign countries, demonstrated by the flight of the king on June 21, 1791, showed that the aristocracy preferred, through class interest, to betray the nation rather than surrender: this appeal definitively unmasked the aristocracy, but it also compromised the upper bourgeoisie, who were incapable of controlling the situation.

The crisis forced a new revolutionary personnel to emerge from the bourgeoisie, one that was socially different. The counterrevolution accentuating its pressure (the first troubles of the Vendée broke out in August of 1791), and the foreign threat multiplying its demands (the declaration of Pillnitz dates from August 27, 1791), a more combative element replaced the great "Feuillants" bourgeois. Recruited in part from the cultivated middle bourgeoisie of lawyers and novelists, in alliance with the bourgeoisie of business—shipowners, merchants, bankers—its most representative type was Brissot. This bourgeoisie of business and the politicians at its service desired an end to the counterrevolution, particularly to reestablish the credit of the "assignat" [bank note] necessary for the smooth functioning of enterprises. The bourgeoisie of business did not abhor the war which the aristocracy, anticipating defeat, desired in order to conduct the interior counterrevolution. Equipment for the armies—wasn't this a source of considerable profits? War against England? Nothing was less sure. The base of power of this bourgeoisie of business rested in the prosperity of the ports—Marseille, Nantes, Bordeaux especially—vital centers of the capitalism of the time, essentially commercial. Having unleashed the continental war in April 1792, the Girondists declared war on England only in February of the following year: the maritime war compromised the commerce of the islands and the prosperity of the maritime cities.

The continental war served the economic and political interests of the Girondist bourgeoisie. It served to bring to a fever pitch the struggle against the feudal aristocracy, to unmask it and to destroy it beyond the borders, where it had sought refuge in emigration, to intensify the class struggle on the scale of the European Ancien Régime. "Mark in advance a place for traitors, and let this place be the scaffold," cried Guadet, on January 14, 1792. But the Girondist bourgeoisie showed itself incapable of conducting this war against the national and foreign aristocracy by its forces alone. Through class egoism, it refused an alliance with the people. Thus the predictions of Robespierre were verified: what was necessary before fighting the aristocracy across the borders was to destroy it in the interior.

The war thwarted the calculations of the Girondist bourgeoisie. Within the existing social antagonisms, a new cleavage occurred. Under the pretext that the war required union, the Gironde had vouched for La Fayette already at the beginning of 1792 and had supported the Minister of Foreign Affairs, Narbonne. They thereby exhibited premature trust for this regime of "notables," of whom Mme. de Stael, the mistress of Narbonne, was one of the theoreticians, and who reconciled the interests of the united landed aristocracy and the bourgeoisie of business. The reverses of spring 1792 forced the hesitant Gironde to envisage the necessary alliance with the popular classes to assure victory: it consented to appeal to the people on June 20, but only to the extent that the people would keep to objectives assigned them. As the national crisis was fueling the revolutionary spirit of the popular classes, the Girondist bourgeoisie, attached unreservedly to economic liberty, was worried to see the sans-culottes demanding the regulation of food prices. On August 10, the royalist government, supporter of the aristocracy and obstacle to an effective policy of national defense, was swept out by the sans-culotterie and the Jacobin middle class. The insurrection of August 10, 1792 was made, if not against the Gironde, if not in spite of it, at least without it: this abstention was its death blow.

The final politics of the Girondist bourgeoisie was the logical consequence of its initial attitude. The war could not be conducted without the people; through fear of the people and to obtain peace, the Gironde (the trial of the king proved this) was disposed to slide toward compromise with the counterrevolution: the great bourgeoisie regrouped behind it. Once again class interest won over national interest. This is what history discreetly calls the "weakness" of the Gironde. Like the monarchy of August 10th, the Girondist bourgeoisie, having become the indirect support of the aristocracy and the hindrance to the national spirit, was eliminated by a popular movement disciplined by the petty and middle bourgeoisie. Jaurès denied the class character of these days of May 31—June 2, 1793.[15] Certainly, if one limits oneself to considering the parliamentary aspect of these days or the political conflict of the Montagne and the Gironde, both came out of the bourgeoisie (once again it would be necessary to specify the nuances) and both had the same conception of property. But the entrance on the scene of the sans-culotterie complicated the playing out of the class struggle. The Girondist, Petion, was not deceived when in April 1793, in his *Letter to the Parisians*, he rallied the bourgeoisie with this call: "Your property is threatened, and you are closing your eyes to this danger."

In 1793-1794, the aristocratic peril—interior and exterior—required the unity of the Third Estate. The meaning of the class struggle was clearer than ever. More than ever in this struggle, the energy of the sans-culotte masses was necessary: this recourse which the Gironde had refused through class egoism, another faction of the bourgeoisie consented to and undertook the supervision and disciplining of popular enthusiasm through the organization of the revolutionary government and the Jacobin dictatorship. From that would come the salvation of the bourgeois revolution.

A complex problem. It would first be a question of specifying the social condition and political position of the Montagnard (upper) bourgeoisie, whom a man like Cambon, the financier of the Convention, represented so well. A waiting game? Politics making necessity a virtue? Rather, intransigent bourgeois refusing all compromise, a course that left their nation and their class (which they identified as one) no other salvation but victory. And who accepted the necessary consequences of this policy? Intransigent bourgeois, having profited from the Revolution, particularly from the sale of national wealth, knowing that they had everything to lose from a successful counterattack by the aristocracy, but who quickly tired of the measures of constraint and terror (let us think of Danton and the "Indulgents")?

But it is also true that the policy of national and revolutionary defense was imposed from outside the Convention by the Jacobins and the sans-culottes. Of this coalition, on which the revolutionary government leaned, the Jacobin middle bourgeoisie, incarnated in Robespierre, was incontestably the ruling element, a necessary link between the lively forces of the sans-culotte people and the faction of the bourgeoisie who intended to push the revolution to its term: a policy not without contradiction, which to a large degree took into account the final failure of the Robespierrian policy. This policy flowed from the social situation of the Jacobin middle bourgeoisie, which it would be appropriate to clarify by numerous detailed studies, but which the "menuisier" Duplay symbolized, good Jacobin that he was: if he still plunged into the world of work, he was also receiving ten to twelve thousand livres in rent from his houses.

Even more than the Jacobin ambiguity, the contradictions of the sans-culotterie acknowledged the rapid ruin of the revolutionary government. But here we touch on one of the complementary currents that increases the complexity of the French Revolution.

That the sans-culotterie first and foremost struggled against the aristocracy is self-evident. The 14th of July proved that with the high spirit of the volunteers. The sans-culottes furnished the bourgeoisie the revolutionary mass indispensable to knocking down feudal society: their sense of class carried them against the nobility and the Ancien Régime. Having said this, it is nonetheless true that through their position in the feudal society, the sans-culottes constituted a social element that on many points was in opposition to the bourgeoisie.[16]

There was a popular movement in the heart of the French Revolution, a specific sans-culotte current. It is necessary to seek its origins in the aggravation of the living conditions of the shopkeepers, artisans and workers well before 1789. The sans-culottes were brought into struggle by the food crises just as much as by the aristocratic plot. This sans-culotte current was specific in its methods and its political organizations: general assemblies of Parisian sections where the sans-culottes reigned alone in the year II, fraternal and popular societies. To take only one example, there is a significative difference between a popular society, and the Jacobin club which the sans-culottes frequented very little, if at all. This popular movement in the year II presented its own crises, such as the one at the beginning of September 1793, which Mathiez qualified as "Hébertist shoving," and which was only a "sans-culotte shove," followed rather than guided by Chaumette, Hébert and the Commune of Paris. These days have no close or exact relation to the overall process of the bourgeois revolution: the sans-culottes demanded regulation of the prices and distribution of foodstuffs, which the Jacobin bourgeoisie would accord them only when forced to on September 29, 1793.

All of this clarifies a fundamental opposition between the sans-culotterie and the bourgeoisie on the political as well as the social plane.

The sans-culottes were the immediate producers. Peasants or artisans, in order to have their own lives at their disposal, it was first of all necessary for them to cease to be attached to the land or under allegiance to someone else. Without them and their inherent hostility to the aristocracy, there would not have been a bourgeois revolution. The artisans, in order to become free producers selling their merchandise wherever they found a market, had to escape from the regime of corporations—with their controls, their oaths and their apprenticeship laws. Immediate producers, the sans-culottes based ownership of property on the personal work of its possessor. Such a concept of private property of the worker based on the means of his activity corresponded to small agricultural and craft production. This mode of production could flower only if the worker was a free owner—the peasant, of the soil he cultivated; the artisan, of his shop and his tools. Here is the explanation as to why the sans-culotterie was the motor of the bourgeois revolution: industrial capitalism, in order to pursue its expansion, also required that all the shackles of seigniorial power be destroyed; the corporative regime or the control of the merchant-entrepreneurs needed to be turned over to the free development of production.

But this regime of small independent producers working for themselves presupposed the parcelling of land and the dispersal of the means of production: it excluded social cooperation and concentration of capital. The sans-culottes were hostile, above all, to commercial capital. Their ideal corresponded to an extremely limited state of society and production. To counter complete freedom of production and distribution, they demanded taxation and regulation: they wanted to prevent the concentration of property and the means of production. In the year II, the Parisian sections unceasingly opposed the concentration of enterprises for arming and outfitting the troops:[17] thus the opposition between the popular movement and the revolutionary government can be measured on a specific point. The sans-culottes could not understand that this regime of small production to which they were attached, having reached a certain degree of development, engendered the agents of its own destruction: the individual, scattered means of production were thus necessarily transformed into socially concentrated means of production, the small property of a crowd of independent, immediate producers supplanted by the large property of a capitalist minority.[18] Attached to private property based on personal work, to the independence of the shop, the workshop, the small agricultural cultivation, the sans-culottes dreaded above all being reduced to the ranks of the proletariat. They did not foresee that private capitalist production founded on the wage system would necessarily supplant private property founded on personal work. They thought that setting a maximum limit on private wealth and limiting inheritance rights were enough to keep private property within the narrow bounds of small independent production.

On September 2, 1793, at the fever pitch of this popular shoving that forced concessions from the Convention, the sans-culottes of the Jardin des Plantes section, renamed the section of the Sans-Culottes, addressed the representatives. "Make haste, proxies of the people... to unconditionally set the price of necessary foodstuffs, the wages for work, the profits of industry and commerce; you have the duty and power to do so... What's that! you will say that for the aristocrats, the royalists, the moderates, the schemers, this is undermining property which must be sacred, inviolable... Without a doubt; but don't they know, these scoundrels, don't they know that property has no basis beyond physical need?... The Republic must assure to each one ... the means of obtaining necessary foodstuffs." And the sans-culottes demanded, beyond regulation of the prices of basic necessities and wages, a strict limitation of the right of property: "That the maximum of fortunes be fixed; that the same individual can possess only one maximum; that no one can lease more land than what is needed for a fixed quantity of plows; that the same citizen can have only one workshop, one shop."[19]

We do not want to emphasize here the contradictions of such a concept or that it is fanciful to claim to maintain private ownership of the means of production and distribution while setting a limit on these. We will affirm the incompatibility of such a concept with the bourgeois concept, which makes property, according to the Declaration of 1789, "an imprescriptible natural right."

On the political plane we note the same opposition between the bourgeois concepts of democracy and the sans-culotte aspirations. The latter were partisans of a political system of direct democracy. This system is first of all characterized by the negation of political rights of those citizens suspected of being enemies of the Revolution, by their elimination from general assemblies of the sections—by violence if necessary. Then by the right that the sans-culottes proclaimed of controlling their representatives and of revoking their mandate if they had lost the confidence of their constituents. Certain procedures are significant, in particular the voice vote and elections by acclamation: voting by secret ballot was for the sans-culotte a mark of incivility and of aristocracy. The sans-culotte intended to apply this political system not only at the communal, but also at the national level: on some occasions, the sections proclaimed their non-acceptance of Convention decisions unless these decisions were approved by the sections. The sans-culotte political ideal was indeed a type of direct democracy, completely different from the liberal democracy that the bourgeoisie conceived—moreover applicable only with difficulty in the general crisis that was gripping the Republic. This explains why Robespierre and the Jacobins finally rose up against this ideal.

The ambiguous position of the sans-culotterie in the Revolution (if it was the most effective instrument in the struggle against the aristocracy, it cannot be denied that at certain moments it was also raised against the bourgeoisie) explains certain errors of perspective. Daniel Guérin wanted to see in the sans-culotterie an avant-garde and in its bid for power in the year II, an embryo of proletarian revolution: thus he would verify the theory of permanent revolution according to which the proletarian revolution of the 20th century was already emerging in the framework of the bourgeois revolution of the 18th century.[20] "In 1793, the bourgeois revolution and an embryo of the proletarian revolution overlapped each other." This would make a proletariat out of the sans-culotterie. As an example of this error, Daniel Guérin writes that the demonstration of September 4, 1793 was specifically *working class*, adding moreover, without being sensitive to the nuance, that it was almost exclusively a demonstration of journeymen. This is treating as a proletarian avant-garde what was only a rear guard defending the positions of the traditional economy.

The sans-culotte movement permitted the installation of the revolutionary government in 1793; it thus permitted the defeat of the interior and exterior counterrevolution, and the triumph of the revolution. But it could not achieve its own goals. It was brought to the final failure by an internal contradiction. Politically, the sans-culottes represented the advanced party of the revolution. Economically, they were attached to small, independent production, to the workshop, to the shop: they were condemned to decline with this whole system of production, as property founded on the personal work of its owner was dissolved and as the immediate producers were expropriated for the profit of capitalist private property, founded on the work of another, on the wage-earner. This contradiction doomed to failure all the efforts of the sans-culottes to found in the year II the egalitarian Republic that would have saved them. Doubtless, it cannot be maintained that the sans-culottes were reactionary on the economic and social plane: while they were fighting the aristocracy they were marching in the direction of history; if they were hostile to commercial capitalism during the Revolution, they were not unfriendly to industrial capitalism.[21] But, once the feudal relations of production had been completely destroyed and the triumph of industrial capitalism assured, the descendants of the sans-culottes—artisans, shopkeepers, small farmers—rose up against capitalism, took an economically reactionary position and tried to reverse the direction of the wheel of history.[22]

A peasant current—similar in some aspects to the sans-culotte current (especially in regard to the impoverished peasantry)—also developed in the framework of the bourgeois revolution though never surpassing it. Hatred of feudalism united the peasantry with the bourgeoisie, and the destruction of feudalism was indeed the most important reform of the Revolution.

The peasant current nonetheless developed autonomously. Just as for the sans-culotterie, the crisis of subsistence was an essential factor of agitation for the peasantry. This agitation developed without any organic link to the bourgeois revolution. From March of 1789, in certain regions, peasants had risen up against their lords. At the news of the taking of the Bastille, they revolted, but spontaneously and often in spite of the bourgeoisie who, being landowners themselves in many places, relentlessly repressed the revolts. These agrarian revolts, whose history remains to be written, continued on the fringe of the bourgeois revolution until the total abolition of seigniorial rights in 1793.

Apart from the big capitalist farmers and the landowner peasants (this rural bourgeoisie of "labourers"), the impoverished peasantry was characterized by the same precapitalist mentality as the urban sans-culotterie; attached to collective rights and controls, it rose up in the course of the Revolution as much against the agents of the capitalist transformation of agriculture and the break-up of the rural commune as against the feudal lords. The multiple petitions against the big farms and for the maintenance of collective rights prove this. The landed aristocracy stuck together in this sphere with the bourgeoisie: the struggle of the landowners—noble or bourgeois—against collective rights had begun even during the Ancien Régime. Once feudalism was abolished, the lord, if he had not emigrated, was nonetheless a landowner. These "cultivateurs à cabriolet" [carriage-cultivators] were the ones who now denounced the "poor sans-culottes" of the countryside and their obstinate demands for the maintenance of common pasture, the rights of gleaning and clearing, the obligation of harvesting with a sickle, the prohibition of herds kept apart, and the maintenance of the common herd.[23] Here again, the absolute right of property, a bourgeois conception, and economic liberty clashed with the traditional concept of limited property and a system of precapitalist production. The strength of this peasant current was so broad that the bourgeoisie had to compromise: the Revolution, triumphant elsewhere, could not succeed in abolishing the rural community.

III

If now, having acknowledged the profound unity of the class struggle during the decade of 1789-1799, but also the social complexity of the complementary revolutionary currents, we are trying to draw up the balance sheet of the Revolution from our point of view, we are also affirming how much every schematic is contrary to reality. Bourgeois, the Revolution destroyed the feudal regime of production; it ruined the feudal relations of production, substituting for them new structures which corresponded to the productive forces under development in the old society. Bourgeois, the Revolution destroyed the antagonistic class, the landed aristocracy: once again it is a question of specifying to what degree. But it also ruined the factions of the bourgeoisie who, on several accounts, were integrated into the society of the Ancien Régime. Bourgeois, it assured the triumph of the capitalist economy founded on economic liberty: in this sense, it precipitated the ruin of social categories that were attached to the traditional system of production, to the workshop, to the shop. But in the domain of agricultural production, the resistance of the impoverished peasantry was such that capitalism could not be imposed incontestably.

The revolutionary bourgeoisie, aided by the sans-culotterie, pursued the destruction of feudalism and the privileges of the landed aristocracy with a relentlessness multiplied by the resistance of the aristocracy. Without speaking here of the measures taken against individuals—the massacres or executions—we can assert that the nobility disappeared as a social order; all distinction between nobles and commoners was suppressed; the personal seigniorial rights, from which flowed the dependence of the peasants, were abolished on the night of August 4. Above all, with the feudal relations of production destroyed, the aristocracy was hit in its economic base. A number of noble families drew a significant part of their revenue from the seigniorial rights which weighed heavy on the land: these rights, first declared purchasable, were irremediably abolished by the Convention on June 17, 1793. Moreover, the Revolution brought an end to the landed property of the nobility: the ancient lords had to restore the communal rights that they had monopolized; the wealth of the émigrés, impounded from March of 1792, was put up for sale in June of 1793. The suppression of the venality of offices ruined the *noblesse de robe*: they were reimbursed at the official price, in devalued "assignats." As the crisis deepened, the nobles were little by little excluded from all public functions, civil or military. Under the Directory (and this shows how much—even after Thermidor—the meaning of the class struggle remained unchanged), the government went as far as to consider banishing all nobles who had exercised any function in the Ancien Régime, and the reduction of others to the status of aliens. However, we should not stretch the point: the nobility was not entirely nor irremediably stripped of its lands. Only the émigrés saw their wealth confiscated. Many nobles went through the Revolution without great damage and conserved their holdings: property of the bourgeois type, to be sure; once feudalism was abolished, seigniorial rights no longer came with property. Moreover, fictitious divorces and repurchases under assumed names allowed the émigrés to safeguard their lands or to recoup them. Thus a certain percentage of the old aristocracy was maintained which would merge with the upper bourgeoisie in the 19th century.

The bourgeoisie of the Ancien Régime shared to a large degree the fate of the aristocracy. The bourgeois who lived nobly off their revenues from the land saw their rental charges and seigniorial rights evaporate. The bourgeoisie of the "officiers," like the *noblesse de robe*, were ruined by the suppression of venality. The great financial bourgeoisie received a mortal blow with the abolition of the collection of indirect taxes; on August 24, 1793, the Montagnard Convention went as far as suppressing companies; finance resented the disappearance of the national bank, as well as the return of taxation and controls in the year II. Finally, in order to measure the blows with which the bourgeois revolution struck certain sectors of the bourgeoisie, think of the considerable repercussions of inflation on acquired wealth. More than in commercial and industrial enterprises, the traditional bourgeoisie placed its savings in mortgage loans or in bonds of the public debt. In the year II, the depreciation of the "assignat" incited the debtors to free themselves of the mortgage debts at little cost. The management of these perpetual and lifetime debts by Cambon under the Convention, the bankruptcy of two-thirds or the Ramel liquidation under the Directory constituted new blows. All these facts account for the rallying of the bourgeoisie of the Ancien Régime to the counterrevolution: it shared the fate of the aristocracy whose cause it had espoused.

Just as much as the destruction of the aristocracy, the revolutionary bourgeoisie obstinately pursued the ruin of the feudal system of production and exchange, which was incompatible with the expansion of its enterprises. It is true that the bourgeoisie had to compromise with the sans-culottes in the year II and submit once again to taxation and controls; but this was merely an interlude that legitimized the struggle against the aristocracy. After the 9th Thermidor, economic liberty was installed triumphant on the ruins of the popular movement.

The consequences were heavy for the traditional popular classes. Already the Constituent Assembly had suppressed the guilds. If the measure appeared democratic, it nonetheless damaged the interests of the master artisans. By allowing capitalism a rapid expansion, economic liberty energized the acceleration of the concentration of enterprises: thus, at the same time that the material conditions of social life were transformed, the structure of traditional popular classes was altered. Doubtless one cannot exaggerate the progress of capitalism during the revolutionary decade: it was slowed to a great extent by events. But conditions were now put together for a broad development of the capitalist economy that would necessarily transform the sans-culotterie into the proletariat: a social transformation which spread out over the course of the 19th century; on this account, it would be interesting to specify what part was played in the revolutionary movements of that century, from the June days of 1848 to the Paris Commune of 1871, by the proletariat—properly speaking—as opposed to the popular classes of the traditional type: thus the degeneration of the latter would be measured to the extent that the capitalist economy triumphed, and one of the causes of weakness in the revolutionary attempts of the working world during the 19th century would be specified. The artisans and journeymen had a foreboding of the fate that was to be theirs, the latter knowing that mechanization increased the risks of unemployment, and the former knowing that capitalist concentration brought with it the closing of their workshops and transformed them into wage workers. But the bourgeois revolution delivered them defenseless to the rulers of the new forms of the economy: the Le Chapelier law of 1791, prohibiting "coalitions" and strikes, was for the industrial bourgeoisie an effective instrument of development.

In the sphere of agricultural production, where the resistance of the impoverished peasantry was more relentless, the Revolution was less radical in its consequences. Even though it permitted the development of a dominating rural bourgeoisie, the Revolution could not completely destroy the rural community nor give free rein to the development of a new agriculture.

If the destruction of the feudal regime of property and the traditional organization of agriculture, along with the abolition of seigniorial dues and the ecclesiastical "dîme", profited the peasantry on the whole, the other agrarian reforms of the Revolution essentially strengthened those peasants who were already landowners. These reforms included augmentation of peasant property through the sale of national lands, extension of the right of property through the restriction of collective rights and the proclamation of freedom to enclose and cultivate. If we set aside the urban bourgeoisie who appropriated a considerable portion of the national wealth and look at the rural population, it was the big farmers and the "laboureurs" who profited from the way the national lands were sold and auctioned. Thus the rural bourgeoisie was strengthened and the gulf between this bourgeoisie and the impoverished peasantry was widened.[24]

But the impoverished peasantry did not come out of the revolution as disarmed as did the urban sans-culotterie facing the triumphant bourgeoisie. The impoverished peasantry did not obtain from the revolutionary assemblies the restoration or strengthening of the traditional rural community that it had desired. But the bourgeois revolution had not irremediably destroyed this community; it had not brutally suppressed the communal properties and the collective usages which constituted the foundation of the rural community.[25] Both lasted throughout the 19th century and still have not disappeared completely: the law of 1892—still in force—subjects the abandonment of common pasture to the will of the peasants of the village. The rural community, traditional framework of agricultural production, was thus maintained, pursuing its slow disintegration.

Doubtless it would be necessary to introduce here some nuances, the same as were perceptible in the social structure of the peasantry of the Ancien Régime. In the regions of large-scale cultivation, where the farmers were active agents of the capitalist transformation of agriculture, the rural community disintegrated rapidly, not by breaking up into antagonistic classes (the big farmers are generally urban capitalists, strangers to the rural community), but as if emptying itself of its substance: the poor peasants, quickly proletarianized, provided the labor necessary to both capitalist agriculture and big industry. In the regions of small-scale cultivation, the evolution was slower. The rural community was eroded from the inside by the antagonism between the rural bourgeoisie of the "laboureurs" and the impoverished peasantry, fierce in the defense of their rights to use the fields and woods: thus two economic forms confronted each other, one archaic, the other new with the affirmation of individualism among capitalist producers. This was an obscure but passionate struggle marked by agrarian troubles of the traditional sort, of which the last (1848-1851) were not the least violent, nor the least characteristic.[26]

Although it destroyed the feudal relations of production in the countryside, the Revolution could not radically destroy the traditional forms of agricultural production: in this domain it only effected a compromise whose significance is measured if one compares the evolution of French agriculture and that of English agriculture. Doubtless, thanks to the Revolution, the capitalist transformation of agriculture—already perceptible during the Ancien Régime—was accelerated. However, its progress was considerably braked by the maintenance of collective usages left to the will of the peasants, the parcelling of property and of exploitation. The autonomy of small rural producers was maintained for a long time, giving to the political evolution of France, particularly under the Third Republic, certain of its distinguishing characteristics. If enclosure and regrouping of lands had been imposed in France, as in England, capitalism would have triumphed in the domain of agricultural production as radically as in that of industrial production: the obstinate struggle of the landed aristocracy, by preventing all compromise with the bourgeoisie, obliged that bourgeoisie to handle the peasantry carefully, even the impoverished peasantry whose resistance made them all the more fearsome.

If we now consider the class who, having prepared and led the Revolution, essentially profited from it, we affirm that it appears radically transformed. For the dominance, traditional in its ranks, of acquired fortune was substituted that of the directors of production and distribution: the internal equilibrium of the bourgeoisie was modified. The bourgeoisie of the Ancien Régime, whether it lived off seigniorial rights and rents or off revenues of its "offices" or fees, to the degree that it shared the privileges of the aristocracy and had defended its cause, suffered rude shocks: if it was not radically destroyed, since its landed property remained for those of its representatives who had not emigrated, its primacy disappeared. A new bourgeoisie now appeared in the front ranks, formed from the heads of industry, the directors of commerce and finance. The equipping, arming and resupplying of the armies, the sale of national wealth, and the exploitation of conquered lands provided businessmen with new opportunities for developing their enterprises; speculation was at the origin of immense fortunes: thus the bourgeoisie renewed itself by incorporating these "nouveaux riches" (of which Ouvard remains the archetype), who set the tone for the "society" of the Directory. True adventurers of the new society, they revived the bourgeoisie by their enterprising spirit and their taste for risks; soon their capital was invested in commerce and industry. On a lower rung of the bourgeois ladder, circumstances had permitted numerous merchants and artisans to enlarge their fortunes, expand their enterprises and to thus come out from the ranks of the people into those of the bourgeoisie. It is at this middle level that the new dominant class soon recruited the bureaucrats for public administration, as members of the liberal professions. Doubtless after ten years of revolution, these traits were not yet definitively fixed, but they were already sketched with enough clarity to characterize the new bourgeoisie; they hardened during the Napoleonic period when the fusion of these diverse elements occurred at the same time that the institutions were fashioned which consecrated the supremacy of the new dominant class: thus the work of the bourgeois revolution was achieved.

*

At the end of this sketch, which has no other goal than that of stimulating reflection on the history of the Revolution, certain points deserve to be emphasized, for they have an instructive value.

If there are laws of historical evolution, they cannot be reduced to a mechanical schematic, as some are led to do by a false application of historical materialism. Social classes, even the dominant ones, are rarely homogenous; in the framework of general evolution, the diverse factions that compose them complicate the game of class struggles, often developing complementary antagonisms: in the bourgeois revolution, the sans-culottes provide one example. Only a precise economic and social analysis will account for the exact place that the diverse social categories occupy in the class struggle, baring the contradictions that may manifest themselves between a political attitude and an economic position: once again we have the case of the sans-culotterie. One must be careful finally not to forget that the class struggles—as they develop—influence the classes which participate in the struggles and transform them: the bourgeoisie which profited from the Revolution was no longer the same as the bourgeoisie which triggered it.

These truths may appear evident. They are nevertheless worth recalling. History is a dialectical movement. To avoid deforming history by schematizing it, those who commit themselves to its study must acknowledge the complexity that provides its richness, as well as the contradictions which provide its dramatic character.

3

Political Aspects of Popular Democracy in the Year II[1]

Politically speaking, the Parisian sans-culottes constituted the most advanced party of the French Revolution. They conceived of popular sovereignty in the total sense of the term, claimed the right of legal sanctions, such as control and recall of elected officials. In their section [neighborhood] general assemblies they practiced direct democracy, using the name "popular republic."[2] But could bourgeois conceptions of democracy be reconciled with the political tendencies of the sans-culotterie? Its behavior was characterized by a certain number of practices setting it in opposition to the bourgeoisie. Conceived and tested in the fire of action, these practices contributed to the progress of the Revolution and to the strengthening of the Jacobin dictatorship. But were the political tendencies and practices of the sans-culotterie compatible in the end with the necessities of the bourgeois revolution?

I

Sovereignty resides in the people: from this principle all the political behavior of the sans-culottes is derived. They conceived of sovereignty not as an abstraction, but as the concrete reality of the people meeting in local assemblies and exercising the totality of their rights. Popular sovereignty is "imprescriptible, inalienable, indelegable" according to the Parisian section of la Cité, November 3, 1792. From that the sans-culottes drew a conclusion that constituted one of the levers of popular action: censure, control and recall of elected officials.

Here it is necessary to go back to Jean-Jacques Rousseau and the social contract. Rousseau had sharply criticized the representative system as it functioned in England. "If the English people think they are free, they deceive themselves; they are only free during the election of members of Parliament; as soon as these are elected, the people are slaves: they no longer count for anything.... The deputies of the people thus are not nor can they be the people's representatives; they are only their commissioners."[3]

The sans-culottes will say their *proxies*. The deputies to the Convention, observed a citizen of the Tuileries section on September 22, 1792, "must not be called representatives, but proxies of the people."[4] Leclerc, paraphrasing Rousseau, develops in *L'Ami du peuple [The Friend of the People]* of August 21, 1793, what the sans-culottes, in a confused way, were thinking: "A represented people is not free ... Don't lavish this epithet of representatives... The will of the people cannot be represented ... any of your magistrates are no more than your proxies." Many sans-culottes, writing to their representatives in the year II, signed their messages *ton égal en droit* [your equal under the law].

In order to reconcile the representative regime and the necessities of a true democracy, the sans-culottes called for the right to approve laws: the control of elected officials by the people tended toward the same goal. This was forcefully demanded by the Parisian sections at the time of the elections to the Convention. Two-tiered elections were multiplying; from the point of view of popular sovereignty and the inconveniences of the representative system, a number of Parisian sections tried to remedy this situation by censuring the choices of the electoral assembly and by exercising their right to control and recall.

The legislative assembly had suppressed the distinction between active citizens and passive citizens, but conserved the system of two-tiered elections; thus direct universal suffrage was called for in the most advanced sections. In his *Methods presented to the Marseilles section to irrevocably establish liberty and equality,* Lacroix denounced two-tiered voting as "immoral, destructive to the sovereignty of the people, favorable to intrigues and cabals."[5] On August 21, 1792, the Quinze-Vingts section adopted a petition plan already approved by the Montreuil section: "that there be no electoral bodies, but that any elections be held in the primary assemblies."[6] On August 27, 1792, the Place-Vendôme, Robespierre's section, in order to prevent the disadvantages of indirect suffrage, demanded that the electors vote by voice vote with the people present.[7] That same day the primary section of Bondy affirmed "that the sovereign people must not commit to anyone the exercise of the rights that they can't delegate without disadvantage; — that representation is true only when it derives immediately from those represented."[8]

The General Council of the Commune approved these votes by deciding on August 27 that the electors would vote by voice vote with the people present, and that the choices of the electoral assembly would be submitted to the approval of the various sections.[9]

Censure or the elimination ballot of elected officials had as a goal not only remedying the disadvantages of the two-tiered ballot: it manifested the indivisible characteristic of popular sovereignty. On August 27 the Place-Vendôme section demanded that the deputies nominated by the electors be "submitted to revision and examination by the sections or primary assemblies so that the majority might reject those who would be unworthy of the people's confidence." The Bondy section accorded the electoral assembly only one right of presentation, "reserving the right to recognize as deputies only those who will be confirmed or approved by the majority of primary assemblies of the department."

The General Council of the Commune, on this same August 27, once again sided with these views. On 31 August, the Maison-Commune section decided that the electors would just nominate the deputies; the sections would accept them or reject them.[10] On September 1, the Poissonnière section "considering that the sovereign people have the right to prescribe the path their proxies should take in order to act according to their will," declared that the deputies will be discussed, approved or rejected by the primary assemblies.[11] Popular pressure was such that on September 12 the electoral assembly of the department of Paris decided to present to the sections the list of deputies elected to the Convention, "in order to prepare the approval of the people by the elimination ballot, and in order to waken the spirit of sovereignty in all members of the body politic."[12]

Whatever the popular conviction in the matter of sovereignty may have been, we cannot conceal the fact that even the most solemnly proclaimed principles were being bent to circumstances. If the principle of censure by the sections was affirmed with so much force before the designation of the deputies, it was to protect against each bad choice by the electoral assembly. Thus the people would be in a position to rectify the vote of the electors. The general assembly of the Quatre-Nations section explained this clearly. On September 9, 1792, recalling the necessity of excluding from all seats "the royalists, petitioners, chaplains and other schemers of this sort," it decided that "if by misfortune one of these designated individuals reached the seat of representative of the people," the assembly reserved the right to reject him and proceed to another ballot.[13] Just as much as the general principle of popular sovereignty, the censure of deputies thus conformed to tactical necessities. When it appeared that most of the deputies nominated by the electoral assembly belonged to the Montagnard faction, the advanced sections modified their attitude and bent their principles. If the censure of deputies were to proceed, it risked going against the desired goal. The General Council of the Commune, who on August 27 had upheld the sections' right to approve the choices of the electoral body, was not afraid of reversing its decision: around the middle on September it published an address "on the disadvantages that would occur in subjecting the deputies of the Convention to an elimination ballot."[14]

Already, in fact, certain sections or certain moderate agitators were challenging the most solid patriotic reputations. The Marches section accepted the nomination of Marat to the Convention on September 19, 1792, only after a long discussion and not without denouncing "the principles of disorganization" of the Friend of the people.[15] Mehee was indignant that they wanted to tear away from the citizens the right to accept or reject the deputies designated by the electors, even if this was only to better attack Robespierre.[16] Faced with this danger, certain sections,
while proclaiming their attachment to the elimination ballot, were opportunistically renouncing it. Thus the Réunion general assembly declared on September 18, 1792 that it would renounce "for this time only" exercising its censure on the nominations of the electoral assembly.[17] The Poissonnière section, in order to reconcile "both the rights of the people and what was necessary to the safety of the country," decided the same day to postpone the *review* of deputies until "after the return of our brothers from the borders."[18]

The censure of deputies as a remedy for the two-tiered elections was not enough to safeguard the principle of popular sovereignty. It was still necessary that the elected officials be faithful to the mandate they had received. Without again formally taking up the theory of the imperative mandate that had been affirmed at the time of the elections to the Estates General and the editing of the "cahiers de doleances," the Parisian sections clearly enunciated, during the elections to the Convention, the principle of control and recall of elected officials by the sovereign people. In this way the disadvantages of the representative system were to a certain degree attenuated.

On August 25, 1792, the general assembly of the Marché-des-Innocents posited as an essential base of a national Convention that "the deputies will be subject to recall at the will of their departments", and that "public officials will be subject to recall by those who appointed them, whose deliberations they will be obliged to execute."[19] That same day the general assembly of Bonne-Nouvelle invited the Paris sections "to remind their delegates of the inalienable right of the sections to withdraw their power and to remind [those elected] of the object of their mission."[20] On September 9, 1792, in the Paris electoral assembly, an elector from the Les Halles section proposed "to declare as a principle that the inviolable sovereignty of the people admits the inalienable right and power of recalling their representatives any time they judge it proper and in accord with their interests."

The electoral assembly which, on September 6 had been content to send back to the primary assemblies the question of recall of deputies "in the event of negligence or corruption," adopted the proposition of the Les Halles section. On September 18, the assembly of the Droits-de-l'Homme declared that it was reserving the right to recall deputies "if, in the course of the session, they demonstrated signs of lack of patriotism."[21] The general assembly of the Reunion declared the same day that "it expressly reserved the recall of elected deputies whenever during the course of their functions they performed some act that made them suspect of lacking patriotism or seeking to introduce in France a government contrary to liberty and equality."[22]

The principle of control and recall of deputies was not affirmed by the Parisian sections in an abstract manner. In the circumstances of the summer of 1792, this principle was adapted to precise tactical necessities, as was the principle of censure of nominations to the electoral assembly. It was a question of assuring the triumph of the patriots. This same principle was recalled each time revolutionary policy was threatened. To take up again the terms of a brochure of summer 1792, the deputies were only proxies, porters of the orders of the citizens. "They must thus strictly follow them, without deviation and must account to their nominators about all they have said, written or done in the exercise of their functions as proxies."

In the conflict that set the Girondists against the Montagnards — from the autumn of 1792 on — the advanced sections demanded the right to censure elected officials and to demand an accounting from them, while the moderate sections protested against this claim.

During the electoral process that began on November 11, 1792, for the replacement of the Parisian authorities, the Quatre-Vingt-Douze section on December 18 invited the electoral assembly to remain faithful to its commitment to submit its nominations to the sections for approval: those elected should not only pass "through the crucible and censure of the sections, but also owe them an accounting."[23] On December 30, the Champs-Élysées section denounced "these decrees dictated by a Machiavellian and disruptive mind: the wishes of the citizens are forced in this direction by threats of banishment, and principles are forgotten to the point of wishing to influence, by publicizing an indiscreet oath, the representatives of the whole nation." This section demanded respect, "in all its fullness," for the freedom of the representatives.[24] Thus is plainly pronounced the opposition between two conceptions of the representative system — one popular, the other bourgeois.

As the crisis worsened in March 1793, the advanced patriots demanded from "the impious faction" the application of the people's right to recall their representatives. On March 10, at the time of the first attempt to eliminate the Girondists, the club of Cordeliers invited the department of Paris, "an integral part of the sovereign" to take hold of the exercise of sovereignty; that the electoral body of Paris might be convened to replace "the members who are traitors to the cause of the people."[25] That same day, the Quatre-Nations section demanded "as the supreme and only effective measure" the convocation of the section to authorize the electoral assembly of the Paris department "to recall the unfaithful proxies, unworthy of being legislators of the public welfare, since they have betrayed their mandate by voting for the preservation of the tyrant and the appeal to the people."[26]

To the principle of the removability of elected officials, the Girondists countered with that of their inviolability. The Tuileries section observed on April 10, 1793 that the principle of inviolability, "having been conceived only under a monarchic reign, deputies could not enjoy it under a republican government; the proxies should be accountable to a free people for their deeds and actions." The Tuileries section demanded in consequence the suppression of inviolability, "as being an odious privilege to betray the interests of the people with impunity, a perfidious cloak with which a corrupt proxy can cover himself."[27] In the name of these same principles, the Finistère section evinced on May 12 its "discontent... with the misfortunes that the negligence, the incompetence or the bad faith of the Convention brings us," and summoned its representatives to "express categorically, yes or no, whether they can save the nation."[28]

This popular conviction against the inviolability of elected officials constituted the theoretical justification of the days of May 31 and June 2, 1793. The Convention did not obey the injunctions of the sovereign people as to the representatives considered traitors to their mandate, so the people again took up the direct exercise of their sovereignty and imposed the removal of the 22 Girondist deputies. On May 21, Luillier, the public prosecutor of the department, charged the Convention, in the name of the revolutionary authorities, to deliver itself to the wishes of the nation; the delegation and a crowd of citizens came to mingle "fraternally with the members of the left party."[29] On June 2, the spokesman of the delegation of the insurrectional authorities declared that the citizens of Paris "demanded from their proxies, their rights, shamefully betrayed."[30] The insurrection constituted the ultimate consequence of the principle of popular sovereignty.

Were the Montagnards, who since August 1792 had supported and clarified the popular demands on the matter of sovereignty, going to make these demands law once they were in power? On May 25, 1793, the Unité section, "given that responsibility is the essence of a Republic," had demanded that a tribunal composed of members from each department make a pronouncement, at the time of the elections, on the conduct of the deputies of the preceding session, "and that those who have badly served the country be... forever rejected from all seats in the Republic."[31]

The Arras sections posed the problem in all its urgency when, on June 18, 1793, they declared to the Convention that five deputies of Pas-de-Calais had lost their confidence; the Assembly made no decision.[32] Responding to these concerns, Herault de Sechelle, in the course of the discussion on the projected Constitution on June 24, 1793, presented a chapter entitled *On the people's censure of deputies and its guarantee against oppression from the legislative body.* It raised sharp opposition and Couthon, in the name of the Committee of Public Safety, had it rejected.[33] Here again tactical necessities prevailed over principles.

The strengthening of the Committee of Public Safety, accompanied by the ongoing establishment of the revolutionary government, did not totally silence the sectional demands on the matter, which were moreover kept alive by the popular press. Leclerc reminded the deputies in *L'Ami du peuple* [August 21, 1798] that they were under the *watchful eye* of the people. "Their arms will be rewarding or vengeful according to how you will have fixed their opinion by your actions." On August 4, the Amis-de-la-Patrie section had asked the General Council of the Commune that the deputies be judged after the session and "that they be paid according to their works."[34] On September 29, 1793, the Halle-au-Blé section affirmed solemnly "that it is up to the sovereign [people] alone to examine the members of the constituted powers which it itself has chosen."[35] In the beginning of Year II, the Observatoire section again recalled "that the sovereignty of the people necessarily included the right to recall unfaithful representatives and all public officials unworthy of its confidence."[36]

This people's control reinforced the authority of those representatives to whom they accorded their confidence. Certain Montagnards realized this. In the crisis of the summer of 1793, they judged it necessary to justify their acts in front of their section. Thus Collot d'Herbois, member of the Lepeletier section, on assignment in the departments of the Oise and the Aisne, wrote to his section from Senlis on September 4 an account of his conduct and a collection of his decrees: the assembly discussed and approved them.[37] This kind of communication permitted the sections to control their elected officials and allowed the representatives to contribute to the formation of public opinion.

Once the revolutionary government and the Jacobin dictatorship were firmly established by the decree of December 4, 1793, affirmation of the principles of popular sovereignty disappeared. The Committee of Public Safety was concerned above all with centralization and effectiveness. It no longer tolerated even a simple reminder of the right of the people to control and recall their elected officials. The popular principles were subordinated to the requirements of the bourgeois revolution.

II

Certain practices of the Parisian sans-culottes in their political assemblies were naturally worrisome to the bourgeoisie, whose opposition to the revolutionary government thus intensified. So it was with the practice of voting by voice or by acclamation. The sans-culotte felt that the patriot had nothing to hide, neither his opinions nor his actions. Political life thus unfolded in broad daylight, under the eyes of the people; the administrative bodies and the section assemblies deliberated in public sessions, the electors voted by voice vote with the tribunes watching: one acted in secret only if one had evil designs. "Publicity is the safeguard of the people."

The practice of the voice ballot was established after August 10, 1792. On the 17th, two municipal officials read the law creating the extraordinary criminal Tribunal to the Théâtre-Français assembly which decided that "given the urgency and the necessity of promptly organizing this tribunal," it would nominate its representative by acclamation.[38] For the elections to the Convention, the voice ballot was imposed for all of the procedures. This permitted an evaluation of the choice of electors and remedied to a certain degree the two-tiered ballot that was considered destructive of popular sovereignty. The Place-Vendôme section decided on August 27, 1792, under the influence of Robespierre, that the electors would vote by voice in the presence of the people; in order to carry out this last prescription, electoral operations unfolded in the hall of the Jacobins.[39] That same day, the Bondy section decided that all elections would be by voice vote, and that the electoral assembly should surround itself with the greatest number of citizens "to be witnesses to the will of each elector," the only measure capable "of confounding intrigues and forcing the electors to not abuse their powers."[40] The General Council of the Commune approved these expressed wishes the same day: ballots would take place by voice vote and by roll call, the sessions would be held in the presence of the people; the bishop's palace not offering arrangements necessary to receive the public, the electoral assembly would be seated in the premises of the Jacobins.[41] The electoral assembly conformed to this decision.

The question of the method of voting was raised again in October, 1792, at the time of the nomination of the Mayor of Paris and municipal officials: the same reasons of revolutionary surveillance led most of the sections to use the same procedure. The electoral law having imposed the secret ballot, the Mirabeau section, reflecting on "the disadvantages and dangers" that would result, called for the voice vote.[42] More prudent, the Champs-Élysées section was content to affirm the sovereignty of the primary assemblies, without prejudging their decision: on October 3 this section posited in principle that "the exercise of the right of voting should not be hampered by any form that did not emanate from the primary assemblies themselves, since it is the only right which cannot and must never be delegated"; they were thus empowered to set their method of balloting.[43] On October 9, the Piques section considered the secret ballot "as a custom destructive to liberty"; it demanded from the Convention a ballot "appropriate to a free people."[44] The Panthéon-Français section, "without regard to the law or the decrees of the municipality," decided that it would vote by voice ballot.[45] The Bondy section hesitated. On October 29, the general assembly demanded the vote "by voice and by open ballot"; the president closed the session. The assembly elected a new president and declared the voice vote "the only ballot appropriate to republicans."[46] In fact many sections hesitated, tending toward the voice vote but observing that the secret ballot was required by law. The situation appeared less serious than in September: public pressure had relaxed. The Piques section, formerly the Place-Vendôme, which had been the first (August 27, 1792) to pronounce in favor of the voice vote, was now conforming to the law.

The influence of the moderates, concerned with legality and attached to the forms of bourgeois democracy, in effect counterbalanced that of the sans-culottes. On the order of Roland, Girondist Minister of the Interior, the Mayor of Paris inquired on October 9, 1792 about the method of balloting adopted by the various sections.[47] The responses that reached him enable us to draw up a political picture of the Parisian sections, unfortunately incomplete, and to thus measure the popular influence on one specific point. Out of twenty-six sections whose responses have been saved, fifteen declared that they had voted by roll call voice vote, certain ones adding that, acting thus, they were going by the example of the elections to the Convention. Eleven sections had used the secret ballot; but, as the Mayor of Paris specified in his letter of October 14 to the Minister of the Interior, they expressed the wish that a law would permit future elections by voice vote.[48]

The renewal of moderate influence in the autumn of 1792 was marked in the sections of the Temple, Luxembourg, Piques, Théâtre-Français: they had voted by secret ballot. The sections of Panthéon-Français, Gravilliers, Finistere, Faubourg-Montmartre nevertheless remained faithful to the voice vote: they were among the most popular and the most advanced.

As the crisis resumed in March 1793, the sans-culottes once again imposed the voice vote as a means of effective struggle against the moderates. Soon even this method of balloting seemed suspect, as not translating the sentiments of unanimity which should animate the sans-culottes: voting by acclamation became widespread during the summer of 1793. Even more than the voice vote, the ballot by acclamation, or by sitting or rising, intimidated those who were hesitating and eliminated all opposition. It soon seemed the only method of revolutionary balloting.

In March 1793 when the Parisian sections, at first spontaneously, then in execution of the law of the 21st, nominated their revolutionary committees, these elections were generally held by voice vote, often by sitting or rising, as occurred on March 29 in the Contrat-Social section.[49] These nominations were subsequently judged illegal and constituted one of the grievances most often invoked against the former commissioners during the repression of the year III. In May and June 1793, in the bitter struggle between the sans-culottes and the moderates for the domination of the section general assemblies, the method of balloting was a tactic that the rival factions fought over. "No closed ballot, or the cabal triumphs," declared a sans-culotte from Mail on May 21.[50] During the election of the commander in chief of the Parisian National Guard, the sans-culottes, in order to sweep along the election of Hanriot, imposed balloting by voice vote in the sections they dominated; the moderates, favoring Raffet, declared themselves for the secret ballot. The Lepeletier section, then led by moderates, stuck to the law; but the sans-culottes there voted by voice vote. The gunner La Merlière declared: "I'm not Joe f... off," I'm voting loud and clear for Hanriot."[51] Where they could not impose their way, the sans-culottes used other means. In the Unité section, on June 27, a citizen denounced the evil-wishers and their cabal, and forced reconsideration of the decree by which the assembly had adopted the secret ballot: the ballots would be signed by the voters, or else be considered null and void.[52] Thus the principle of the public nature of debate, considered essential by the sans-culottes, was maintained.

In the course of the summer of 1793, balloting by voice vote spread to the extent that the political influence of the sans-culotterie grew. The Society of Free Men of the Pont Neuf section adopted it on August 7, 1793: it is the *ballot of free men*.[53] In the autumn of 1793, moderate societies adopted the voice vote favored by the sans-culottes. Moderates who persisted in wanting to use the secret ballot were arrested as suspects. Thus a certain Bourdon of the Bonne-Nouvelle section was arrested for "voting in the swamp in a low voice at the moment of nominations."[54] The same fate met Louis Maillet, printer and line engraver of the Panthéon-Français section, arrested December 2, 1794 "for fiercely opposing the desire of the patriots to vote by voice in the general assemblies."[55] The practice of the secret ballot, considered unpatriotic, thus disappeared from the political life of the sections at the beginning of the year II.

As masters of the general assemblies, the sans-culottes imposed a method of nomination corresponding even better to their revolutionary temperament and their ardent search for unanimity: voting by acclamation. Certainly it was not unknown. The sans-culottes had already used it in moments of acute crisis. Thus on August 2, 1792 the general assembly of Postes designated its president by acclamation and rejected a call for a ballot.[56] From September 1793 on, voting by acclamation became widespread. About this time, the general assembly of Beaurepaire, "not wishing to waste its time in elections by ballot," got used to naming its president by acclamation, "a procedure it also hastened to use when the president of the committee received orders ... that necessitated a prompt decision."[57]

Urgency was not the only motive for the vote by acclamation. It was, apart from a means of annihilating opponents, a manifestation of revolutionary unity dear to the sans-culottes. This practice was the rule until spring of year II, concurrently with the vote by sitting or rising, less used, but just as effective. The general assembly of Butte-des-Moulins decided on November 10, 1793 to proceed to nominations *in a revolutionary manner by sitting and rising*; on December 15 it reelected its officers *in a revolutionary manner by acclamation.*[58] Voting by acclamation was finally imposed, under popular pressure, on the General Council of the Commune. On February 20, 1794 Lubin, its president, asked to be replaced. *Lubin! Lubin!* shouted the members of the Council, almost unanimously, and the gallery took up the cry: *Lubin! Lubin!* Lubin observed that such a nomination would not be legal. The laws of the provisional government were consulted; it was determined that the General Council had the right to name and to reelect its president when it pleased and *in the manner in which it pleased*. "Nominate canvassers, proceed to the ballot? That would take up too much time." Lubin was proclaimed elected.[59]

The sans-culottes were not satisfied with having imposed a method of voting on sectional politics corresponding to their temperament and their political interests. Their wish was to extend it to all domains. For example, to the domain of justice. Already the jurors of the Revolutionary Tribunal gave their verdicts by voice vote. But in the jury of the Criminal Tribunal of the department, the old rules persisted. On December 20, 1793, the Society of Free Men of the Revolutionaire section expressed astonishment at this situation. "The magistrate, the judge, the citizen juror, which the law calls to pronounce on offences whatever they may be, owe the people an explanation of the motivations that determined their judgment; they owe to public opinion an accounting of all their thoughts so that the public may in turn judge them." The Society demanded that all jurors be obligated to give their verdicts by voice vote and to give the reasons for their opinion. "The public nature of proceedings, this fundamental principle of liberty, of justice, of equality, will give them all the energy they must have."[60]

The Convention was loath to abandon the habitual forms of justice for ordinary tribunals: the petition was sent back to the Committee on legislation. On March 11, 1794, according to the observer Boucheseiche, various groups of people in the Palace of Justice were astonished by the voting method of the jurors in the criminal Tribunal. "It was observed that this secret method saved the life of more than one hoarder, because a juror who would have said out loud that the accused was guilty would in secret absolve him."[61]

By this date, the sans-culotte practice of the open ballot was ready to disappear. It was not to survive the crisis of February-March 1794 and the condemnation of the *cordelier* group. With the strengthening of the Jacobin dictatorship, a return to bourgeois forms was in operation: voting by acclamation or even out loud was formally proscribed for the nominations of the general assemblies by Payan, national agent of the purged Commune. The sections had to obey. But the sans-culottes deserted the general assemblies rather than use a balloting method they deemed favorable to their adversaries. For the election of two clothing commissioners on July 18, 1794, a discussion arose in the general assembly of the Invalides: should we proceed by acclamation or by secret ballot? "With the decision that the commissioners in question should be named by ballot, many citizens left the assembly, not wishing to take part in the deliberation."[62] The return to the secret ballot was one of the measures marking the reaction in the spring of 1794. It contributed to some extent to the disaffection of the sans-culottes from the revolutionary government.

The reactors of the Thermidorian period maintained the policy of the Robespierrist Commune on this point. In spring of 1795 they even prosecuted those who had advocated the voice vote, by sitting or rising or by acclamation, as well as those who had benefitted from it. The last mention of this popular practice concerned the Parisian section of Indivisibility. At the meeting of its primary assembly on the first complementary day of year III (September 17, 1795), a certain Berger proposed that voting should be only by voice vote: he was expelled "almost unanimously by the assembly, as one of the most obvious agents of terrorism."[63]

These few notes shed light on the opposition between democracy as practiced by the sans-culottes and democracy as understood by the bourgeoisie, even the Jacobins. The sans-culottes implemented their rights to the letter. For bourgeois democracy, the rights of the sovereign people are exercised only during the nomination of their representatives and by their intermediaries. Speaking in the name of the Gironde, Vergniaud rose on March 13, 1793 against the abuse that the anarchists made of the word sovereignty: "It very nearly happened that they overturned the Republic, by making each section believe that sovereignty resided in its breast." Likewise, the practical politics of the sans-culottes, essentially characterized in 1793 and 1794 by voting by acclamation, was the expression of a concept of democracy fundamentally different from that of the bourgeoisie.

Doubtless the popular conceptions in the matter of sovereignty furnished the Montagnard bourgeoisie the justification for the insurrections of August 10, 1792 and May 31–June 2, 1793. The bourgeoisie itself also used certain popular practices. For instance in Paris during the elections to the Convention, the voice vote was used. Events legitimized this infringement on the habitual conceptions of bourgeois democracy, as did class interest. This same interest and events prevented the continuation of these conceptions and practices once the revolutionary government and the Jacobin dictatorship were installed in power. If it corresponded to the political interests of the sans-culottes, the popular practice of democracy was incompatible with the behavior and the conceptions of the bourgeoisie: it threatened its interests and its supremacy. This contradiction could be resolved, in the conditions of the period, only by the pacesetting of the Parisian sections. But this meant breaking the spirit of the popular movement that had brought the revolutionary government to power and which alone could sustain it.

Thus the road to Thermidor was laid, where the popular dream of an egalitarian revolution foundered.

4

From Feudalism to Capitalism—A Contribution[1]

In the light of the controversy on "the transition from feudalism to capitalism" led by the journal *Science and Society*, profiting in particular from the precious remarks of H. K. Takahashi, but also taking into account the suggestions of Georges Lefebvre (that one shouldn't be content with a theoretical debate and that our task as historians is to study concrete cases), I would like to emphasize here certain aspects of the French Revolution: particularly, the social condition of the sans-culottes, their position in regard to commercial capital and their rôle in the revolutionary movement. This broad discussion will allow me to return to certain problems and to qualify certain oversimplified assertions.[2]

I

The French Revolution does indeed constitute a classic bourgeois revolution: the class struggle essentially pitted the capitalist bourgeoisie against the feudal aristocracy. But what was the social element of the former Third Estate which, in this struggle, represented the decisive factor in the destruction of the old relations of production? The large capitalist bourgeoisie or the small and medium merchant-producers and independent peasants?

In the society of the Ancien Régime, the bourgeoisie holding the commercial capital was in large measure tied to the power of the monarchical State and the feudal aristocracy: financiers, wholesale merchants, manufacturer-entrepreneurs were integrated, from the point of view of the relations of production, into the social and political system of feudal reaction. Think of the "fermier généraux," the suppliers of armies, the principal agents of the privileged financial companies. Think of the ties of dispersed rural workshops, under the control of merchants and manufacturers, with the feudal organization of agricultural production.

This social group of the upper bourgeoisie tied to commercial capital quickly took a counterrevolutionary position. This was expressed from

September 1789 on by the endeavors of the "Monarchiens." Mounier, their principal architect, will later write that his design was "to follow the lessons of experience, to oppose reckless innovations and to propose in the existing forms of government only those modifications necessary to maintain freedom:"[3] that is, to maintain the existing relations of production and the monarchical State that guaranteed them. The "Monarchiens" were replaced by the "Feuillants" (1791), then by the Girondists (1792-1793).

On the subject of the Girondists, we will take an example to illustrate their position in relation to commercial capital and to clarify their political stance. Isnard, the son of a merchant from Grasse, was elected deputy to the Convention from the Var. Sitting with the Girondists, he made himself famous with his apostrophe of May 25, 1793 against Paris ("Soon people would be searching on the banks of the Seine..."). Ordered to be arrested on October 3, 1793, arrested on March 9, 1794, he returned to the Convention on February 26, 1795. On April 19, 1795, he presented a memorandum seeking compensation for the losses suffered during his proscription.[4] This document informs us about the fortune of the Girondist Isnard and his economic activities. "I found myself," Isnard wrote, "at the head of a house of commerce passed from father to son, organized and developed by a half century of assiduous work, backed up by wide acceptance and an extended correspondence." This house of commerce specialized in the wholesale trade of oils, "for the shipment of which were supplied annually four to five hundred barrels." This trade in oils was linked to a manufacture of soap. "This house of commerce manufactured and shipped each year around 3,000 crates of soap of 225 'livres' each, which makes 7,400 'quintaux' (hundred-weights), to which were added about 1,600 'quintaux' of white soaps shipped in bars, not crates, or which were sold on the premises, making a total of 9,000 'quintaux' manufactured annually." Moreover, Isnard observed that "these two branches [soaps and oils] which were the most important products of my trade were not, however, the only ones; to these I joined among others the importation of grains, the manufacture of silk threads, the purchase of wine and other foodstuffs." Let us finally add two houses of commerce at Draguignan whose value Isnard estimates at 1,300 livres, and "some ships" for which he gives no precise information. Isnard claimed and obtained for losses suffered 152,047 livres.

This document calls for several comments. Isnard is first of all a wholesale merchant specializing in the commerce of oils and grain; his economic activity is founded on commercial capital; but, in this particular case, the commercial capital is not subject to production; he serves simply as an intermediary in the exchange of merchandise (oils, grain) which he does not produce. Isnard possesses in addition factories for soap and silk threads. The merchant has thus become an industrialist. The development of commercial capital to a certain degree is indeed the historical condition for the development of capitalist production: to a certain degree only, for this development unfolds without modification in the relations of production. This development could not therefore explain the passage from the mode of feudal production to the mode of capitalist production. In all of the businesses of Isnard, commerce always dominates industry; the economic base of production remains intact. There is no revolution there, as Marx emphasized.[5] The economic position of the merchant Isnard coincides well with the political position of the Girondist Isnard.

The medium and small bourgeoisies led a vigorous struggle against the upper bourgeoisie in 1793-1794. This struggle was as much against the top echelons of the bourgeoisie based on commercial capital as it was against the feudal aristocracy to whose social-political system the upper bourgeoisie were tied by the relations of production. It would be appropriate here to specify who the *Montagnards*, the *Jacobins* and the *sans-culottes* were from a social point of view: the problem of the transition from feudalism to capitalism would thus be clarified.

Danton symbolizes the Mountain: he could be characterized as a purchaser of national wealth. The abolition of feudalism was the essential condition of his new position of deriving income from the land, of living a life of ease as a capitalist. Among the Jacobins, the *carpenter* Duplay is a representative example: he was not a journeyman carpenter, but a boss of some importance. The words of Duplay's daughter, the wife of the delegate to the Convention Lebas, are often cited; according to her, her father, careful of his bourgeois dignity, never invited one of his "servants" to share his table. By servants he meant workers. Jaurès recalls in his *Histoire socialiste* that the *carpenter* Duplay collected ten to twelve thousand "livres" a year in rents from housing.[6] It is thus a question of an independent producer on the way to becoming a capitalist; on the political plane it is a question of one of the most active revolutionary elements.

I would like to here pay particular attention to the "sans-culottes." This term is vague; it encompasses diverse social categories, from the lowest popular strata to the small bourgeoisie. The framework of the Parisian "sans-culotterie" in 1793 and 1794 consisted of the personnel of the revolutionary committees. What was their social composition?

The personnel dossiers of the Committee of General Safety[7] provide us with a census of 454 revolutionary commissioners for Paris. Among these 20, or 4.5 % lived on private income: 4 men of leisure collecting income from land and investments (0.8 %), 11 retired from the liberal professions (2.4 %), 6 former shopkeepers or artisans (1.3 %). On the opposite side, we count 22 wage earners, workers, journeymen or "boys" (that is, workers working off debts to a master), and 23 servants or former servants—9.9 % of the total. The liberal professions are represented by 52 commissioners (10.5 %): the most numerous are the artists, sculptors, painters, musicians; then the school teachers; there are relatively few lawyers. To this group we could add 22 office workers, 7 of whom worked for the post office (4.8 %).

The bulk of the commissioners were artisans or shopkeepers: 290 of the 454 surveyed, or 63.8 % of the personnel of the revolutionary committees. Of these, 84 (18.5 %) can be considered as part of small or medium commerce, but 206 (45.3 %) come from the artisan class; that is, essentially small or medium merchant producers. Among these artisans, shoemakers were the most numerous: 28 shoemakers (6.1 %), followed by 18 carpenters (3.9 %), then by 16 wigmakers or coiffeurs (3.5 %). But it is to the whole of the trades of art and luxury that 42 commissioners belonged (9.2 %). The group of building trades comprised 37 commissioners (8.1 %), 29 were woodworkers or cabinetmakers (6.3 %).

Over and above these 454 revolutionary commissioners of the year II, a small group had already gone beyond the stage of artisan to enter into capitalist production. Along with the 8 commissioners classified as entrepreneurs (7 masons and 1 locksmith), we must look closely at the situation of 8 manufacturers of gauze, ribbon, stockings, wallpaper and plaster. Let us make it clear that "manufacturer" is not used here in the sense of manufacturer-contractor (commercial capital), but as the head of an enterprise employing a concentrated, wage-earning work force (industrial capital). The passage to capitalist production is accomplished here by the transformation of the producer into merchant and capitalist.

Several individual dossiers allow us to clarify the relations of production. In the section of the "Gardes-Françaises," the commissioner Maron is identified as "manufacturer and merchant" of plaster; he owns a quarry where he employs twenty workers.[8] This precise information gives us a glimpse of an industrialist who became a merchant producing directly for the market. Likewise, in the section of "Faubourg-du-Nord," the commissioner Mauvage is already an important industrialist, directing the manufacture of fans in a workshop that employed more than sixty workers.[9]

The members of the revolutionary committees of Paris in the year II were the most active agents of the revolutionary government, the most zealous executants of the Terror, whose "terrible hammer blows," to use Marx's expression,[10] rid France of the feudal ruins. We certainly don't want to deny the leading role of the big bourgeoisie in the Revolution. But it was indeed the petty and middle bourgeoisie (small and middle producer merchants) who constituted in year II the most efficient element in the struggle for the abolition of the former means of production.

II

At the end of the Ancien Régime, commercial capital was integrated into society, serving as the simple intermediary in the exchange of merchandise while dominating industrial production; the opposition of the small independent producers thus crystallized against commercial capital. This accounts for certain aspects of Montagnard policy and certain demands of the Parisian sans-culottes in the year II.

The sans-culottes attacked the institutions that supported commercial capital. They demanded the closing of the stock exchange and the suppression of joint-stock companies. On May 1, 1793, the Parisian section of Faubourg-du-Nord demanded the closing of the stock exchange; the next day the Contrat-Social section supported this petition.[11] It was necessary to wait for the elimination of the Girondists: the Convention ordered the closing of the Paris Stock Exchange on June 27, 1793.[12] As for joint-stock companies, they had proliferated by the end of the Ancien Régime. In July 1793, a citizen of the Sans-Culottes section was astonished to see appear "here a mutual aid association, over there a commercial bank, in another place a savings bank, farther on a subscription insurance office for the elderly, here a life insurance office, at this address the patriotic Lottery of the street of the Bac. (These are nothing but businesses to grab money.) These rich men, owners and entrepreneurs of banks, are the ones to fear most."[13] On August 24, 1793, the Montagnard Convention banned financial companies; on April 15, 1794, it prohibited all companies without distinction.[14]

Even more significant was the position of the Parisian sans-culottes on the subject of the manufacture of war materiel. Since nationalization had been adopted only for the manufacture of weapons, the revolutionary government was forced to turn to private enterprise for equipment and supplies. Following the tradition of the Ancien Régime, the government ordered from a handful of businessmen—wholesale merchants, important manufacturer-contractors—instead of dispersing orders among many small workshops of independent producers: commercial capital would still dominate industrial production, not the reverse. This situation was a source of conflict between the revolutionary government and the Parisian sans-culottes throughout the year II and contributed to the worsening of their relationship.

In certain sections, militants started a fund to raise the capital necessary to start manufacturing and thus escape their dependency on manufacturer-contractors and commercial capital. Toward this end, the Tuileries section issued a significant proclamation on February 4, 1793. "First of all, the greedy suppliers, ill-intentioned or ill-skilled, will no longer be able to hinder the movements of the armies, halting our successes; the fate of liberty will no longer be at the mercy of speculations of monopoly. Secondly, a small number of rich contractors will no longer appropriate all the profit from these immense supply orders; it will be shared by all our merchants, all our workers, all of us. Thirdly, partial enterprises, having always been managed with intelligence and economy, having smaller expenses, will supply us more, and the supplies will be better."[15]

Higher praise could not be given to the "partial enterprise"; that is, the small independent production controlling the commercial function. In fact, work will remain organized following the most widespread mode of this era. The manufacturer-contractor had skilled workers in scattered places; he was thus manufacturer in name only; in reality he was a merchant. The administration furnished the raw material to the contractors who had the clothing and the equipment made. This system raised even more protests because it aggravated the situation of the immediate producers, transforming them into simple wage earners.

The sections kept on protesting; but, without capital, they could not free themselves from their dependence on the contractors. On June 15, 1793, the Finistère section decided to establish a workshop under its control. However, it had to turn to commissioners capable of furnishing security equivalent to the value of the raw material allocated to the section and to advance the wages of the workers. Only one citizen came forward to pay the security of 6,000 "livres": he was an entrepreneur. The freedom of his enterprise was limited, however, by the control of the section commissioners.[16]

The same problem arose when the Invalides section organized a sectional workshop on September 9, 1793. Two commissioners were given the charge of directing it, overseeing the manufacturing, proposing the price of the tailoring and the piecework so that the overhead costs were covered, yet taking into account the prices paid by the Administration of the Outfitting of the troops. The general assembly of the section did indeed run the enterprise, naming the commissioners and recalling them, fixing their salary and the price of the finished products, verifying the accounting and regulating the expenses: thus the supervision of the manufacturer-contractors was rejected. But this enterprise had an irremediable weakness: it lacked operating funds. On August 12, 1794, the general assembly of the Invalides was obliged to invite rich citizens to lend the necessary funds free of charge.[17] The sectional workshops were finally obliged to turn to commercial capital, thus falling under the supervision of the manufacturer-contractors once again, a dependency that the sans-culottes claimed was over and done with.

So the solution was not in the utopian establishment of sectional workshops: the time was not ripe. The solution was in the subordination of commercial capital to industrial production, in the destruction of the old means of production and in the establishment of new structures of production.

Certain petitions indicate that the independant artisans sensed this solution. On October 1, 1793, a delegation of shoemakers went to the Convention demanding that they alone be accepted as providers of shoes for the troops and that merchants and manufacturer-contractors be excluded.[18] On January 23, 1794, the popular Society of the section of Unité demanded "a law to abolish and suppress all the tenderers of the Republic who, by shrewd maneuvers, worked their way into the supplying of equipment to the troops... Who suffers at the hands of all these suppliers? The Republic, the indigent artisans, the workers without savings, who, in order to eat bread, are forced to go to these egoists to ask for a piece of work to do for a vile wage."[19] The petition denounced the scandalous profits of the *tenderer monopolizers*. The deals they concluded seemed to be to the advantage of the Republic; in fact the *monopolizers* are paying 16 to 18 sous for the manufacture of a pair of gaiters, 10 to 12 for a shirt, while they receive 30 sous for each of these pieces; moreover the workers are supplying the thread, which absorbs an important part of their pay. We find in these petitions the anguish of the small independant artisan being transformed bit by bit into a simple wage-earner under the thumb of commercial capital.

On May 4, 1794, the Bonnet-Rouge section took up again the same subject and denounced a new *aristocracy*, "that of the contractors." "One alone, always the richest, is sure to absorb everywhere all the lucrative enterprises, the just sharing of which would offer to a multitude of good citizens the means of living for their families and the allowable profits."[20] In order to prevent "this monopolizing which all these financial contractors contemplate," the Convention must decree that no one will be able to participate in tendering without a certificate of public-spiritedness. Since these certificates would be granted by the general assemblies of the sections, the manufacturer-contractors were sure not to receive any. The sans-culottes intended to turn the Terror against commercial capital, for the refusal of a certificate of public-spiritedness would place a citizen in the category of suspects.

But times were changing. Since the trial and execution of Hébert (March 24, 1794), the revolutionary Government had parted company with the Parisian sans-culottes and revised its social policies; it was relaxing the economic Terror to benefit the propertied classes.

After 9 thermidor, reaction accelerated rapidly economically as well as politically. The crushing of the Parisian sans-culottes during the spring of 1795 put an end to the sections' demands against the manufacturer-contractors and commercial capital. On June 13, 1795, the Committee of Public Safety authorized the Commission of Supplies to order the uniforms of the troops from the contractors:[21] this was a concession to commercial capital. By this time, the Girondists were again seated in the Convention; the upper bourgeoisie was regaining its influence.

Also by this time, the Terror had thrown down the old relations of production: the field was open for the installation of new relations. The petty bourgeoisie of artisans and shopkeepers, Jacobins and sans-culottes who imposed the Terror and supported the revolutionary Government, certainly appear to have been the essential motor of the French Revolution. In the capitalist society which ensued, industry would dominate commerce, while in the society of the Ancien Régime commerce dominated industry. In the 19th century commercial capital no longer had an autonomous existence, being no more than the agent of productive capital, of industrial capital, to which it was henceforth subordinate. As for the small and medium producer merchants, who in year II had formed the major part of the Jacobin party and the sans-culotte movement, economic evolution brought a clear differentiation to their ranks: some succeeded and became industrial capitalists; others were eliminated and swelled the ranks of the wage-earning class. Thus once again the dramatic character of the class struggles during the Revolution is demonstrated by the final consequences of those struggles.

5

Problems of the Revolutionary State[1]

We are acquainted with the famous formula of Marx from his analysis of the political nature of the Paris Commune in *The Civil War in France*: "It was essentially a working-class government, the product of the struggle of the producing against the appropriating class, the political form at last discovered under which to work out the economical emancipation of Labour."[2] In *The State and Revolution*, Lenin repeated this formula and amplified it: "The Commune is the first attempt by a proletarian revolution to smash the bourgeois state machine; and it is the political form 'at last discovered' by which the smashed state machine can and must be replaced."[3] These texts present the Commune as both the outcome of a long historical experience and the point of departure for a critical reflection which was to result in the Leninist theory and practice of the dictatorship of the proletariat.

"The political form *at last* discovered": Lenin, after Marx, makes implicit reference to the historical French experiences and the solutions to problems of the revolutionary state, particularly those of the revolutionary dictatorship, which were tried or suggested during almost a century of revolutionary struggles from 1789 to 1871. This influence or relationship of the French Revolution to the Russian Revolution, passing through the Commune of 1871, has been emphasized by historians. Among others, Georges Lefebvre writes in *The Directory* about the Conspiracy of Equals: "He [Babeuf] arrived at a clear idea of this popular dictatorship that Marat and the Hébertists had talked about without defining; through Buonarroti, he passed it on to Blanqui and to Lenin who made it a reality."[4]

Thus a line of practical politics and critical reflection on the problems of the state and the revolutionary dictatorship would be established that would lead from Marat and the Hébertists to Babeuf and Buonarroti, then to Blanqui, and finally to Lenin through the experience of the Commune.

It is a seductive hypothesis, generally accepted, without worrying about developing it more specifically or supporting it. It is also a somewhat simplistic hypothesis that by equating Marat and the Hébertists masks the fundamental opposition of two revolutionary temperaments facing the problem of the state and the dictatorship, an opposition which was concretized historically in the antagonism between "sans-culottism" and Jacobinism. In fact two fundamental lines of revolutionary theory and practice were established that ran through the whole 19th century, intersecting in the Commune of 1871: mass popular movement and dictatorship or organization of a revolutionary party and concentration of power in the hands of a ruling group?

It seems useful to clarify these problems in regard to the French Revolution. In so doing we will perhaps also clarify certain aspects of the problem of the state during the period of the Commune: what part fell to one or the other revolutionary traditions? Was the Commune "the form at last discovered" of the revolutionary state or was it only one stage?

If we confine ourselves to the French Revolution, it seems that the reflection on the revolutionary state and on the notion of dictatorship was clarified and specified from Marat to Babeuf: from the dictatorship of one man to that of a revolutionary party, from the dictatorship of a tribune of the people to that of, if not yet a class, at least the "plebians" and the "poor."[5] But it would not be possible to isolate the individual reflection of a Marat or a Babeuf on the revolutionary dictatorship and state from history itself. On the one hand, all individual thought and ideology depend on their relation to the existing ideological field and to the social and political structures that support it. And on the other hand, real history is necessarily reflected in this individual development following the complex ties of the individual to this history. It is through revolutionary struggles that the notions of the revolutionary state and dictatorship were clarified. Action often precedes and furnishes the theoretical justification, which in turn strengthens the struggle. Neither the thought of Marat nor that of Babeuf could be isolated from two great ideological currents, two revolutionary practices of the time: "sans-culottism" and Jacobinism. If Marat disappeared too soon to clarify his conception of the revolutionary dictatorship and state in the light of solutions suggested or tried by the popular sans-culotte movement or by the revolutionary government under Jacobin leadership, Babeuf at least could enrich his critical reflection with this double experience: he finally passed on to the 19th century a revolutionary theory and practice that showed its relationship to Marat's but had nonetheless overtaken earlier concepts in many fertile ways.

I

From 1789 on, the exigencies of the Revolution gave rise to reflection on the nature of revolutionary power and the necessity of the dictatorship. From the beginning this reflection was oriented in a double direction: necessity of the concentration of power, certainly, but resulting for one, Sieyes, in the collective dictatorship of an assembly; and for the other, Marat, in the demand for a dictator or a tribune of the people.

Sieyes, who had an excellent political mind, as early as 1789—in his famous brochure *What is the Third Estate*—laid the cornerstone on which the men of 1789 and then those of 1793 supported their whole revolutionary struggle: the theory of *constituent power*, foundation and justification for the concentration of all powers in the hands of the Constituent Assembly, then the Convention, and the dictatorship.[6]

Constituent power resulted from a special and direct delegation of the nation, the only sovereign; its object was the drafting of the Constitution. When a nation wishes to give itself a new constitution, it names "extraordinary representatives [who] will have such new powers as it will please the nation to give them." These extraordinary representatives who form the constituent power replace the nation itself and are not bound by earlier law. "It is sufficient that they desire what individuals in the state of nature desire ... An extraordinary representation [that is, the constituent power] does not in any way resemble the ordinary legislature. These are distinct powers. The latter can only move in the forms and conditions imposed on it. The former is not subjugated to any form in particular; it assembles and deliberates as the nation itself would if, being composed of only a small number of individuals, it wanted to give a Constitution to its government." The will of the nation is sovereign and independent of all civil forms, even those of the assembly which holds the constituent power: "All forms are good and its will is always the supreme law."

By virtue of this theory, the Constituent Assembly, then the Convention assumed all powers without exception: former constituted powers disappeared before the constituent power representing the popular sovereignty as a whole. The theory of constituent power conferred to the Assembly, then to the Convention, a dictatorship without limit in all domains: they both administered and governed through their committees, and the separation of powers disappeared. Doubtless the dictatorship of the constituent power could be applied only with force: the taking of the Bastille was necessary to force the king to recognize the union of the three orders and the National Assembly. In moving from theory to practice, the dictatorship of the constituent power became also a dictatorship of violence: "it was necessary to use force to bring forth right."[7]

Sieyes was to write in year VIII that his brochure had been "the theoretical manual by which the great developments of our Revolution were implemented." The theory of constituent power was to exercise a decisive influence on the whole course of events from 1789 to 1793, revealing a singular revolutionary effectiveness. It finally was used as one of the theoretical justifications of the Jacobin dictatorship.

Marat's political reflection was engaged in a totally different direction. As early as *The Chains of Slavery* (1774), the notion of dictatorship seems to be clearly linked in Marat's works to an obvious distrust of the revolutionary spontaneity of the masses. "What can be expected from these unfortunates? ... Their measures are poorly devised and above all lack secrecy. In the heat of resentment or agony of despair, the people threaten, divulge their plans and give their enemies time to abort them." Marat already has a pessimistic vision of history: "Thus freedom shares the fate of all human things; it gives way to time that destroys all, to ignorance that confuses all, to vice that corrupts all and to force that crushes all." A leader was needed to direct the movement, "someone bold who would put himself at the head of the malcontents and rally them against the oppressor, some great character who would captivate the people, someone wise who would direct the actions of an unbridled, floating multitude." Fifteen years before the storming of the Bastille, Marat had prepared the ground for the reflection on revolutionary power that would take shape under the weight of revolutionary necessity.

It was during the course of the crisis of September 1789 that the idea of a necessary concentration of revolutionary power became clear in Marat's mind though such a concentration did not become a reality until the summer of 1793, in the hands of the Committee of Public Safety.[8] Dispersed in too many hands, revolutionary action languished. "We must not surrender France," comments J. Jaurès in his *Socialist History of the French Revolution*, "neither to the anarchy of the overexcited and blind crowds nor to the anarchy of the too numerous assemblies." Marat proposes the constitution of a revolutionary jury, which will exercise in the name of the people but with more exactitude than the people would, the necessary repressive powers (this is already the "coactive force" of '93); the purging of the Constituent Assembly, reducing it to a quarter of its members; the substitution of a Committee with a few determined members for the incoherent and impotent Assembly of the Hôtel-de-Ville [City Hall]. "The political machine will never be raised except by violent jolts." We will not follow the critical commentary of J. Jaurès; rather, subscribing to the work of J. Massin, we will willingly underscore the clairvoyance, even the prescience of Marat.[9] The Friend of the people caught a glimpse of the only road for the safe passage of the Revolution at a moment when such a road was not yet conceivable.

Doubtless, the Maratist notion of dictatorship remained summary and without precise social content in the early days of the Revolution. It is straining the case to write as J. Massin did: "For him [Marat] the revolutionary dictatorship is tied to the class struggle," when for Marat the struggle was most often reduced to the struggle of the poor against the rich and the plebeians against the patricians. As for the dictatorship, if it is the necessity of the concentration of power in the hands of a limited group or a single man, is it not just as much the exigency of revolutionary violence? "It is the height of folly to claim that men who for ten centuries have had the power to berate us, to fleece us and to oppress us with impunity will resolve in good grace to be only our equals." (*The Friend of the People*, July 30, 1790.) From this understanding came the recourse to violence and the famous phrase on the poster of July 26, 1790, *C'en est fait de nous* [It's all over for us]: "Shooting down five or six hundred heads would have assured you repose, freedom and happiness; a false humanity restrained your arms and suspended your blows: it will cost the lives of millions of your brothers." Extreme violence, brief dictatorship. "If I were the people's tribune and supported by several thousand determined men," writes Marat in *The Friend of the People* on that same July 26th, "I would see to it that in less than six weeks the Constitution would be perfect and that the well-organized political machine would be working at its best." A people's tribune or a dictator, according to *The Friend of the People* of July 30, for six weeks or for three days ... To curb the audacious counterrevolutionary, it would be necessary "above all to set up a true tribune of the State..., then to institute the office of dictator, elected by the people in the times of crisis, whose authority would last only three days."

Marat's political thought had difficulty disengaging itself from memories of Roman Antiquity idealized through school manuals of the good Rollin. Tribune of the people or dictator, it mattered little. But "elected by the people" or "supported by several thousand determined men"? Were these simple antiquarian reminiscences or was Marat hesitating between the two paths history was to adopt: dictatorship by plebiscite or the dictatorship of a revolutionary minority? Moreover it is necessary to emphasize (and here we measure the distance from Marat to Babeuf) that the Friend of the people in his anxiety to give a leader to the conquering revolutionary movement seems to leave victory to the spontaneity of the masses despite a certain initial distrust. He calls them to action with hardly a thought to constructing the future: there is no specific political program. A tribune of the people or a dictator: all would be swept away in six weeks, nay in three days, and "the nation would be free and happy ... For that I would not even need to act; my known devotion to the country, my respect for justice and my love for liberty would suffice."

We are reaching the limits of Marat's political thought. Doubtless it would be necessary to push the analysis further. It does not seem, however, that Marat went beyond his affirmations of 1789-1790 ("I arrived at the Revolution with ideas all formed," he declared in 1790): necessity of revolutionary violence and of the concentration of powers in the hands of a dictator for a short time, sufficient to break the resistance and install definitive prosperity and happiness.

Marat the prophet, it has been said. Yes, certainly more than theoretician. We must acknowledge that his calls for a dictatorship roused scarcely an echo: the masses were instinctively hostile to the idea, while it recalled unfortunate historical memories among the political personnel. The Maratist justification of violence was more in accord with the revolutionary temperament and comportment of the masses.

Over and above individual positions, collective conceptions and practices must be examined: sans-culottism and Jacobinism were effective for the progress of the Revolution. The antagonism of their orientations toward the problem of the revolutionary state nonetheless contributed to the ruin of the system in the year II.

II

If they could not conceive of an original and efficient social program, the popular Parisian militants put into place a coherent set of ideas and practices in the political domain from 1792 to 1795. They tended toward the practice of a direct government and the installation of a popular democracy.[10] Taking popular sovereignty as a given absolute, they deduced the principles of the autonomy and permanence of the sections, the right to approve laws and to control and recall elected officials. A conception of revolutionary government and the state was thus affirmed in year II that ran counter to the Maratist conception of the dictatorship and to the Jacobin practice of the concentration of powers and centralism. And thus as early as year II one of the specific lines of the French revolutionary temperament and practice was sketched, a line that would continue in the 19th and 20th centuries: the libertarian line, the line of "spontaneity."

Sovereignty resides in the people: from this principle all the behavior of the popular militants derives; for them it was not an abstraction but the concrete reality of the people in their neighborhood assemblies exercising all their rights: the revolutionary concentration of powers occurred at the base and was not delegated for fear of alienation.

From this experience arose the mistrust and hatred of all personal or collegial dictatorship; in the popular mentality, dictatorship could only be usurpation.

Since popular sovereignty was "imprescriptible, inalienable, indelegable" even in times of revolution, the Cité section concluded on November 3, 1792 that "any man who claims to be wrapped in a cloak of popular sovereignty will be regarded as a tyrant, a usurper of public freedom, worthy of death."[11] When a citizen declared in the general assembly of the Panthéon-Français on March 13, 1793 that "They are threatening us with a dictator," the whole assembly stood up and swore to stab "every dictator, protector, tribune, triumvir, regulator and all others, no matter what their title, who would try to destroy the people's sovereignty."[12] This trait of the popular mentality and this concern with keeping revolutionary power in the hands of the people doubtless explains the little success Marat had, in diverse circumstances, with propositions to name a people's tribune or a dictator; likewise the accusation brought against Hébert and the "cordelier" group that they were planning to create a "grand judge" lowered their popular esteem.

Since the exercise of popular sovereignty could not tolerate any restriction, the sans-culottes meant to enjoy total sovereignty even during revolutionary times. First, as far as legislative powers were concerned, they insisted that the law of the central government was valid only if made or approved by the people. The sans-culottes in fact took back from the Constituent Assembly the exercise of legislative power in exceptional circumstances such as the acceptance of the Constitutional Act on July 6, 1793, and as they naturally would have had there been an insurrection. The establishment of the revolutionary government does not seem to have attenuated these claims, at least not until the spring of 1794 when the Jacobin centralism was strengthened. In the Marchés section a moderate declared, "When a decree hampered the schemers, they said: 'we are the sovereign, we alone have the right to make laws, and as a consequence to not execute those that do not suit us.'" A revolutionary commissioner in the Contrat-Social section was not afraid to declare to the gallery in the summer of 1793: "The moment has arrived when the sections must rise and appear en masse at the Convention; they must tell the Convention to make laws for the people, laws that suit them; they must set a deadline of three months and warn the Convention that if the laws are not made by this time, the whole Convention will be put to the sword."[13]

From the principle of popular sovereignty confusedly extended to the practice of direct government, the popular militants also deduced approval of laws by the people, the popular exercise of justice and the unrestricted arming of all citizens. Thus a genuine popular dictatorship—so effective in the process of establishing the revolutionary government—was affirmed in the crucial moments of the Revolution in the summer of 1792 and the spring of 1793. We will not insist on these popular aspects, developed elsewhere; rather we will emphasize the consequences in regard to the problem of the dictatorship and the concentration of revolutionary power in the year II.

From the summer of 1793 there was evidence of antagonism between the popular behavior and demands and those of the Montagnard or Jacobin bourgeoisie: was revolutionary power to remain in the hands of the people or was it to be concentrated in the hands of a collegial dictatorship? This was essentially a problem of political direction; but can the politics be abstracted from the interplay of social forces opposing each other? This was also a problem of the duality of powers. Who does not recognize there the problems posed to the revolutionary movements of the 19th century, not to mention those of the 20th?

The Jacobin revolutionary government was being consolidated, then stabilized from the summer to the fall of 1793, thanks to the installation of popular power in the Parisian sections; sovereignty and therefore power would soon be concentrated in the Convention, then in the hands of its government committees, essentially the Committee of Public Safety. The very expression "popular sovereignty"—so widely used by the government in 1792 and 1793—disappeared from official vocabulary in the year II. One would search in vain for this expression in the October 10, 1793 speech of Saint-Just on the necessity of declaring a revolutionary government until peace was won; neither can it be found in the decree of December 4 constituting this government, nor in Robespierre's speech of December 25 on the principles of revolutionary government. Representative democracy, the base of the Jacobin dictatorship, was substituted for direct democracy, the foundation of the popular dictatorship. Appointment replaced election.

The evolution of revolutionary committees is significant in this regard. Essential organs of the popular dictatorship in the spring of 1793, they were originally elected by the section general assemblies, according to the terms of the March 21 law which legalized their existence (a certain number had been formed spontaneously by the militants). Reelected under an application of the law of suspects of September 17, 1793, they were purged by the central [Paris] Commune. In the course of the winter they fell under the control of the Committee of General Security. Finally in spring of year II their members were appointed by the Committee of Public Safety, which was tending to concentrate all power. It went the same way for the General Council of the Commune: purged after the spring of 1793, its authority was terminated by the Committee of Public Safety without consulting the sections. On May 5 [1794], Payan—the national agent of the Commune and good Robespierrist—reminded the sections that "under the revolutionary government, there are no primary assemblies, we know only general assemblies."[14] This statement informed the sans-culottes that their sovereign rights had been transferred to the revolutionary government; thus the inescapable evolution was completed: the end of popular power and the concentration of all power in the hands of the Jacobin dictatorship.

It is still necessary to place this evolution in its general social and historic context in order to better understand it. The bourgeoisie held the upper hand—at least that fraction who saw an alliance with the people as the only way to save the Revolution. If popular power reigned in the sections, it was *that* bourgeoisie who had prepared and organized the days of May 31–June 2, 1793. These days of popular insurrection were in a sense revolutionary bourgeois days: they accelerated the march of history toward the Jacobin dictatorship. Could it have been otherwise? The vague insurrectionary impulses of the isolated sans-culotterie ended in the tragic failures of March 1794 and April-May 1795, as if popular violence left to itself was destined to impotence. But deprived of popular strength, didn't the Jacobin revolutionary government sink in the night of Thermidor 9-10?

There was a contradiction between the popular conceptions concerning the revolutionary government and state and those of the Montagnard or Jacobin bourgeoisie. Should the constant control by organizations based in the sovereign people be maintained once the revolutionary government was in place? Or should power be concentrated in the hands of an assembly and finally in a ruling committee? The latter solution was proposed in the name of the principles of representative democracy that had been more or less explicitly enunciated. In the circumstances of the times this Jacobin concept carried the day; but it was to break the spirit of the popular movement that had carried this revolutionary government to power. Jacobinism could only outlast sans-culottism by a few months. Problem of the duality of powers: who does not recognize there the essential problems that were posed to the Paris Commune [of 1871] and that are still posed?

The revolutionary practice of sans-culottism was no less original and specific. Two essential principles guided the political action of the popular masses for whom violence constituted the last recourse. First there was publicity [openness], safeguard of the people, with its corollary of revolutionary surveillance in the year II. Next there was unity founded on the unanimity of sentiments and convictions that permitted united action to be achieved and thus appeared as an essential factor of success. From these principles came a certain number of practices through which the specificity of the popular movement was affirmed, but these practices placed the popular movement in irremediable opposition to even the revolutionary bourgeoisie.[15]

The publicity principle was derived from the simple and fraternal concept of social relations held by the common people. "The patriot has nothing personal," according to a letter from the Fontaine-de-Grenelle section to the popular society of Auxerre on March 15, 1794. "He brings everything to the mass community: joys, sorrows, all is vented on the bosom of his brothers; there is the source of the publicity that distinguishes the fraternal, that is to say republican, government."[16] On the political plane important consequences of publicity were demonstrated: the patriot having only the public good in view must not hide his opinions or his actions. Public life unfolded in broad daylight under the eyes of the sovereign, the people; administrative bodies, like general assemblies, deliberated in public sessions and electors voted by voice vote under the watchful eye of the tribunes. Since only bad citizens acted in secret, denunciation became a civic duty.

We will stress the practice of the open ballot that appeared after the victory of the popular movement in the summer of 1792 and was generalized in the course of the following summer to the degree that the political influence of the sans-culotterie swept it along. Voting "by voice vote and open ballot" was the "ballot of free men," proclaimed the popular society of the Pont-Neuf section on August 7, 1793.[17] The sections went on to endorse voting by acclamation, a method that responded better to that ardent and obscure desire for unanimity that animated the sans-culottes, but that also constituted a simple means of annihilating opponents. Voting by acclamation and the equally effective method of voting by sitting and rising were common practices until the spring of 1794. This popular practice of voting did not survive the February–March crisis in 1794 and the condemnation of the cordelier group. As the Jacobin dictatorship grew stronger, the return to bourgeois forms of balloting was implemented: voting by acclamation—even voice votes—was prohibited in the general assemblies by Payan, the national agent of the purged Commune. The sections had to obey, but the sans-culottes deserted the general assemblies. The return to the secret ballot, which also marked the Jacobin reaction of the spring of 1794, contributed to the popular disaffection with the revolutionary government.

True to the principle of publicity, voting by acclamation represented at the same time the ardent desire for *unanimity* which animated the sans-culottes. They sought unity among citizens as well as among popular organizations. On the sectional level the unitarian practice was expressed by incessant appeals for regular attendance at the general assemblies, then by denunciation of absenteeism and finally by condemnation of indifference. On the communal level it was a matter of coordinating the action of the sections and the sectional societies, an autonomous force with respect to the Commune. Petitions in the name of the collective and correspondence between sectional organizations were for a long time useful procedures. In the spring of 1793 the militants perfected a tactic effective in its very ambiguity: fraternization from section to section; the fraternal embrace was its symbol and an oath conferred on it a quasi-religious value.

"To be always in agreement," "to be together fraternally," "may we never be separated and may we all be brothers:"[18] in the tragic days of May 1795, these moving words from an obscure militant of Popincourt underscore the essential exigency of popular unanimity. The sans-culotte had a hard time envisaging an isolated individual: he thought and acted *en masse*. Fraternity was not an abstract virtue inscribed at the base of monuments, but a warm feeling, an almost physical sensation of popular unity. "To be together fraternally"—the combatants of 1871 also wanted this and they were during the great hours of the Commune, as the most beautiful pages of Lissagaray's *History* and Valles's *The Rebel* document.

Finally it seems useful to stress certain traits of popular social behavior that were to be retained for a long time and still appeared in the revolutionary movement of the 19th century.

First of all, the "tutoiement" [using the familiar form "tu" for "you"] and the designation "citoyen" [citizen].[19] These usages became imperative in the course of the summer of 1793 with the entry of the sans-culottes into political life. On December 4, 1792 the general assembly of the Sans-Culottes section, formerly the Jardin-des-Plantes, banished the [formal] "vous"—"remnant of feudalism"—and imposed the [familiar] "tu"—"the true word worthy of free men."[20] On the preceding October 3rd the *Chronicle of Paris* had written that "if 'vous' is appropriate for 'Monsieur' [gentleman], 'toi' [emphatic form of the familiar 'tu'] is appropriate for 'citoyen': in the happy reign of equality, familiarity is simply the image of philanthropic virtues carried in one's soul." This point of usage, which may seem a mere detail, allows us to grasp one of the lines of division in social behavior: like Brissot, who declared this "impropriety" useless, Robespierre was hostile to "tutoiement." On November 11, 1793, the Convention refused to make this usage obligatory.[21] If "tutoiement" was in general use in the sectional and municipal organizations throughout year II, the Jacobin repugnance for this usage was affirmed after April 1794, when the ebb of the popular movement began.

Even more important for distinguishing social behaviors and their consequences for the revolutionary movement is the attitude toward women. Without discussing here the role of women in the great days of popular uprising, we must recall the important position they held in many sectional organizations, general assemblies and popular societies from the summer of 1792 to the autumn of 1793; sometimes staffing offices, actively participating in discussions, they were granted voting rights by certain sections. The Society of Revolutionary Republicans, led by Claire Lacombe, called for political equality: "The declaration of rights is shared by both sexes." Vain appeal. The Jacobin and Montagnard reaction asserted itself by September 1793; on October 29, Fabre d'Églantine, speaking to the gallery of the Convention, denounced societies composed not of mothers of families but "of adventurers, wandering knightesses, emancipated girls and female grenadiers."[22] Language of Versailles [the seat of the bourgeois government during the Commune] before the expression was coined! The Convention at once decreed the dissolution of women's clubs and societies. Thus the action of women in the revolutionary movement of year II came to an end, and the antagonism between sans-culottism and Jacobinism was asserted on this specific point.

The absence of antifeminist prejudices among the sans-culottes doubtless corresponds to one of the characteristic traits of the life of the common people: the frequency of free love. This accounts for the insistence of the militants' call for equal rights for both natural and legitimate children. In practice the sectional authorities made no distinction between women and children—legitimate or not—in the year II. But in the year III, honest men and traditional morality swept this practice away, women "who won't offer proof of a legitimate marriage" were excluded from receiving assistance for the families of soldiers, so the Maison-Commune section voted on July 8, 1795.[23]

Sans-culottism, as we have tried to define it here, has passed into history under the convenient term "Hébertism"; actually this is designating the popular movement by one of its spokesmen, an echo rather than a guide. This revolutionary tradition was exalted in 1864 by G. Tridon's brochure, *The Hébertists, Complaint against a Scandal of History*; a new edition was issued in 1871. "The Revolution," writes Tridon, "is not this theater of phrases, continually surpassed by the Parisian movement ... It resides in the entrails of the plebeians, the pikes of the working-class districts, the bellowing of the sections and clubs, in these obscure or execrated men, always in action, who exasperated the strong, revived the weak, sowed everywhere hatred of tyrants and dogma ... Paris is the furnace where metal is fused, the flaming mold from whence will come the great statue of Liberty." The revolutionary spontaneity of the masses could not be better glorified. The Revolution: "This seething of men, this outpouring of ideas, this torrent of passions, admirable and terrible melee where all the aspirations, all the principles and all the sorrows of humanity were found face to face." Such is the image of the Revolution that at the end of the Second Empire was forced on the "neo-Hébertists" and that they set up against the "sterile and savage idol called Robespierre."[24]

The popular tradition of the Revolution was indeed confronted with the Jacobin tradition.

III

Jacobinism: historically we can talk about it with no other specification, even though the club evolved in the course of its four years of existence. Michelet, clairvoyant in his anti-Jacobin bias, notes the entry into the Society of a third generation at the end of 1792. Thus "begins the Jacobinism of '93, that of Couthon, Saint-Just, Dumas, etc., which must use Robespierre, and abuse itself with him."[25] The Jacobinism of '93, therefore, to take up the expression of Michelet, was the same that when associated with Rousseau crystallized the hatred of tradition and counterrevolution as well as sans-culottism (baptized "Hébertism") and associated currents. Let us think of Proudhon enveloping in the same hatred "the charlatan of Geneva" and Jacobinism defined as "a variety of doctrinairism." Let us think of Tridon, of his attempt to rehabilitate the Hébertists, of his anti-Robespierrist imprecations.[26] But let us think also of Taine, writing in *The Origins of Contemporary France*, after a long analysis of *The Social Contract*: "On that point practice accompanied theory, and the dogma of the sovereignty of the people—interpreted by the crowd—will produce perfect anarchy (for sans-culottism and popular power), until the moment when, interpreted by the leaders, it will produce perfect despotism (for Jacobinism and the dictatorship of public safety).[27]

Just as much as by a political temperament, Jacobinism was defined by a revolutionary technique.

Attachment to principles, certainty and the pride of being right: the rigidity of the attitude often masked the fuzziness of the doctrine. Easily intolerant, sometimes sectarian, Jacobinism nevertheless applied itself, not without a certain contradiction, to a passionate search for unity: but wasn't this also one of the characteristic traits of sans-culottism? We must clarify the opposition between the sectional militant—the man of the masses—and the Jacobin—the man of the office—who was easily disoriented by contact with crowds.[28]

The mechanism of the revolutionary practice of Jacobinism was taken apart a long time ago, not without a certain hostility.[29] The Jacobins perfected the practice of restricted committees fixing doctrine, clarifying the political line, and concretizing it with simple and effective language. Elections were corrected by purges and their corollary, infiltration. Once competition had been limited by means of the purged ballot, permitting only affiliated Jacobin members to judge the aptitude of the candidates to live up to their mandate, freedom to choose was left up to the electors. If pushed, cooptation or nomination replaced elections. The citizen was hemmed in by the network of affiliated organizations which received the signal from the mother society, "unique center of public opinion," as was the Committee of Public Safety for governmental action. From these centers emanated "flashes of light and life which will enlighten, animate and fire up patriotism," according to a circular of the popular society of Belleville in the year II.[30]

This political practice and this revolutionary technique, combined with the popular violence, proved to be very efficient; in 1793 they assured the conquest of power, the installation of the revolutionary government and the dictatorship of public safety, and finally in the spring of year II, the victory of the armies of the Republic. But they were established in flagrant contradiction to the political practice and revolutionary behavior of sans-culottism. Jacobinism could not survive its victory.

The problem of the revolutionary state and its orientation was posed at the beginning of August 1793: dictatorship of the popular masses or centralized dictatorship? Issuing from the Convention—the sole possessor of national sovereignty—the Committee of Public Safety intended to be obeyed, by virtue of the principles of representative democracy, while the sectional militants claimed that the Committee followed their leadership. If the militants succeeded in imposing a series of revolutionary measures in the summer of 1793, the Committee quickly turned these to the profit of the State and the reinforcement of the dictatorship of public safety. "Popular movements are only just when tyranny makes them necessary," wrote the unofficial *Journal of the Mountain* on September 19, 1793; "fortunately, the people of Paris have always felt this necessity ..." In fact, the Committee of Public Safety wanted to put an end to the pressure of the masses and popular forms of dictatorship in order to perfect the concentration of powers in its own hands.

A first stage was achieved when on October 10, 1793, based on the report of Saint-Just, the provisional government was declared revolutionary until peace was achieved. The Committee of Public Safety gained control over executive power, not only over the ministers, but over local administrations, to say nothing of the armies.[31]

A second stage was set up, after the sharp check on dechristianization, by the decree of December 4, 1793 that crowned the efforts of the Committee of Public Safety to consecrate its dictatorship in principle.[32] All constituted bodies and public functionaries were placed under immediate inspection of the Committee of Public Safety: they were forbidden from issuing extensive, limited or interpretive decrees in the literal sense of the law, a direct blow to the natural penchant of the popular authorities for direct government. The prosecutor of the commune became a national agent, a simple delegate of the revolutionary state, under the control of the government committees. The power to send agents or commissioners was reserved exclusively to the organs of the central power: it was all over for the commissioners of the Paris Commune who, at certain moments, had played such a large role in the revolutionary movement. Constituent authorities were prohibited from communicating through commissioners or delegates and from forming central assemblies, a common procedure used by the Parisian sections, a major source of their strength. The same restrictions applied to the popular societies who were, moreover, forbidden from federating under the form of a committee or a central club, an action considered subversive to the unity of governmental action. Thus the evolution toward the dictatorial concentration of powers was legally completed.[33]

The task remained to introduce this concentration into practice by the reduction of all autonomous powers: the elimination of factions provided this, and even more the destruction of the essential organ of the popular dictatorship, the sectional societies.

Solidly planted in the general assemblies and the revolutionary committees, popular power had been concentrated in the sectional societies since the suppression of the section committee rooms and the reining in of the committees in the autumn of 1793. These societies rapidly became the organs of direction and control of popular political activity, rising up as rivals for power; more precisely, their influence counterbalanced that of the Jacobins.

Thus from the beginning the revolutionary government declared a secret war against the societies, demonstrated by a significant intervention of Robespierre starting on November 9, 1793. A draft decree, appearing in the papers of the Committee of Public Safety, dating from the winter of

1794, leaves no doubt as to the government's intentions: "1) that in order to maintain unity in the Republic there cannot be new societies otner than those affiliated with the Society of the Friends of Liberty and Equality [the Jacobins]; 2) that in order to conserve unity in each large city no new societies can be formed other than those in conformity with the first society affiliated to that of Paris and forming a section with it."[34] This draft gave the Jacobins control and direction of all societies: a centralized network of popular societies, organized into a hierarchy, under the thumb of the revolutionary government.

The Committee of Public Safety had its way after the fall of the factions. The sectional societies were denounced by Saint-Just on March 13, 1794 in his report on foreign factions; then again on April 10, 1794 by Collot d'Herbois in the name of unity and efficacy; four days earlier they had been accused of *federalizing* opinion.[35] In April–May 1794 the debate spread to the Jacobins. On May 15, Couthon stigmatized these societies in Paris that were offering "the hideous spectacle of federalism"; it was necessary to reestablish the *unity of opinion*; all patriots must *be concentrated* on the Jacobins. According to Collot d'Herbois, on this same day, the sectional societies "were visibly tending toward the establishment of a new federalism ...; they would make of each section a little Republic."[36] Collot d'Herbois was attacking the popular practice of revolutionary power, underlining its incompatibility with that of Jacobin centralism. Unity of opinion should be reestablished under the aegis of the mother society, the Jacobins, themselves both the expression and support of the dictatorship of public safety; thus the last obstacles to the concentration of powers in the hands of the Jacobin State disappeared.

Finally, 39 societies were dissolved—31 from May 14 to May 24, 1794, after the Jacobin offensive of May 12-15—underlining the authoritarian aspect of the operation. The societies were dissolved under Jacobin and governmental pressure, on the initiative of a functionary of the revolutionary committees or some such official. The framework of the popular movement was thus broken. Having knocked down the factions, and holding the popular militants in check by the threat of repression, the revolutionary government unified all forces and concentrated all powers. The revolutionary state, resting on the network of the Jacobins and their subsidiaries, was the sole center of opinion as well as the sole center of action.

This logical but rigid construction did not take into account the social nuances of the revolutionary forces. By forcibly integrating a popular movement that had been autonomous—with its own aspirations, organizations and democratic practices—into the Jacobin cadres, the revolutionary government alienated itself from the militants in the sections. Thus the implacable antagonism between sans-culottism and Jacobinism was established, and through the division of the revolutionary forces, the road to Thermidor was laid.

The Jacobin heritage that the French Revolution handed down to the 19th century was finally embodied in two contradictory figures: Robespierre and Marat. It would be interesting to follow the embodiments of one and the other in the revolutionary currents of the 19th century. Let us limit ourselves to the image that emerged in the last years of the Second Empire and thus in all likelihood to the combatants of the Commune.

Robespierre had been exalted by the republicans in the 1830s. Laponneraye published a volume of *Selected Works of Maximilien Robespierre* in 1832 and a *Historical Notice* in 1840 that characterized Robespierre as "one of the most powerful personalities of the French Revolution, the militant leader of the Jacobin Party, of which Rousseau was the theoretician and Jesus the initiator." Let us recall the Robespierrism of Buchez and of his *Parlementary History of the French Revolution* (1834-1838).[37] The exaltation of Jacobinism in the person of Robespierre did not outlive 1848. Michelet did not hide his preference for Danton, whom the adherents of positivism were rehabilitating at the same moment. It was as if Robespierre were enveloped in the discredit that the revolutionaries attached to the men of '48, particularly to the "ex-preacher of Luxembourg," to borrow Tridon's expression.

Blanquism asserted a fierce anti-Robespierrism. Blanqui's notes, composed in August of 1850 when he had been detained at the chateau of Doullens after being condemned for his participation in the uprising of May 15, 1848, are significant in this regard: "Robespierre was a premature Napoleon. The same plans by different means, but with passions in common: hatred of the revolutionary spirit and of incredulity, antipathy for men of letters, especially a thirst for power. I am not speaking of the insensitivity of the heart: neither one nor the other belonged to the human race. Both wanted to construct society on an old metaphysic." And further on Blanqui wrote: "There were no longer any people at the 9 Thermidor. Robespierre had demoralized and dumbfounded them with his plans of a reactionary dictatorship and a religious reconstruction." It seems that here is the essential argument: Blanqui, anticlerical and atheist, could not forgive Robespierre for the Cult of the Supreme Being.[38]

The fact remains that while Robespierre had been the idol of the revolutionaries until 1848, Blanqui taught them to hate him. *The History of Robespierre* by Ernest Hamel, which appeared in three volumes from 1865 to 1867, hagiographical and somewhat soothing, could not redress the current. From that time on it was the Hébertists, idealized—for whom

Blanqui's disciple Tridon was the apologist—who in 1864 become the models for these revolutionaries to follow. But, if Blanqui expelled Robespierre to the hell of the counterrevolution, his own centralist, elitist revolutionary practice appeared nonetheless as a direct descendant of Jacobinism.

More precisely we see the persistent influence of Jacobinism in its elementary form: Maratism. One year after Tridon had rehabilitated Hébert, Alfred Bougeart exalted Marat, in an otherwise solid work, calling for "the cessation of an iniquitous judgment." Writing about the evening of the assassination of the Friend of the people, Bougeart asks: "Don't we wonder involuntarily, pondering the events to come, what obstacle Marat would have posed to Maximilien Robespierre, to this dictatorial authority much more concerned, it seems, with the necessity to get rid of personal enemies than with the duty to put an end to the enemies of public liberty?" Going back to a judgment of Camille Desmoulins in number 2 of the *Vieux Cordelier* (December 10, 1793), Bougeart answers: "Marat alone could save the Republic, Liberty and the Revolution, because he alone had stopped at the point beyond which there is only extravagance, short of which there is only reaction."[39] This is a centrist position par excellence, between exaggeration and moderantism, which was indeed the position of Jacobinism. But isn't this attributing a lot to Marat?

IV

The Jacobin dictatorship of public safety had failed because it had cut itself off from its social base, the popular movement. "The revolution is frozen," Saint-Just had noted in July. The crisis of the Revolution after Thermidor and the horrifying trial of 1795 prompted the revolutionary militants to examine their experiences critically. If the fall of the government gave rise to an anti-Jacobin reaction and "neo-Hébertism" (more precisely a renewal of sans-culottism) during the summer and autumn of 1794, the defeat of the sans-culottes in the spring of 1795 rehabilitated Jacobin policies to a certain degree. From this double experience emerged a new revolutionary practice and a new conception of the revolutionary state, not a conciliatory synthesis, but a true mutation. Babouvism constituted this essential stage, beyond sans-culottism and Jacobinism. Babeuf, hero of thought and action, was able to conceive the revolutionary ideology and practice for the new society born of the Revolution. Particularly fertile was his critical reflection on the problems of the revolutionary dictatorship and state.

In the course of the winter of Year IV (1795–1796) the organization of the Conspiracy of Equals accentuated the rupture with the various methods used up to then by the revolutionary movement, whether Jacobinism or sans-culottism.

Until 1794, Babeuf, like all popular militants, had been an avowed partisan of direct democracy. From the end of 1789 he had voiced his distrust of the representative system and elected assemblies: "the people's veto *de rigueur*"; in 1790 he defended the autonomy of the Parisian districts. Here Babeuf's thought was hardly original: his debt to Rouseau, whose *Social Contract* he often paraphrased, is obvious, and his conformity with the political tendencies of the Parisian militants is clear.[40] The principles, organization and methods that he led the conspirators to adopt in 1796 are thus all the more remarkable.[41]

The goals of the conspiracy were clarified during the winter of year IV (1796) in a series of meetings of a secret committee held at the residence of Amar, a former member of the Committee of General Security[42]: first, the destruction of the Constitution of 1795, "as illegitimate in its origin, oppressive in its spirit and tyrannical in its intention"; next the reestablishment of the Constitution of 1793, "rallying point necessary to overthrowing the existing authority;" finally, "the preparation from afar of true equality."[43] In the light of this analysis, among revolutionary requirements appears the necessity of the destruction of the old State, as well as the necessity of an intermediate stage before attaining a social system to be definitively installed. These necessities had not appeared in Jacobin practice.

Two fundamental problems remained: "the means of implementing (the destruction of the Constitution of 1795)" and "the public form to quickly substitute for the government to be defeated."

As for the organization of the Conspiracy, the mutation seems less clear than has often been claimed in regard to the methods, up to then characteristic of revolutionary action, whether sans-culotte or Jacobin. It has been asserted that the conspiracy was organizing par excellence. Doubtless, but it emerged from a popular insurrection, not a coup d'état nor a raid. But had not the insurrection of August 10, 1792, been prepared by an insurgent Commune, secretly formed? And the popular days of May 31–June 2, 1793 by the secret Committee of the bishop's palace? It seems indeed that the difference here is one of degree, not nature. The requirement of secrecy was nonetheless very clearly affirmed, the rules necessary for the clandestine action having been decreed by the "First instruction of the secret Directory to its principal revolutionary agents."[44]

At the center of the clandestine organization was the small group of collegial administrators; these men "reattached the scattered threads of democracy to a central point in order to uniformly direct these toward the reestablishment of the sovereignty of the people." Thus the necessity of centralism, already the centerpiece of Jacobinism, was reaffirmed. Beyond the leading circle was a smaller number of tested clandestine militants: the revolutionary agents of the twelve Parisian zones and the intermediate agents for liaison with the Directory.[45] Beyond these was the fringe of sympathizers, patriots and democrats in the sense of year II, kept outside the secret and apparently not sharing the new revolutionary ideal. The revolutionary agents were charged with "organizing, each in his 'zone', one or more meetings of patriots in order to nourish and direct the public spirit by readings of popular journals and by discussions of the rights of the people and the present situation." And finally there were the popular masses themselves who must be led. An organizing conspiracy, without a doubt; but the problem of the necessary links with the masses seems to have been resolved in an uncertain manner. If the "Instruction to the agents on the order of the movement"[46] regulated the training of the insurgent people, nothing seems to have been foreseen for the next stage: no text specifies how the link between the "meetings of the patriots" and the masses was to be established at the level of the 'zone.' As M. Dommanger remarks, "the Babouvist conspiracy was above all equipped with a powerful leadership."[47] We are still a long way from the conception of a tightly structured party. The revolutionary vanguard appears detached from the popular masses that it wishes to lead, a trait which also characterized the revolutionary Blanquist organization.

Once the insurrection triumphs, the problem arises of the revolutionary power to substitute for the old state that has been destroyed. At this point, according to Buonarroti in his history of the *Conspiracy for Equality*, the idea of an intermediate stage is advanced, necessary for the success of the enterprise, "between the fall of aristocratic power and the definitive establishment of the popular constitution."[48] This intermediate stage of a revolutionary dictatorship was defined by Buonarroti as "extraordinary and necessary authority, by which a nation may be placed in full possession of liberty, in spite of the corruption which is the consequence of its former enslavement, and cutting through the traps and hostilities of interior and exterior enemies conspiring against it."[49] Three solutions presented themselves to the conspirators, the same that the experience of the Revolution had revealed since 1789. "Some proposed that we recall the remnants of the National Convention, which they regarded as still rightfully existing; others wanted to entrust the provisional government of the Republic to a body named by the people of Paris in insurrection; still others thought that the supreme power and charge of instituting the Republic should be given, for a determined time, to a single man named *dictator* or *regulator*."[50] The recall of the purged Convention, proposed by Amar, constituted the Jacobin solution; the dictatorship advanced by Debon affirmed the Maratist tradition; the nomination of a provisional government by the insurgent people was in the tradition of the sans-culottes (called Hébertist).

In the first days of March 1796, the secret Directory of Public Safety was instituted. Debate resumed on the question of knowing "by what form of authority would that authority whose destruction was mediated be suddenly replaced." Here it is important to follow attentively Buonarroti in his history of the *Conspiracy for Equality* in order to clarify the distant origins of the notion of the dictatorship of the proletariat.[51]

Here is the first evidence: the necessity of "a certain interval ... between the insurrection and the installation of the new constitutional authority," understanding that "it would be the greatest imprudence to leave the nation without a director or a guide for a single moment." The arguments reported by Buonarroti are the same that the history and experience of the French Revolution suggested to the conspirators: "a people, so strangely separated from the natural order, were hardly capable of making useful choice, and needed extraordinary means which could place them in a state where it would be possible for them to effectively and not in fiction exercise the plenitude of their sovereignty." Thus the necessity of "a revolutionary and provisional authority, constituted in a manner to forever shield the people from the influence of the natural enemies of equality and to give them the unity of will necessary for the adoption of republican institutions."

What will that authority be? The three propositions discussed by Amar were reproduced.

Recalling the Convention, the only legitimate authority—following the revolutionary line of the Jacobin tradition—was rejected: the necessary purges posed problems that were too complex, since many Montagnards and Jacobins had taken part "in the crimes of 9 Thermidor." The necessity of revolutionary efficacity took precedence over concern for legitimacy.

The dictatorship was defined by Debon and Darthe as an extraordinary authority, entrusted to a single man, charged with a double function: "to propose to the people a simple legislation that will assure equality and real exercise of sovereignty, ... to dictate provisionally the preparatory measures tending to dispose the nation to receive such sovereignty." Such an important task required unity of thought and action: thus a single head. Collegiality could have only dire consequences: the divisions within the Committee of Public Safety on the eve of 9 Thermidor proved that. Doubtless, the exercise of such power could entail dangerous abuses; these would be avoided by the virtue of the citizen invested with the power, by the clear exposition of the goals to be attained, and by the limits—imposed in advance—on the duration of the power. These arguments were rejected by the secret Directory, who invoked the difficulty of the choice [of the citizen-dictator] and even more "the general prejudice that it seems impossible to conquer"; that is, the popular animosity against all form of personal power, even if it had its origin in the revolution.

There remained the third solution, in the sans-culotte path: have the insurgents of Paris nominate the provisional authority to which the government of the nation would necessarily be entrusted. This solution was in harmony with the principles of popular sovereignty to which the masses were profoundly attached. Did it present the necessary guarantees of revolutionary efficacy? Even the secret Directory had its doubts since it decided to conduct a careful search for democrats to propose [for the provisional authority]; and, "having made the revolution, it would not cease its work and would watch over the conduct of the new assembly."[52] This meant returning, in some ways, to the practices of Jacobin centralism.

If we stick to these texts, it would be an exaggeration to say that Blanquist practice was derived from Babouvist theory. Let us say more accurately that when Blanqui called for the postponement of elections and for a provisional revolutionary dictatorship in 1848, he was clarifying Babouvist theory based on a careful analysis of the social and political conditions of his own time. Certainly Babeuf and his conspirators affirmed the necessity of installing a dictatorship immediately following the revolutionary conquest of power, but they don't seem to have arrived at a clear definition of the instruments of this dictatorship. A mutation of the revolutionary ideologies that had preceded it, Babouvism had a hard time extricating itself from both sans-culotte and Jacobin practices.

*

Thus we have the double legacy that the French Revolution gave to the 19th century. It left its mark on the revolutionary movement and on the Commune itself, with the tragic contradictions that ensued. The sans-culotte tradition, characteristic of popular behavior, lived on steadfastly for its final expression in the "neo-Hébertism" (let us say the neo-sans-culottism) of Tridon and his friends; thus a libertarian line crossed all of the 19th century. So also did a centralist line, incarnated in the neo-Jacobinism of a Delescluze. But didn't Blanquism, through its Babouvist heritage, belong to the same revolutionary family? Consider its authoritartarian practice, its concept of a centralized dictatorship, its "elitist" concept of the Revolution.

The French Revolution had bequeathed the problem of the revolutionary state to the 19th century. Was the state to be based on a popular dictatorship of the masses or a concentration of power in the hands of a vanguard minority? Torn between contradictory tendencies, some of which were tragically reflected in history, the Commune does not appear to have clearly resolved the problem. According to Edouard Vaillant, "The revolutionary Commune in power possessed neither unity of thought nor action nor energy. It was a deliberative assembly without sufficient coherence." And cannot the same be said of the Central Committee of the twenty 'zones' of Paris—a discussion club rather than an organ for action? Here it would be necessary to measure exactly the portion of the history of the Commune of 1871 that reverted to the revolutionary traditions of 1793 and those of 1795-96. We would thus measure the degeneration of the traditions while stressing one of the causes of the failure of the Commune.

The political form of the revolution could not be "at last discovered" until the heavy handicap of this double revolutionary heritage was overcome. But isn't this double heritage in the very nature of all revolution, and of the human heart?

6

Problems of work in year II[1]

The Revolution of 1789, unlike the 1848 Revolution and others that followed, did not have problems of work at the center of its concerns. As a bourgeois revolution it was much more concerned with property, which the Declaration of 1793, like that of 1789, had placed in the rank of the imprescriptible rights of man; the abolition of feudalism made property an absolute right.

The bourgeoisie of the 18th century had rehabilitated "the arts and the professions," and the spirit of invention blossomed incomparably. Especially sensitive to problems of technique and production, the bourgeoisie had not thought of the social function of work. From 1789 to 1794, they had not envisioned the problems of work in themselves nor in regard to the workers but only in relation to their class interests. The Le Chapelier law of June 14, 1791 prohibited unions and strikes; in the name of freedom, workers were disarmed in their confrontation with employers. Although on September 29, 1793, the Convention granted the general price controls demanded by the sans-culotterie, the Montagnard bourgeoisie always saw that as a tactical concession: controls were seen as necessary for subsistence, and wages were not at all viewed as representative of work.

How could workers, divided between the dominant craft economy and the nascent industry, lacking in class consciousness, set their views against those of the bourgeoisie? In the struggle against the aristocracy, they had to a large degree entrusted the representation and defense of their interests to the bourgeoisie. On the problems of work they could have only a position influenced by the dominant social and political structures. The development of production and trade had carried the bourgeoisie to the first rank. Traditional forms of production still prevailed, as large industry was just being established. The economic evolution was insufficient to make workers aware of the place they held in society as a group or of the place that work held as a function; all the more reason for them to be unaware of the role of work in the development of the individual.

If the bourgeoisie placed property at the heart of the social problem, the sans-culotterie, under its influence, never considered work as other than a function of property.

I

The vocabulary of the era bears witness to these limitations of consciousness.

Workers were not designated by their social function, but simply by their dress. Workers adopted pants buttoned to the jacket and this costume became characteristic of the people: the sans-culottes. We do not know who thought of making a social and political distinction from this manner of dressing. It is enough to note that the bourgeoisie did not mistake the social significance of this term: "In speaking of the sans-culottes," Pétion declared to the Convention on April 10, 1793, "we don't mean all citizens except nobles and aristocrats; rather we mean men who have nothing, in order to distinguish them from those who have [something]."[2] Property, not work, set the line of demarcation.

The property owners, aristocratic or bourgeois, designated the masses who worked with their hands at the end of the 18th century by the somewhat disdainful term of "people" [peuple]. Actually from the petit bourgeoisie to the proletariat, the nuances were numerous, as were the antagonisms. Jean-Jacques Rousseau had already written in his *Confessions* that he had been born into a family whose means distinguished them from the "people": his father was a watchmaker. As an echo we hear the carpenter Duplay, the host of Robespierre: the words of his daughter, the wife of Lebas, a member of the Convention, are often quoted. According to her, her father, concerned with his bourgeois dignity, had never invited to his table one of his "serviteurs"; that is, his workers. As to the "carpenter" Duplay: Jaurès reminds us that he received ten to twelve thousand livres from rents of homes, without counting the profits of his business.[3] The vocabulary acknowledges the imprecision of social boundaries and the indelible mark that the artisan class imprinted on its members: it was the profession or the corporation that determined the qualification, not the notion of work. The "carpenter" Duplay, actually a rather big boss in carpentry, had he in his youth handled a plane? Had his father? Or his grandfather? A small detail, perhaps, one it would be necessary to clear up in the interest of a true social history of work. The head of the enterprise kept his professional qualification, always calling himself "carpenter" [menusier or charpentier], even when he employed a dozen workers. Likewise we have the "fan-maker" [éventailliste] Mauvage, a good sans-culotte of the

Faubourg-du-Nord section; we have to examine his dossier carefully to find out that he owned a fan factory employing more than sixty workers.[4]

In the documents of the period, it is often impossible to make a distinction between a journeyman, a small craftsman, and an entrepreneur. From one to the other the nuances were multiplied and with many intermediate gradations. The notion of work is scattered in words; it is poorly defined. This linguistic aspect corresponds to social reality.

Paris in 1789 was a city of 500–600,000 inhabitants, about half of whom depended on manual work for their existence. In the beginning of 1791 the exchange of large bank notes by the employers for "assignats" of five pounds to pay wages permits an accounting of the distribution of workers in 41 of the 48 sections of Paris:[5] they totalled 75,000, or with their families about 300,000 persons.

Workers were much more spread out in the various quarters of the capital than they are in our day. With the exception of certain areas in the west, workers were found in all sections, but it was not the most famous sections in the history of the Revolution that had the most workers. The Saint-Antoine district contained 4,519 workers, or on the average 14 per employer; the Saint-Marceau district had 5,577, or 20 per employer. The large popular masses were in the heart of the capital. The sections between the Seine and the Boulevards and beyond to the Barrières counted 21,844 workers; there were the textile and hosiery factories which employed up to 200 or 300 workers; the mean was established, however, at 19 per enterprise. The center sections (Louvre, Oratoire, Halles) comprised 5,897 workers, or about 20 per employer. Finally on the south bank of the Seine, from Pont-Neuf to the Saint-Michel bridge, the sections of Quatre-Nations, Théâtre-Français, Thermes-de-Julien had 5,656 workers, on the average 16 per enterprise.

The Parisian working population at the end of the eighteenth century was thus characterized by wide dispersal and multiple nuances. It is remarkable that the districts of Saint-Antoine and Saint-Marceau possessed neither a dense working population nor large enterprises, Saint-Antoine having an average of workers per employer even lower than the mean for Paris, which was 16 or 17. Among the popular urban classes, the most revolutionary element was not composed of a factory proletariat, but of small artisan employers and their journeymen: this artisan milieu formed the marching wing of the sans-culotterie, the nerve of the social group of workers.

These social conditions caused a definite pattern of behavior, as well as certain contradictions resulting from an ambiguous situation.

Working and living beside his journeymen, very often a former journeyman himself, the small artisan employer exercised a decisive ideological influence over them: through him, bourgeois influences penetrated the world of work. Even if the journeymen were in conflict with their masters, since they had been trained by them, often living under their roof and eating at their table, they had the same conceptions of the great problems of the time. Thus the artisan petit bourgeoisie shaped the workers' mentality. Doubtless it would be necessary to introduce some nuances. In particular, alongside the independent artisan class, the dependent artisan class had always thrived: the classic type is still the silk worker [canut] of Lyons. The artisan worked at home, under the control of the merchant [négociant] who furnished the raw material and sold the finished product. The artisan owned his tools: he could even take on some journeymen. Legally he was free and the head of an enterprise; he was looked on as a boss. Economically, he was only a wage earner strictly subordinate to the merchant. The interest of the dependent artisan and that of the journeyman were the same: confronting merchant capitalism, they demanded the *tarif*; that is, a living minimum wage. But they didn't go so far as to establish a relation between the labor rate and the wage rate; wages were determined in relation to the price of subsistences, not in relation to the value of the labor—more proof that the social function of work was not clearly conceived. The dependent artisan thus appeared in an intermediate position between the journeyman and the independent artisan who adjoined the petit bourgeoisie.

As for the wage earner in an already concentrated and incorporated manufacturing sector, he sometimes acted more independently, thus foreshadowing the behavior of the proletariat of large contemporary industry. Note the strike at the Reveillon wallpaper factory which turned into the riot of April 27, 1789. But very often the wage earners of big business had started in little workshops: they remained impregnated with artisan attitudes reinforced by the milieu where they lived—among journeymen in relation to whom they constituted a weak minority. The world of work is deeply marked on the whole by the petit bourgeois mentality, participating in the bourgeois ideology. Neither through thought nor action did the workers constitute an independent element during the Revolution.

Still the ideas that the sans-culottes had about their work and their political activity pose serious contradictions. Tied to their journeymen by their conditions of existence—often extreme poverty—the artisans nevertheless owned their workshops, their tools, and were thought of as independent producers. Having journeymen and apprentices under them accentuated their bourgeois mentality. But the system of small production and direct sales put them in irremediable opposition to the new bourgeoisie. Thus there arose among these artisans and shopkeepers who formed the bulk of the sans-culotte movement a social ideal in contradiction with economic evolution. They rose up against the concentration of the means of production; but they themselves were proprietors. In the year II when the most advanced demanded a *maximum* on wealth [controls on personal income], the contradiction between their social position and this demand escaped them. The demands of these artisans were sublimated in passionate complaints, surges of revolt, without ever specifying a coherent program on the rights of work. The same can be said for the political groups who shared this mentality: the Enragés, then the Hébertists and finally the Robespierrists themselves.

The workers were much more attentive to their interests as consumers than to the general problems of their condition; it was not strikes and wage demands that aroused the sans-culotterie, but the question of subsistences. Raising or lowering the price of the main products of popular consumption—grains, especially bread which represented at least half of family expenses—constituted the decisive factor which tightened or relieved the wage-earner's budget. The sans-culottes demanded price controls on food, their only demand for controls: a significant insight into the economic and social conditions as well as the ideology of the period.

II

In the ensemble of traits by which the sans-culottes defined themselves as a social group, work did not necessarily appear in an explicit manner; the sans-culotte defined himself through social opposition.

The social antagonism most clearly affirmed in popular consciousness was that which opposed aristocracy to sans-culotterie. Privilege, landed wealth, seigniorial rights—in short everything that characterized a still feudal society, personified by the aristocrat—that was what the sans-culotte, both worker and peasant, rose up against. The nobleman was also, but only secondarily, the one who did not engage in any productive activity, who did not work with his hands for fear of demeaning himself; thus the social opposition was reinforced. The speech of the Society of Sans-Culottes of Beaucaire to the Convention on September 8, 1793 is significant in this regard: they defined themselves as "artists" (we understand artisans) and peasants. "We are sans-culottes; ... poor and virtuous, we have formed a society of artists and peasants...; we know our friends, those who have delivered us from the clergy and the nobility, from feudalism, from the tithe, from royalty and all the scourges which make up its procession."[6]

From 1789 on, the economic crisis contributed to a clarification of social antagonisms: as the crisis deepened and the patriotic party of 1789 split apart, an antagonism between the sans-culottes and the higher levels of the former Third Estate was added to the fundamental antagonism of sans-culotterie/aristocracy. A note sent to the Committee of General Security in January-February 1794 signals the existence of two parties in the Brutus section: one of the people, of "sans-culottism"; the other composed of "bankers, stockbrokers, moneybags."[7] Here again the notion of manual work appears only implicitly. The same is true for the speech to the Convention of March 17, 1794, which opposed to "the brave sans-culottes" not only the clergy and the nobility, but also the public prosecutors, lawyers and notaries, plus "these fat farmers, these egoists and all these fat rich merchants."[8] Opposition of owners and non-owners? We cannot affirm that: among the sans-culottes, the artisans and shopkeepers were proprietors. Rather it was an opposition of the followers more or less conscious of a certain conception of limited and controlled property and the partisans of an absolute right to property as was proclaimed in 1789. Even more it was an opposition between the followers of regimentation and controls and the partisans of economic freedom. Finally, but secondarily, it was an opposition between those who work with their hands and those whose activity does not rest on manual work.

Beyond these elementary reactions, certain texts permit both the qualification and clarification of the position of the sans-culottes as a social group.

They denounced "decent people," meaning those who possessed at least ease and culture, if not wealth. The expression appeared after June 2, 1793 and the elimination of the Gironde when the moderates and the sans-culottes clashed on the political and social plane.[9] It essentially designated the bourgeois as opposed to equality. If the sans-culottes ironically termed their adversaries "decent people," the latter saw no fault in treating them as "riffraff":[10] thus two expressions clarify the social antagonisms. One text from the year III gives us the key to the expression "decent people." On February 4, 1795, the surveillance committee of the VIth arrondissement noted the stormy scenes in the general assembly of the Lombards section when the men with forty coins and the decent citizens confronted each other.[11] The men with forty coins were workers to whom the law of September 9, 1793 accorded an allowance of forty *sous* to permit them to attend the section assemblies without hardship; the "decent people" did not receive the forty sous.

Just as significant was the animosity of the sans-culottes toward the persons of independent means [rentiers], which was especially apparent in the fall of 1793 when the economic crisis and difficulties of daily life exacerbated the antagonisms. The position of "rentier" constituted a reason for suspicion from that time on, therefore for arrest. On September 18, 1793 the revolutionary committee of the Mutius-Scaevola ordered the arrest of Duval, the first secretary of the Paris police, as suspect on two counts: spurning the section assemblies and drawing 2000 livres of private income.[12] Jean-François Rivoire, former colonist in Santo Domingo, was arrested on March 22, 1794 by the revolutionary committee of the Mont-Blanc section; besides his political conduct, he was accused of possessing 16,000 livres of private income.[13] As an extreme case, a certain Pierre Becquerel was arrested on March 9, 1794 during a police operation in the Palais-Égalité gardens simply "for having said that he lived off his property."[14] Here again, the sans-culotte who worked with his hands defined himself in opposition to those who did not work.

The hostility of the sans-culotterie toward the "rentiers" constituted only one more emphatic aspect of their instinctive opposition to the rich. The most conscious sans-culottes were not far from considering, as did Babeuf in the year IV,* the revolution as a war declared "between the rich and the poor."[15] But most often they had only a cursory knowledge of the rich, their attitude being purely subjective. In the Amis-de-la-Patrie section, Pierre Fotier was arrested during the anti-terrorist repression on May 29, 1795 for having displayed "jealous sentiments against the rich."[16] There are few texts that allow a glimpse of any more in-depth analysis on the part of the sans-culottes. Rare were those who had a clear conception of what lay at the base of this wealth that they both scorned and envied: the exploitation of the labor of others. There are however a few examples. On March 16, 1794, Godefroy, a hat merchant, was arrested by the revolutionary committee of the Lombards section. Besides his political conduct he was accused of possessing a cotton mill at Vernon in the Eure where "120 women, old men and children" worked.[17] In the Faubourg-du-Nord section, Santerre, a former gauze merchant, was arrested on April 13, 1794. He lived from his income, having "fattened himself continuously from the sweat of the lowest-paid workers."[18] Here is evidence of an inkling of the truth that the antagonism between the sans-culotterie and wealth rested on the relations of production, function and activity; thus the position of the diverse social classes is specified in relation to work.

A few sans-culottes on the fringes of the middle bourgeoisie tried to go beyond the negative positions of the sans-culotterie and define them through explicit reference to their social function, work. In this difficult

*Began September 22, 1795

realization they were aided by representatives of the Montagnard bourgeoisie who saw in an alliance with the people the salvation of the Republic. It was the same with the Robespierrists and on another level Hébert who through conviction, though not without a touch of demagogy, exalted in his [newspaper] *Père Duchesne* "the most precious class" for the nation, the sans-culotterie. "There is nothing as valuable as the sans-culottes." he wrote in September 1793, "... they are the ones who with their sweat water the soil that nourishes us, they are the ones who make the fabric which clothes us, they are the ones who work the metal and make the arms that serve in the defense of the Republic."[19] And he contrasted the bankers, the financiers, the merchants, the men of law, "in a word all the leeches of the sans-culotterie" to "these industrious artisans who wear themselves out with work."

In the same style as *Le Père Duchesne* the Poissonnière section in their address to the Convention on September 24, 1793, opposed "the rich egoists" to "this industrious part of the people who live only by their work."[20] Sometimes these texts pressed the eminent dignity of work and workers. On July 4, 1794, the revolutionary committee of the Bon-Conseil section suspended three commissioners who were manufacturers of saltpeter, proclaiming: "they lived in great comfort and pride out of proportion with the condition of their workers."[21] When the sans-culotte Vingternier—arrested on April 6, 1795—was interrogated about his section, he answered that he had no section other than "that of the people and the workers."[22] While repeating the same imprecise definitions of the sans-culotte, this militant nevertheless introduced a new notion. Responding in May 1793 "to the impertinent question: but what is a sans-culotte?", he declared: "A being who always walks ... and who lives quite simply with his wife and children, if he has any, on the fifth or sixth floor."[23] Jacques Roux will also speak of the attics where the sans-culottes live, and *Le Père Duchesne* will write: "Do you want to meet the finest flower of the sans-culotterie? You must visit the garrets of the workers."[24] Vingternier did not stop with the material conditions of the workers' existence; he introduced a new notion of social utility: the sans-culotte knows how to "work a field, forge metal, saw, file, cover a roof, make shoes." Here work is defined in relation to social utility.

During the repression of the year III, the former terrorists saw themselves accused of having exploited the popular feeling that work introduced a differentiation into society for political ends. According to a notation on January 6, 1795, the former commissioners of the Bonne-Nouvelle section were only seeking "to mislead the numerous class of workers lodged in rooms."[25]

In denouncing former terrorists on April 9, 1795, the "decent people" of the Bon-Conseil section essentially accused them of having placed citizens into two antagonistic classes. "In the first class, as if there were supposed be two classes among republicans, the malevolent ones placed the merchants, the shopkeepers, the tradesmen, the men of law, the "rentiers," the men of letters, the clerks and the artists. In the second, ... they admitted only those citizens judged as being accustomed to working with their hands."[26]

As difficult as it was for the sans-culottes to see their position in society as workers, they had no clear, distinct notion of work itself and its social role. They did not think that work in itself could have a social function; they conceived of it in relation to property.

Work, i.e., manual work, creates property in proportion to the amount of work. Artisans, journeymen, and peasants with small plots of land—the sans-culottes were small independent producers whose personal work legitimized their property: a field for the peasant, a shop and tools for the artisan. So the sans-culottes were strongly attached to, and never questioned, the right to hold small property. What they feared above all was the concentration of property which would reduce them to the rank of dependent workers, proletariat. The popular society of the Poissonnière section asked the Administration of subsistences to reimburse a baker of the section, declaring on January 16, 1794 that "the small fortunes acquired through work useful to society cannot be too strongly respected and preserved from all attack."[27] In all periods of crisis the sans-culotterie affirmed more or less confusedly the demand for appropriate legislation to render impossible the concentration of property and the means of production and to thus maintain the independence of work.

The clearest demand was formulated on September 2 at the height of the popular upsurge in the address to the Convention of the Sans-Culottes section, formerly the Jardin-des-Plantes. After having affirmed the workers' right to a living and defined property as "the extent of physical needs," they demanded that the Assembly "set without variation the price of necessary foodstuffs, wages for work, profits of industry and commerce," a broad program of regulation of economic life which finally resolved itself in the fixing of the maximum wealth allowed. "That one individual will be able to possess only the maximum; that no one will be able to hold for rent more land than is necessary for a set quantity of plows; that one citizen will be able to possess only one workshop, one store." These radical measures, concluded the Sans-Culottes section, "would cause the too great inequality of wealth to disappear little by little and the number of proprietors [independent workers] to grow."[28]

At no other moment of the Revolution do we find so concise and clear a formulation of the sans-culotte ideal regarding the regulation of property and the organization of work, an ideal suited to the artisans and shopkeepers who formed the bulk of the Parisian sans-culotterie and who exercised a decisive ideological influence on their journeymen and clerks. It was also an appropriate ideal for that mass of urban consumers and small producers who were hostile to all merchants of basic foodstuffs and at the same time hostile to all entrepreneurs whose capitalist initiatives threatened to reduce them to the state of dependent workers.

What were the theoretical and political sources of this social ideal of property implicitly founded on work and maintained at its limit? Many Montagnard or Jacobin leaders formulated similar propositions. In his *Elements of Republicanism* Billaud-Varenne states that "the accumulation of great masses of wealth in the hands of a small number of individuals leads progressively to all social calamities"; on the contrary, "the comfort of the largest number, the fruit of work in industry and commercial speculations brings a nation to the highest degree of prosperity and conveys to its government a real grandeur."[29] Saint-Just in his *Institutions* assigned the Republic the goal of "giving all French people the means to obtain the basic necessities of life without depending on anything but laws and without mutual dependence in the civil state";[30] in other words, every French person would be a small proprietor, an independent producer, a free worker, and property would be based on work. As for Robespierre, who on April 24 had defined property not as a natural right but as a social institution, his ideal was a society of small producers: the peasant possessing his field, the artisan his workshop, each sufficient for the support of a family. Georges Lefebvre has noted—and justly so—a double moral and social concern in this ideal. "The man living from his work without owing anything to anybody is the one Robespierre calls *poor*; individual production and very little property guarantee him independence; but the acquisition and conservation of this property requires a certain initiative and personal virtues of work, frugality and savings."[31] Although rarely made explicit, this moral concern was not foreign to the sans-culotterie, who declaimed against idleness and luxury.

Nevertheless the sans-culottes went beyond the Montagnard leaders on one point. The Montagnards were above all interested in agricultural production and landed property; they intended to maintain a total freedom of enterprise in the domain of commerce and industry. In his Declaration of Rights of September 1792, Momoro, while limiting by law "territorial properties," declared "industrial properties" inviolable.[32] About the same time an essay on popular government set a maximum for landed property but assigned no limit "to the increase in wealth consisting of purely personal or movable property, such as money, government securities, merchandise, ships, etc."[33] The sans-culottes—consumers of agricultural products but also small urban producers attached to the independence of their shop or their workshop—went further: they were just as hostile to the concentration of commercial or industrial property as to large landed property. The demands of the Sans-Culottes section derive from this hostility.

III

The ideological ambiguity based on a contradiction of function and representation was translated into a social and political contradiction: this popular demand for independent work that legitimized small property was not in harmony with the historical necessities of the period. An example will prove this. The national defense policy in year II required resorting to large private industry for supplies of uniforms and equipment since nationalization of the manufacture of arms had not been adopted. Concerned with efficiency, the government committees directed most of their orders to capitalist entrepreneurs instead of dispersing them among the multiple small artisan workshops. In year II this became a source of conflict between the revolutionary government and the Parisian sans-culottes.

The crisis at the beginning of 1793 gave rise to enlistments, increasing the need for equipment. The sections contrived to equip the volunteers; some sections, like the Tuileries, opened workshops. The considerations set forth as motivating this decision reveal the hostility of the sans-culottes to concentrated big business and commercial capital, as well as their attachment to independent work. "First of all, the avid suppliers, whether spiteful or clumsy, will no longer be able to hinder the movements of the armies or stop our success; the fate of liberty will no longer be at the mercy of monopoly speculations. Secondly, a small number of rich entrepreneurs will no longer appropriate all the profit from immense supplies; it will be shared among all our sellers, all our workers, all of us. Thirdly, since small enterprises are always managed with intelligence and economy, with less cost, we will supply more and the supplies will be better."[34] Higher praise could not be made of small independent production. But was it reconcilable with the immense needs of national defense?

The government branch in charge of outfitting the army was of course directed to organize large workshops where planned production was established. This met with constant opposition from working women used to unrestricted work, who never ceased demanding the organization of small sectional workshops. Thus the confrontation between two concepts of the organization of work was also a confrontation between the government policy and popular demands. On July 30 (1793) the commissioners of the 48 Parisian sections explained to the general council of the Commune "how many disadvantages arose from bringing together in a single workshop a large number of female citizens."; they regarded the distribution of work among sectional workshops "as much more advantageous."[35] If the work was in the end distributed among the sections, the difficulties and the complaints still didn't stop. If sectional workshops corresponded to the popular ideal of the organization of work, they presented an irremediable weakness: lacking working capital, they had to turn to private capital, thus once again coming under the supervision of the entrepreneurs and tenderers that the sans-culottes hoped to shake off. The popular demands resumed.

On October 1, 1793 a delegation of shoemakers petitioned the Convention to be the exclusive providers of shoes for the army.[36] On January 23, 1794 the popular society of the Unité section proposed a law to abolish and suppress all tenderers of the Republic who, through shrewd maneuvering, were working their way into supplying equipment for the army. Who suffered from this? "It's the Republic, the indigent artists, the workers without means who, in order to eat bread, are forced by life's needs to go to these egoists to ask for a piece of work to be done at a very low price."[37] The working women of the Invalides section returned to the attack on February 18, 1794 and demanded that "the uniforms to be made for the soldiers of the Republic be distributed among the workshops of the section and not to greedy tenderers." The general assembly promised to support them, deeming that "it was just that the profits to be made from public works turn to the advantage of the greatest number and the poorest."[38] The assembly did not say: to the advantage of the workers.

On April 20 the Bonnet-Rouge section again denounced the aristocracy of entrepreneurs: "One alone, always the richest, is sure to absorb everywhere all the lucrative enterprises, the just division of which would give the means of existence and allowable profits to a multitude of good citizens and their families." A few entrepreneurs must not monopolize all the work: the Convention should decree that no one will be able to tender if he has not obtained a certificate of public-spiritedness. The big entrepreneur had little chance of obtaining such a certificate from a popular assembly. As for the sans-culotte, no difficulty, and he will take "only the portion of work which belongs to him, without harming his brother sans-culotte."[39] The militants of Bonnet-Rouge intended to turn the Terror against commercial capital and big business, for the refusal of a certificate of public-spiritedness most often led to arrest. But times had changed; in the spring of 1794 the popular influence was declining, and the government committees were relaxing the economic Terror to the advantage of the propertied classes.

The sectional workshops for uniforms were not immediately swept away by the Thermidorian reaction, but they did not survive the smashing of the Parisian sans-culotterie in June of 1795. On June 13 the Committee of Public Safety authorized the supplies commission to liquidate the workshops and the distribution offices of the Commune of Paris and to order army uniforms from private entrepreneurs.[40] History resumed its course. It could not be a question of favoring craft labor and small independent production when economic freedom had been attained and war production belonged to the bourgeoisie of business, a domain reserved for capitalist initiatives. The concentration of work, characteristic of developing industry, still remained in its technical and social aspects the antithesis of the ideology of craft labor.

*

The inability of the sans-culottes to see their position as workers in terms of a social class or group, and work in terms of function was a characteristic in harmony with the conditions of the time, as suitable as the conception of limited property based on individual work.

Whether peasants or artisans, in order to freely dispose of their persons and their work, the sans-culottes first had to break the ties that bound them to another, on the land or in a corporation. This explains their hatred of the feudal aristocracy, whom they detested even more as unproductive and scornful of manual work. This also explains their bitterness toward the Ancien Régime and its corporative organization. They were direct producers, and in their view individual work alone legitimized property. They dreamed of a society of small proprietors. In order to maintain a relative equality, the State should intervene. Through laws of inheritance, progressive taxation, and social assistance, it would protect work and restore small property to the extent that economic evolution tended to destroy it. It was above all a question of preventing the establishment of a monopoly of wealth along with a dependent proletariat. The sans-culottes did not understand that having reached a certain degree of evolution, this system would engender the agents of its own destruction and that the individual, parcelled-out means of production must necessarily be transformed into socially concentrated means of production, with the small property of a host of direct producers being supplanted by big capitalist property.

In the spring of 1794, when the ultimate crisis of the Revolution was building up despite all the efforts of the revolutionary government and the Robespierrists in particular, the failure burst like a bombshell in the eyes of the people. Had the confiscation of the holdings of the clergy and the emigrés, the impoundment of the property of suspects allowed the distribution of a plot of land to peasants without land? Had the abolition of corporations allowed journeymen to establish themselves on their own account? Had the Revolution made the sans-culottes independent producers?

The bourgeoisie—being more clear-sighted—took a stand against the artisan ideology, affirming that it was impossible to want to maintain production founded on individual work when capitalist production was developing. In 1789 the parish register of Augny in the Metz bailiwick, doubtless edited by some large proprietor, protested against the division of communal [lands] already carried out in Lorraine and in the bishoprics. "These cleared plots are ruinous for the public [interest] in that the individuals, occupied with their individual portions, can be of no help to our cultivators, our manufacturers or our entrepreneurs."[41] On January 19 (1794), the representative Delacroix wrote: "We thought that in a large population, the poor should find resources not in agriculture but in industry, commerce and the arts."[42] The observations of Lozeau, deputy to the Convention from Charente-Inférieure, are particularly noteworthy. On September 8 (1794) he stated: "A great society only forms a respectable whole because all its members are linked to each other by the mutual services they render; ... it is impossible for the majority of the nation to be proprietors, because in that case each would be obliged to cultivate his field or vinyard to survive, and commerce, arts and industry would soon be obliterated."[43] It was impossible to eliminate wage-earning labor; it was in fact essential to maintain it. If all the peasants and all the artisans had lived from the product of their labor, on their plot of land or in their workshop, where would the big farmers, the manufacturers, the pioneers of big industry have found the labor essential to their enterprises? The Montagnard bourgeoisie considered the transformation of independent workers into wage-earning workers inescapable, a necessary condition of the economic order as they conceived it. As for those, like the Robespierrists, who considered state intervention in favor of free labor and small property essential, they could not free themselves from their own contradictions. And thus they perished on July 27, 1794.

The sans-culotterie wrestled with equally insoluble contradictions. Hostile to the capitalism that threatened to reduce them to proletariat, they were nevertheless tied to the bourgeois order because they were already proprietors of their fields or their workshops, or hoping to be. They demanded price controls, limitation of property and that property be based on personal work, but at the same time they demanded the independence of the shop, crafts and rural property, thus followers in this regard of the economic liberalism dear to the capitalist bourgeoisie. These contradictions reflected the social composition of the sans-culotterie who, since they did not constitute a class, could not conceive of their exact place in society nor could they establish a coherent economic and social program. Attached to the traditional system of production and property founded on personal work, they were condemned to decline as the capitalist organization of production based on wage work progressed.

Such are some of the essentially social aspects of the problem of work in year II. Many others could have been envisioned: technical and economic aspects, purely psychological aspects... Let us emphasize the research difficulties. Without mentioning the absence of documents that would permit a precise social analysis of the world of work for the period that interests us, we must state that the popular classes left few documents and for this reason it will always be difficult to write their history. Many aspects thus escape us, and we would not presume to reason by analogy. One could assume with some likelihood conflicts among the workers; for instance, between the unskilled worker or the day laborer and the art worker—jeweler, engraver, or carver—conscious of the value of the object he produces. We detect this differentiation if not this opposition in the split among the political personnel of the sections: specialized workers, more conscious and more educated, are found among the civil and revolutionary commissioners, while unskilled workers rarely rose above the rank of simple militants. But lacking documents, we cannot carry the research any further, and entire sections of social reality remain in the shadows.

These were brought to light with the development of the new economic organization. Still scarcely apparent at the end of the 18th century, defined by receding traditional structures, the notion of work emerged little by little under the influence of economic evolution, as workers became conscious of their place and role in society. Work finally appeared as an essential social function in the political debate.

7

The "Maximum" of Parisian Wages and 9 Thermidor [July 27, 1794][1]

No one today disputes that economic and social discontent in the spring of 1794 and the resulting disaffection of the sans-culotterie from the revolutionary government constitute one of the underlying causes of 9 thermidor. Once again what is needed is an exact measurement of this discontent and clarification of government economic policy, particularly in regard to wages. The publication of the maximum wage by the Paris Commune on July 23 brought popular discontent to a peak and explains the passive attitude of many of the sections during the night of July 27-28. The discovery of this document permits us today to throw a new light on the attitude of the Committee of Public Safety in the spring of 1794 and to better appreciate the class bias behind its economic and social policy after the fall of the Hébertist Commune.

In a note in the *Annales historiques de la Révolution française,* Albert Mathiez wrote in 1927: "It would be interesting to find this new 'maximum' for a day's wages promulgated by the Commune on 5 thermidor [July 23] and to compare it to the earlier rate. I have searched for it in vain."[2] Yet an economist, Léon Biollay, claimed in 1886, in a work rarely cited in the bibliographies, to have found a decree of the General Council of the Paris Commune of July 9, 1794 containing "a table of wages of almost all professions."[3] This is the table that was published on July 23, 1794. Three copies of this document, to our knowledge, are conserved in the National Archives. Two copies are found in the series F^{12} (commerce and industry), carton 1544^{30}:[4] covered with corrections, erasures and marginal annotations, they are part of a dossier drawn up for the revision of the maximum wage on July 23. A third copy, doubtless the one Biollay was aware of, is kept in the Rondonneau Collection with the classification mark AD XI 75[5]. A fourth copy, with the classification mark LB^{40} 1154 M*, is found in the Bibliothèque nationale [National Library].[6]

This document is presented in the form of an undated brochure of 62 pages, printed *In Paris by the citizens Nicolas and Desbrieres, printers of the Municipality of Paris* and as an extract of the register of deliberations of the General Council of the Commune of Paris, signed *Lescot-Fleuriot*, mayor, and *J. Fleury*, secretary-clerk. Let us emphasize that the deliberation is not dated. "The General Council of the Commune enters the text, in execution of Article VIII of the law of September 29, 1793 (v.s.) (here follows the text of the article)[7] after taking into account the prices [compensation] paid in 1790, decrees what follows." First comes the "Maximum Rate of Wages of all Occupations in the Area the Paris Commune," the professions being classified in alphabetical order, the wages divided into two columns, the 1790 "price" and the "maximum" according to the new law:

A.	1790 Price	Maximum under new law
[Billposter] Affïcheur	liv. s. d.*	liv. s. d.
Per hundred notices	1 8	1 7
[Refiner] Affineur		
The first worker per month	80	120

Following is the rate applicable to transport workers, first those at ports (p. 46), then those at central food markets (p. 59). Article VI decrees that "working men, working women, carters and others will be held to the customary working hours followed for each position in 1790." Finally, Article VII shows the importance of this decree by requiring the members of the General Council to go out into each of the 48 Parisian sections for its proclamation.

I

An analysis of the rates of July 23 not only permits a clarification of government policy in regard to salaries after the fall of Hébert and Chaumette, but it also throws light on the wage policies of the Commune before April of 1794.

Until the law of the general maximum of September 29, 1793, wages remained "free."[8] Diverse political circumstances (particularly the fall of the Gironde—proprietors and producers, partisans of economic freedom), mass conscription and war production (the first making workers in short

*Livres, sous, derniers

supply, the second requiring more and more workers) had, since June 1793, improved the position of workers and brought about higher wages. Certainly there were inequities among different occupations, and the increases were in any case insufficient to compensate for the rise in prices of basic foodstuffs. It is significant that, if the sans-culottes obstinately demanded a fixed price for foodstuffs from the beginning of 1793, rarely did they petition for a fixed wage rate.[9] This is explained first of all by the large proportion of small shopkeepers and master artisans among the sans-culottes who obviously had no interest in raising wages. Moreover, the workers feared that the application of an upper limit on wages would wipe out any advantage from fixing the price of foodstuffs. Much more than higher wages, they were inclined to demand lower prices, due to their economic and social position and their lack of professional organization. The absence of class consciousness led journeymen and workers to ally themselves with small shopkeepers and master artisans rather than to unite against the employers.

In order to maintain a margin between wages and prices favorable to the workers, the law of September 29, 1793 raised wages by half relative to the 1790 rates, while prices were raised only one-third. Nevertheless, the setting of an upper limit to wages certainly reduced the nominal increases won by workers during the preceding months. Georges Lefebvre established in his *Peasants of the North during the Revolution* that the September 29 law led to a considerable lowering of wages in the countryside.

The fear of displeasing the workers explains why Article VII of the September 29 law was not implemented by the "Hébertist" Commune, which showed so little attentiveness to posting the general table of wage limits that the law died before being published.[10] Historians who have dealt with the question, and especially Albert Mathiez in his *Vie chère* [High Cost of Living], have discussed this "maximum" of wages without giving any proof of its existence. Neither the *Journal de la Montagne* nor *Le Moniteur* mention this subject. When the police observers are scandalized by the excessive, from their point of view, wages demanded by the workers, they make reference not to wages set by a nonexistent schedule, but to compensation "practiced in the past." For example, laborers who carry up wood are asking 8 livres for carrying a load "that used to cost 1 *livre* 4 *sols*" [sous]; such a worker "who used to draw 4 or 5 *livres* from his day's work" now demands 20 or 24; a day-worker is not ashamed to ask 100 *sols* for a job that would have paid 10 *sols* "a year ago."[11] Certainly if there had been a decree of the Commune setting an upper limit of wages, these police observers—small bureaucrats with modest salaries, jealous of the workers—would have taken a malicious pleasure in comparing the compensation practiced with that of the schedule.

The Paris Commune was certainly not the only one to consider Article VIII of the September 29, 1793 law—charging the general councils with the establishment of a "maximum" of wages—a dead letter. If the municipalities of towns where the bourgeoisie dominated were more zealous in putting up the table of the rate for daily wages than the municipalities in the country, as Georges Lefebvre has shown for the North region, the towns where the pressure from the sans-culottes was strong were not aware of the table before the spring of year II. On June 10 the Committee of Public Safety, acting on the inapplication of the law by numerous general councils, ordered the national agents to fix the "maximum" of wages according to the established rules.[12] It is remarkable that the decree of the Paris Commune of July 9, fixing the "maximum" of wages published July 23, carries no reference to a preceding rate which it would have been necessary to annul before publishing a new one. The decree only mentions Article VIII of the September 29 law and cites the wages "that had been paid in 1790."

The "Hébertist" Commune, under pressure from the sans-culottes, had thus resolutely practiced a policy favorable to workers and consumers, applying controls on food prices while showing no interest in wage controls to the point of not respecting the law. Noting this class position, we can understand the satisfaction the proprietors and producers felt when the Commune fell.

II

With the execution of the cordelier group on March 24 and of Chaumette 20 days later, the Commune was purged and the sans-culotte movement was contained, then suppressed. The new attitude of the revolutionary government was reflected in its policy on wages. Concerned with reestablishing the [as yet] fragile equilibrium that was the base of their action, the government inaugurated a policy favorable to proprietors and producers with workers and consumers bearing the brunt of the costs. Likewise the committees endeavored to reassure commerce by relaxing the system of control and repression,[13] while the Committee of Public Safety was anxious to reestablish in favor of the employers the traditional social balance of power that for a moment they had believed shattered in favor of the sans-culottes. In this domain the class concerns of the governmental authorities conclusively prevailed.

This policy, which was to further widen the gulf that the drama of germinal [the spring executions] had created between the sans-culottes and the revolutionary government, first manifested itself by the proclaimed willingness to repress all worker agitation, then by the publication of the "maximum" of wages on July 23. If the obstinate refusal of the Robespierrist Commune to consent to wage increases displeased the sans-culottes, the new rates July 23 made them indignant, and they determined to act. It was no longer a matter of raising wages, for the new rates, by strictly applying Article VII of the September 29, 1793 law, reduced wages by a considerable proportion.

After the executions, workers participated in agitation for wage increases. This agitation was incited by a new upsurge in food prices. The publication of a general price control on foodstuffs, impatiently anticipated by the sans-culottes, was a bitter disappointment for them. "People are impatiently awaiting the new 'maximum,'" noted the surveillance report of the Paris police on March 24 and 25; on the following days this report provides evidence of popular discontent. "The 'maximum' is the business of the day," the report of March 29 stressed, "and the general opinion is that it favors the merchants and not the people."[14] Barère had declared on March 4 that it was a question of *curing* commerce and not *killing* it.[15] The tables posted by Concedieu, acting national agent of the Department of Paris, replacing Lulier, attenuated the strictness of the law: the new wages were higher than those set by the first "maximum." What is more, the new limit was applied to the disadvantage of the sans-culottes since the commissioners of monopolies, who had strictly applied the controls on foodstuffs, disappeared with the reform of the law on monopolies adopted on March 29.[16] Henceforth the price controls on foodstuffs were violated with impunity. Responding to members of the Commune who were denouncing the numerous infractions of the controls on June 19, the national agent Payan saw no other remedy than to invite the citizens to report the evaders to the police commissioners of their respective sections.[17] The authorities were almost becoming accomplices to violations of the law.

It is understandable that the workers would demand wage increases to reestablish the equilibrium. Agitation began on April 20, 1794.[18] Without going into all the details, we must stress the proclaimed willingness of the authorities to maintain wage stability. This further increased the disequilibrium as the price controls on foodstuffs were being applied to the advantage of the producers and tradesmen in sharp contrast to the policies of the Hébertist Commune. The workers' demands were met with police repression. On April 21, when a delegation of tobacco grinders from the Robillard factory, backed by close to 200 workers, presented itself to the general council of the Commune, Payan called for the application of the Le Chapelier law on professional associations; the matter was referred to the police administration. It proceeded to make five arrests the following day.[19] The brutality of this repressive action did not escape some men in the government. Saint-Just noted in the margin of the police bureau report of April 24: "Write to the police to become acquainted with the organizers of this gathering and the legitimacy of their demands, and tell the police that it is the causes of the gathering that must be dispersed and that justice must be rendered to those to whom it is due."[20]

From that time on, agitation was continuous. On April 23 a gathering of plasterers formed to present a petition to the National Convention.[21] On May 2, a decree of the municipal Corps intended to put an end to the demands of the bakers' assistants, stating that any baker's assistant who demanded a wage above that fixed by law (without specifying what that wage was), who demanded an extra ration of meat or who left his employer without a month's notice would be considered as a suspect and treated as such.[22] On May 7, the pork butcher's assistants demonstrated at the general council of the Commune.[23] The agitation reached the port workers. "Interest alone is the cause of this disorder," stated the police surveillance report of May 3. The wood merchants don't want to pay the day laborers the wages they demand, "on the contrary, they want to lower them." Seventeen to eighteen day laborers were arrested that day, two more on May 5, on the Rapée quay.[24]

The persistence and size of these movements, and the diversity of professions involved, worried the government committees. On May 4 they had the Convention pass a decree requisitioning "all those who contribute to the handling, transport and sales of foodstuffs and other basic merchandise"; the public prosecutor of the revolutionary tribunal will seek those "who would make a criminal coalition against the people's subsistence."[25] The next day the municipal Corps addressed a severe warning to the workers: "Malicious people have spread among workers employed in basic production a spirit of revolt and insubordination that the revolutionary laws punish by death. We have seen almost simultaneously the tobacco grinders, the bakers, the workers employed in sorting, transporting and stacking floating wood demand from the citizens who employ them daily wages above those fixed by law, form illegal assemblies, threaten to no longer continue their work and finally carry their malevolence to the point of entirely abandoning work." The municipality threatened to bring before the tribunals those "Who, scorning the laws, would abandon their work, which must be even more dear to them than it is necessary to public survival."[26]

The determined attitude of the authorities and the threats of heightened repression led to a period of calm as worker agitation cooled in late May. The emotion incited by the assassination attempts against Robespierre and Collot d'Herbois, by overexciting the revolutionary ardor of the sans-culottes, for a moment turned their attention away from the problems of daily survival. When the emotion subsided and the same difficulties remained, the agitation began again, continuing until thermidor, contributing in a major way to the general crisis that swept away the revolutionary government.

Discontent was asserted at the beginning of June in a particularly dangerous way among the workers subject to conscription and working in one way or another in war production. Tightly supervised, under the strict surveillance of government agents, they did not have recourse to leaving their individual workshops in order to ameliorate their wages, fixed by decree; their only recourse was to form coalitions and to strike, both illegal actions. The agitation of the war production workers, coupled in February and March with the general movement of the sans-culotterie and the endeavors of the leading cordeliers, began again in early June; the government turned again to repression. On June 7, the Committee of Public Safety ordered the arrest of the ringleaders; the revolutionary committee of the Fontaine-Grenelle section proceeded on June II to incarcerate Louis Barre "as agitator and suspect for refusing to carry out the laws relative to armament workers' wages in the Jacobins' workshop"; on the 12th, they arrested two workers "from the arms workshop of the house of Ainé on Dominique Street charged with being instigators of the troubles in that workshop."[27] On June 10 Barère had made a statement to the Convention about movements in the factories for assignats, powder and arms; severe police measures restrained them in time; three ringleaders were arrested in the workshop for assignats; on June 9, at the powder factory, certain workers who wanted to stop work before the prescribed time were incarcerated. On the basis of this report, the Convention charged the public prosecutor of the revolutionary Tribunal to pursue "the counter-revolutionaries who have used criminal maneuvers in the workshops manufacturing assignats, arms, powders and saltpeter" and that they be immediately placed under the surveillance of the Committee of Public Safety.[28]

While the government authorities were committed to a course of repression, the municipal authorities were showing their willingness to lower wages. On June 7 the municipal Corps decreed that the wages paid to workers employed in outlet stores could not exceed the rate of 3 livres per day; now, in two out of three stores, the workers were receiving 4 livres. Despite complaints, the municipal Corps upheld its decree.[29] In the June 13 report to the municipal Corps on the suppression of window displays, we read this revealing passage on the intention of the authorities regarding wages: "Our factories are short-handed, rich harvests are calling workers from all quarters ... we must fill our workshops with women who will take up the needle, the card, the spindle, who will busy themselves with preparing raw material ... It is by multiplying workers that we will lower the exorbitant price of manual labor."[30]

Toward the middle of June, the worker agitation was generalized, affecting numerous craft groups. In several workshops, construction workers demanded a wage increase. On June 12, all those of the Louis Ballu enterprise, Grange-aux-Belles Street, who were receiving six livres per day, demanded eight, threatening to leave the workshop "all unanimously." The 18th, the construction workers of the Pierre Quantinet workshop in the Martin district made the same demand. On June 19, eight journeymen carpenters abandoned the Kempft and Pouillay workshops after their demand for eight livres a day was rejected. Faced with this general movement, the employer-carpenters who were tenderers of work for the Republic declared they were no longer responsible for delays in the completion of their orders; some admitted to having granted the increase demanded in order to fill their commitments to the government, but they intended by their declaration "to protect themselves against exceeding the 'maximum.'"[31] The workers' demands reverberated in the national defense works. According to the police bureau report of June 18, the revolutionary committee of the Popincourt section declared that it could not carry through on the work undertaken for the Republic, due to "the enormous increases" demanded by the workers.[32] On June 29, the administrators of the Commission of agriculture and arts for the Department of Paris registered the same grievances: workers employed in the Department refused to work at the fixed rate of 48 sous for laborers, demanding 3 livres 15 sous and a reduction in the length of the working day.[33]

Worker agitation continued throughout June and into July. On June 25, the Quinze-Vingts revolutionary committee repeated at the police bureau its denunciation of the journeymen carpenters "who demand too considerable wages from the tenderers at whose homes they work." On June 29 this same committee condemned "the avarice of the porters and the carters who demand exorbitant wages, and of merchants who hide their merchandise for anyone who is willing to pay the utmost."[34] Workers were all the more led to demand wage increases when the price limit on foodstuffs was not observed. The report of the police bureau to the Committee of Public Safety notes on July 6 a denunciation made by the earthenware manufacturers of Paris: their workers decided to work no longer "unless they are allotted twice the wage of 1790, threatening those who would not conform to their decree." Saint-Just noted in the margin of the report: "refer to the public prosecutor, then the revolutionary Tribunal."[35] The movement for higher wages tended to expand all the more as some employers preferred to meet the workers' demands rather than lose their work force. The revolutionary committee of Popincourt reports the case of a worker who had left his workshop when he learned that in a neighboring workshop the daily wages had just been raised from 7 to 8 livres; in the Mutius-Scoevola section the revolutionary committee attributed the raises obtained in certain workshops to the agitation that was occurring in others.[36] The movement even affected the workers in the printing works of the Committee for Public Safety. On July 7 the Committee ordered the arrest of three employees of the print shop of the *Bulletin des lois*, accused of having "violently forced their comrades to quit work before the prescribed hour and before the task was done."[37]

Thus the worker agitation for wage increases persisted, becoming all the more dangerous as it was combined with political agitation incited among the sans-culottes by the reactionary measures taken against their organizations.[38] The only reaction of the administrative or governmental authorities was that of repression. In a report in messidor Payan asked the police bureau of the Committee of Public Safety if it should bring before the revolutionary Tribunal a conscripted worker who had left his work "under the pretext that he was not earning enough."[39] It was in this atmosphere of discontent, heightened by repression, that the "maximum" of wages was published on July 23.

III

In order to evaluate the precise impact of this rate for a day's work, it would be necessary to compare it with the preceding rate in force. Since a complete schedule of the earlier rates does not exist, we must use the fragmentary evidence that it is possible to glean here and there. We thus arrive at the table giving an approximate idea of the evolution of wages for certain occupations in the months preceding July 27.

The comparison of certain figures speaks for itself: the rate for a day's work published on July 23 imposed an authoritarian, often considerable, wage decrease on workers since it reduced the wage of a first class carpenter from 8 *livres* to 3 *livres* 15 *sous* and that of a blacksmith or a metal worker in an arms workshop from 16 *livres* 10 *sous* to 6 *livres* or 5 *livres* 5 *sous*.

OCCUPATION GROUPS [wages per day]	1790[1]		Feb. 19 - March 20, 1794 VENTÔSE YEAR II		June 19 - July 18, 1794 MESSIDOR YEAR II		July 23 5 THERMIDOR YEAR II	
	livres	*sous*						
I. Building: Carpenters (1st class)	2 l.	10 s.	6 l.[2]			8 l.[3]	3 l.	15 s.
Stone-cutters at building site of the Pantheon	1	16[4]	4[5]		. . . .		3	8
Layers (id.)	2	5	4	5				
	. . . .		5		. . . .		3	15
Masons (id.)	1	12	3	10	. . . .		2	8
	1	16	4	5			2	14
Scaffolding (id.)	1	18	3	10	. . . .		2	17
Roofers (id.)	1	12	3		. . . .		2	8
Laborers (id.)	1	8	3		. . . .		2	2
II. Arms Workshops:								
First Class[6]	3	10	. . . .		16	10[7]	5	5
Second Class	2	10	. . . .		8	5	3	15
Laborers	1	16	. . . .		3		2	14
			NIVÔSE PLUVIÔSE Dec.21 — Feb.18		PRAIRIAL MESSIDOR May 20 — July 18		THER-MIDOR July 19	Aug.17
III. Various; Brush makers[8]	2	10	. . . .		3	15	5	3 15
Asst. Bakers	4		15[9]		. . . .		. . .	6
Carters	1	12	[10]		. . . .		. . .	2 8
Delivery men (average route)		10	5[11]		. . . .		. . .	15
Carriers of one load of wood	. . . .		8[12]		. . . .		. . .	3
Chimneysweeps (per chimney)		6		18	. . . .		. . .	9

1. All the wages for 1790 are drawn from the "maximum" of July 23, 1794.
2. A.N., F^7 4662, d. l. This is the wage "fixed by the law"
3. *Ibid.* This is the wage demanded by the workers.
4. A.N., F^{13} 1137, workers' wages at the building site of the Pantheon in 1790.
5. *Ibid.*, F^{13} 1138, workers' wages at the building site of the Pantheon set by the Department of Paris, (March 5, 1794).
6. According to the "maximum" of July 23, the first class included blacksmiths and metal workers, the second casters and moulders.
7. Camille Richard, *Le Comité de salut public et les Fabrications de guerre sous la Terreur*, p. 720.
8. R. Cobb, "Une coalition de garçons brossiers de la section des Lombards", *A.H.R.F.*, 1953, p. 67.
9. R. Marion, "Les lois du maximum et la taxation des salaires sous la Révolution", *Revue internationale de sociologie*, 1917, vol. XXV, p. 485.
10. According to a report of Grivel and Siret of December 28-30, 1793, "the carter ... is demanding triple the wage owed for his work." (Mathiez, *La Vie chère...*, p. 587).
11. "The public delivery men are not ashamed to demand 100 *sols* [sous] for a light job that would have been generously paid 10 *sols* a year ago." (Grivet and Siret, cited by Mathiez, *La Vie chère...*, p. 587). Naturally we cannot take these figures literally.
12. According to Grivel and Siret (Mathiez, *La Vie chère...*, p. 586).

Combining with the political malaise which had been developing in the Parisian sections since germinal, the discontent aroused by the "maximum" of wages of July 23 accentuated the divorce of the sans-culotterie and the revolutionary government: at the height of the crisis, the Robespierrist authorities of the Paris Commune lacked popular support.

Worker discontent immediately after the publication of the new rate of daily wages is vouched for by the precautions that the Robespierrist Commune felt obliged to take. On July 25, Hanriot was warned that "several workers, doubtlessly misled by enemies of the people, have left their workshops."[40] In the morning of July 27 [9 thermidor], Lescot-Fleuriot, mayor of Paris, ordered for the next day, a holiday, an armed contingent "especially necessary in these times when malicious persons would be able to take advantage of the proclamation on the 'maximum' of workers' daily wages to mislead some citizens."[41] On the very day of 9 thermidor, workers indifferent to the political struggle unfolding, or unaware of it, demonstrated their discontent against the new "maximum." In the Unité section about three o'clock in the afternoon, there was "a sort of rumbling among masonry workers and stone-cutters working in the refinery (of salt-peter) occasioned by the daily wages set by the 'maximum' proclaimed on the 6th (5th) of this month by the Commune."[42] About four o'clock, while the Convention was ordering the arrest of Robespierre, a gathering was forming at the square of the Hotel-de-Ville "that was said to be on account of the 'maximum' of workers' wages."[43] About the same time Fouquier-Tinville heard the call to arms. "They came to tell me," he later wrote, "that it was because of the gathering of workers at the port, regarding the 'maximum.'"[44] The Robespierrist authorities of the Commune finally realized the political importance of these worker demonstrations. About eight o'clock in the evening, in a proclamation to the people of Paris signed by Lescot-Fleuriot, the Commune lay the responsibility for the "maximum" of July 23 on Barère: "This Barère who belongs to all factions in turn and who had the workers' daily wages set to make them perish from hunger,"[45] But it was too late...

The *Messager du soir* reported on August 1 that the workers showed "a little humor toward the municipal rebels on their way to Revolution Square by pleasantly calling them: 'f... maximum.'"[46] This was in effect the meaning that for the moment the workers gave to the fall of Robespierre and the Robespierrist Commune. Seeing in Robespierre and his friends an obstacle to their movement demanding the preservation of their standard of living, the workers, once Robespierre had been eliminated, again called for a revision in the rates of July 23. On July 29 or 30, the journeymen of Pierre Ramossin, master brushmaker on Denis Street, began forming a coalition to obtain a wage increase: "And there you are, the 'maximum' in the garbage can", one of them declared.[47]

The thermidorian authorities demagogically gave the same interpretation to the events. The Committee of Public Safety issued a proclamation on July 30 "to the workers of Paris, on the 'maximum' of daily wages" recognizing that most of the objections were "just and well-founded, given that this 'maximum' was not based on that of foods or basic necessities." The Committee would thus take care of "the means necessary to rectify this process, so that the compensation for a day's work would be proportionate to the price of subsistences."[48] Workers were urged to return to their workshops and take up their work, more evidence that the protest movement had grown after July 27. On the 31st, the enforcement of the rates of July 23 was suspended: "If proof is lacking of the counter-revolution of the 'triumvirs,' it is sufficient to present this rate. The insufficient wages which it shows and the moment that the Commune chose to publish it, several days before the fall of the conspirators—don't they obviously prove a deliberate plan to excite a movement in Paris?"[49]

The government authorities had, however, ordered a revision of the July 23rd rate. The Bureau of the maximum of the Agency of the maximum and interior commerce undertook a survey of wages actually paid and on August 2 heard from employers of various crafts groups: their information agreed that actual wages were generally much higher than the theoretical wages of the "maximum." The compilers rapidly completed their task. On August 9 they transmitted their report and the revised rate[50] to the Committee of Public Safety, through the intermediary of the Commission of Commerce and Supplies to which the Agency of the "maximum" was answerable. One part of the report was immediately published: on August 15, the Committee of Public Safety decreed "the maximum of salaries and daily wages for workers and employees working on bridges, quays and ports throughout the Commune of Paris."[51] As for the rate of other wage-earners, on August 26 Lindet prepared, in the name of the Committee of Public Safety, a report and a draft of a decree to submit to the Convention based on the proposals of the Bureau of the "maximum." On September 10, the report, draft decree and table of revised rates were communicated to the Commerce Committee of the Convention which discussed them that same day and decided to file the dossier with the bureau so that all the Committee members might read it. On September 14, the Bureau of the "maximum" again transmitted parts of the dossier to the Commerce Committee.[52]

The Bureau's revisions merit attention. The report to the Committee of Public Safety begins by criticizing the method of the compilers of the July 23 rate: in order to set the wages of the workers of the first class, they had taken as a base the wages paid to workers of the third or even fourth class. A whole other method guided the revision. "The workers' daily wages have been calculated in this new work according to the current value of food, especially of vegetables and fruits which are the workers' principal consumptions." The compilers were especially interested in workers whose earnings were the most modest: they were increased because "their needs surpassed the funds previously allotted them." On the other hand, the increase was less considerable for the workers of the first class "because workers who earn 6 livres a day are in no condition to complain and such wages appear proportionate to their work and able to satisfy all their expenses." Finally workers working on "non-maximés" [uncontrolled] products were not included in the revised rates "for the simple reason that manufacturers or merchants who have retained or acquired the right to sell their merchandise by mutual agreement cannot demand that we assess the citizens they employ in the manufacture of this merchandise." Consequently, the new rate had only 43 articles, "established in proportion to work, to the necessary expenses of the workers and to the high price of foodstuffs in Paris." This was a long way in letter and spirit from Article VIII of the law of September 29, 1793.

Similar augmentations were established for different occupation groups.

Thus conceived, the revised rate of August 9, 1794 entailed a definite improvement in wages in comparison with the rate of July 23 as the following figures—for the categories cited earlier—illustrate:

	July 23		August 9	
Construction workers (1st class)	3 l.	15 s.	5 l.	
Stone-cutters (id.)	3	8	5	
Layers (id.)	3	15	6	
Masons (id.)	2	14	4	
Roofers	2	8	3	
Laborers	2	2	3	10 s.
First class	6		7	
Second class	3	15	5	
Carters	2	8	3	5
Chimneysweeps		9		12
Saddlers:				
Assistant cutters	4 l.	10 s.	6 l.	
Grooms	3	15	5	
Day laborers	3		4	
Saddlers	3		4	
Ropemakers:				
Journeymen	2	14	3	15
Tinsmiths:				
First Class	4	10	5	10
Second Class	3	15	5	
Third Class	3		4	
Fourth Class	2	5	3	10
Tanners:				
Workers	2	8	4	10
Carpenters:				
Heads of workshops	5 l.	5 s.	6 l.	10 s.
Journeymen (1st class)	3	15	5	
(2 nd class)	3	8	4	10
Pit sawyer	3	15	8	

The wages set down in the schedule of August 9 have documentary value as they were actually in force. They are noted in the margin of the dossier of the rate printed on July 23 often with the address of the enterprise where they were applied: for carpenters: "Mrtreil (?) rue Antoine"; for tobacco workers: "Felipon, tobacco factory at Gros Caillou, Robillard, maison Longueville." The rate of August 9 did nothing but sanction actual conditions, maintaining the advantages won by the workers.

This explains why this schedule was never decreed: the report, the draft decree and the table of the "maximum" remained in the files of the Commerce Committee. Reaction was rapidly taking over the Convention, which had only accepted the "maximum" in September 1793, under pressure from the sans-culotterie. Once freed from this pressure, it returned to liberalism. With the dismantling of the revolutionary government and the reestablishment of the social and political preponderance of the proprietors and producers, wage and price controls could not survive. The "maximum" for foodstuffs disappeared on December 19, 1794. The price of subsistences rose at a breathtaking rate, reducing the sans-culottes to extreme misery. When the people rose up in the spring of 1795, they demanded the reestablishment of controls.

Recalling these events, Albert Mathiez in his discussion of Parisian workers stresses "the exclusive concern with their particular interests, their lack of a political education."[53] This is of course true, but we could just as well emphasize the political error of the Robespierrist Commune taking measures of anti-worker repression and publishing the maximum wage of July 23. These actions reveal the lack of economic understanding of Robespierre and his group, who were incapable of drawing up a coherent social program. But how could they?

We cannot lose sight of the fact that the Revolution whose battles were directed by the Committee of Public Safety remained a bourgeois revolution. Having agreed, under pressure from the popular masses and in order to support a national war, to control the [prices of] products supplied by the possessors of the means of production, it was also necessary to control the wages which entered into the production costs. The policy of the "Hébertist" Commune regarding wages tipped the balance in favor of workers and consumers, at the risk of destroying the equilibrium. After its fall, the Committee of Public Safety sought to reestablish the balance. Monetary necessities and the needs of national defense, moreover, dictated that the increase in wages be stopped; otherwise it would have been necessary to raise the price of war supplies.

The Robespierrist authorities, by publishing the maximum wage of July 23, were thus responding to the requirements of the bourgeois revolution. But at the same time they were alienating the sans-culottes at the very moment when the offensive of the bourgeoisie—eager to be rid of their yoke—made the support of the sans-culotterie more necessary than ever. The Robespierrists paid with torture and death for the inescapable contradictions of their politics.

8

Sectional personnel and Babouvist personnel[1]

In order to measure the precise impact of the Conspiracy of Equals, it is necessary to study, beyond the political documents, the social composition of the Babouvist personnel, not just the Conspirators themselves, the leading group of the conspiracy, but the men whom they intended "to use in the movement," like those who, for having been arrested in the spring of 1796 or compromised from Ang. 18–Sept. 16 in the affair of the Grenelle camp, merited being considered Babouvists. It would therefore be possible, by reference to the political personnel of the Paris sections in the year II, to better place the Conspiracy for Equality in the general movement of the French Revolution.

In this study, the documentary base contains a certain number of lists of names drawn up by Babeuf and his conspirators for propaganda purposes or for revolutionary action, and conserved in the archives of the High Court of Justice of Vendôme, instituted on August 7, 1796 in order to judge the Tribune and his conspirators. Of particular interest are the lists in carton W561 of the National Archives: lists of subscribers to the *Tribun du peuple* and lists of "patriots appropriate to command."[2] The bill of indictment, drawn up after the arrests, which were spread out from April to June 1796, includes a list of 56 names.[3] Finally the attempt at the Grenelle camp resulted in 132 arrests; the list for these was drawn up by the administrators of the central office of the Paris district on September 10, 1796.[4]

Obviously we cannot consider all these lists of equal importance. A rapid examination reveals diverse ranks among the Babouvist personnel, an expression that is too general to give an accurate picture of reality. Likewise, in the sectional personnel of year II, political and social differences are expressed which differentiate the militants from the masses they trained and which, among the militants themselves, underscore the specific characteristics of different ranks—for example, civil commissioners and revolutionary commissioners. Certainly, as we have already demonstrated for the sectional personnel of year II, the nature of the documents can hardly allow a study of exact social statistics. Often no occupation is given.

Vocabulary remains imprecise, reflecting the social boundaries themselves; quite often the same term encompasses different social realities—the employer and the wage-earner—more precisely, the small proprietor and the journeyman. Once again we assess to what extent all studies on the social composition of the popular masses and middle layers of the former type (included at the end of the 18th century in the expression "sans-culotterie") are condemned to remain vague and imprecise. It has nevertheless seemed possible to draw certain characteristic traits from these ciphered approximations, traits which throw some light on the Conspiracy for Equality, its structure and its limits.

I. Subscribers to the *Tribun du peuple*

We count a total of 590 suscribers to the *Tribun du peuple*,[5] a figure which may seem low, but it is necessary to take into consideration conditions of reading at the end of the 18th century, particularly in the popular milieu. We cannot mechanically deduce the influence of the newspaper from its circulation. It is true that the popular societies, which in year II and still in year III increased the audience for patriotic papers, no longer existed in year IV. But it would be necessary to research, particularly in the archives of the police stations, whether or not public reading at the great building sites like those of the Pantheon had completely disappeared.[6] Also, in year IV as in year II, the cafés and bars played a not inconsiderable role from this point of view. Seven innkeepers or cabaret owners figure among the subscribers in the departments, a dozen among those of Paris. For example, Pierre Nicolas Chrétien—café owner Neuve Saint-Marc Street, Lepeletier section, revolutionary commissioner and juror at the revolutionary Tribunal in year II, accused with Babeuf in year IV—whose very name symbolizes the revolutionary continuity of the sans-culotte personnel.[7]

Out of a total of 590 subscriptions, 238 (40.3 %) come from the departments; 345 (58.4 %) from Paris.[8] Thus we again verify in year IV one of the lasting traits of the revolutionary movement since 1789, marking an essential continuity: the preponderance of Paris and its leading role.

The geographical distribution of the departmental subscribers is characterized by the preponderance of the group from Nord and from Pas-de-Calais (18 and 20 subscribers), and by the importance of the Mediterranean group: Var and Alpes-Maritimes (21 and 8 subscribers), Vaucluse (10), Hérault (12), but only 5 subscribers in Bouches-du-Rhône, and only one in Gard. Coming next in order of importance are the departments of Saône-et-Loire (8 subscribers), of Mont-Blanc,[8] of Morbihan and Moselle

(6 subscribers each), of Dordogne, of Rhône, of Seine-et-Marne (5 subscribers each)[9]...

It does not seem possible to draw up from this numerical data a valid political map of Babouvist influence in France in the year IV: too many factors intervene which are purely fortuitous, particularly when we consider the human mingling characteristic of all revolutionary periods. If the Moselle had 6 subscriptions, 5 of these at Metz, is this not due to the influence of Bouchotte, sans-culotte War Minister in year II, who on leaving prison withdrew to his native town?[10] If the Nord and Pas-de-Calais head the list for the number of subscribers, is this not in part due to the familial ties of the revolutionaries of year II or of year IV, to ties of friendship which at the same time create political alliances and strengthen them? Is the subscription of the farmer of Bouret (Pas-de-Calais) explained by that of the "citoyenne" Lebas, who lived right nearby, at Frévent, native village of Saint-Just's friend? Does the residence of the "citoyenne" Darthé account for the three subscriptions at Saint-Pol? And do the ten subscriptions at Arras show fidelity to the memory of Robespierre or Lebon?[11] Let us note in this regard the name of Duhem fils [son] among the four subscribers at Lille, native town of Duhem, member of the Convention.[12] But on the other hand, it is surprising to count only two subscribers to the *Tribun du peuple* in the Somme—one a merchant at Amiens, the other a health officer at Rosières—in the Santerre region that Babeuf had stirred up, five years earlier, in his struggle against the feudal rights of "aide" [indirect taxes] and "champarts" [portion of the harvest].

If we glance rapidly over the lists of departmental subscribers, the towns appear as points of refuge or of settling for victims of events or adversaries of the regime of the Directory, particularly in the regions where the counterrevolution and the White Terror had held sway, as in the Rhône Valley or the departments of the South-East. But can we conclude that there was a notable influence of the Babouvist paper on local opinion? Two Corsican refugees were among the 8 subscribers of Alpes-Maritimes, both living in Nice.[13] Of the 21 subscribers of Var, 8 lived in Toulon (among them a chief engineer and two Navy employees), 3 at Fréjus (one an employee of military material), 3 at Saint-Raphael (one a lieutenant).[14] The 10 subscribers in the Vaucluse were all inhabitants of Avignon.[15] Of the 6 subscribers of Morbihan, 4 lived in Lorient, one an employee of the Navy, and two in Vannes, one a soldier doubtless called there by the hazards of war.[16] On the other hand, in a department like Hérault, spared by the counterrevolution in year II, the dispersion of the 12 subscribers is remarkable, even more so, considering that apart from an ex-priest at Villemagne, there were none in the countryside.[17] The six towns of the department are represented:

Montpellier with 3 subscribers, Béziers and Adge with 2, Cette, Lodève and Pézenas with one each. Likewise the 8 subscribers of Saône-et-Loire are divided among Mâcon (3), Autun (2), Charolles (2) and Châlon (1).[18]

In order to give an exact account, however, of the geographical distribution of the subscribers of the *Tribun du peuple*, a precise knowledge of the turns taken by the revolutionary struggles and political personnel in each of the departments would be necessary—knowledge which we cannot claim. To what extent did the Jacobin personnel and cadres of year II show their opposition to the regime of the Directory by subscribing to Babeuf's newspaper? How many of these departmental subscribers are former militants or state employees of the revolutionary government? We need meticulous research and collation which only local scholars could successfully carry out. It would then be possible, by identifying the personnel of year II and the subscribers of year IV, to underscore individual continuity and revolutionary fidelity. It would also be possible, by process of elimination, to spot slow evolutions or brusque choices under the influence of events, like the sudden consciousness among the new generation matured in the course of the dramatic year III, through whom the revolutionary personnel partly renewed themselves.

If, from the study of the geographical distribution of the departmental subscribers of the *Tribun du peuple*, we pass to that of the social and occupational distribution (the lists indicate the social rank or occupation for 163 subscribers out of 238, or 68.4 %), we cannot help but be struck by the preponderance of well-off, even rich, proprietors. Conversely, the proletarian element is absent.

Of these 163 registered departmental subscribers, only one is listed as "rentier."[19] Three socio-professional groups belong uncontestably to the propertied categories. The group living off landed property comprises 10 subscribers (6.10 %) who on several accounts come under the rural bourgeoisie.[20] The group of merchants comprises 23 subscribers (14.1 %) listed simply as "négociants": it is thus a question of commercial enterprises of a certain importance. Finally there is the group of heads of enterprises: 7 manufacturers or entrepreneurs (4.2 %).[21] Altogether these groups have 40 subscribers, almost a quarter (24.5 %) of the total. If the sources permitted, it would be advisable to specify at what level of comfort or wealth these subscribers to the *Tribun du peuple* were situated.

Of the group in the liberal professions (26 subscribers, or 15.9 %) 13 notaries or men of the law stand out; then come 9 subscribers in the medical professions and 2 engineers.[22] Here also is the bourgeoisie, well-off at the very least. It is also to this social category, if we refer to the eligible voter structure of the regime [suffrage based on property qualification], that we must attach the 21 subscribers (12.8 %) who belong to various categories of administrative personnel: political personnel (3 commissioners with executive power), judiciary personnel (5 judges or public prosecutors), municipal personnel (13 officers or presidents of municipal administration).[23] In sum, these 5 groups that we can consider as part of the bourgeoisie form more than half (53.2 %) of the departmental subscribers whose occupation is known.

For the military group (14 or 8.5 %), we cannot gather any precise information on the point of interest here. It is a heterogeneous group, going from subaltern officers to leaders of brigades and a general of a division (Turreau, in Conches, Eure), whose social origins are difficult to pinpoint. More characteristic is the group of 13 state employees (7.9 %) generally belonging to lower administrative personnel, with the exception of the director of customs at Besançon. Finally, there remain the tradesmen and the shopkeepers: 47 out of 163 subscribers, or 28.8 %, among which 16 (9.8 %) seem to qualify as merchants rising above the simple boutique, without however meriting the designation of "négociant".[24] Among the 31 artisans and shopkeepers remaining are 7 printers and 2 booksellers, 7 café owners or innkeepers.[25] We know the role of the latter in the popular movement of year II and how the cabaret could constitute a center of diffusion of revolutionary ideas. From this point of view, we should also underline the importance of the booksellers and the printers.

By reference to the sans-culotte personnel of the Parisian sections in year II, we cannot but be struck by the lesser importance of the artisan-shopkeeper group among the departmental subscribers to the *Tribun du peuple*: less than a third of the whole, while that group comprised nearly two-thirds of the Parisian committees (58.6 % in the civil committees, 63.8 % in the revolutionary committees).[27] The proprietary bourgeoisie prevails here over the world of crafts and shops. But didn't it go the same way in the year II? Wouldn't we find, for the period of the revolutionary government, the same social disparity between the Parisian sectional personnel and the departmental political personnel? That is to say, between the artisan and shopkeeper sans-culotterie on one hand and the Jacobin bourgeoisie on the other? This would tend to further verify for year IV one of the fundamental traits of the revolutionary movement since 1789: the gap—not only political but also social—between Paris and the departments.

The social and occupational analysis of the lists of Parisian subscribers to the *Tribun du peuple* in fact reveals characteristics close to those of the sectional personnel of year II; here the specific groups of the sans-culotterie regain their importance.

A study of the geographic distribution of the subscribers, section by section, would certainly be useful. But besides the rather large difficulties such a study would present, as the lists only rarely include an indication of the section, it would permit no valid comparison with respect to year II, particularly given the multiple changes in residence forced on numbers of former "sectionnaires" [participants in sectional politics] by police harassment or the anti-terrorist repression of year III. As for the socio-occupational analysis, the results attained have only informational value, since the occupation or social rank is indicated for only 94 subscribers out of 345, or less than a third—apart from 32 deputies or former deputies[28] and 5 directors.

At the two extremes of the social scale, we note on one hand the absence of the proletarian element, properly speaking (who formed 9.9 % of the personnel of the revolutionary committees in year II). On the other hand the weakness of elements coming out of the proprietary bourgeoisie. The commerce group in fact includes only 7 subscribers described as "négociants" (7.4 % of the 94 registered subscribers), whereas the group of heads of enterprises includes 3 entrepreneurs or manufacturers[29] (3.1 %), a proportion close to that of the revolutionary committees (2.8 %). The liberal professions are represented by 7 subscribers (7.4 %, but 10.5 % in the revolutionary committees), 4 belonging to the medical professions,[30] only 2 to the juridical professions.[31] Thus, these three groups make up only 17.9 % of the Parisian subscribers, whereas comparable elements account for 53.2 % of the departmental subscribers.

More characteristic of the Parisian sans-culotterie is the group of 9 low-level state employees and civil servants (9.5 %) and especially the group of artisans and shopkeepers: 68 subscribers (72.3 %), an even higher proportion than that of the year II revolutionary committees (63.8 %). Among the shopkeepers, 11 merit the description of "marchand" (dealer).[32] The most numerous element is formed by the 6 café-owners[33] and the three wine merchants; next come 6 painters and 6 carpenters, and 4 shoemakers.[34] Printers, relatively numerous among the departmental subscribers, are represented here only by one printer in Honoré Street.[35] As in the revolutionary committees, the artisan element seems to prevail here over the strictly shopkeeper element, although it is often difficult to distinguish one from the other. On the other hand, still in reference to year II, the art crafts, numerous in the revolutionary committees, are here represented by only 5 subscribers.[36]

Despite these slight differences, social continuity is clearly expressed between the sectional personnel of year II and the Parisian subscribers to the *Tribun du peuple* in year IV: both were recruited from the ranks of artisans and shopkeepers who constituted the framework of the Parisian sans-culotterie. It would doubtless be necessary to examine each individual case in order to determine the exact social level of each subscriber, a difficult task in the absence of sufficient documentation. But in year IV as in year II, the social range of the sans-culotterie fanned out from abject poverty to assured affluence. We see social continuity, but also personal or familial loyalty to a revolutionary past. The widows of the martyrs of liberty—Lepeletier, Marat (or his sister), the mother of Goujon, martyr of prairial—were subscribers to the *Tribun du peuple* and also the "citoyennes" Lazowski, Ronsin, Brochet. Without claiming to have set up a thorough statistical analysis, we have also found on these lists the names of 4 former civil commissioners and 10 former revolutionary commissioners; they symbolize the revolutionary continuity from year II to year IV of the Parisian sectional personnel.[37]

II. "Patriots appropriate to command"

An examination of the lists of "patriots appropriate to command" brings new evidence that the revolutionary avant-garde, which Babeuf and his conspirators believed they could count on, was still constituted in year IV not by a manufacturing or factory proletariat but by this coalition of small employers [artisans] and journeymen, working and living together. The nature of the documents, very incomplete for most of the sections and in some disorder, certainly do not permit a study of the Babouvist personnel in the precise sense of the term. More than lists of militants, they appear as lists of sympathizers on whom the leaders thought they could base the Conspiracy, either because of their revolutionary past or because of their present political reputation: "patriots appropriate to command," "patriots certain and appropriate to regenerate," "patriots appropriate to be employed in the movement," "patriots good for administering and revolutionizing," according to the texts, generally dating from April 20–May 19, 1796.

A comparison with the lists of the sectional personnel of year II present the same difficulties already pointed out in regards to the Parisian subscribers to the *Tribun du peuple*: the mobility of the population and changes in residence due to the repression of year III lead to a mingling that makes identifications difficult. Taking into account the repetitions from one document to another and the multiple cross-checkings, it is possible to characterize this personnel for two districts of Paris—the VIth (Lombards, Gravilliers, Temple and Amis-de-la-Patrie sections) and the VIIth

(Réunion, l'Homme Armé, Droits-de-l'Homme and Arcis sections)—as well as several sections scattered in various other divisions.

In first considering the social and occupational composition of these lists drawn up by Babeuf's agents, we always note the same dominant trait: crafts and the shop prevail. For the Lombards section, in the VIth district, 13 patriots are listed; of the 9 whose occupation is indicated, 7 are artisans or shopkeepers, 1 an employee and 1 a teacher. For the Gravilliers section, out of 13 patriots "appropriate to take charge" there are 10 artisans or shopkeepers, 1 teacher, 1 health officer, 1 silk worker. For the Temple section, of the 9 patriots whose occupation is indicated (out of 13) there are 5 artisans or shopkeepers, and 1 employee, but also 1 "rentier" and 2 patriots of liberal professions.[38]

For the VIIth district, the lists are both more extensive and more precise. For the Réunion section, out of 43 "democrats," 28 are artisans or shopkeepers and 7 are employees. For l'Homme-Armé section there are 41 artisans or shopkeepers and 10 employees out of 62 "democrats" noted.[39] In the Arcis section there are 26 artisans or shopkeepers and 1 employee out of 32 "democrats." Finally, among the 36 "patriots" which make up the list of the Droits-de-l'Homme section, 20 are artisans or shopkeepers and 5 are employees (but no occupation is given for 7 names). In considering the whole of the VIIth district, we find that out of 173 patriots or democrats noted (with the occupation indicated for 157 or 90.7 %), the artisan or shopkeeper element reaches almost three-quarters (73.2 %): a higher percentage than for the revolutionary committees of year II (63.8 %).[40] The group of employees, situated at the same social level, attains 14.6 %. Coming from bourgeois affluence are 13 patriots or democrats (8.2 %): 7 belong to liberal professions, 2 seem to be heads of enterprises, 4 are described as "rentiers" (probably retired artisans or shopkeepers).[41] Conversely, the proletarian elements comprise only 7 names (4.4 %), 6 of whom are in one section, l'Homme-Armé; they are wage-earners of clientele (4 day workers, 1 water carrier, 1 delivery man) rather than wage earners in manufacturing (only 1 worker, with no other qualification).

There is no need for further examples. The lists available for certain isolated sections convey this same predominance of artisans and shopkeepers.[42] There is no rupture in regard to year II: it was indeed the world of the shop and the workshop which imposed its social mark on the revolutionary personnel of year IV. Should we conclude that it had an ideological influence? At least the problem is posed of the diffusion and penetration of Babouvist ideas in a social milieu characterized by its petit-bourgeois mentality and its attachment to small property based on individual work.

In glancing over these lists of patriots and democrats, however, we are compelled to make another observation. Although there was without a doubt social permanence with respect to year II—continuity of artisans and shopkeepers, that is to say sans-culotte—there was also a rupture if we look at individual names. The lists of men appropriate to lead reveal, within the same social category, a renewal of revolutionary personnel.

In the VIth district, if we find, out of 13 "patriots proper to take charge" in the Gravilliers section, 9 former commissioners or militants from year II, the Temple section includes only 6 out of 13, the Amis-de-la-Patrie section 3 out of 12, and the Lombards section 2 out of 13.[43] For the whole of the VIth district, there are 20 former members of the political personnel of year II out of the 51 patriots noted by Babouvist agents (39.2 %): 13 revolutionary commissioners predominate, far outweighing 4 militants, 1 member of the Committee of Public Safety of the Department of Paris, 1 justice of the peace, and 1 civil commissioner.

For the VIIth district, the lists of patriots and democrats contain 173 names: there we find 43 members of the former sectional personnel, the proportion dropping to less than a quarter (24.8 %). The 24 revolutionary commissioners attain the first rank; the civil committees are represented by 8 names; then come 8 militants, 2 second commanders from the sectional army, 1 justice of the peace, 1 president of a popular society.[44]

Among this former sectional personnel, the revolutionary commissioners are in the first rank. They constituted in year II the most active element of popular power, the most devoted support of the revolutionary government. As they were recruited more democratically than the civil commissioners and represented the more popular and more conscious categories of the sans-culotterie, the Babouvist agents were certain to find among them reliable patriots, "good for administering and revolutionizing." But the whole problem of the adhesion of these men of year II to the Babouvist ideology remains. And the same for the new men that the lists reveal. This renewal of the revolutionary personnel in year IV is explained only too well by both the anti-terrorist repression and by the crisis of year III, the crisis leading some to a clear awareness of the necessity of political action, the repression throwing others into the shadow of inaction. Was this renewal of men (for the VIIth district three-quarters of the patriots listed are new) accompanied by a renewal of ideas? We have noted social permanence; was there an ideological rupture?

We must assume there was not, if we refer to the methods of organization that the lists reveal: lists of sympathizers rather than militants; even more, lists evidently drawn up on the strength of acquired reputations and sectional renown without the knowledge of the interested parties.

Particularly significant in this regard is the case of Varlet, the former Enragé, appearing on the Babouvist list of the Droits-de-l'Homme section. After Thermidor, Varlet's activity was developing parallel to that of Babeuf and popular organizations like the Museum section and the Electoral Club, against the left Thermidorians and the revolutionary government. His arrest on September 5, 1794 brutally ended this activity. Varlet was not freed until a year later, doubtless following the amnesty proclaimed by the Convention.[45] This long detention broke the Enragé: his political career was finished (yet prison reinforced the energy of the indomitable Babeuf). During his stay in the Plessis prison, however, Varlet had known some of the future conspirators, in particular Germain and Brutus Magnier. Is it to these acquaintances or to his reputation that he owed being inscribed without his knowledge on the list of "democratic patriots" of the Droits-de-l'Homme? The fact remains that Varlet retired from revolutionary action and played no part in the Conspiracy for Equality.

This example is as significant for the lack of connection on the level of revolutionary organization as for the absence of ideological unity. The "patriots appropriate to command," former members of the sectional personnel of year II or new men of year IV, both coming from middle layers of the Parisian sans-culotterie, appeared to be firmly situated, apart from a few cases, in the line of the traditional popular ideology rather than in that of the new ideology.

III. Bill of Indictment and the Affair of the Camp of Grenelle

This impression is reinforced by an examination of the list of the bill of indictment drawn up following the mandates of induction and arrest issued from May 8 to July 3, 1796, and from the list established the following September 10 by the administrators of the central bureau of the Paris district of "men arrested in the camp of Grenelle and its surroundings."

The bill of indictment, written by André Gérard, one of the directors of the grand jury of the Paris district, is directed against 56 "charged with conspiracy to overthrow the Constitution and the government and to reestablish the Constitution of 1793." At the head of the bill are the staff of the Conspiracy: Babeuf, Germain, Darthé. The personnel of the Convention are represented by Amar, Laignelot, Lindet, Ricord, Vadier. Others among the accused belong to military personnel: the generals Fyon, Parein and Rossignol...

From the former sectional personnel of year II—retaining only incontestable identifications—we discover 12 accused: 7 revolutionary commissioners and 1 civil commisioner;[46] 1 justice of the peace of the Marchés section—Bouin, stocking worker; 1 commander of a sectional battalion—the shoemaker Thierry, moved from the Amis-de-la-Patrie section to Lombards; finally 2 militants of the popular society of Arcis.[47] These form close to a quarter of the whole (23 %). With these, putting aside marginal cases like those of the two Duplays, 17 other defendants, craftsmen and shopkeepers, belong to the sans-culotterie.[48] That is to say, more than half of the list. It would also be appropriate to add to this group a man like Rossignol, the sans-culotte general.

If, from the plane of social adherence, we pass to that of ideological formation, we must note that only 9 of these 29 defendants, all sans-culottes, were subscribers to the *Tribun du peuple*.[49]

The list of the men arrested for the affair of the camp of Grenelle is important to us because it indicates the occupation for 127 names out of 131.[50] Since it was a question of a revolutionary action, we are tempted to consider this list as more characteristic of the Babouvist personnel than the lists of "men appropriate to command," taking into account a margin of error ensuing from the provocateur and police aspects of the affair. But can we mechanically conclude adhesion to an ideological system from involvement in the action?

It does not seem that we can draw any lessons from the geographical distribution, section by section, of the men arrested in this affair;[51] still we should note that in the Antoine *faubourg* [inner working-class suburb] the sections of Popincourt and Quinze-Vingts are represented by only two arrests each, while from the Montreuil section there are none.

We discover here again, with several slight differences, the same traits characteristic of the sectional personnel of year II, particularly of the active personnel, that of the revolutionary committees dominated by artisans. The well-off, if not rich, social categories are represented by 2 merchants and 2 men from liberal professions (3.1 %) to which we may add 2 men "sans état" [without profession]. The case of the 6 "rentiers" (4.7 %) is more doubtful, though they are probably former artisans or tradesmen retired from business, living off a small acquired profit, but still products of the kind of life and the mentality of the world of the artisan class. On the other hand, the percentage of proletarian elements is higher, 7.8 %, while they were only 4.4 % of the "men appropriate to command" of the VIIth district; they are still wage-earners of clientele: 10 day-laborers or unskilled laborers, porters, stablemen or water carriers. The "employee" element is very small: 2.3 % (it formed 14.6 % of the lists of the VIIth district). The 97 artisans and shopkeepers constitute more than three-quarters of the men arrested in the Grenelle affair: 76.3 %, a higher proportion than for the men appropriate to command (73.2 %) and for the revolutionary committees of year II (63.8 %). Let us emphasize that crafts are largely predominant over shops: 15 shoemakers (11.8 %), 12 carpenters (9.4 %), 8 locksmiths... independent artisans, likely to turn to violence and ready to lend a hand.

The preponderance of craftsmen, the relative importance of proletarian elements, the smaller percentage of the more prudent office workers and shopkeepers—all this is very normal since it was a question of attempting an insurrectionary struggle. The affair of the camp of Grenelle is from this point of view inscribed in the revolutionary continuity: from 1789 to year IV, the avant-garde of the struggles was not constituted by a factory proletariat but by a coalition of artisans and journeymen leading the lower strata of the sans-culotterie, who furnished the main body of combatants.

Among the men arrested in this attempt, 14 members of the former sectional personnel of year II stand out. Even if we take into account the many difficulties of identification, this is a rather low proportion (11 %). There were 7 revolutionary commissioners, 6 militants and 1 army captain, all tested on several accounts by the anti-terrorist repression of year II.[53] But beyond this continuity the question again arises of the penetration of the Babouvist ideology among these men who belong socially to the sans-culotterie: out of 131 detained from Grenelle, we discover only 6 subscribers to the *Tribun du peuple*.[54]

*

What can we conclude from these few encoded data? The nature of the documents permits us to accord only an approximate value.

If we refer first to the revolutionary technique characteristic of the Conspiracy of Equality, we cannot but be struck on the one hand by a concern for organization, pushed to the extreme as the lists of patriots appropriate to command evince, revealing a certain Jacobin style, and on the other hand by the uncertain method by which the essential problem of the connection with the popular masses was approached and resolved. Without returning to the manner in which these lists were drawn up, illustrated by the Varlet case, the non-concordance of the four series of lists examined denote a real stratification of the diverse categories of Babouvist personnel and their isolation one from the other. This is an essential requirement of any conspiratorial action, but here it is pushed to an extreme. For example, in the Réunion section (VIIth district), special lists were drawn up including the name of one man "having our confidence in case the leader responsible for the VIIth district is arrested," six patriots appropriate for command, and some men designated to represent the section at the municipality, the General Council of the Commune and the Department of Paris after the Babouvists had seized power.[55] Yet only one of these ten men in whom the leaders of the Conspiracy placed their trust appears on the lists of subscribers, none on those of the Grenelle affair or the bill of indictment. Conversely, the shoemaker Bouvard of the Réunion section, arrested in the Grenelle affair, does not appear on the list of patriots of the Réunion appropriate to command. This throws some light on the structure of the Conspiracy.

At the center the leading group appears, relying on the support of a small number of tested militants; then the fringe of sympathizers, "patriots" and "democrats," kept out of the secret plans and who do not appear to have shared the new revolutionary ideal. Finally the popular masses themselves who were to be led. One of the essential problems of revolutionary practice which was thus posed to the Conspirators was that of their connection with the popular masses, by the intermediary of these sympathizers, cadres not of the Conspiracy, but of the revolutionary government that would follow the seizing of power. One could write that at the prairial insurrection, "movement of masses without organization or real leaders of the action" was followed by the Conspiracy for Equality, an "organizing conspiracy par excellence, but whose leaders could not and did not know how to make a mass movement."[56] This judgment seems harsh. In the minds of the leaders of the Conspiracy, there was without a doubt a contradiction between their conspiratorial methods and the popular movement as it had developed in year III. Nonetheless they sensed the necessity of a close connection between the basic cadres and the masses, perhaps in the light of the organized days of struggle of August 10, 1792, or of May 31–June 2, 1793, which led to those lists of "patriots appropriate to be employed in the movement." But an examination of the lists of the Babouvist personnel does not permit us to affirm that this problem, sensed by the Conspirators, was solved in practice in any effective way.

In the second place, if we refer to the social continuity and permanence in the heart of the sans-culotterie, from the sectional personnel of year II to the Babouvist personnel of year IV, a discrepancy must be stressed over and above the renewal of individuals. On one hand, the social mentality of these men who formed the base, patriots and democrats, remains incontestably in the ideological line of the sans-culotte, characterized by attachment to small property based on individual work. The ideology of the leaders of the Conspiracy, accepting the communality of wealth and work, constitutes on the other hand a renewal or more precisely—a brusque mutation—a first form of the revolutionary ideology of the new society born of the Revolution itself.[57]

The contradiction between the Babouvist ideology and the sans-culotte mentality demonstrates the antagonism that there may have been between the aspirations of an avant-garde and the objective state of historical necessities, but it also underscores the dramatic character of the revolutionary endeavor of the Conspiracy of Equals. That Babeuf and the Conspirators conceived, through the experience of year II and the drama of year III, "those ideas that led beyond ideas of the old state of things," to repeat a phrase of Marx,[58] is to say enough of their greatness.

9

Religious Sentiments and Popular Cults: patriot saints and martyrs of liberty[1]

For a long time, the historians of the French Revolution saw the revolutionary cults only as political endeavors appropriate to the circumstances. Reacting against this tendency, Albert Mathiez wanted to underscore the specifically religious character of these cults.[2] Then it became a question of agreeing on the nature of the religious occurrence. On this question, Mathiez is a strict follower of Durkheim who affirms that it is essentially by their form that we recognize religious phenomena. Like his predecessors, Mathiez seems little concerned with studying the religious sentiment manifested by those who participated in the ceremonies of the revolutionary cults; it is there, however, that their nature can be discerned, whether political expediency or true religion.

We cannot conceal the difficulty of this enterprise. The documents do allow us to be present at the creation of new ceremonial ensembles, but to what extent do they clarify the exact beliefs of the followers of these new rituals? Here we grasp the difficulty of studies of historical psychology, yet the relative abundance of popular documents concerning in particular the cult of the martyrs of liberty seems to legitimize this first attempt.

I

Catholic writers have naturally denied any religious character of the revolutionary sects in order to see them only as an instrument of war against the Church. In his *History of the Sects,* Grégoire insisted on the persecution [of the Church].[3] More recently, the abbot Sicard endeavored to analyze the dogma of this *civil religion* that the revolutionaries, according to him, were trying to install;[4] but if he has described the symbols, rites and ceremonies of this "religion," still he considers it a political creation with no true religious character.

Michelet was the first to sense the religious character of the great demonstrations of the Revolution, of the Federations in particular—which he rightly considered as the first step in the formation of the revolutionary cults.[5] But in the end he reproached these various endeavors for being only political forms devoid of dogma. "Fertile in laws, sterile in dogma, [the Revolution] did not satisfy the eternal hunger of the human soul, always starving for, thirsting after God... The two parties of reason, the Girondists and the Jacobins, paid little attention to this. The Gironde completely dismissed the question, the Jacobins evaded it. They thought they could pay off God with a word."[6]

Aulard attached enough importance to the revolutionary cults to consecrate a special study to the Cult of Reason and the Cult of the Supreme Being. But he emptied them of all religious content, seeing in them "the necessary political consequence of the state of war into which the Revolution had been thrown by the resistance of the Ancien Régime against the new spirit." The men of year II, "by enthroning the goddess of Reason in Notre-Dame, or by glorifying the God of Rousseau at the Champ-de-Mars, were envisaging a *political* goal, and, for the most part, were seeking in these undertakings against traditional religion, as in their other drastic attitudes and words, only an expedient for national defense."[7]

Mathiez, while expressing his agreement with Aulard that these religious endeavors represented not only the struggle against the Church, but more essentially the defense of the new France, nevertheless went on to claim that the revolutionary cults constituted a true religion.[8] To delimit the religious occurrence, Mathiez relies on the analyses of Durkheim,[9] for whom, as we know, the religious occurrence is above all defined by its form: obligatory belief and obligatory exterior practices—these are the two essential characteristics retained by Durkheim and Mathiez after him. Taking these premises as a point of departure, Mathiez is less interested in a study of the common creed of the revolutionaries than in the demonstrations of the new faith, in its practices and ceremonies, in the revolutionary symbolism. "If I show all that, won't I have the right to conclude that a revolutionary religion existed, analogous in its essence to all other religions?"[10] And Mathiez affirms at the end of his study: "There exists a revolutionary religion whose object is the social institution itself. This religion has its obligatory dogma (the Declaration of Rights, the Constitution), its symbols wrapped in mystical veneration (the three colors, the trees of Liberty, the altar of the Fatherland, etc.), its ceremonies (the civil holidays), its prayers and its songs."[11]

Mathiez's study nevertheless remains on the surface of things. Not that we could reproach his staying on a purely historical plane: that's also a distinctive feature of the history of religions. But Mathiez does not properly characterize the religious occurrence when he assimilates the religious and the collective. He applies to the 18th century an assimilation that is justified in the context of Durkheim's study. The latter was describing archaic societies in which the diffused religious beliefs impregnated everything; the social and the religious were to a rather large extent merged. Can we say the same for the end of the 18th century? With the development of rationalism beginning in the preceding century, the religious was specialized and occupied only one sector of collective life. It is thus necessary to characterize it in itself and to consider both religious beliefs and specifically religious ceremonies as distinct from civil ceremonies. Doubtless it is not false to affirm as does Mathiez that the religious event is distinguished by its form. It is still necessary to specify that form and to consider the religious event in its totality: rites, symbols, dogma and beliefs; the latter, like all mental occurrences, only capable of being approached indirectly.

The problem of the revolutionary cults seems to have been poorly posed by their two most important historians, who have both ignored the specificity of the religious event, their perspective distorted by political preoccupation with Aulard, or by sociological deformation with Mathiez. They both follow more closely the official creations of the ruling bourgeoisie than the popular cults; not that any one cult was at that period the property of any one class, but the popular cults do allow us to grasp real-life manifestations of the religious spontaneity of the revolutionary masses. Aulard and Mathiez both insist on the rupture between traditional religion and the new religion; thus agreeing, though for different reasons, with the Catholic historians of the revolutionary cults. The rupture is hardly contestable; the innovation constitutes the interesting occurrence: it is still a matter of knowing how to characterize it and what factors were in play.

Whatever the importance of the political upheaval from 1789 to 1794 may have been, the Revolution could not destroy traditional religion in the soul of the people. To a certain extent the Revolution imprinted its mark and gave rise to certain aspects of Catholicism as it evolved toward a new popular religion. There is no doubt that, once the revolutionary crisis had passed, the men and women who, through a deep-felt need, had embraced the new cult returned to the tradition. Although the momentary abandonment of Catholicism constituted a rupture, it is all the more necessary to place the study of revolutionary cults in the perspective of traditional religion.

Certainly the study of new rituals on which Mathiez bases his reasoning is important, but it would be necessary to specify how the syncretism was established with old forms and what the new ceremonies borrowed from the Catholic form of worship. Moreover what were the beliefs and to what extent were they related to traditional beliefs? A religious cult implies on the part of the believer (especially if we place ourselves in the perspective of 18th century Catholicism) veneration of its object—a transcendent, supernatural object—which appears to be endowed with a virtue efficacious both down here and in the beyond. The believer participates in this efficacious grace through ritual worship, which constitutes in a certain sense an exchange of services between human beings and the supernatural. The religious event implies finally its participation in all personal life. These traits characterize traditional religion: to what extent do they apply to the revolutionary cults?

II

The cult of patriot saints enables us to clarify one aspect of the passage from the Catholic religion to the revolutionary cults: it joined new political aspects to the former religious context, aspects which became integrated into the traditional religion.

Perrine Dugué belonged to a family of small farmers from Thorigné, a village of the Mayenne department on the borders of the Sarthe. The whole family (Perrine had five brothers) were strongly attached to the Revolution and did their best in the struggle against the *chouans* [royalist insurgents]. Two of the brothers were recruited at Sainte-Suzanne, a village north of Thorigné, into the free companies defending the region against the "brigands." On March 22, 1796, Perrine, 19 years old and scorning threats she had received (she was accused of providing information to her brothers), started off for the market fair at Sainte-Suzanne. There she would also see her brothers. Halfway there she was attacked by three *chouans*; her body was found the next day and she was buried in a nearby field. The two sides accused each other of murder and perhaps these reciprocal accusations united all the elements of the population in a common commiseration—the murder had vividly struck the popular imagination. Three laments of the period make no allusion to Perrine's republican ideas, seeing in her only a good Christian who preferred death to rape. Her sentiments were generally known, however, and Perrine came to be regarded as a republican saint. According to the report of the priest Coutard, people had seen her "ascending to heaven with tricolored wings." Crowds rushed to her grave, where healings took place. Rumors of these miracles spread and pilgrims came from the neighboring departments of Orne, Sarthe and Maine-et-Loire. In 1791 a chapel was built. The restoration of the Catholic religion put an end to the cult of the republican saint whose miracles were not recognized, but the memory of Perrine was not erased for a long time.[12]

The example of Perrine Dugué is not unique. The Taillay forest, on the border of the departments of Loire-Inferieure and Ille-et-Vilaine, contains a famous grave known as "the tomb of the girl." This is Marie Martin, originally from Tresboeuf. Either for having pointed out the refuge of a royalist band to the *blues* [revolutionary soldiers], or for not wanting to divulge the hiding place of her masters, she was abused and massacred by the *chouans*. She was buried on the spot. According to an account related in 1950, two crosses were seen on her head. On nearby oaks are nailed small niches containing statuettes; one of these niches served to collect monetary offerings, which a woman came to gather on Sundays and days of pilgrimages until the war in 1914. Still today, people from all the neighboring rural districts make pilgrimages to this tomb, especially on Saint-Jean day in summer and on Easter and Pentecost Sundays. "Sainte Pataude" (as the natives call her, from the name given to the republicans by the *chouans*) is thought to grant all the favors asked of her. Mothers bring young children so that they will walk early, making them walk around the tomb three times with normal steps. The tomb is always maintained by persons who leave ex-votos. According to the woodcutters, no ax has been able to cut into the trunk of the tree to which the saint was tied and martyred.[13]

These two examples indicate how syncretism with old forms was established. The traditional religion was broadened by the integration of republican and patriot saints. The old religious forms clearly prevailed over the new political aspects. Religious belief, though here condemned by the Church, could not be denied. The patriot saints appeared endowed with efficacious virtue: they enacted miracles. The revolutionary cult still remained very close to Catholicism.[14]

III

The cult of the martyrs of liberty seems to mark the completion of the evolution of revolutionary religious sentiment from the traditional religion. Here the new forms and political aspects, secondary in the cult of patriot saints, clearly prevail over the old religious context.

Historians of the revolutionary cults, by concentrating on the Cult of Reason and the Cult of the Supreme Being—artificial creations of the leading revolutionary elements—have neglected the spontaneous development of the popular cult of the martyrs of liberty, of Marat in particular. That would have enabled them, however, to specify the evolution of religious sentiment at the time of the Terror. Starting in July 1793, this popular cult developed in the Parisian sections, the basic organizations of the sans-culotterie. Its objects of veneration were three illustrious victims of the counterrevolution: first Marat, assassinated on July 13, 1793; then Lepeletier de Saint-Fargeau, assassinated January 20, 1793 by the Paris guard; finally Chalier, condemned by the reaction and guillotined at Lyon on July 17, 1793.

Marat enjoyed enormous prestige among the Parisian sans-culottes for his role from the beginning of the Revolution. His assassination (without speaking here of its political consequences) aroused a popular veneration which remained one of the most original traits of the sans-culotte mentality. The formation of the new cult was marked in the days following the assassination by a veritable competition for the remains of the Friend of the people. Who will keep these "precious remains"? The Théâtre-Français section, Marat's section, which would soon take his name, claimed them. Jacobins and Cordeliers argued over his heart, which finally stayed with the Cordeliers. The women of the Society of Revolutionary Republicans took an oath on July 17 to raise their children in the *cult* of Marat and to not put in their hands any other *gospel* but the collected works of Marat.[15] On July 26, the Cordeliers decided "to raise an altar to the heart of the incorruptible Marat."[16] The ceremony took place at the beginning of August: Marat's heart was placed in a vase and following the invocation of a patriot, these "precious remains of a god" were hung from a vault in the meeting hall.[17] Was this the imitation of an old rite or the creation of a new one?... Several days beforehand a popular brochure featured a lengthy comparison of Marat and Jesus, who also fell "under the blows of fanaticism, while working with all his energies to carry out the salvation of humankind."[18] It was doubtless a case of making Jesus a revolutionary; but as a consequence Marat participated in the divine nature of Jesus.

We must stress here the equivocation that weighed on many words, transposed directly from the religious vocabulary, and the mental contagion which resulted.[19] When the leaders declared that Marat was immortal, they meant that he lived in their memory; but for the sans-culottes raised in Catholicism, the word *immortal* is inseparable from the immortality of the soul. For the same sans-culottes, *saint* applied to Marat could not be separated from *sacred.* Among the saints ordinarily invoked, martyrs held an eminent position: to say that Marat was a martyr was assuredly for the sans-culotte to promote him to sainthood. While the militant looked to the Friend of the people, living on in his memory for strength in the struggle, the sans-culotte hoped that Marat, promoted to the rank of Saint, would bring success to the Revolution. The Revolution was *good news*, the *gospel*, assuring the salvation of humanity. For the sans-culotte, nurtured with Catholic practice, salvation also had a temporal meaning: the ex-votos in the churches proved this. Now we haven't found any ex-votos dedicated to the Friend of the people; but to invoke Marat, martyr of liberty because he had offered his life for the Revolution, thus for the salvation of humanity, should, in the popular mentality, lead to the same result.

During the month of August, several sections and popular societies celebrated funeral ceremonies in honor of Marat or proceeded with the installation of busts of Marat and Lepeletier—ceremonies where the characteristics of the new cult began to be clarified.

On August 4, the Fraternal Society of the Patriots of the Two Sexes unveiled busts of the martyrs in their meeting hall.[20] On August 8 the Social Contract section displayed in Saint-Eustache Church, their meeting place, "the reenactment of this representative of the people stretched out on his death bed"[21]—a spectacle which borrowed the framework of traditional religion and was made to strike the popular imagination. The Hommes-du-Dix-Août society heard the Marat funeral oration on August 15 at Filles-Dieu [Daughters of God Church] where they met.[22]

How do we characterize these ceremonies? Certainly the simple unveiling of a bust and a speech do not constitute a religious rite. The sans-culottes found new energy in these pageants, which generally ended with a civil sermon. It was not a question of supernatural help, but the normal comfort that the group obtained. We can assume, however, that for many of the participants these funeral ceremonies in honor of Marat and which most often took place in churches, were the equivalent of a Mass for the repose of his soul.

At the same time, the exterior characteristics of the new cult were being manifested. Here is the description of the funeral ceremony in honor of Marat held on August 18, 1793, in the Bonne-Nouvelle church. "The image of Marat was displayed in the nave on a sarcophagus decorated with blue drapery sprinkled with stars; at each end were two antique candelabras; in front, on another tiered sarcophagus was the bust of Lepeletier: said sarcophaguses, draped with garlands of cyprus, with inscriptions containing the virtues of these great men. Behind Marat was the representation of his bathtub... [Marat was killed while bathing.] The principal altar of the church served as a throne for the figure of Liberty. The perimeter of the church was decorated with wide draperies in the national colors and with candelabras topped by girandoles. On top of the main door of the church was a transparency in the national colors, on which one read these words: "Entry to the *Temple of Liberty*."[23]

Here we are witnessing the creation of a new ceremonial ensemble and we see the syncretism with the old forms of the Catholic ritual taking shape. Draperies, candelabras, sarcophaguses come from the traditional ceremony; but the national colors replace the funeral black. The garlands of cyprus and the inscriptions invoke memories of antiquity. To strike the imagination of the faithful, plastic arts, painting and sculpture are used. The representation of Marat's bathtub somewhat recalls those of the instruments of the passion; the statue of Liberty replaces that of the Virgin. Thus a ceremony is composed little by little, with elements borrowed from the Catholic religion or from antiquity and with revolutionary elements; a symbolism is sketched out. But the new cult remains essentially revolutionary: if the documents permit a clarification of what these new ceremonies borrowed from Catholic pomp, nothing indicated the influence of Catholic beliefs themselves. The new ritual tended above all to exalt the civic sentiment of the sans-culottes: sermons, invocations, prayers—the oral rite had an essentially political content.

Toward the end of August 1793, the popular upsurge became stronger. During September, the sans-culottes definitively prevailed in the sections which had still eluded them. The cult of the martyrs of liberty became widespread and at the same time took on a more specific form. Lepeletier was now always linked with Marat. The ceremonial ensemble was amplified; choirs (but patriotic choirs) and soon processions began to give a truly religious pomp to the new cult.

On the first of September, the Fontaine-de-Grenelle section conducted the unveiling of the busts of Marat and Lepeletier.[24] On the 15th the Moliere-et-Lafontaine section, now called Brutus, celebrated a ceremony in honor of the martyrs in the Saint-Joseph Church, Montmartre Street.[25] That same day, in the *regenerated* (that is to say, taken over by the sans-culottes) Montagne section the "apotheosis" of Lepeletier and Marat took place.[26] These ceremonies were usually celebrated on Sundays in the churches where the general assemblies met: thus the new form of worship was little by little supplanting the old, not without borrowing many exterior elements from it. On September 22, the Panthéon-Français section broke new ground with the creation of a true republican trinity, by joining Brutus to Marat and Lepeletier.[27] On the following Sundays, September 29 and October 6, these ceremonies multipled and without a doubt their public was in part a public there for Mass. The Halle-au-Blé and Guillaume-Tell sections, on October 6, added to the now habitual speeches and choirs, a procession through the streets of their quarters, with Brutus preceding Lepeletier and Marat. The addition of Brutus, like the consecration of a stone from the Bastille bearing an engraved inscription of the Declaration of the Rights of Man, underscored the civic nature of the ceremony.[28] On October 9, in the Piques section, a genuine procession took place, thus confirming a new element in the cult of martyrs.

The processions of the Catholic religion had taken place in the various quarters of Paris until spring of 1793, especially that of the *Fête-Dieu* which had nevertheless been marked here and there by incidents and was the last Catholic procession. The corteges of the cult of martyrs imperceptibly took their place. Since religious processions had constituted an important element in the traditional popular life, the militants of the sections and the clubs adapted them to their views. But to what extent did the faithful transfer Catholic beliefs to the new ceremonies? The documents are mute on this important point, or difficult to interpret. To the traditional procession with chants and stations in front of portable altars and images of saints, the sans-culottes added, besides the republican themes and symbols, elements borrowed from national holidays which since 1790 had celebrated the great republican anniversaries; in particular, military trappings. Thus a popular art of the cortege was developed in honor of the martyrs of liberty whose inspiration was both religious and patriotic and which in the fall of 1793 contributed to an expansion of civic sentiment. But how can we establish the exact share of strictly religious sentiment among the followers of the new ritual?

The first processions, still scanty, were the work of the Halle-au-Blé and Guillaume-Tell sections on October 6 and of the Piques section on October 9. On Sunday, October 13, in the Révolutionnaire section, formerly Pont-Neuf, a long cortege with banners and statues of martyrs, patriotic choirs and military music wound through the streets of the quarter.[30] In the afternoon of October 16, the procession of the Museum section (soon to be renamed in honor of the painter David) ran through the streets that encircle the Louvre, then penetrated the Square Court through the Colonnade.[31] At the head were two rows of drummers and gunners; then the popular societies with their emblems, followed by the banners of the Parisian sections and their constituted bodies; an armed detachment followed them headed by the flag and drums, then the section, en masse. A "musical corps" preceded a deputation from the Convention, followed by young men of the first conscription carrying oak branches and surrounding the "citoyennes" of the section who, dressed in white, were holding their children by the hand and carrying flowers. An army detachment brought up the rear. In the courtyard of the Louvre, sarcophaguses had been set up which displayed the original David paintings of the assassinated Lepeletier and Marat; a funeral service was celebrated with hymns and civic speeches colored by a vague religiosity. As in the Catholic ceremonies, all the arts contributed their prestige to the exaltation of the faithful. The sans-culottes communed in the memory of their martyrs. But to what extent did these ceremonies imply an attitude of veneration regarding their object? To what extent, in other words, was religious sentiment coming to exalt civic spirit? One senses a religious fervor while reading these documents, but one cannot grasp precise demonstrations of that fervor.

The new cult gradually won over all the sections, clarifying its form as it advanced. On October 30, the Bonne-Nouvelle section started up some new forges for the manufacture of arms; after the works had been inaugurated, the section consecrated busts of Marat and Lepeletier,[32] patriotic effort and civic exaltation going hand in hand. That same day the Temple section celebrated "this holiday that patriotism has created. The benefactors of the people must obtain altars... Paris raises temples to the martyrs of liberty... If priests and all enemies of the Republic dare to debase the solemn beliefs that we give them, may the representatives of the people avenge this slander."[33] Here for the first time appeared a clear formulation of the opposition to Catholicism and the role of the new belief in dechristianization. If the new ceremonial ensemble borrowed certain aspects from Catholicism, it does not seem that there was, at least in the spirit of the promoters, any reconciliation with old beliefs. Reference is made not to the saints of the Catholic Church (even though Marat and Lepeletier are described as *apostles*), but to the heroes of antiquity elevated to the ranks of gods: "the inventor of the plow and the courageous mortal who dared to avenge humanity for the outrages of tyrants." Likewise, the syncretism appears to be purely formal as when the Champs-Élysées section asked the Convention on October 31 "if the first two days of the republican era shouldn't carry the names of its first two martyrs."[34]

The cult of the martyrs of liberty completed its form by adding Chalier, guillotined on July 17, 1793, at Lyon by the counterrevolution. Marat, Lepeletier and Chalier composed the revolutionary triad or trinity, depending on whether reference was made to antiquity or Catholicism. But here it was a question of a political initiative, with no popular spontaneity, and all sentiment of religious veneration seems to have been excluded from the beginning. The addition of Chalier represented one more turn toward the non-religious and, despite his association with the two other martyrs, this was a third stage of evolution toward non-belief, beyond the cult of patriot saints and the cult of Marat.

The initiative for the cult of Chalier came from Chaumette, public prosecutor of the Commune of Paris. Doubtless a political maneuver on his part. The cult of martyrs had developed spontaneously in the sections, without intervention by the municipal authorities; it conveyed, on the religious plane, the revolutionary spirit of the sans-culottes exalted by the ceremonies. It is significant that the Commune, during the summer of 1793 while the new cult was taking form, had not organized any ceremonies.

Only toward the middle of brumaire, when the cult of martyrs had become widespread with no backing from the authorities, did Chaumette intervene to link a martyr more in keeping with his politics to Marat and Lepeletier. On November 1, 1973, Chaumette delivered before the General Council of the Commune the funeral eulogy for Chalier, portraying the Jacobin from Lyon more as a hero of antiquity than as a saint of the new religion.[35] The exaltation of Chalier's republican virtues, the *simple and true account* of his last moments, his last remarks—in a Socratic tone—all contributed to draw a picture of the new martyr capable of striking the popular imagination and of making him worthy of joining the republican Pantheon; but nothing in the eulogy incited veneration or exaltation of religious sentiment.

We grasp here the difference in behavior between the sans-culottes, properly speaking, and the militants coming out of the middle or petit bourgeoisie. The latter, endowed with a classical education, made references to Antiquity; the former borrowed ritual elements from the Catholicism that nourished them. But once again, to what extent did the syncretism go beyond ceremonial aspects and affect the belief itself? No document constitutes an affirmation of the cult of Marat as a saint. His tomb did not become an efficacious site where miracles were produced—a marked difference with the cult of patriot saints and the evolution of belief.

Nevertheless, it seems that the demonstrations in honor of Marat must be considered as more than simple testimony of esteem for a political man. Certainly the sectional militants, who were the officiating priests of the new cult, emphasized its civic aspect. If they kept the exterior forms of the traditional litany, invocation and prayer, the new content was essentially political.[36] But it must be noted that the audience for the revolutionary ritual was essentially the same one that had attended the ceremonies of traditional religion; was there also in their minds a transfer of old beliefs concerning the saints to the new martyrs? The reports of police observers most often concentrate on the crowds at the revolutionary ceremonies into which the cult of martyrs was integrated. For example on February 28, 1794, in the Bonne-Nouvelle section, "there were a considerable number of people, especially women" at the temple of Reason, formerly the Bonne-Nouvelle church. In the Gravilliers section that same day, "the former church of Saint-Nicolas des Champs was almost completely full, with many youth." On March 20, 1794, a police observer noted in his report: "In the past we saw many more women than men in the churches: it's the same in the temples of Reason. Few men and many women."[37] Did these women think of the martyrs of the new trinity as saints enthroned in heaven? We might assume so, but no document allows us to affirm that. The framework of the religious demonstrations had not changed; the pomp of the new could be compared to that of the traditional. It is not implausible that for these women of the people, who formed the majority of the faithful, the adoration of the Catholic saints had simply given way to the adoration of republican martyrs.

The dechristianization movement that developed in the autumn of 1793 had origins far from the popular movement, but it gave a new impetus to the cult of martyrs. The sections that had been slow to embrace the cult now hurried to establish it. The cult of martyrs now appeared as one of the elements of the republican ideology that the sectional militants intended to install on the ruins of traditional religion. Devotion to the republican trinity was integrated into the cult of Reason, a too abstract deity, which at the same time was taking on traits of a young lady of the Opera.

The religious sentiment underlying the new forms would not disappear, however, without arousing opposition. Catholic believers accused the new cult of idolatry. On November 16, 1793, the revolutionary committee of the Arcis section arrested a candlemaker's assistant under charges of fanaticism: he had refused to attend a ceremony in honor of Marat, saying "that he would a thousand times rather suffer death than attend a celebration like that."[38] Yet this man was a good sans-culotte, who had taken up arms on all the great days of revolutionary struggle. His was not an isolated case.

On the other hand, the cult of martyrs aroused attacks from atheists, political purposes combining with ideological motives. On November 28 (1793), in front of the Jacobins, Hébert angrily challenged the cult of Marat: "Already it is being said that the Parisians have substituted Marat for Jesus."[39] And in number 315 of his *Père Duchesne*: they would have us believe that "Parisians wish to know no other god than Marat." On December 2, Danton rebuffed a petitioner who, in front of the Convention, began to read a litany to the glory of Marat.[40] Did this reaction show political or personal hostility, or a conviction that the new belief, since it was religious, was overall still too close to the traditional religion? All these motives doubtless explain the sharp rebuke delivered by Danton.

The cult of martyrs, integrated into the cult of Reason, nonetheless lasted until spring 1794, the weekly [every ten days on the revolutionary calendar] ceremonies attracting large crowds, especially women and children. The reaction that began with the trial and execution of Hébert (March 24, 1794) dealt it a deadly blow. Marat was to a certain degree included in the discredit attached to "Père Duchesne," the moderates striving hard to sow confusion in the minds of the people. On March 17 (1794), a police observer heard it said that "if Marat was still living at this moment, he would be charged and perhaps guillotined." Rumors were flying on

March 25 that the Marat section was ready to cover the portrait of the Friend of the people. According to the testimony of one police observer, on March 28 the inhabitants of the villages around Paris were disconcerted by the rumors circulating about Marat: "If it is possible that Marat deceived them, they could no longer have confidence in anyone."[41]

This campaign was brutally stopped by the authorities of the Commune of Paris on March 29 when they threatened to declare suspect all those who sought to alter the esteem "justly owed" to the "martyrs of liberty."[42] But esteem is far from veneration. The Robespierrist authorities of the Commune thus indicated the strict limits under which they would allow the cult of Marat to survive. There was no longer any question of religious fervor, but simply civic spirit. The spring reaction of year II (1794) foreshadowed the reaction of year III; counterrevolutionaries and Catholics felt free to throw statues of the martyrs of liberty out the window. On August 17, 1795 in the Nord section, "the statues established by terrorism and placed in the choir of the Saint-Laurent church" were destroyed;[43] it was the same in all sections.

*

At the end of this sketch, without examining in detail the political aspect of the popular cults, we can observe that the political and social crisis in 1793 had a profound effect on the religious sentiment of the revolutionary masses. But [as part of the general evolution of religious sentiment at the end of the 18th century] how should we interpret the popular cults that conveyed this effect? Should we think that there was, on the whole, dechristianization in the course of the ten years of revolution and that the popular rituals studied here represent stages of this dechristianization? Or should the cults be considered new forms—sects through which the traditional religion was regenerated? This implies a larger problem: when Christian faith is lost, is it through the intermediary of a sect that one arrives at non-belief? We can only ask these questions. Doubtless, for a better approach to the reality of the situation, it would be necessary to consider the social categories that created these cults or who simply participated in them: the first, middle or petit bourgeoisie, seem to be non-believers, while the others, sans-culottes, remain, in all likelihood, believers in the traditional religious context.

Now we understand the mortal obstacle for the popular cults. If we look at the factors which have at all times contributed to the birth of religions, we see that they have always had theologians, whereas cults could not have any. The militants who organized these sects were doubtless rationalists;

but the people transposed their thought into the framework of the religious education they had received. Did the orators at the ceremonies in honor of the martyrs of liberty suspect this transposition? In that case they would certainly have turned against this survival of clerical education, which they specifically wanted to destroy through dechristianization. The people were naturally incapable of formulating the theology of the new cults; their leaders were just as unwilling to do so.

The ephemeral character of the revolutionary cults explains why there was no independent and critical intellect to observe the popular transposition and leave us a written account. Without any documents, we can only indicate these problems and take a few steps.

10

On the "Red Priests" in the French Revolution[1]

On June 5, 1790, C. Fricaud, deputy of the Third Estate from the bailiwick of Charolles, presented to the Constituent Assembly, in the name of the Committee on Relations, an affair offering "the most astonishing peculiarities: After the account of the events, you will see that there's something absolutely delirious about them."[2]

"Last October 6 (1789), M. Abbot Carion, the priest of Issy-l'Évêque (in the bailiwick of Autun), under pretext of establishing a food loft for the poor, convened a parish assembly. The session began with the reading of a register entitled *Formation of the Committee and Administrative Council of the town and commune of Issy-l'Évêque*. This register contains the laws governing the town police, the maintenance of prisons, the administration of justice, the national guard, fines and confiscations, imprisonment of citizens under simple written order of the committee, alignment of streets and public squares, forced labor, the price of grain, in a word all that the exalted imagination of this pastor had been able to bring together to give birth to a body of legislation. The priest, a helmet on this head and a sword at his side, was always going to the laborers to seize their grain; in accordance with his rules, he set the price for grain. This new legislator did not recognize the separation of powers; for he ordered, judged and executed his own judgments... One day, M. the priest departed, beating a drum, and arrived in the Grandes-Bruyères; he immediately executed his agrarian laws, allocating to himself a portion of the territory under the pretext that this was a former commune. His sermons were a mixture of acts of war, seditious threats, and ample explanations of his regulations so that they would be enacted. With the aid of his troops (for he had some), he has established and collected a city toll, knocked down outer walls, torn out hedges... it's up to us to disarm this fearsome priest."[3]

The matter was sent back to the Committee on Relations. Under an arrest decree, Abbot Carion was transferred to Paris. On February 10, 1791, a delegation from Issy-l'Évêque and five other municipalities ("we have come 80 leagues on foot") demanded his freedom from the Constituent Assembly. "We must make known to this august Assembly, in whose bosom he has been falsely charged, the true facts about this person. He sold wheat for 50 *sous* that he had bought for a very high price; he sacrificed a part of his garden for the use of the community; he gave aid to workers who were without work; he gave the commune money for leases it could not pay." As for the permanent committee and the national guard established "for subsistences and for police, ... our priest was only carrying out decisions taken by the general assembly of the commune."[4] On March 17, 1791, the National Assembly decreed the release of Abbot Carion.[5]

Was the priest of Issy-l'Évêque a "red priest"? Through the denunciation and accusations made by Fricaud, a lawyer and former subdelegate from the Bourgogne district, we note that by 1789 the essential traits of the "red priests" of '93 had been traced. Demands for price controls on grain and sharing of communal goods: these are very ordinary demands and certainly we could cite many other analogous cases from 1789 on. The same goes for the appeal to the popular practice of direct democracy. Moreover, we note the prophetic tone ("His sermons were a mixture of acts of war, seditious threats..."), the exalted imagination, the utopian vision inciting the legislation and regulation of everything from the system of prisons to the "alignment of streets and public squares." Even more, the abbot Carion was a man of action. He was the mayor of his commune, president of the permanent committee, member of the staff of the national guard. There he was "a helmet on his head, a sword at his side," knocking down walls, tearing out hedges, in a word "carrying out... his agrarian laws." The time had finally come: the people would recover the fullness of their rights.

Looking beyond this sketch which suggests a text from 1790, we need to press the analysis further and clarify the "red priests" of '93.

I

"Red priests"—in the case of the French Revolution, the expression is anachronistic. Red was never the symbolic color of the revolution. The name and the sign of the "red flag" refer to the martial law of October 21, 1789 whereby it should be deployed whenever the law is exercised. "This declaration will be made by exposing at the main window of the town hall, and by bearing in all the streets and squares, a *red flag*."[6] We know what happened with this at the Champ-de-Mars on July 17, 1791. If there was talk on the eve of the August 10, 1792 insurrection of having the insurgents march under a red flag bearing the inscription "Martial law of the sovereign people, against the rebellion of executive power," there was no follow-up on that proposition.[7] As for the red bonnet, although it was widely worn by the popular masses during the summer of 1793, it never enjoyed unanimous respect. Marat wore a cap, not a red bonnet, and the day that Armonville sported a red bonnet in court, it raised such a storm that he was compelled to take it off. At the Jacobin Club on March 19, 1792, Robespierre said that imposing the wearing of the red bonnet on orators and staff of the society would be "weakening the energy" of the only national emblem, the tricolored cockade [red, white and blue rosette of ribbons worn on a cap].[8] We will not press the point any longer; it was not until the Second Republic that the political symbolism of the color red was affirmed. *Red* according to Littre (1876): "Advanced Republican accepting the red flag as a symbol."

The expression "red priest" does not appear in the works of Lichtenberger on "socialism" in the eighteenth century and during the Revolution, nor in the work of Aulard. It seems to have been used for the first time by Brégail in 1901.[9] Campagnac repeated it in 1913 to describe Métier, the priest of Saint-Liesne of Melun, whereas in 1903 this same author (who likely was unaware at this time of Brégail's study) described Petit-Jean, the priest of Épineuil (Cher) as a *communist priest.*[10] Let us note that neither of these two authors made an effort to clarify exactly what they meant by *red priest.* In 1937, the expression appears in quotation marks—with no commentary—in F. Brunot, *History of the French language.*[11] In the sphere of revolutionary studies, it would seem that it was M. Dommanget who popularized the expression when in 1948 he published a pamphlet entitled *Jacques Roux, the red priest* and in 1955 an article in *L'École libératrice* entitled "Red Priests and Worker Priests."[12]

In the light of these works, we will be wary of all unwarranted associations in our endeavor to formulate a definition, starting by specifying what a red priest is and simply is not.

The first such association is often presented by traditional religious historiography for which all married priests, stripped of their authority, are necessarily red: see Bridoux's *Religious History of the Seine-et-Marne Department during the Revolution*[13]; but was Parent, parish priest of Boissise-la-Bertrand near Melun and dechristianizer, really a red priest? Another example is the work of Abbot J. Gallerand who drew up a list of 77 married priests from which Gabriel Bayeux and Alexandre Dubreuil emerged as prime examples.[14] But to be identified as red priests is it enough that Alexandre Dubreuil was the right arm of Hésine, one of the defenders of the Babouvists during the Vendôme trial, and that Gabriel Bayeux persisted in giving revolutionary names to children until 1810? And we would also question the case in Louhannais of Antoine Thomas who burned his letters of priesthood at the foot of the Liberty tree at Chalon and of the priest Maître [Master] who laicized his name to Égal [Equal][15]...

Broadening this notion, Campagnac likens red priest to patriot priest. "Métier suffered the fate common to all patriot priests who merited the appellation red priests."[16] His accusers reproached him for being a priest, even though he had sent back his letters of priesthood. Born in 1758, Métier had become a priest and practiced his vocation in various communes of the Seine-et-Marne department, Melun being the last place. "A firm and energetic character and a revolutionary head," according to representative Du Bouchet on assignment in the department, Métier had been the secretary of the meeting of electors of the Melun bailiwick in 1789, a member of the first Melun municipality in 1790, and one of the two secretaries of the Society of Friends of the Constitution in 1791. A constitutional priest, Métier occupied a top-ranking position in the town of Melun. When Du Bouchet arrived, Métier was judge of the tribunal, president of the departmental administration, and president of the popular society. There he was on September 11, 1793, as the delegated commissioner of the representative of the people, with unlimited powers that his revolutionary energy would exercise fully—an exemplary revolutionary career. If Métier finally recanted, it was not until November 12, 1793, the day after Gobel's renunciation. "Métier's antireligious statements are rather rare," remarks Campagnac, "and those that he makes are expressed in moderate terms." Métier: a Jacobin priest who, even before Robespierre, had protested the violence of the dechristianizers, understood the danger of antireligious propaganda—red priest, certainly not.

Likewise, the former priests who were relentless dechristianizers cannot be described as red priests. Take the case of Parent, priest of Boissise-la-Bertrand, "a red priest of the first instance," according to Campagnac; "the most apostolic and most obstinate" of the red priests of Seine-et-Marne according to Dommanget. It is he who, on November 4, wrote to the Convention: "I am a priest, a parish priest, that is to say, a charlatan." Commissioner of the Melun district, Parent was a patriot priest, but his militant action was essentially dechristianizing and did not go beyond that. Parent: a dechristianizing priest—red priest, certainly not.

These are the same dechristianizing priests whom Bianchi describes as "democratic priests."[17] Even though the term *democratic* is ambiguous (were they advocating political democracy or social democracy?) can we place the dechristianizer Parent in the same group with the true democrats like Petit-Jean, priest of Épineuil, or Dolivier, priest of Mauchamps? We are forced to attempt a more precise definition: what was a "red priest" of '93?

We will borrow elements of the definition from Dommanget. In his 1955 article "Red Priests and Worker Priests," he remarks that "certain terms coined by historians as representative of a mass movement or of a current of ideas are historically false. Such is the case with the term *jacquerie* [epithet for peasant revolts] to designate what at that period people called *effrois* [terrors]; such is also the case with the term *curé rouge* [red priest] to designate the priests who, during the 18th century and especially during the Revolution, were in the avant-garde of the clergy in deed, in speech and in what they wrote." Having stressed the vagueness and ambiguity of the term, Dommanget distinguishes between the red priests "keeping to the philosophical plane; that is, priests who had rid themselves of religious prejudices, but held on to social prejudices," and the red priests "who had rid themselves of all or a part of social prejudices, but held on to religious prejudices." Finally there were those whom Dommanget calls the *complete* red priests, "rid of both religious and social prejudices."

We certainly agree that the red priest fought on the social plane; still it would be appropriate to clarify the meaning of this fight. But, commiserating with the people's misery, enamored with charity, full of the teachings of the Gospel, the red priest held on to his "religious prejudices." He was not a dechristianizer. It was both as Christian and patriot that he carried on his social battle.

II

In trying to sketch a portrait of the red priest, we see him first of all in the prime of life. In 1793, Croissy, parish priest of Étalon in the Montdidier district (Somme [department]), was thirty-nine years old; Jacques Roux, of the Gravilliers section [Paris] was forty-one; Dolivier, parish priest of Mauchamps in the Étampes district, was forty-seven; Petit-Jean, parish priest of Épineuil in the Saint-Amand district (Cher), was fifty-three.[18]

Here is the priest Petit-Jean, according to the description sent to all the departmental districts after the troubles in Épineuil. "Fifty-two years old (the date is 1792), but appearing younger; very erect, naturally carrying his head high, chestnut-colored hair and eyebrows, beard of the same color, well-shaped forehead...; in sum a handsome man who looks as if he knows it by his glance and his bearing." We also know that Jacques Roux was a handsome man, animated and courageous, in full possession of his faculties.

Drawing from these four examples, we say that these red priests had been or were still priests of rural parishes. Before being "vicar" of the Saint-Nicolas des Champs parish, as he declared to the Police Department of the Commune of Paris, during his interrogation of August 23, 1793, Jacques Roux had been the parish priest of Cozes, then of Saint-Thomas de Conac in the diocese of Saintes. Before serving the parish of Mauchamps, Dolivier had been the vicar of Condat in Auvergne. All had direct experience with the people of the countryside, their needs, their mentality, their demands. There is no doubt that peasant egalitarianism was one of the living sources of the militant vocation of the red priests.

All preached sermons and kept the faith. Constitutional priests, they did not renounce their oath, or they did so only under constraint.

In the case of Jacques Roux, Dommanget remarks that "he does not seem to have been as bold on the religious plane as on the political and especially the social plane." If in fact he condemned the "ultramountain charlatans,"* Jacques Roux was just as hard on "bloodthirsty atheists." "The religious vocation is a state," he wrote in number 264 (September 1793) of his *Publicité de la République française*; "you can't make it a crime for a man to exercise it, if he publicly professes the principles of true morality, if he inspires the horror of tyranny. A priest of this nature is not odious to society, all the more so since we can't suddenly make twenty-five million men philosophers."

Petit-Jean, who lived through dechristianization, did not renounce the priesthood, never detaching himself from religion, a believer among the believing peasants, "especially the women," in the words of the prosecutor of the commune writing to the Saint-Amand district on September 26, 1792. Arrested on the following December 19, condemned to a year in prison, Petit-Jean was liberated on September 27, 1793 by the representative Laplanche on assignment in Bourges. Laplanche named Petit-Jean the parish priest of Saint-Caprais "to shield him from the malevolence of his enemies and prevent all discord." Petit-Jean refused, writing to Bishop Torne that he wished to be the parish priest of Épineuil or not be a priest anywhere. He finally offered his resignation, but he never renounced his calling.

You may know the story of the parish priest of Étalon, Louis-Pierre Croissy, told so well by Georges Lefebvre. At Montdidier, the municipality decided on November 28, 1793 to close the churches. "That the priest of Étalon," writes Georges Lefebvre, "felt offended in his faith, there is no reason to doubt." He continued to celebrate the rituals, supported by part of his parishioners, bringing communion and extreme unction to the dying. He declared later, while being interrogated, that he had not carried the the good Lord in his pocket, as had been claimed, but in the customary

*Montagnard reactionaries

manner, that is of course by ringing bells and bearing the cross. Finally the district had the church's silver plate taken away and closed the church; then on March 7, 1794, Croissy turned in his letters of priesthood to the municipality, on the invitation of the representative on assignment, André Dumont. But he did not hide the fact that he would have liked to keep his parish and pursue his calling. The high-ranking *notables*, who had completely different grievances against him, took advantage of dechristianization to rid themselves of him. It is very probable that the jurors of the Revolutionary Tribunal who condemned him to death on June 9 (1794) did not attach great importance to the accusation of preaching agrarian reform, but condemned in Croissy a priest who had greeted dechristianization with anger.

Abbot Dolivier, parish priest of Mauchamps, was one of the first priests to marry. We are struck by the philosophical tone of the speech he delivered on October 21, 1792, at the close of vespers, to announce his marriage to his parishioners.[19] It was the result of a long evolution and not some sudden brainstorm or the desire to imitate his colleagues who, like Abbot Cournand, had preceded him in his path. Just like the petition of the preceding spring in favor of the rioters of Étampes, the October 21, 1792 speech was nothing less than a manifesto of natural law applied to the problem of the celibacy of priests, this "superstition," this "imposture" contrary to the laws of nature. Remaining profoundly religious, Dolivier only renounced the priesthood under constraint and with the greatest discretion. He censured the dechristianization carried on with a great uproar by Couturier, on assignment in the district of Étampes from October to December 1793, who on November 29 ordered the closing of all churches. For Abbot Dolivier, religious "sentiment" was necessary to the harmony of the social edifice. It is impossible to set the exact date of the renunciation of the priesthood by the priest of Mauchamps, but it became effective on December 1, 1793. Abbot Dolivier left Mauchamps to take refuge with his brother in Paris.

Men of faith, the red priests were also men of action. It should be sufficient to recall the role of Dolivier in the affair of Étampes in March and April of 1792, that of Petit-Jean in the Épineuil riot of September 23, 1792, and the militant life of Jacques Roux. On Sunday, September 23, at the close of High Mass, Petit-Jean assembled the peasants whom he had brought together through posters. In front on the altar he placed a table that served as a platform. About a hundred of his partisans surrounded him and he presented them with a petition to sign... In the brawl that followed, Petit-Jean aroused the peasants: "Kill all those rogues!" The agitation resumed at the close of vespers. Petit-Jean once again assembled his partisans and led them to the lands of Clermont, municipal officer and one of the richest landowners of Épineuil, to tear down the hedges. Toward the end of the day, the rumor spread that a detachment of the national guard of Saint-Armand was advancing; Petit-Jean ordered the ringing of the *tocsin* [alarm bell]...

More than rebels, the red priests were by temperament revolutionaries. From this point of view we cannot compare them to the priest Meslier, as Dommanget invites us to do. The priest of Étrépigny was more a rebel than a revolutionary. Meslier lacked the enriching influence of deed and action that we find in Jacques Roux. There are both similarities and contrasts in these two temperaments: in both there is revolt. But with Jacques Roux there is the audacity of action, the sense of revolutionary agitation, perseverance and courage unto death. The prudent conduct of Meslier, apart from the 1716 scandal, is astonishing, confronted with the daring nature of his thought.[20]

Meslier was called a prophet. Pursuing the comparison with the red priests of '93, we observe how far the latter went beyond the prophesying of the priest of Étrépigny. Both denounced with the same force all injustices, all abuse, all oppression; both revolted with the same vigor against great men and kings, aristocrats and monopolizers. Both had the same compassion for the poor and the disinherited, the same demand for total justice, the same thirst for the absolute, the same intolerance for the times. The same prophetic breath animated them. Let us listen to Petit-Jean. On September 1, 1792, he announced that "the general massacre of all aristocrats will be carried out to establish equality," that "before a month is out the houses of the rich will be destroyed." In a piece of writing addressed to the district, to the department and to all of France, we find these words: "It is a priest who lost France (Abbot Maury?); it is a priest who will save her"—Petit-Jean himself. "That the counterrevolution would begin at Épineuil, from there it would spread to all of France and he would place himself at its head; that the name of Petit-Jean would be memorable; that equality and division of wealth would soon be enacted; that we have seen the rivers overflow, but that we would see them flow with lots of blood."

If the prophet denounced the ignominy of the present and announced the future, he did not concern himself with constructing that future. The red priest on the contrary launched himself into action with complete boldness and helped history give birth to the future.

The revolutionary action of the red priests was characterized in practice by constant recourse to direct democracy. To his enemies who were threatening him with judges, Petit-Jean responded "that he did not recognize the competency of any judge; the natural judge is the sovereign people." Scorning official institutions, he convened on his own authority an assembly of villagers; to the mayor who asked him why he convened this assembly when it was a violation of the law, he responded that it was to obey "the law and humanity." As for Croissy, he had often said to his friend Dumont that "the people being sovereign could take what was suitable for them without needing to have recourse to arbitrators or courts, and that the communes were absolute masters." Such remarks, conforming to popular mentality and behavior, and which legitimized at the very least the taking back without formalities of the usurped communal wealth, could not but fundamentally displease the *notables*.

The political thought of Abbot Dolivier had been expressed from 1790 on with *Le Vœu national* [the National Vow],[21] a severe critique of the political organization elaborated by the Constituent Assembly and a sketch of an original system of popular democracy. The constituents spoke of equality of rights only to better maintain the *natural* inequality of means. "I would like, on the contrary," affirmed Dolivier, "the social state to establish a just equality of means... so that each associate could reach the full enjoyment of the right that belongs to him." This formulation implies: "I don't understand this distinction when what is called a mean is precisely what constitutes a right." The principles of equality had scarcely been proclaimed when they hastened to infringe on them. "It must be confessed that if they intended to establish an aristocracy of the rich, they could not have found a better way."

The political practice of Jacques Roux in the framework of the Gravilliers section is too well known for us to go over it here. Let us just recall the constant concern of Jacques Roux to find support in the basic popular organizations. It was thus in his famous petition of June 25, 1793. On June 20, at the Cordeliers Club, he proposed that an article be added to the Constitution, already almost entirely voted on, directing the death penalty be used against speculation and usury. The next day, at the General Council of the Commune, Roux proposed that they go over to the Convention en masse to demand that it decree as a constitutional article that "freedom does not consist in starving your fellow creatures." Jacques Roux obstinately returned to the attack at the Cordeliers Club on June 22. On the 23rd he succeeded in getting his petition adopted by the general assembly of the Gravilliers and Bonne-Nouvelle sections and by the Cordeliers Club. Perhaps even more than by its content, the tone of his petition angered the

Assembly. In the name of the sovereign people, he berated the representatives: "For a long time you have promised to end the calamities of the people; but what have you done for that?... Deputies of the Mountain, establish the bases of prosperity for the Republic; don't end your career in ignominy." He ordered: "Pronounce then, once again... The sans-culottes with their pikes will carry out your decrees."[22]

Leaning on the practice of direct democracy, the social demands of the red priests, in profound harmony with popular sympathies, essentially dealt with the right to existence and thus with the critique of the right to property, though apart from Dolivier, we do not find a theory elaborated. It was simply a matter of a visceral egalitarianism, essentially agreeing on certain conditions of existence. They could speak of egalitarianism of consumption. "Each must have what is necessary to live peaceably," wrote the priest Meslier. At the other end of the century, Jacques Roux answered him: "Equality is nothing but a hollow phantom when the rich, through monopoly, exercise the right of life and death over their fellow creatures." The right to existence prevails over the right to property. "What! The property of rascals would be more sacred than the life of men?" The right of property could not exist for the "leeches of the people."

Exercising their calling in the heart of rural communities, the red priests could not help but be sensitive to the problems of the land, essentially problems of property and exploitation. "The land taken in general," wrote Abbot Dolivier in his *Essai sur la justice primitive*, "should be regarded as the great communal of nature where all living beings have originally an indefinite right to the products it holds... (in the social order) each individual must find his right to share in the great communal." From this theory came very concrete demands: the taking back of usurped communal wealth, the division of the great farms.

In order to have an accurate appreciation of the militant action of the red priests in the heart of the village community, it would be necessary to have a precise analysis of the social structures of Épineuil, Mauchamps and Étalon. Let us recall that the parish of Mauchamps comprised 135 to 140 inhabitants grouped in 34 households: a small peasantry of wine growers and laborers dominated by two plowmen who by themselves were paying, at the end of the Ancien Régime, 800 livres in taxes, and 18 day laborers paying only 600. While the villagers held for themselves or to rent hardly more than 86 *arpents* [about 72 acres], the farmers as a group cultivated 92. From this situation came the essential demand of the small peasantry that Dolivier transcribed in his *Essai sur la justice primitive*: "The division of the land among all citizens who have none or who don't have enough," so that a farming concern "would not exceed the plowing of one plow."

At Épineuil, the village community was dominated by three well-off peasants who, moreover, appropriated for themselves a portion of the national estates that had been put up for sale. They were doing so well that the priest Petit-Jean was able on several occasions to treat them as monopolizers and to arouse the jealousy of the small peasants against them. As political power went hand in hand with landed property, these rich peasants dominated the municipality. When did the militant action and egalitarian propaganda of Petit-Jean begin? We cannot be precise. The first traces appear, according to later denunciations, in August of 1792. "He tells them every day that property is going to be communal; seeks to persuade them by the most ingratiating remarks, by telling them that there will be only one cellar, one granary where each one will take all that is needed." There we recognize one of the essential themes of egalitarian utopia. Petit-Jean advised his parishioners "to form warehouses in the cellars and granaries where you will go to draw from as a community," adding that "you will no longer need money." On September 1, 1792, he addressed a lampoon to the district, the department and the legislative Assembly "where he announces that the general massacre of all the aristocrats is going to be carried out to reestablish equality; and he invites the citizens to follow his counsel, to freely consent to abandoning all their property and to a general division of all their goods."

This egalitarian preaching, however utopian in nature, could not help but frighten the landowners. "He was preaching the violation of property." According to the report of the national guard commandant at Saint-Amand, "Master Petit-Jean makes the most incendiary and unconstitutional remarks while preaching, as is his wont, on agrarian reform." The priest Petit-Jean was not content to preach; he acted. He counselled his parishioners not to pay "the indemnity of the *dîme*," meaning the church tax (called *colonique* in Auvergne) over and above the sharecropping payment (Berry was a land of general tenant farming). At the time of the riot of September 23, in the afternoon, Petit-Jean took charge of peasants armed with "pitchforks and fence boards," and led them to the lands of Clermont to tear out the hedges. The texts do not permit us to specify if it was a question of national lands or taking back usurped communal land. The meaning of the action is nonetheless clear: for the red priest, it was the deed heralding the coming of the egalitarian society; for the peasants, the seizure of the land they coveted so.

We will not take up again here an analysis of the case of Croissy, the priest of Étalon. (See the work of Georges Lefebvre.) Accused of having preached the agrarian law, Croissy denied it, and it may be that was sincere. "Never have I spoken of this law except to fight it...; observing that it was necessary to make a distinction, that it was not personal property, but tenant farming lands that would be divided into several plots so that the people could claim them... People have confused the tenant farming lands with private lands." Croissy carefully sets the division of the great farms apart from the agrarian law, just like Dolivier who, at Mauchamps, had limited his propaganda to the first object. But it is clear that in the eyes of the well-off peasants and the big farmers, cocks-of-the-village or matadors, as they were called in the North, there was certainly confusion between division of farms and general sharing of the land. Moreover, hadn't Croissy justified the restitution to the communes of the brushwood from trees along the roads, seigniorial property under the Ancien Régime, and thus legitimized, in the name of popular sovereignty, the taking back of usurped communal goods? There was enough there to worry the *notables*. The members of the municipal government of Étalon, well-off peasants like the mayor Hadingue, were perhaps Jacobins, but conservative Jacobins. They loathed the agrarian law, along with everything that could undermine their domination of the land and thus their profit. Dechristianization furnished them with a pretext for getting rid of the priest Croissy, who, if he was not a communist, was certainly an avowed partisan of social democracy.

*

At the end of this sketch on the red priests, a double direction for research seems necessary: the historical origin and the social impulse for the ideas and action of these priests. What were the sources of their agrarian egalitarianism? Book sources, certainly, but also lived experiences.

The Gospel is certainly the primary book source for these priests who kept the faith and the mythic memory of "the communion of the first christians," evangelical communities of primitive Christianity. Other likely sources for these men imbued with classical culture would be the myths of the golden age as they appear in Virgil or Ovid or in similar modern works such as the description of Bétique in Fénelon's *Télémaque*.

As for lived experiences, certainly the red priests, like Meslier in Champagne or Babeuf in Picardie, took from the village communities in whose heart they lived their strong feeling for social rights and their egalitarian demands. The Picardie of Croissy (Étalon is a few kilometers north of Roye, in Babeuf's general neighborhood) and the Berry of Petit-Jean were provinces where the rural communities always steadfastly maintained the defense of their collective rights and their communal traditions, and had withstood a bitter struggle against their feudal lords for the ownership of communal goods. The village community conserved a very active sentiment for social rights, doubtless from the earliest times: the just needs of the community, all of whose members have the right to survive, take precedence over property, which consequently must be managed. We still need better information on the communities of Épineuil or Étalon and those where Jacques Roux exercised his vocation before settling in Paris. What exactly were their social structures? As opposed to the well-off peasants, what were the burdens weighing on the peasants with tiny plots or no land at all, whose cause the red priests espoused? How did village democracy function before the municipal reform of 1787? These experiences could only reinforce memories from books and nourish critical reflection.

We must, however, stress the gap between the violence of social denunciation, the boldness of abstract affirmations, and the proposed remedies. At the end of his *Essai sur la justice primitive*, Dolivier reassures the landowners: "As for the present, it must be only a question of provisional remedies such as the current state of things entails." And to demand the division of rented farmlands, of sharecropping plots, not of all landed property. The sans-culottes of the countryside were not asking for anything more. Thus the general ideological climate was imposed on even the most daring. From this point of view we can only underscore the realism of the petition presented by Jacques Roux on June 25, 1793. He repeated the essential demands of the most conscious sectional militants, fashioning them into a coherent program, but we can't speak of a doctrinal basis for this program. "The socialist priest," A. Mathiez writes of Jacques Roux. This is an anachronism. Let us say an egalitarian priest, a militant connected to the people, who knew how to express their aspirations with uncommon perceptiveness, sincerity and warmth.

Petit-Jean disappeared from the political scene at the end of 1793, Dolivier in January 1794. Jacques Roux committed suicide, Croissy was guillotined. But whatever the setback, these red priests, confronting a world of imposters and exploiters, wanted to construct the fraternal community of the future. By their denunciation of the present, by their courage, they advanced history. Jacques Roux committed suicide in despair, but the Convention approved the law of the general maximum [limit on property] on September 29, 1793. A copy of Dolivier's *Essai sur la justice primitive* was seized among Babeuf's papers.

11

Militant Women of the Parisian Sections (Year II)

Here it is not at all a case of feminist practice, meaning a specific doctrinal movement demanding the social and political equality of women and men; such a movement was in the minority throughout the Revolution. What concerns us is feminine practice, meaning the active participation of women in the general movement of the Revolution, even though the political action of women constituted the best argument—formulated or not—for the feminist demand.[1]

Nor will it be a question of the "famous women" of the Revolution, demi-mondaines, or great ladies who occupied the national stage: Olympe de Gonges or Théroigne de Méricourt, Mme. Roland or Mme. de Condorcet.[2] Claire Lacombe and the Society of Revolutionary Republican Women will not concern us either, for their action unfolded on a city-wide level.[3] Both groups have aroused the attention of historians on several counts. On the sectional level, numerous women, particularly in 1793, participated in intense militant activity in the framework of the basic organizations of the popular movement—general assemblies of the section, popular societies—as well as in mass demonstrations. The most intense period for Parisian feminine practice was from spring to autumn of 1793, until the banning of women's clubs on October 30, 1793; this was the period of the full flowering of the popular movement. To help during the crisis, feminine action was launched again in the spring of 1795, affirming itself for the last time during the prairial days [May 20—June 18].

In these popular Parisian milieux, feminine practice naturally prevailed over feminist demands which, in the precise sense of the word, only appeared episodically. In the case of women coming from the sansculotterie, battling the difficulties of daily life, the struggle against high prices and food shortages obviously had a higher priority than political action: daily bread ranked higher than the right to vote. There was nonetheless convergence between the orders of action; the social demands of women, specifically the political responsibilities they sometimes claimed, tended to give higher esteem to their social role and thus reduce the inequality between feminine and masculine status.

*

The sources for this investigation of the militant activity of women in the Parisian sections in 1793, although scattered, are relatively numerous. In the National Archives, the addresses or petitions sent to the Convention or to its Committee on Legislation are preserved in the series C and DIII. Even more important is the alphabetical series of the Committee of General Security, F7 4577-4775[53]—an inexhaustible gold mine of individual dossiers on the sectional personnel of year II that would require a systematic perusal with an exact study of feminine practice in mind. Likewise, such a study would require systematic research in the important series of statements of the police commissioners preserved in the Archives of the Prefecture of Police (A A/48 to A/265), an indispensable source for the study of daily life in Paris during the revolutionary period.

Numerous women participated in the general movement of the Revolution. In this sense, their action is hardly distinguishable from the men's: same demonstrations, same organizations. Women did, however, have a clearer consciousness when the question of food supplies was at stake. Here we are not speaking of occurrences of feminine action for their own objectives but of the situation of the popular masses as a whole. It should be sufficient to recall the march of women on Versailles during the October days of 1789 or their presence in the great demonstrations of September 4-5, 1793.

From this point of view, the mentality and behavior of women and men are very similar; nevertheless, the mentality is more emphatic and the behavior is more marked in women, who were of course consumers but also mothers and housewives. Significant in this regard are the dossiers of the antiterrorist repression from the spring of 1795, which abound in denunciations of terrorist remarks directed by women in 1794 against tradesmen, all considered monopolizers and speculators. Perhaps even more than men, women linked terror with subsistence.

The widow Barbau, from the Indivisibilité section, a veritable *furie* according to her denouncers, was in the habit of declaring that "as long as the egotistical merchants, the former aristocrats, the rich, etc., are not guillotined or dispatched as a whole, all will not go well."[4] The widow Barbau quite naturally put merchants before aristocrats. Many women shared this intense terrorist excitement. If we must guard against taking the denunciations and police reports literally, we cannot deny the fact that for certain women it was a question of pure violence. The wife Baudray, café owner in the Lepeletier section, was heard to declare that "as for those who opposed the sans-culottes," she wanted to "have their hearts to eat;" she appeared to raise her children with the same principles. "You no longer hear them talking about anything besides cutting off heads," and that "not enough blood was flowing,"[5] as one informer testified.

The examples could be multiplied. Let us simply say that women participated in the popular mentality and that their terrorist remarks are not typical of women's action, except perhaps by their tone and stress. Yet it is a significant characteristic of the social and mental structures of the period that we do not find in the flood of addresses and petitions to the revolutionary Assemblies, and to the Convention in particular, concerning the problem of subsistence, documents emanating from women, from women alone. There are a few exceptions, all the more significant. After the president of the Bondy section had presented to the Convention the address of adherence to the Constitution of June 24, 1793, the woman citizen Mouroy, *speaking in her own name*, demanded "a harsh law" against monopolizers and that the prices of basic foodstuffs be controlled.[6] Along the same lines, we find among the numerous protests from the sections demanding rent control the address of the citoyenne Barbot, retail haberdasher, 17 Transnonain Street, Gravilliers section, September 5, 1793, denouncing "the tyranny of landlords" and demanding "a general law that would quell (their) cupidity."[7]

If women's demands regarding food supplies were, with a few exceptions, lost in the protest actions of the mass movement, there was however on occasion a new awareness of the specific conditions of feminine alienation and action demanding political equality for women, an implicitly feminist demand. This awareness was strengthened from spring to autumn of 1793, from the acceptance of the Constitutional Act of June 24, with the demand for political equality and the right to vote, until the Jacobin counteroffensive and the Convention's banning of women's clubs on October 30, 1793.

At the time of the primary assemblies at the beginning of July 1793 for the ratification of the Constitution, women participated widely in the "sanction en masse," that is, the vote by acclamation or by sitting and rising, but none took part in the roll call votes. However, several delegations of women came to the Convention to declare their acceptance of the Constitution: they represented the sections of Beaurepaire, l'Homme-Armé, Faubourg, Montmartre, Croix-Rouge, Marchés, Théâtre-Français, and Bon-Conseil.[8] "And we too," declared the republican women of the Marchés section on July 5, 1793, "we accept the Declaration of the Rights of Men and the Constitutional Act that you have presented for the approval of the sovereign people. If our husbands and our brothers have sworn to defend [the Constitution] by armed force, we ourselves swear to defend it, some by raising our children in the principles of liberty and equality which form the base of this Constitution, and the others by giving their hand only to true republicans who will have done something for the country."[9] As for the women citizens of the Théâtre-Français section, on July 6 they declared that they could not "remain insensitive to the republican sentiments that their husbands, their brothers and their friends have just expressed."[10] "The wives, the mothers of the Piques section, on this same July 6, also came to swear to make the future (of the Constitution) the object of their domestic devotion; they swore that the French Constitution would from now on and for always be the catechism of their children."[11]

These women's declarations fit into the general movement of acceptance of the Constitution that swept the Parisian sections in the first days of July 1793; they did not present any specifically feminine, much less feminist, vows or demands. There was however an exception. After the president of the Beaurepaire delegation had presented to the Convention his section's approval of the Constitution, he yielded the floor to a citoyenne who loudly demanded political equality. Why shouldn't the Constitution, sanctioning a *de facto* state, mark the legal entry of women into political life? Men, under the constitution, enjoy all the rights of liberty. "But women," declared the citoyenne of Beaurepaire, "are far from being at that height; they are not counted in the political system. We are asking you from the primary assemblies, and since the constitution rests on the rights of man, we demand today the full exercise of those rights."[12] Thuriot, who was presiding that day, merely responded that the Convention would examine this demand.

Logic would certainly have it that, despite the prejudices of the times, the principle of popular sovereignty would apply to women. Women did not fail to take advantage of that concept. As the popular movement expanded during the summer of 1793, women in many of the Parisian sections participated in the sessions of the general assemblies with voting rights. The most militant were not content with this *de facto* situation; they demanded the recognition of their political rights. Decisive here was the action of the Society of the Revolutionary Republican Women that echoed the sectional militants. As proof of this connection, we have the "Discourse delivered to the Society of the Revolutionary Republican Citoyennes by the women of the Droits-de-l'Homme section, giving them a banner on which is [inscribed] the Declaration [of the Rights of Man]" (September 1793).[13] The women of the Droits-de-l'Homme denounced the prejudice "that made half of the individuals passive and isolated beings." "And why should women endowed with the faculty to feel and express their thoughts accept the pronouncement of their exclusion from public affairs? The Declaration of Rights is common to one and the other sex."

The political equality loudly demanded by the most conscious militants had in fact been won by women in July of 1793 in the framework of the sectional organizations, general assemblies and even more in the popular societies, although we must make a distinction between the formerly established instructional societies and the action societies, both formerly and newly established.

As an example of a formerly established instructional society, let us take the Fraternal Society of both sexes meeting at the Jacobin Club, founded in 1790 by the schoolmaster Dansart. It had, from its beginnings, excited the witty eloquence of the Fayettist bulletins, for whom the presence of women seemed as agreeable as it was dangerous.[14] Meeting in the shadow of the mother society [the Jacobins], the Fraternal Society offered every guarantee of legitimacy. But when the campaign against the sectional societies raised doubts about the admission of women, the Society came to question the principle of its institution. Its "purifying" commission wrote to the Committee of Public Safety on April 10, 1794 to inquire if the law of October 30, 1793, which dissolved the Society of Revolutionary Republican Citoyennes, forbidding women to debate, was applicable to the Fraternal Society. Its members were divided. "Citizens who desired to withdraw into the terms of the law have given some the idea of forming a party, while others wish to lead the society [with its present composition]." Here again the Jacobins and the sans-culottes confronted each other. It was hoped that a decree from the Committee interpreting the law would put an end to this disunity.[15] The request was transmitted to the Committee on Legislation, which seems to have refrained from responding. In fact, the sectional societies had fallen into wide disfavor since the preceding autumn, which had become focused on the participation of women in the political life of the basic organizations.

As for the action societies, whether they had been established prior to the summer of 1793 or newly created in the autumn, most seem to have admitted women as members. The Society of Free Men decided on September 19, 1793 to open its ranks to women; they were to sit to the left of the president, the men on the right. On October 30 the society passed over the order-of-the-day proposition to exclude women whose husbands were not members of the society, and they decided to add four more women to the presentations committee.[16] The Luxembourg patriotic society, in its regulation of February 19, 1793, admitted women from the age of fourteen with the same rights as men and the same formalities; but their number could not exceed one-fifth of the total number of members; they were eligible in the same proportion to hold posts in the society, except for those [working] in the office.[17]

The political activity of women in the sectional organizations was maintained at a high level until October 30, 1793, when the women's clubs were banned. There was only one club that was exclusively feminine, the Society of Revolutionary Republicans; its dissolution marked a turning point, from tolerance to repression. In fact, women's militancy did not cease for all that, as is evidenced by the reports of police observers published by Pierre Caron[18] and the dossiers of the antiterrorist repression of spring 1795 conserved in the National Archives in the alphabetical series of the Committee of General Security. Popular mentality differed on this point from that of the Jacobin bourgeoisie: militants admitted women to active participation in the political life of the sections. Indeed it seems that following the passage of the law banning women's clubs, the most militant women fell back to the popular societies, particularly those in the sections.

In the Cité sectional Society, "it is women who make the law," according to the observor Mercier on January 16, 1794; "they meddle in all the political business, such as certificates of public-spiritedness and others."[19] In the course of the winter of 1794, the acuteness of the subsistence crisis naturally contributed to intensifying sectional political life. General assemblies, sectional societies and weekly revolutionary ceremonies, attracted great throngs where the women were not the least numerous. According to the reports of the observor Bacon, always very attentive to sectional political life, women frequented the general assemblies and popular societies more than ever. On February 20, 1794, at the Bonne-Nouvelle popular assembly (that is, the sectional society), there were many women in the galleries; same remark on the 22nd for the l'Homme-Armé Society. There were large crowds on February 26 in the societies of Indivisibilité and Droits-de-l'Homme, where Bacon noted many women in the galleries; "the popular assembly of the Lombards section was as full as it could be and there were considerable numbers of women in the former church." The next day, at the l'Homme-Armé popular assembly, there were still many women in the galleries. Still according to Bacon, on February 28, in the Temple of Reason, Bonne-Nouvelle section, the crowd was considerable, mostly women.[20]

This militant activity of women persisted after the trials of germinal and despite the repression against sectional personnel suspected of "Hébertism." When, on May 1, 1794, the Revolutionary Committee of the Contrat Social section suspended one of its members, suspect for his remarks in favor of Hébert, "a muffled excitement" followed, notes the Committee in its report of May 3rd. "The women of the galleries are in all confidence the ringleaders of the society."[21] At the meeting on May 1st, a woman named Millet had called the president *scélérat* [villain] "because he had said that there were Hébertists, agitators and schemers in the Society."

This latent opposition [to the law and the government] that was favorable to the presence of women in the popular organizations, a trait characteristic of the sans-culotte mentality and behavior, continued throughout the spring of 1794, in spite of the intense Jacobin campaign against sectional societies not affiliated with the mother society, a campaign that finally ended with the dissolution of 31 societies between May 14-24, 1794. Certain societies openly resisted despite the violence of the attacks. An example is the Fraternal Society of Two Sexes of the Panthéon-Français section, denounced on May 30 in a letter to Collot d'Herbois. It is "the germ of all hatred. There are at most 60 men and as many women, and with this tiny minority, they would lead the section of 8000 to 9000 men."[22] Described as *hermaphrodite* by its opponents, the Fraternal Society of Two Sexes refused to dissolve; women continued to intervene in debates and to staff the office. Meetings went on throughout 1795 and on May 29 the society was denounced as "a hearth of insurrection."[23]

Women's militancy did not manifest itself only on the political plane. There were in 1794 protest actions that were specifically feminine, that is connected to problems of work or family, the woman expressing herself as a mother or producer.

Characteristic of the protest action of women were the soap riots of June 26-28, 1793. On the 26th, in ports from the Seine at Grenouillère to port Saint-Nicolas, the laundry women unloaded soap from boats and sold it at a price of 20 *sous* a pound. The next day the gatherings began again. Meanwhile as if to legitimize their action, the laundry women protested the same day on the floor of the Convention against the excessive price of soap, candles "and other necessities." The riots continued on June 28: women gathered around a cart of soap at the Saint-Lazare gate, a meeting was held in the Poissonnière section, a delegation of women went to the General Council of the Commune to demand that the seized soap be delivered to them at 20 *sous* a pound. The Council refused, Hébert having presented "the frightening picture of the misfortunes which would follow closely on the violation of property in Paris."[24]

There were soap riots again on April 15, 1794. In the Temple section a group of women forced their way into the office of the civil committee, indignant that pieces of soap were no longer distributed. The women complained about the "very offensive" attitude toward them of the committee and the guard; the guardsmen declared that they had been "ill treated and scratched"; one young seamstress, twenty-two years old, was arrested.[25]

Evidence of a more specific social sense was the action of the women workers of the Midi cotton mill workshop at the former Jacobin [society] of Saint-Jacques Street. At the end of February 1794, they protested a new wage rate imposed by the Department of administrators of public establishments, at the same time that a daily allocation of two pounds of bread was cancelled. The women workers drew up a petition, alerted the Popular Society of the Friend of the People, Marat section, and sought the support of Père Duchesne [Hébert]. To certain remarks of the director of the workshop, on the lack of public spirit evident in their demands, they responded "that they didn't give a d..." They tried to bring along the women workers of the workshop of the Nord section in the Saint-Martin district: two of them introduced themselves there, asking the women if they were happy with their leaders, and presenting the petition adopted by the Midi mill.[26]

In early June of 1794, when the social crisis was becoming clearer and the repression more pronounced, the affair was taken up by the revolutionary committee of the Chalier section. On the June 2, 1794, it proceeded to interrogate a dozen of the women workers. Benoîte Tribel, the wife of Jennison, who in March had presented the demands of her companions and drawn up the petition, was arrested. There was an aggravating circumstance: Benoîte Tribel was said to have declared out loud after the execution of Hébert that he was condemned because he was a good patriot. Bound over to the Revolutionary Tribunal, she was acquitted on June 23, 1794, her neighbors on Perdrix Street near Maubert Square having attested to her patriotism.[27] This case is significant for the awakening, in a woman, of political consciousness through social protest.

As mothers, the militant women did not stop with the demands for price controls on basic foodstuffs or increases in the wage rate. As sectional militants, they placed education high on their list of demands, equal with other social rights. As the Declaration of June 24, 1793 had placed education among the rights of man (article 22), numerous sections demanded its prompt organization. Women participated widely in this movement; sometimes they were the whole movement. For example on July 7, presenting to the Convention "the wish of the citoyennes" of the Contrat-Social section, the citoyenne Bayard demanded a "national education" which develops in children "the germ of Spartan virtues that we have placed in their hearts."[28] That same day, "the citoyennes flower sellers from different sections of Paris" demanded "a national instruction (organized) according to popular principles."[29] Just as much as a general instruction, it was a question of civic education; this demand was integrated into the social action of the most conscious women; in the end, it characterized that action.

*

An attentive search through the dossiers of the antiterrorist repression of the spring of 1795 would doubtless enable us to sketch the portrait of the militant sectional woman who appears to have been characterized by two essential traits: a visceral egalitarianism and an intimate conviction that women, also, constituted the sovereign people.

The citoyenne Auxerre had been noted for her militant fervor toward the end of February 1794, when the women of the cotton workshops started a protest action against the new wage rate that had been imposed on them. Employed in the workshop for bags for the flour store on Temple Street, the citoyenne Auxerre tried to engage her co-workers in the struggle. She was said to have declared "that they were the sovereign, that the municipal officers and authorities were only their agents," adding "that it was really astonishing that the sovereign lacked wood when its agents were abundantly provided with it."[30] She was denounced on February 24 (1794) at the committee of the Amis-de-la-Patrie section for counterrevolutionary remarks.

Look at the citoyenne Chalandon of the l'Homme-Armé section. She was arrested on May 27, 1795.[31] Among the grounds for arrest, three were essential. First, the demand for political equality: a sentry having prevented her from entering the general assembly and having sent her to the galleries, she declared that "such orders could have been given only by aristocrats." Second, social egalitarianism: she is reported to have said "regarding the houses of Grand Chantier Street and the announced project of some citizens to buy one as a national property, that she was opposed to it, that the houses would not be sold, that they would be given to them, and that she, wife Chalandon, hoped to have her share." Finally, terrorism: "That all would go well only when there are permanent guillotines in all the crossroads of Paris."

But these "female grenadiers,"[32] these "furies of the guillotines" were good mothers, for whom solidarity was not an empty word. Examples are not lacking of this civic virtue, a characteristic trait of popular mentality and sociability. Françoise Ravinet, innkeeper, was arrested on May 24, 1795; she was known for her active participation in all the days of revolutionary struggle. Mother of four young children, she had not hesitated to take charge of a fifth, "by adoption and humanity."[33]

In the spring of 1795, after more than five years of revolution, the courageous action of a minority had not succeeded in making society leap over the cultural barrier of social and political inequality between the sexes. After May 1795, the Convention banned women from "attending political assemblies," urging them to withdraw to their homes and ordering "the arrest of those who would gather together in groups of more than five." Woman was sent back to her natural and legitimate role, that of wife and mother inside the family circle. For the revolutionary bourgeoisie, Thermidorian as well as Jacobin, the subordinate condition of women was obviously natural. Feminine demands, and even more, feminist ones, were still utopian. But it cannot be denied that the awakening of feminine consciousness was manifested through the protest actions. The militant Parisian women of 1793-1794 had advanced history, opening the doors to the future by their boldness.

12

From the Ancien Régime to the Revolution: the regional problem and social realities[1]

It has been said about the principle of nationalities that it was "a very simple and clear notion" (E. Boutroux) and also "the classic example of an obvious idea that is, however, false." (H. Hauser). Couldn't these same contradictory judgments be applied to the living realities of provinces or regions, provincialism and regionalism? Provincialism, particularism, federalism, regionalism: the multiplicity of words demonstrates the difficulty of defining the problem, which needs to be placed in its historical evolution.

Provincial sentiment—or regional, in the current sense of the word—was aroused very early. If the word *province* is relatively recent (its use had hardly become widespread before the end of the Middle Ages), the reality is much older. The province appears as a historical category perpetuated throughout the centuries, but what concerns us here is the content more than the framework. The provincial or regional question has assumed various aspects in the course of its evolution, depending on the historical tradition and the political context, and even more on the social group involved. Here it is a question of the historical turning point from the 18th to the 19th century; the influence of the French Revolution, generally simplistically considered to be unifying and centralizing, should be accurately measured and situated in relation to the Ancien Régime. It is certainly evident that provincial realities and regional sentiment could not be cut off from social conflicts and political struggles. This discussion must also take into account class antagonisms, leading to contradictory developments in different regions. While the revolutionary necessity of equality and the unifying national sentiment were mutually strengthened from 1789 to 1793, the concern for social preservation found support in the traditional provincial values. But at the time of the federalist insurrection, popular regional sentiment was also turned to the advantage of the counterrevolution. This was particularly true in Marseille, which up to then had played a vanguard revolutionary role in Provence.

This is a general problem, but one that varies according to historical tradition, economic development and social evolution. Thus, for the period we are studying, it is determined by the specific reactions of various social groups to the ideology and action of the Revolution.

I

At the end of the Ancien Régime, the regional units, the provinces, were still very much alive. Hadn't Mirabeau defined the kingdom as "an unconstituted aggregate of disunited *peoples*"? The institutional vagueness of these regional realities is conveyed even by the vocabulary.

The province in the legal sense did not in fact exist under the Ancien Régime. The word was used officially for the first time, with its rigorous administrative connotation, in the June 1787 regulation creating the *provincial assemblies* in the "pays d'état" [lower regional subdivisions].[2] The word had no precise meaning, except in ecclesiastical matters: "The jurisdictional expanse of a metropolis is called an *ecclesiastic province*. There are eighteen ecclesiastic provinces in the kingdom. In this sense, people ordinarily say *province* without qualification. *The Lyon province, the Sens province*."[3] The word had been preserved by the royal power for its very imprecision: it served the ignorance of an administration which, in its public acts, never gave a clear indication of the jurisdiction aimed for, first because it most often was unaware of these jurisdictions, and also because they were tangled up in the greatest disorder.[4]

In the absence of the word *province*, whose usage was hardly in the common language before the 15th century and was not established administratively until the end of the Ancien Régime, several Latin or French terms have long been used that in a general sense may be considered synonyms of *province*, but which are distinguished by particular nuances.[5]

In the Middle Ages, *regio* was applied in a very precise way to those living realities which were Brittany, Normandy and Provence. But of all the terms designating what historians have since called provinces, the most widespread in the Middle Ages was incontestably the word *pays*: the chronicles and texts repeat it constantly to apply to all the French provinces. The inquiry should be extended to words like *langue* [language] and *nation*, even though their use as a synonym of *province* may at first seem strange. The expression *langue d'oc* came to designate a province with precise geographical boundaries, those of the three feudal bailiwicks [seneschalsies] of Toulon, Carcassonne and Beaucaire-et-Nîmes. What were called at the end of the 15th century the *langue de Normandie* and the *langue de Flandre* corresponded quite closely to the duchy of Normandy and the earldom of Flanders. Let us underscore this essential trait: a regional unity designated by the language spoken by its inhabitants. As for the word *nation*, among numerous meanings, it still designated province in the expressions *nation of Brittany* or of Normandy, of Burgundy or even in *nation provençale*.*

At the end of the Ancien Régime, there were thus many words which tended to express in various ways what today we understand as province. The synonymy is not complete, however. If all these words commonly designate province, each one preserves its own personality to suggest to the mind some particular trait derived from history. The persistent use of words like *nation* or *pays* reflects the specific vitality of certain regional entities. On the other hand, the preponderance of the word *province* at the end of the Ancien Régime expressed the progress of the political and administrative unification of the kingdom, as if each one of these provinces resembled its neighbor. That unity was not yet achieved is shown by the very imprecision of the word *province.* At the Constituent Assembly in October 1789, at the start of the discussion on a new administrative division of France, M. de Tracy, deputy of the nobility from Moulins, proposed that the Assembly "define what was meant by the word *province*, before concerning itself with any new administrative division."[6]

Scholarly research and critical reflection must go beyond this survey of vocabulary, for resorting to linguistic methods does not, as some claim, constitute a panacea. Behind the straw man of words is the living reality of people and things. From primitive structures to Roman boundaries, then to feudal divisions, finally to the "provincial nationalities" of the Ancien Régime, the "region, regionalism" problem requires a historical approach and analysis. Regional sentiment, in the modern meaning of the word, was clearly expressed at the end of the monarchy. The years 1787-1788 therefore appear singularly important. This was when the attempt to establish provincial assemblies often clashed with the leanings of the aristocracy toward autonomy and the centralizing authority of the administrative officers. The social content of regionalism was evident from the beginning.

Beyond this episode, however, it is important to follow closely the provincial realities in themselves in order to discern their essential components. By what criteria was a province defined at the end of the Ancien Régime?

Rousillon was held in 1789 as a "foreign province," not integrated into the kingdom.[7] According to Arthur Young in his journal entry dated

*A Romance language, with several dialects, in southern France.

July 21, 1787, "Rousillon constitutes in fact a part of Spain; the inhabitants are Spanish in their language and customs, but they are dependent on the French government."[8] Catalans are not Spanish, but Arthur Young was right to emphasize the particularism, or sense of political identity, of Roussillon. Reunited to the kingdom of France in 1659 by the treaty of the Pyrenees, it had resisted all attempts at decatalanization no matter how systematic. The Catalan culture persisted, even though it was considered popular in a somewhat pejorative sense.

The components of Catalan particularism are to be found not so much in geography as in history and language. Roussillon, that is the "earldoms" of Roussillon, properly speaking, and Cerdagne, is a historical designation covering a complex geographical reality of varied landscapes and climates, even though this diversity is of a somewhat complementary nature. But these lands possessed a deep human unity: their inhabitants were and wanted to be Catalans, differentiating themselves from their neighbors of Languedoc, the *gavatxos*, a somewhat pejorative term, like their word for foreigners (*foraster*). The Catalan language forms the cement of this particularism, remaining the language of the large majority of the population who knew no other; sermons were preached in Catalan until 1874 in the cathedral of Saint-Jean de Perpignan. This was in spite of the monarchy's Frenchification efforts, which favored the Jesuit actions of proliferating small schools, and requiring the use of French in official acts in 1700 and in civil acts in 1735.[9]

The weight of the historical past is no less important. The earldoms of Roussillon and Cerdagne had maintained a particular status in the kingdom of Aragon and—since the 15th century—in Spain, as did the Catalan lands as a whole. After annexation they were still governed by the Constitutions of Catalonia: French laws were not in current use, as the Sovereign Council established at Perpignan was charged with overseeing the application of the *Usatges* as long as they were not in contradiction with French legislation. On the social plane, annexation brought about an exile movement, essentially among the nobility, accompanied by an important transfer of property from the earldoms to the princedom of Spanish Catalonia. Those nobles who remained were decimated when the movements resisting Frenchification, in which they widely participated, were repressed—so much so that Roussillon had practically no old nobility left by the 18th century.

In the final analysis, history and language had formed a specific mentality reinforced by the maintenance of ancient institutions, the insurrections that followed annexation, and then the latent but stubborn resistance to Frenchification. All these characteristics finally wove a Catalan personality and culture. No one factor was most important; the specificity of Roussillon arose from the interaction of them all. Yet this Catalan consciousness was not expressed by nationalism nor renewed desire of union with the princedom [Spain].[10] The registers of grievances of 1789 do not question the annexation with France; but the overriding idea is that the hardships suffered by Roussillon came from the abandonment of traditional liberties and the excesses of monarchistic centralization. If Roussillon supported the Revolution and the Republic, it could hardly tolerate Jacobin centralism.

The case of Gascony, a counterexample to Roussillon, would suffice to demonstrate that language alone cannot fuse the unity of a province.[11] With the exception of the three Basque provinces (Labourd, Basse-Navarre and Soule), the lands to the west and south of the Garonne did in fact preserve a common linguistic patrimony: the domain of Gascon which a certain number of irreducible traits distinguish irremediably from central Occitan [Provençal French]. (If the Catharist or Albigensian heresy did not penetrate Gascony, wouldn't it be because the preachers coming from Languedoc and speaking central Occitan were not understood by the Gascons?) In the 18th century, Gascon remained the common spoken language, at least in the popular milieus, though less common as a written language. Gascon literature, established in the 16th century, bloomed in the first half of the 17th, then declined during the personal reign of Louis XIV; it lived on in Bearn until the end of the Ancien Régime. But other forces were in play to counter this strong and vibrant linguistic unity: geographical dispersion, a broken-up historical past, institutional diversity and the absence of economic unity.

If the term "Gascony" has been preserved, the territory to which it refers presents very vague boundaries, uncertain to the east on the Languedoc side, and to the west of the Guyenne side. Inside these uncertain boundaries, the compartmentalization of the valleys of the Pyrenees, the southwestern orientation of the Adour basin, and the north-south direction of the Gascony valleys do not favor a solid political unity, but rather facilitate the breaking up of the region into little lands [*pays*]. Certainly it had known real political unity under the Gallo-Roman Novempopulanie in Vasconie, then as the duchy of Gascony in the Carolingian period, which brought together most of the territories between Arrats and Ocean, the Pyrenees and the Garonne. This unity did not survive the death of the last duke in 1032. Feudal divisions, suzerainty conflicts and the distant ambitions of the houses of Armagnac and Albret prevented the consolidation of a unified Gascony.

The institutional diversity of the modern period could only favor dispersion. The Gascon *pays* came under different jurisdictions: for some the Bordeaux Parlement,* for others the one at Toulouse; for some the Governor of Guyenne-et-Gascogne, for others the one of Basse-Navarre; for some the tax district [*généralité*] of Mantauban, for others that of Bordeaux. In the 18th century however, the creation in 1716 of the district or *intendance* of Auch, and the strong, active administration of the intendant d'Etigny (1715-1767), appeared to have revived the notion of Gascony and given a new life to the ancient province (in fact expanded to include Basse-Navarre and Bearn).[12] The regeneration of Gascony, paradoxically enough, was due to an act of sovereign power and the action of an intendant, the agent of monarchistic centralization, later saluted as the true "creator of the province." The events that followed bear witness however to the contradictions of this rediscovered unity: the creation in 1768 of the *intendance* of Pau-Bayonne, then the territorial reorganizations of 1775, 1784 and 1787. The geographical imperatives were compelling. The unifying action of Etigny and the creation of a modern network of roads had not succeeded in forging a viable economic unity.

The word and the idea of Gascony appeared again at the very end of the Ancien Régime when the intermediary commission of the provincial assembly of the *intendance* of Auch received permission for the body to be called the provincial assembly of Gascony. In January 1789, it demanded that Gascony be established as a higher regional subdivision [*pays d'état*]. A similar project was taken up by the permanent committee of Auch in September 1789: the constitution of a large administrative district grouping together all the Gascon *pays*. But at the end of September, when Thouret was preparing to present his plan to create 80 departments to the Constituent Assembly, it was no longer a question of asking for a true province of Gascony as vast as the old *intendance*.

Could not the case of the French Netherlands, which were to form the departments of Nord and Pas-de-Calais, be linked, relatively speaking, to that of Gascony? Or again, does one single criterion, whether it be the language or the spirit of political independence, permit us to define a regional unity?[13] A strong particularist spirit survived in the Netherlands, deeply rooted in the towns that had experienced an incomparable development at the end of the Middle Ages. Integration remained unaccomplished, for the autonomy enjoyed by these lands freed them from certain taxes such as the salt tax [*gabelle*]; the customs gate of the Grosses Fermes separated them

*Parlement: a regional Court under the Ancien Régime.

from the rest of the kingdom, and the judicial organization as well as the religious again underscored this particularism. This was demonstrated in the registers of grievances of 1789, bursting with hostility against monarchistic centralism and its agents, intendants and delegates. But is a particularist state of mind enough to form a province when everything diverges?

The French Netherlands present no geographical unity; they form a true mosaic where almost thirty "pays" can be distinguished.[14] Nor do they have any historical unity. No name could be given to this ensemble of territories, with shifting borders and submitting to successive dominations. No royal house had been able to bring together this "borderland" between Picardy and the Netherlands in any lasting way, despite the successive importance of the counts of Flanders and the dukes of Burgundy. The uncertainty of their historical destinies is reflected in the absence of a name. The French Netherlands were far from presenting themselves as a strongly constituted province like Brittany or Franche-Comte.

At the end of the Ancien Régime, this mosaic persisted. The various *pays*—historical, political and administrative units—were distinguished by their language, traditions, life style and temperament. Without attaching a scientific value to these cultural stereotypes, we must note that the district administrators perceived clear differences between the Flemish and the Hennuyer; nor did travellers such as Arthur Young confuse the two. Above these complex administrative divisions—constantly undergoing reorganization, with enclaves and jurisdictions running into each other—the two administrative divisions of Lille and Valenciennes really formed the administrative framework of this border area; they were not enough to establish a coherent regional unity.

This confusion appeared shocking to enlightened minds who recognized the necessity of a reform that would substitute a logical and voluntarist design for this traditional empirical reality. In the simplifying and unifying spirit of the century, plans proliferated. But while the monarchy was striving to accentuate the centralizing tendencies, a "provincialist" movement was expressing itself, tending to safeguard traditions, customs and privileges. One could speak of a "provincialist reawakening." Let us underscore its social content: it was the act of the privileged, at least the "notables," in the framework of traditional *pays*, and thus of a very localized autonomy. This is indeed a case of "localism."

Finally, the geographic heterogeneity, historical vicissitudes and cultural specificities of the Netherlands are reflected in the demarcations of the departments of Nord and Pas-de-Calais where astonishing continuity was expressed. The unifying work of the Revolution could not erase the local particularisms where multiple social and historical factors were interwoven. Once again it is a question of specifying which social category is embodied in particularism and which social and political usage dominates in each historical stage. The example of Provence and the case of Franche-Comte at the end of the Ancien Régime are enlightening on this score.

The example of Provence at the end of the Ancien Régime illustrates the importance of social criteria. The various factors which make up the personality of a province do in fact differ for different social groups: was the Provence of the "notables" really the same as the Provence of the common people?[15]

Provençal survived as the popular language, but was it still the language of the elites? According to the president of Brosses, in 1760 the people spoke hardly any French. This persistent predominance of the provençal language is accounted for in the first place by the bad state of roads, which encouraged people to take the coast highway (though even in Marseille, provençal dominated) and condemned the interior to a life of drowsy connections. The countryside lived intensely, but withdrawn into itself, true conservators of traditions. To this were added the deficiencies in education (the known literacy rates are low) and the indecision of the clergy as regards preaching (at the Charité hospital in Marseille. prayers were said in provençal and it is in this language that Father Nicolas was preaching in 1790).[16]

But speaking provençal was not an act of the elites. If they remained to a certain degree faithful to their culture, this attachment was expressed as "the scholar's taste for the past language"; in particular this was shown by the popularity of the troubadours, which peaked in 1780. If the "notables" used provençal, it was out of necessity, to have contact with popular opinion. Indifference to the living provençal but worshipping the linguistic past, passion and pride for provençal history, literature and traditional institutions: such was the "provençalism" of an elite otherwise concerned about French culture and philosophy.

Through a reappraisal of regional history, this elite began to express a vague awareness of what might have been the "provençal nation." At the end of the Ancien Régime, historical works were published that exalted the centuries preceding the union with France and which expressed a latent sentiment of "the crushing of the *pays d'oc*".[17] Specifically provençal history seems to have stopped during the reign of Louis XIV with the province's loss of privileges and the end of the autonomy of Marseille. The *Traité sur l'administration du comte de Provence* of Coriolis published from 1786 to 1788 expressed even more clearly than the historical works the frustration felt by the provençal "notables," their rancor and their demands; in fact it was a breviary for a certain regionalism, that of the privileged in the society of the Ancien Régime.

The "provincial constitution," dear to these "notables," is thus represented by a collection of texts progressively elaborated since the Middle Ages that confirm a certain number of privileges and organize regional power. The nation agrees to taxation through the intermediary of its Estates or, after their suspension, of the Assembly of Communities. Nation here means the "notables." This regime was perfectly fitting for at least the upper layers of the Third Estate who held the majority in the Assembly of Communities. Thus the convocation of the Estates demanded by the nobility in the summer of 1787 could not be agreeable to the "notables," for if the traditional forms were respected, they would be a minority. So from the summer of 1787 to the spring of 1789, there was a divergence of the "notables" who had been identified with a provençal nation from which the people were excluded.

Provence as a political entity, but not as a culture, disappeared in the social and political struggles of 1789. The renunciation of the traditional "constitution" and integration into the new national unity seemed the only way to end the society of privileges and go beyond the Ancien Régime. In order to destroy the traditional social structures, it was necessary to break up the old political and administrative frameworks; Provence split into three departments. The people regained their rights. Until 1792, the citizens of Marseille were the spearhead of the Revolution in southern France. But at the same time provençal culture was preserved by the old and new elites, while the "notables" of Marseille were embittered by the memory of their former autonomy, and those of Aix by the memory of their lost preeminence. While provençal was kept alive in the still isolated countryside and in the popular milieus, provençalism was reinforced among the "notables" by the evocation of an idealized history of a prosperous, glorious and poetic—that is, mythical—Middle Ages. Already the episodes of federalism were being presented as the incarnation of Félibrige [character created by the 19th century Provençal poet, Mistral].

Just as illuminating is the case of Franche-Comté.[18] The problem of the social content of regionalism is posed at once by the appeal of a noble of the region to Emperor Leopold of Austria in 1791.[19] "If the emperor has any designs on Franche-Comté, it could be his in a very short time: he will be powerfully seconded by a party of gentlemen who miss the domination of the kings, his predecessors. This party of the nobility will even be aided by the people, already weary of the anarchy into which they have been plunged." This was undoubtedly the appeal of an émigré, but the question is still clearly posed: through nostalgia for its provincial autonomy and its lost privileges, was Franche-Comté ready to give itself to the Emperor in 1791? Were the *people* ready to follow the *gentlemen* in this adventure? One of the interesting features of Count Faverney's proposal is the important distinction he makes between the nobility and the people.

Franche-Comté has always been a land of French language and civilization. At the moment of the Revolution, it had been definitively joined to France for more than a century.[20] It was thus one of the first provinces to develop the federation movement among its towns and villages, culminating in the celebration of July 14, 1790.[21] If there ever was a moment when the citizens of Franche-Comté might hesitate between France and the Empire, it was not during the Revolution.

Although Louis XIV had taken Franche-Comté from Spain, the historic past tied the region to the Austrian Empire, to which it had belonged for more than six centuries. The ravages of the 17th century wars, the fiscal regime imposed by France, regular taxation instead of free gifts—all caused the faraway past to be idealized and made valorous. The blessed times of Charles V, both Count of Burgundy and Emperor, were deeply missed. Thus a resident of Franche-Comté, unhappy with the Revolution, would turn toward the Hapsburgs of Austria, not the Bourbons of Spain—not because of dynastic ties or simple loyalty to old masters, but because of a particularist spirit and attachment to privileges.

If the people of Franche-Comté remained, if not hostile, at least uncertain [of their ties to France] at the beginning of the 18th century, some among the "notables" were rallying around, especially the newly ennobled, families ascending the social ladder, an ascent accelerated by their purchase of State offices; some were implacably opposed because they were kept out of administrative offices or the army; most remained undecided while the outcome of the armed struggles appeared to be in the balance. The treaties of Utrecht and Rastadt put an end to the uncertainties: Franche-Comté would remain French.

In the course of the 17th century the province was gradually integrated into the kingdom but a local patriotism, a regionalism, persisted. These were exploited at the end of the Ancien Régime by the Parlement of Franche-Comté, in its conflict with royal power. The attachment to ancient exemptions and local privileges, especially fiscal ones, were most clearly expressed; it was in this area that the members of the Parlement at Besançon were sure to have public opinion on their side. But in Franche-Comté as elsewhere, the accord between the Parlement and public opinion was ruptured on the eve of the Revolution when there was a clear indication of the social content that the "notables" meant to give to their proclaimed particularism and claimed autonomy. The boldness of the language destroys all illusions; the position of the members of the Parlement was determined more by egotistical considerations than by any profound conviction: the appeal to a regional past was only an argument in favor of maintaining the old order and of jealously guarding privileges.

The social oppositions were finally shown to be stronger than provincial solidarity in defense of traditions and exemptions. Confronted by the privileged, who were united with those of the rest in the kingdom, the Third Estate of Franche-Comté felt a solidarity with the whole of the Third Estate: the national (and social) solidarity of the people clashed with the social solidarity of the privileged. On the night of August 4, with "the abolition of the particular privileges of the provinces," the union of Franche-Comté to France was sealed. Furthermore, the abolition of privileges and feudalism brought the peasants of Franche-Comté into the French nation. Social solidarity and national sentiment were reciprocally reinforced. "To believe that the Franche-Comté of 1791 was ready to give herself to the Emperor," concludes Gresset, "one would have to be an émigré traumatized by the revolutionary upheaval. If the nobles of Franche-Comté could address the Hapsburgs in this manner, it was because they expected from them the restoration of the old social order. The past history of the region only offered them a convenient pretext. But the peasant masses would never have accepted a return of the feudal lords."

Particularism, provincialism, regionalism, demands for autonomy: the key to these problems is found, at any moment in historical evolution, in social analysis. They are ultimately defined by their social content, as the revolutionary events should help to demonstrate, if proof is needed.

II

It would be banal to recall here the progress of French unity in the course of the Revolution. The new institutions formed the framework of a State administratively and economically unified. National consciousness was strengthened at the same time in the revolutionary struggles against the aristocracy and the [European] coalition. From 1789 on, the word *nation* had been charged with a new value of faith and hope. The nation was the mass of citizens molded into a single block. There were no more provinces, *pays*, communities, no more orders or classes: all privileges and all particularisms were disappearing "in the natural law of all the French people."[22] The Revolution could not, however, make a clean sweep of the historic past, of the provincial or regional specificities. Their persistent reality was affirmed in the new administrative division of France; it imposed itself on the linguistic policy of the Constituent Assembly, then of the Convention; it brought on a federalist crisis in 1793. But here again the content is more important than the framework or the form: wasn't the French Revolution a social revolution *par excellence*?

The new administrative division of France into departments was not, as has often been written, an arbitrary and hasty undertaking, without historical foundation. On the contrary, it appears to be a skillful compromise between the necessities of a modern administration and the given realities from geography and history: it respected, much more than is generally said, the ancient particularisms.

On November 3, 1789, Thouret proposed a plan of geometric division (with departments of 320 square leagues each). Mirabeau replied that same day that it was necessary to take traditions and history into account. "I would like a material, de facto division, appropriate to the localities and the circumstances, and not a mathematical division, almost ideal, the execution of which appears impractical... Finally, I ask for a division that does not appear in any way to be too great a novelty; that, if I dare to say it, allows groupings with prejudices and even with errors; that would be equally desired by all the provinces and founded on relations already known."[23] It was to this position that the Constitution Committee and finally the Assembly itself were won. "The Committee is bound to respect the decisions made by the deputies of the provinces... It thought that the new division of the realm should offer to the mind the idea of an equal and fraternal sharing and never that of a dislocation of the body politic, and consequently the ancient borders of the provinces should be respected in all cases where there would not be real public utility" [in forming new ones] (February 15, 1790).[24]

France was finally divided into 83 departments. The essential framework of the ancient provinces was preserved, as Mirabeau had asked. The Constitution Committee had distinguished "the provinces that can be organized in their own borders" from those "who are invited to unite with several others to be in keeping with the division of the realm".[25] The great provinces were easily divided: Provence formed three departments; Brittany and Normandy, five each. It was more difficult to regroup the small territorial units, the "pays": it was necessary to join a part of Auvergne with Brioude at Velay to form Haute-Loire. We must nevertheless emphasize that very often in these cases there was continuity from the

Ancien Régime to the Revolution: the eight districts of the Nord department corresponded to the ancient divisions of the French Netherlands.

From the point of view of the history of regionalism, it would be necessary to study the discussions and conflicts which, at the end of 1789 and at the beginning of 1790, gave rise to the new territorial division; thus we would be able to measure more exactly the intensity of particularist sentiments at the beginning of the Revolution. In his critique of the "Division of France into Departments" in the year IX, Pinteville de Cernon, deputy of the nobility from Chalons-sur-Marne, one of the four "commissioners added (to the Constitution Committee) for the division of the realm," recalled "the claims of the former provinces who were still acting very much like guilds... All the ambitions supported by members of the Assembly and by numerous extraordinary deputations made the Committee an arena in which people fought with the greatest obstinacy...; then they negotiated, they bargained... The guild system which had still not been extinguished made it impossible to dismember the former provinces; the Committee has been forced to yield against its better judgment. Indeed, Brittany has been divided into five departments, but no part of its territory, not so much as a village, has been dismembered to be amalgamated to another province. Franche-Comté, Dauphiné, Provence, Alsace, Auvergne, etc., are in the same category."[26]

In fact, whether the departmental division had respected the borders of the ancient provinces or whether it had regrouped neighboring *pays* "united by commercial relations, by a conformity of language and customs,"[27] it would appear as a compromise between the century's requirement of rationality and the centralizing spirit inherited from the monarchy on one hand, and, on the other, the unconscious traditionalism of the Constituents naturally inclined to respect the geographical imperatives, the historic traditions, the economic ties, habits and usages. The thought of the Constituent Assembly was not, as has been too often written, to break all ties and divide all interests. It was inspired above all by the necessity of putting the administrative chaos in order. In his report of January 8, 1790, Bureaux de Pusy, one of the four commissioners, explained their work. It was a question of presenting the idea of an equal and fraternal sharing beneficial to all concerned, and never that of a ripping apart or dislocation of the social body. The ancient borders should in consequence be respected in all cases when it would not be in the public interest or an obvious necessity to destroy them.[28] The division of France into departments was not the work of a geometric philosophy, but a work of realistic wisdom, not going against the grain of tradition and history.[29]

The question of language seems to have played only a minor role in the formation of the new districts, for example in Flanders, despite the observations of certain deputies that no consideration was being given to language affinities in the regrouping of populations. The majority of the Assembly intended to erase "all divisions which prevent the fusing of the spirit and particular interest of the provinces with the spirit and interest of the whole nation." Moreover, the majority triumphed over reservations, thus rejecting the claim of the German-speaking deputies from Lorraine to form a separate department.[30]

We should not attribute to the creation of departments, however, linguistic consequences that it could not have: it could not destroy a state of affairs that didn't exist; that is, the conformability of linguistic zones to administrative districts. The problem of the national language and that of regional dialects were posed on a whole other plane during the Revolution.

It is not in our province to retrace here the turns taken by the linguistic policy of the Revolution, but to underscore their social content.[31] In 1789 the French language entered a new phase of its history. It became national, from that time on appearing as an essential element of "nationality"; the language became an affair of the State; local or regional dialects became dissidents. It goes without saying that we could not abstract this linguistic policy from the political and social struggles of the Revolution.

If the Constituent Assembly had a liberal attitude in linguistic matters, respecting regional languages, the national fervor and unity of hearts that characterized '89 along with the strengthening of political ties led to a unity of language. We cannot conceal the social content of this evolution: speaking French appeared to be one of the more important ways of asserting oneself as a patriot. The fact still remained that in the interest of the revolution itself, there was no other way to enter into relations with those who didn't know French than to speak *their* language. This explains the decision of the Constituent Assembly on January 14, 1790 to translate its decrees, and the claim of a genuine linguistic regionalism put forward in a message to Montauban on December 18, 1791: "After having demonstrated the absolute impossibility of succeeding to any degree in familiarizing our peasants from Gascony, Languedoc, Provence, etc. with the French language, I believe that the only means left to us is to instruct them exclusively in their native language."[32] But wasn't this tending toward linguistic federalism? The crisis of the Revolution, in 1793, brought to the forefront the problem of language and its social implications.

At the beginning, the Convention followed the tradition of preceding Assemblies: nothing was changed in the policy practiced in regard to dialects. "In order to give an accelerated impulse to the public spirit," Roland wrote in his report of January 6, 1793, "we must multiply the channels of instruction to the people. At least one-eighth of the French people do not understand the language; we should therefore translate both our laws and our documents into the different dialects of these inhabitants."[33] It still seemed that in the regions with dialects, the difference in language caused serious difficulties in the development of the Revolution. This necessitated translation into regional languages. "Fanaticism dominates," a commissioner in Ustaritz (Basses-Pyrénées) noted on October 22, 1792; "few people know how to speak French; the Basque priests and other bad citizens have interpreted the decrees to these unfortunate inhabitants according to their own interests... Unless we give instruction in Basque, pure patriotism will have a hard time spreading."[34]

As the crisis deepened in 1793, the dialects became suspect: linguistic particularism favored the counterrevolution. On September 17, 1793, Carrier and Pocholle, representatives on assignment at Rennes, sent the news that "They [the evils and ravages of fanaticism] are all the more difficult to smother when, in the most fanaticized cantons, we cannot make the language of reason understood. The inhabitants of the countryside only understand and know how to speak one dialect: it can be understood only by them."[35] These dialects, despite all the efforts that could be made, offered an insurmountable obstacle: they lent themselves to counterrevolutionary propaganda. "They [the Bretons]," wrote Prieur de la Marne to the Committee of Public Safety on November 13, 1793, "have all the inclinations necessary for freedom, but they speak a language as removed from ours as German and English; they have no kind of instruction and are thus delivered up to fanatic priests... In general the towns are patriotic, but the countryside is a hundred leagues from the Revolution, and everything, down to their bearing, their costumes and especially their language, are notice enough that great efforts will be necessary to bring them up to that [revolutionary] level."[36] Isore, representative on assignment, made a similar observation in a letter from Cassel on December 2, 1793: "If the people of Maritime Flanders are not at the level of the revolution, we must blame the language that they still cultivate in secret."[37]

As the danger increased to the point of urgency, the question of language became a problem of public safety. On January 22, 1794, Grégoire proposed the doctrine: "The unity of the Republic demands the unity of dialects, and all French people must be honored to know a language that henceforth will be *par excellence* the language of courage, virtues and liberty."[38] The requirements of public safety; that is, maintaining the social and political conquests of the Revolution, entailed war on linguistic federalism.

On January 27, 1794, in the name of the Committee of Public Safety, Barère denounced to the tribunal of the Convention the dangers to the Republic from "the ancient Welch, Gascon, Celtic, Wisigoth, Phocaean and Oriental [eastern] dialects."[39] "What we need is to prevent the formation of a new Vendée in the former Brittany where the priests exercised the most cruel influence by speaking only low Breton. What we need is to repopulate a district of the Bas-Rhin department that the émigrés have carried because they were speaking to the inhabitants in their language and used this means to make them stray. What we need is to stop Paoli from operating the counterrevolution in Corsica by the means offered to him by the Italian language which is uniquely spoken on that island." We could not better underscore the political and social utilization of linguistic particularisms by the counterrevolution. This famous diatribe is well-known: "Federalism and superstition speak low Breton; emigration and hatred of the Republic speak German; the counterrevolution speaks Italian and fanaticism speaks Basque. Let us break these instruments of fanaticism and error. It is better to teach than translate... We owe the citizens the instrument of public thought, the surest agent of the Revolution, the same language."

The social content of this unitary linguistic policy could not escape our attention. Language, whether national or regional, also represents a tool in social struggles and political conflicts. Now the question is posed of knowing, at each stage of these conflicts and struggles, what political use is made of linguistic particularism, what social class is using for its own ends regional languages or local dialects.

In 1793 linguistic particularism favored political federalism with an obvious social content. Doubtless the persistence of regionalist sentiments partly explains this, but even more important was the solidarity of class interests. As early as May 15, 1793, Chaset, deputy from Rhone-et-Loire, was writing: "It is a question of life and then property";[40] after June 2, he won over Lyons in revolt against the Convention and put himself at the head of the movement.

A preliminary remark is necessary, however, on the history of the word *federalism.*[41] In 1790, the *federations* had sealed the fraternal ties between the regions and their populations. Demonstrations of unity, they affirmed at the same time the very existence of these regions. Thus we have the ambiguity in the words. *Federal, federative*, applied to the State, continued to designate a decentralized organization. "We believed that there was a design formed to make a federative Republic," declared Robespierre, in opposition to the Girondins on September 25, 1792.[42] Soon this meaning prevailed and gradually expressed the predominance of the idea of division over that of unity. From May 1793 on, federalism, accused of separatism, was combatted with as much violence as the counterrevolutionary insurrection in the Vendée or foreign invasion. Still it is a question of specifying its exact nature: was federalism in the circumstances of the revolutionary crisis of the summer of 1793 simple regionalism or real separatism? Two problems are posed: the more general one of Girondist federalism, and the more diverse one of federalist insurrections.

The so-called Girondist federalism was in fact only a "departmentalism," excessive at times, but with no idea of real dismemberment.[43] The texts coming from the Girondists in 1792-1793 did not include any plan to form a state of the American type. We find no program for federalism in the minutes of the meetings of the Girondist commissions created in the departments after May 31, 1793, such as those of Calvados, Gironde or Gard.[44] The text of the oath taken by the popular commission of public safety of the Gironde is characteristic in this regard: "To wage eternal war on tyrants, traitors and anarchists, to maintain liberty and equality, unity and indivisibility of the Republic, and to use the powers confided in it only to reestablish the respect due to the sovereignty."[45]

Without being federalists, properly speaking, the Girondists were ardent partisans of a policy of decentralization, although neither they nor their leaders had any nostalgia for the ancient provinces. Of the Girondist group, seventeen had been deputies to the Estates-General and had participated in the work of the Constituent Assembly; none had defended the privileges of the former *pays d'états* or advocated autonomy for the former provinces; for example, not one put forward the plan to group together the Breton, Normand or Languedoc departments to reconstitute the ancient provinces of Brittany, Normandy or Languedoc. The Girondist demand for decentralization was set on the departmental level: the departmental administrations must have a certain independence in relation to the central power and retain real powers. Significant in this respect is the *Critical Examination of the 1793 Constitution* by Salle, deputy from Meurthe.[46] He reproached the Constitution for taking away from the departments numerous powers that the Constitution of 1791 had granted them and that the Condorcet proposal had respected, in order to concentrate all powers centrally in Paris. "The constitution must allocate the details of interior administration to the administrative bodies of the departments, leaving to the center only supervision."

The Girondists' desire for decentralization was crystallized in their hatred of Paris. The popular commission of public safety of the Gironde declared on July 1, 1793 that "liberty was born in Romans and not in Paris."[47] (An allusion to the birth of the federations movement at Romans-sur-Isère in Dauphiné.) The Bouches-du-Rhône department echoed the statement of the Gironde department.[48] The departmental council of Pyrénée-Orientales was even more violent. "Does this city that prides itself for giving birth to liberty assume today to put the French nation in chains and to put itself in the place of the despot who no longer lives?... No, Paris will not make the law for the French universe."[49] Condorcet, in an appeal to the French citizens in July of 1793, accused the Montagnards of wanting to "favor Paris with an outrageous advantage over the other cities of the Republic by setting the capital as the site of the sessions of the Legislature."[50]

Distrust of the central power was expressed again by even sharper attacks on those representatives on assignment to the departments: "cowardly despots endowed with unlimited powers, who dare to establish an atrocious dictatorship in the departments."[51] According to the Girondist popular society of Nimes, "these proconsuls have done the greatest harm to the Republic."[52]

The social content of Girondist "departmentalism" is not in doubt. It was an avowed mixture: denunciation of "anarchy" and "horror of Maratism"; reaction of the *notables* of property and money against the democratic evolution of the Revolution and the beginnings of popular power in Paris. In the end, Girondist federalism was the act of the bourgeoisie in control of the departmental administrations, worried about property. It received the support of all the partisans of the Ancien Régime, but the town councils, recruited more from the people, were generally hostile to it. In the departments that the Girondists stirred to revolt against the Convention, the troops under their command encountered indifference or hostility: allowing for some exceptions, the men of the people were loath to fight for the rich.

The federalist insurrections of the summer of 1793 varied according to the intermingling of regional particularities, political factors, social motivations and historical traditions. If a Girondist "departmentalism" existed, on the other hand there was not, despite several attempts at coordination, any common platform for the various insurrectional movements. Reactions to the Paris uprisings of May 31–June 2, 1793 varied according to region. Situations that were initially connected eventually evolved in different directions.

A general observation must, however, be made: the federalist insurrections affected the towns much more than the countryside, thus dissociating themselves from the Vendee insurrection and the Chouannerie [royalist insurrections in western France]. This characteristic is particularly clear in the southern departments, from Bordeaux to Marseilles and Toulon. Here we are faced with the problem of the influence of federalist propaganda on the propertied strata of the countryside. There is no doubt about their anti-Jacobin state of mind. Already aroused by the fear of agrarian reform, "a phantom created by rascals to terrify imbeciles," as Robespierre told the Convention on April 24, 1793, this state of mind was reinforced by the May 4 decree setting a departmental maximum on grains and flour, and even more by that of June 10 authorizing the sharing of communal lands among the heads of families. But to what extent was this anti-Jacobin state of mind counterbalanced by the proclamation of the freedom of property and economy in the Declaration of Rights adopted as a preamble to the Constitution on June 24,[53] and even more by the decree of July 17, 1793 abolishing without compensation seigniorial taxes and feudal rights? Our first impression is that the efforts of the federalists to create a united front of the propertied classes in the towns and the countryside did not have much success. Federalism appears as essentially the act of the urban bourgeoisie.[54]

The full extent of the federalist insurrection in the departments of Brittany is still unknown.[55] After the strong unitarian upsurge of the federations in Brittany, after the part played by federated Bretons in the Parisian insurrection of August 10, 1792, which made it a day of national importance, wouldn't the federalist attempt be seen as the resurgence of a particularist current against which, until the end, the administration of the Ancien Régime had worn itself out and of which the local bourgeoisie had now taken charge? This is the angle insisted upon by Sevestre in particular, the representative on assignment in the five departments of what was formerly Brittany.[56] The "Central Committee of deputies" formed in Rennes on June 10, 1793, brought together the delegates of the departmental administrations, and those of certain towns and districts: essentially the departmental "notables," most often lawyers. For Sevestre, himself a former commissioner to the Estates of Brittainy, these unfaithful administrators were walking "in the path of the former parlements." The reality seems more complex: if the framework remained similar, the content was nonetheless different.

In fact, if, at the occasion of the mobilization of the Breton departments against the days of uprising in Paris of May 31 and June 2, the provincial framework was vital and if Rennes spontaneously rediscovered its function as regional political capital, it was not so much as the seat of the former Estates of Brittany, but as the home of that patriotism it had nourished from November 1788 until the establishment of the new administrations in March 1790: a prestigious patriotic past that had made Rennes the center of the surge of Breton federations. Rennes was therefore the capital of federalism, but in the sense of 1790; that is, the passionate refusal of the ancient provincial structures that the privileged insisted on defending. The counterrevolutionary pressure in the flatlands contributed to maintaining the patriotic tradition of the first years of the Revolution. If the Commune in Paris was denounced and the "anarchistic" danger feared, the counterrevolution was no less welcome; the struggle unfolded on two fronts. This gave rise to the concern of the Rennes authorities to "push away all suspicion of federalism, all suspicion of wanting to be isolated from the rest of the Republic."[57]

Breton separatism nevertheless certainly existed in June 1793, but as the essential theme of the counterrevolution. Since 1789, the Breton aristocracy denounced in violent and frenzied lampoons the institutional levelling in the decrees of the night of August 4 [abolishing feudal rights] and exhorted Bretons to return to the contract of Duchess Anne.[58] They insisted that it was necessary to refuse integration with the French nation and thus to refuse the personal taxes levied. It would be important to know to what extent this propaganda effectively influenced the peasants who gathered together in March 1793 against the Convention. Without a doubt they also wished to recover the fiscal privileges of the former province, defended by the Breton nobility, and to return to the status of the Ancien Régime, at least in their relations to the central power.

Separatism was thus not the act of departmental authorities embarked on a federalist adventure; rather they were grappling with a counterrevolution that covered itself in a flag of provincial particularism. The failure of federalism here appears to be closely linked to the counterrevolutionary pressure on the local authorities. These latter were no less hostile to the Parisian sans-culotterie and what they symbolized socially and politically. Thus the position of Breton federalism is clarified: a center, facing two extremes, that refused to deny the principles of '89.

The driving force was nonetheless hostility to the Parisian sans-culotterie on the part of the lawyers—jurists strongly attached to an elitist conception of society and to the constitutional principle. For them, the sans-culotterie represented only a dangerous class without any political ability—victims of brutal urges or manipulated by demagogues. This was the mentality of the moderates, the "notables," the Thermidorians, transformed into supporters of the Directory, then of Napoleon's coup d'état. On one side we have the bourgeois moderates, on the other the Parisian sans-culotterie. Breton federalism would be, in the last analysis, dissociated from truly particularist movements linked to the survival of a bygone past; it appears essentially to be the result of the clash of different social structures.

Sevestre finally comes around to this interpretation in his report to the Convention on August 26, 1793. Abandoning the accusation of federalism, properly speaking, he underscores the incurable moderantism of the Rennes authorities: "these moderates, 100 times more dangerous in this land than confirmed aristocrats."[59]

The case of Lyons illustrates the social content of federalism, obviously in the specific context of that city: "Lyons, unique and exemplary."[60]

This is not the place to reexamine the social components of manufacturing in Lyons, except to recall the long-term antagonisms that set master-workers, journeymen and apprentices against the merchant-manufacturers. Even if the structures remained essentially artisan in their form, their spirit and economic reality were going in another direction. While the master-workers were seeking recognition for an intermediate status of master-merchant that would be composed of independent artisans selling their products, in the course of the 18th century they went from disappointment to failure, gradually being driven back toward the journeymen.[61] The ties of merchant wealth to nobiliary fortune were numerous, the origins of the Lyons nobility being both recent and modest, and entry into the nobility did not mean a break with the commercial milieu nor completely abandoning merchant activities. Impervious to the Enlightenment, generally thought of as "the real aristocracy, the ruling class,"[62] the merchant bourgeoisie of Lyons appeared at the end of the Ancien Régime much more as "the class of enslavement" than the class "of emancipation." "The Revolution in its bourgeois form," writes M. Garden, "could not bring real solutions to the most important problems posed in the 18th century."[63]

The events of 1789 reinforced the power that the oligarchy of Lyons already held and exercised with an obvious concern for conservatism. But at the same time, the initiative was passing more and more to the popular strata, tending to assure them of political hegemony. The very conservative author of *The Enfranchised Commune* in 1789 contrasts "the open joy, the exaltation of the middle class who offered nothing seditious" to "the threatening, even outrageous, attitude of the workshops (that revealed) more hatred than could have been seen up to now in the struggle between the worker and the merchant."[64] In fact, from July 1, 1789 on, the bourgeois consular powers mobilized decent folk against "the brigands that are infesting the city."[65]

We could not show here, even briefly, the events which gave a certain rhythm to the Revolution at Lyons. Let us remember that serious social unrest occurred in June–July 1789, followed by episodes on February 7, 1790 and July 19 and 26 of bourgeois "notables" confronting popular masses. The high cost of living and unemployment stimulated the class conflicts and agitation that started up again in the spring of 1792. L'Ange published his *Simple and Easy Ways to Set Up Abundance and a Fair Price for Bread* on June 9, 1792.[66] Finally the "Jacobin" city council of Chalier was carried to power by the sans-culottes of Lyons during the February days of uprising (1793). On May 29, it was the popular sections that defended the city hall against the federalist attack inspired by the merchant bourgeoisie; the political geography of the sections matched up with the social geography of the city. The social content of this so-called federalist insurrection is emphasized by the authors of the *History of Lyons* edited by Kleinclauz. "Behind a Vitet who will hold his bench on the right side of the Convention, behind the *rolandin* [Girondist] bourgeois who had no interest in the subversion of the social edifice, suddenly loomed up the men of the Central Club (the "Chaliers"), turbulent, fanatic, full of hatred, who get drunk on their incoherent and brutal language and want to play a leading role despite the poverty of their minds, and try to substitute class struggle for the struggle of political parties." The conclusion is pertinent to our study: "It became inevitable at Lyons, city of commerce and industry, that poverty would rise up against fortune, the wage-earners against the employers."[67]

The Lyons bourgeoisie had been all the more quickly overtaken for having so slowly advanced along the revolutionary path; integrated into the ancient system of production and exchange, they had not been led to break the social and political framework. The workers, on the other hand, who were supporting the whole weight of the old system, had the advantage of a social consciousness enlivened by practice, already tested in the struggle for wages, with recourse to strikes and violent action; this very quickly gave them the means to accede to an autonomous revolutionary practice. Against the "Jacobin" city council, the employers and wealthy were assured, therefore, of the support of the moderate forces of the department and succeeded, with the help of the royalists, in provoking the insurrection; the anti-Parisian, federalist mask could not hide the social realities. But, having lost the strength to maintain exclusive political domination, having looked for allies with whom to share power, the Lyons bourgeoisie was finally forced by the circumstances to completely surrender it; the leadership of the insurrection passed into the hands of the royalists.[69]

At Lyons as in Rennes, the federalist movement of 1793 was thus defined by its social content as much as by its political aspects. Certainly it was an anti-Parisian movement, departmentalist and decentralizing, but just as much a defense movement of the propertied classes against the threat of the popular masses. "Your property is threatened," hurled the

Girondist, Pétion, in his *Letter to the Parisians* at the end of April 1793, "and you close your eyes to this danger."[70] The provincial bourgeoisie saw the danger and was strong enough, in many departments, to try to prevent it, with the various forms of the federalist movement corresponding to the diversity of the regional structures. Was the federalism of 1793 a regionalism? Yes, certainly. More exactly, federalism was the political form that cloaked the defensive reaction of "those who have (against) those who don't," to quote Pétion again, in the specific circumstances of the social and political struggles of 1793.

III

This analysis of concrete historical cases of the problem of regionalism at the end of the Ancien Régime and during the Revolution cannot stand without arousing some methodological reflections. Theory is not "a morbid fortress" as some have claimed.

It is the case with regionalism as with any other problem that the study of concrete historical cases, with their diverse forms and particularities, requires a common interpretation and thus an explanatory schema that would be both coherent and complete; that is, not leaving out any aspect of historical reality. It would also be dynamic, as no structure is eternal (there is no such thing as "immobile history").

The common characteristics of the various concrete cases presented here both require and allow a schema capable of characterizing and explaining regional occurrences. We don't intend to refer to any *model*, an artificial construction, theoretical and abstract; but, by using a comparative method, we intend to grasp the essential traits and the fundamental process, over and above the regional diversities and the unevenness of the rhythms of development. Thus we will be able to move beyond the disquieting hesitation of historical research and political thought when faced with the "region" phenomenon and the problem of regionalism.

From its first appearance, the regional question has covered many aspects, varying according to historical tradition and political context, and the social category formulated. This gives rise to extreme diversity. In the course of history, regional sentiment has been combined sometimes with a concern for social conservatism, sometimes with a revolutionary exigency; within the same province, the same region, social antagonisms often brought about more or less contradictory variations. This is a general problem, but one that varies according to economic development, social evolution and historical tradition. Thus we have various criteria, but none of them taken in isolation would allow us to define a region. The use of the

Gascon language, however sharply distinguished from that of Provençal French, not to mention Basque, was not sufficient, in the absence of geographical, historical, administrative and economic unity, to make Gascony a province. Conversely, at the end of the Ancien Régime, Roussillon asserted itself as a province that was not integrated into the realm. Everything converged there. Certainly there was geographical diversity but it was clearly demarcated and strongly fused together by a real human unity founded on a common language, the historical past and particular institutions. This unity was further strengthened by the consciousness of an economic situation critical by comparison with neighboring Catalonia.

The traditional concept of the origin of regional community sentiment gives greater importance to the historical past on the one hand; on the other, to those "stable" structures of land, race and language. Looking again at the Roussillon example, there did exist a Catalan land, *nostra terra*, a Catalan temperament, a linguistic community, and a long common historical past. All these factors need further discussion.

Without a doubt, geographic and human criteria play a role in the constitution of provincial or regional groups. But although they are necessary foundations, they are in no way sufficient. Geographical diversity did not prevent Roussillon from constituting itself as a province, while it broke Gascony up into multiple *pays*. As for temperament, how do we assess it? P. Vilar recalls that the Spanish for Catalan is "man from the North," an incarnation of market egoism, whereas for a French geographer, he is "a peasant from the South, exuberant and generous".[71]

The linguistic criterion also adds to the problem. The unity of language could not make a province of the various Gascon *pays*. Language nevertheless constitutes one of the principal factors of the affective crystallization of regional sentiment. Even more, when the written language taught in the schools is not the language learned at home, the official language is marked as foreign. Speaking Catalan, the inhabitants of Roussillon could preserve a group consciousness which in turn encouraged them to not abandon the use of Catalan. But the value of a language as a regional act is also measured by its social use. In this sense, a literary renewal is not able to have great linguistic significance on the level of a strengthened regional consciousness. The literary renaissance of Provençal in the 19th century was brilliant; nevertheless Mistral failed, for Félibrige could not bring the masses to the movement. Here social and political factors interfered and we must ask what political and social use is made of the regional language at each stage of the history of a region.

Beyond the criteria traditionally invoked, it seems necessary to clarify the relations between economic unities and regional unities. From the idealism of a Renan faced with the phenomenon of the "nation" to the oversimplification of the German historian of the *Zollverein*, would there not be a place for a median position, far from economism? In the case of Roussillon, the complementary nature of interests has been emphasized; the province or region was also affirmed by the voice of its merchants, by its corporate authorities. Paraphrasing the Marxist formula,[72] could we not propose that if the marketplace is not the first school, at least it is one of the schools where one learns regional particularism?

Finally there are the psychological factors that hard times make evident. It is significant that the way a province or region looks at itself is expressed in times of oppression or misfortune, when the group feels threatened and in danger. Would not regionalism also be the act of an unhappy consciousness? A clearer consciousness of the province appeared in the second half of the 18th century, when the crisis of the Ancien Régime was deepening, as it did in Provence. Again it would be necessary to take into account both the structural and circumstantial conditions which explain this clearer consciousness. Would not the region, like the nation, be a "fully conscious solidarity"?... It would be necessary, from this point of view, to establish a precise chronology of the occurrences of regionalism, of its sources and the works dedicated to it. There are strong times for regionalism and weak times, drowsiness and rebirth, a whole range of nuances that it is essential to date. It is not without significance, for purposes of comparison, that Renan and Jullian wrote on the "nation" in the France wounded after 1870. We could thus establish the curve of regionalism from the 18th to the 20th century, with its dips when the consciousness of the group seems to have disappeared and its peaks when a need for local autonomy, sometimes sovereignty, is expressed; each stage indicated would thus correspond to a certain stage of development of the material and spiritual forces of the region.

Thus geographical and historical, linguistic and institutional, economic and psychological factors are all linked up to define the region. That being the case, paraphrasing the definition of the concept "nation" given in 1913 by a classical text forgotten today—I mean the Stalinist theory of the nation,[73] the recall of which, I hope, will not be considered out of place—couldn't we define the region as "a stable community, historically composed of a language, a territory, an economic life and a psychological formation, finding expression in a community of culture"?

This attempt at a definition is not without difficulties. The region is, of course, a phenomenon of long duration, a stable structure where material solidarities and linguistic and cultural permanency are expressed in a certain geographical framework. But isn't the region also a historical category, most certainly plunging into a faraway past, but affirming itself with a strengthened consciousness at the end of the Ancien Régime, and linked to the movement of contemporary history? Again it is necessary to specify the social content of a historical category. The historical stability of the regional group, the more or less clear consciousness of community, constitute a framework and an instrument in the course of its evolution that various social classes successively have been able to use for their political ends. The regional question, like any other, serves various interests at various periods, takes on various nuances, all according to the class that poses it and the moment when it is posed. The avatars of particularism in southern France are in this regard enlightening, from Félibrige in the 19th century to contemporary Provençal literature. There was a bourgeois regionalism, of an often aggressive conservatism; there is a popular regionalism, a defensive reflex, occasionally transforming itself into a social and political protest movement.

The problem of regionalism is thus clarified as a problem of the relations of the "region" occurrence with the underlying social structure, and with the historical circumstances that determine it. Region, regionalism—these notions are not defined once and for all. At each stage of the movement of history, they, like the nation, are affirming themselves under a mask which may appear immutable, in new social realities constantly in motion.

13

From the Ancien Régime to the Empire: The National Problem and Social Realities[1]

The French Revolution filled certain words with the breath of its inspiration. *Nation* was one of those. At Valmy when an enemy cannonade threatened to shatter the French ranks, Kellerman, on his feet, sword in hand, called out to the astonished Prussians: "Vive la Nation!" The revolutionary word echoed from rank to rank; under fire from the most highly regarded troops in Europe, not a man budged. Goethe witnessed the scene. His words, as reported by Eckermann, are engraved on the Valmy monument: "On this day and at this place begins a new era in world history."

From 1789 on the word was charged with a new value clarified in the passionate surges of the heart, in the spontaneous collective movements animated by feelings of faith and hope. The nation—this was the entire body, the mass of citizens fused into a single block; there were no more orders, no more classes; all who are French make up the nation. This key word resounded in the depths of the collective soul, liberated latent strength, raised men up from their former state, guided them or led them astray.

But what was the reality beneath the emotional outburst of the word? *Nation*—wouldn't that be one of those "illusion words" discussed by the author of the *History of the French Language*?[2]

I

The idea of "nation" was clarified in the course of the 18th century with the spread of the enlightenment and the advance of the bourgeoisie. In 1754 d'Argenson noted in his *Journal* that the word was in fashion: "We observe that never have the words *nation* and *state* been repeated as much as they are today: these two nouns were never pronounced under Louis XIV and people didn't even have a notion of them."[3]

Doubtless there is some exaggeration in d'Argenson's claim that the words *nation* and *state* were never spoken under Louis XIV. The word *nation* appears in the 1694 *Dictionary* of the Academy where it is given a definition based on the unity of government, administration and language: a nation is made up of "all the inhabitants of the same State, of the same land who live under the same laws and use the same language." With its particular insistence on governmental and administrative unity, this definition appears in harmony with the political state of France under Louis XIV and in a certain sense conveys the progress of the absolute monarchy towards bureaucratization and centralization. Here we should stress how closely the idea of nation is still associated with that of State.

The 1740 and 1762 editions of the *Dictionary* of the Academy reproduce the 1694 definition. Furetière, in his *Dictionary* published in 1690, before that of the Academy, while noting the political factor, had insisted on geography but omitted language: *nation*,"said of a great people living in a certain expanse of land, enclosed by certain borders or even under a single rule." Trevoux's *Dictionary* of 1771 reproduces Furetière's definition, and the *Encyclopedia* in 1765, the year when the last ten volumes were published, used a similar definition: *nation*, "collective word used to express a considerable number of people, who live in a certain expanse of land, enclosed by certain borders, and obey the same government."

While the definition of nation was limited even in the second half of the 18th century to the idea of geographical unity and a common government, the closely connected idea of *patrie* (homeland)—defined by the *Littré* dictionary of 1876 as the nation to which one belongs—began to take on new meaning. In Chapter X of his *Characters* (1688), entitled "Of the sovereign and the Republic," La Bruyère writes, "There is a *patrie* under despotism; other things take its place, interest, glory, service to the prince." And again, in the same chapter, "how would I be served, how would all the people... how would my *patrie* be powerful and great, if, sad and worried, I was living in oppression?" Thus the two ideas of homeland and liberty already appear linked together at the end of the 17th century.

The English example soon illustrates La Bruyère's affirmation that "there is no *patrie* under despotism." This was one of the themes frequently discussed by Enlightenment philosophy. Voltaire and Rouseau agreed on this point and Jaucourt followed their reasoning in the article *patrie* in the *Encyclopedia*: "There is no *patrie* under the yoke of despotism," he wrote paraphrasing La Bruyère. The idea was enriched, however, for Jaucourt added the notion of happiness to that of liberty. "Those who live under oriental despotism have no homeland and do not even know the word that is the true expression of happiness." D'Holbach is even more assertive when he writes in his *Ethocracy or Government founded on Morality* (1776): "True patriotism can only be found in lands where the citizens, free and governed by equitable laws, feel happy."[4]

Near the end of the Ancien Régime, the social and political movement further contributed to the development of the idea of homeland when national sovereignty became one of its components. "Whatever one may say about it," we read in the article *patrie* in the *Methodical Encyclopedia* of Panckoucke which began to appear in 1782, "true patriotism cannot arise under a monarchy unless citizens are accorded the right to share a part of the sovereign authority."

At the same time that the ideas of *nation* and *patrie* were being enriched by a new political content, their social sense was being clarified by the evolution of the economy and the society. If the nation remained divided territorially and socially, if variations in weights and measures as well internal customs barriers hindered the formation of a national market, progress in language, culture and enlightenment, as well as material progress, multiplied the ties that bound the people together. But the words had different connotations in different social categories.

In his *History of the French Language*, Ferdinand Brunot stresses the significance of the appearance of the adjective *national* in connection with economic problems.[5] The physiocrats were the first to use this word. In the texts of Quesnay it is a question of "national consumption" and "national traders." In his *Element of Commerce* (1766), Veron de Forbonnais speaks of "national supply" and Mercier de la Rivière, in his *Natural and Essential Order of Political Societies* (1767), writes about "national agents" of commerce. The use of this word soon became widespread. In his treatise *On the Legislation and Commerce of Grains* (1775), Necker uses the expressions "national prosperity," "national industry," "national work" and "national population." The development of production and the problems it posed, the growing importance of promoters of technical progress and economic leaders in the nation gave the words a new meaning. "One is a patriot," writes Ferdinand Brunot, "when dying for France, but also when sowing turnips. M. de Chamey raises fowl and mullets along with bread. Parmentier considers him to be *animated with patriotic zeal*."[6] The connection of the ideas of nation and homeland with productive activity was thus affirmed.

This connection merely conveyed on a certain plane the profound conviction of the bourgeoisie that property owners alone belonged to the nation, for only they had homeland. "What therefore is the homeland?" asks Voltaire in his *Questions on the Encyclopedia* (1771). "Wouldn't it be by chance a good field, about which the owner, lodged comfortably in a well-kept house, would be able to say: 'this field that I cultivate, this house that I built, are mine; I live here under the protection of laws that no tyrant can break. With those who own, as I do, fields and houses assembled for their common interests, I have my voice in this assembly; I am a part of the whole, a part of the community, a part of the sovereignty: there is my *patrie*.'" Introducing a young baker's assistant to the scene, who gives himself airs of loving his homeland without owning anything, Voltaire concludes that "in a country of some area there were often several million men who did not have a homeland."[7] The proletariat has no *patrie*, it will be said in the following century.

Considering the homeland and related political rights as a function of property, Voltaire excluded not only the popular classes but also the aristocracy. "Where was the homeland of the Duke of Guise, the scarred one?" he continues. "Was it at Nancy, Paris, Madrid, Rome? What homeland did you have, cardinals of La Balue, Duprat, Lorraine, Mazarin?" It was of these individuals that Voltaire wrote a few lines farther that "the homeland is everywhere where one feels confortable."

Certainly we should try to clarify here the idea that the excluded classes had of the homeland. Yet the texts on the development of this concept among the popular classes necessarily contain some gaps. As for the aristocracy, there is no doubt about their sentiments. "A gallant man," according to Abbot Coyer in his *Dissertation on the Word "patrie"* (1782), "will not write the word *patrie*. It would be even worse if he spoke it." "Patriot," writes the Prince of Ligne to Joseph II in 1788, "an honorable word which is beginning to become odious."[8] The aristocracy excluded itself from the nation, opposing nationalism to the cosmopolitanism, mental disposition and social behavior that made it a class able to find a homeland elsewhere as well as in their own country. "*Nationalism* took the place of love in general," Abbot Barruel wrote in his *Memoirs Serving as a History of Jacobinism* (1798). "Thus it was permissible to scorn foreigners, to deceive them and offend them. This virtue was called patriotism... And that being the case, why not give this virtue even narrower limits? Thus we saw *patriotism* give birth to *localism*, clannishness and finally egoism."[9]

On the eve of the Revolution, the idea of *nation* moved along with the rapid expansion of the bourgeoisie but was slowed down by the persistence of feudal structures in the economy, society and the State, and by the resistance of the aristocracy. National unity remained imperfect.

The development of the economy and the formation of a national market were hampered by the interior customs and tollgates, by the multiplicity of weights and measures, by the diversity and incoherence of the fiscal system, and just as much by the persistence of seigniorial rights and ecclesiastical tithes. There was the same absence of unity in the society. The social hierarchy was founded on privilege, not only that of the nobility and clergy, but also those of the multiple "corps" and communities that divided the nation, each one possessing their "franchises," their "liberties," in a word, their privileges. Inequality was the rule and from one body to another, as Cournot wrote, there was a "cascade of contempts"; the division was accentuated by "corporative" mentality. In his *Picture of Paris* (1781), Sébastien Mercier devotes a chapter to the *Egoism of the Corps*. "The corps [trade associations] have become opinionated, stubborn, and claim to be isolated though they have ties to the political machine: today every association feels only the injustice done to one of its members, and regards the oppression of the citizen who is not of its class as foreign to its interests."[10]

The structure of the State, as of society, constituted a negation of national unity. The historical mission of the Capetians was to give administrative unity to the State they had established by gathering together the French provinces around their domain, a factor as favorable to the awakening of national consciousness as to the exercise of royal power. In fact, the work remained uncompleted and the nation separated from the State, as the monarch himself admitted: "In a moment when," Louis XVI said on October 4, 1789, "we invite the nation to come to the aid of the State."[11] The organization of the State had scarcely been improved in the course of the 18th century, Louis XVI governing and administering with almost the same institutions as his grandfather, Louis XIV. The attempts at structural reform, whether undertaken by Machault, Maupeou, or Turgot, had failed in the face of the resistance of an aristocracy solidly planted in its institutions—the Parlements, the provincial Estates and the Assembly of the clergy. The realm was still divided into "pays d'états" [important regional divisions] and "pays d'élections" [lower regional subdivisions]. The multiple administrative, fiscal, judicial and religious districts overlapped each other in an indescribable chaos. The law was not unified, as it was Roman in the South and customary in the North, without mentioning the canon law according to which Church officials judged. Like the subjects, provinces and towns had their franchises and privileges, ramparts against royal absolutism, but also fortresses of an obstinate particularism.

In fact, the failure of the absolute monarchy to achieve national unity cannot be dissociated from the persistence of an aristocratic social structure, the very negation of national unity. To complete the monarchial work of national unification would have meant to question the structure of the society and therefore privilege. It was an insoluble contradiction, for

Louis XVI would never resolve himself to abandoning *his faithful nobility*. Even if he had wanted to, he would have collided against the obstinate resistance of the aristocracy. The aristocratic reaction that marked the end of the Ancien Régime, by making reform of the State and the society impossible, prevented the accomplishment of national unity. The persistence and even the intensification of the aristocracy's feudal and military mentality again contributed to excluding most of the nobles from the nation, tying them instead to the person of the king. Incapable of adapting, rigid in their prejudices, often living as needy country squires rather than lose rank and title, most nobles were isolated in a congealed exclusivism, while within the framework of outmoded institutions, the new order was already being affirmed. "If one finally considers," writes Alexis de Tocqueville, "that this nobility was entirely isolated in the middle of the nation, separated from the middle classes [the bourgeoisie] it had pushed away from its breast, and from the people whose heart it had let escape, and appearing to be at the head of an army that was in reality an officers' corps without soldiers, one will finally understand how it could be overturned in the space of a single night after having stood tall for a million years."[12]

Although national unity had been checked by the aristocratic reaction, certain progress was made nonetheless in the second half of the 18th century by the development of the network of royal highways and of economic relations, by the attraction of capital—"France," writes Tocqueville, "was already, of all the countries of Europe, the one where capital had acquired the most ascendancy over the provinces and best absorbed the whole empire"[13]—and by intellectual progress. The diffusion of Enlightenment philosophy and the education offered by the colleges incontestably constituted factors of unification. But underscoring these features underscores the development of the bourgeoisie, who had become the essential social factor for national unity, and began to identify itself with the nation. "Who then would dare to say that the Third Estate does not have in itself all that is necessary to form a complete nation?" writes Sieyes in his famous brochure. He makes it clear that the aristocracy would not know how to take part in the nation. "If the privileged order were removed, the nation would not be anything less, but something more... It is not enough to have shown that the privileged, far from being useful to the nation, only weaken it and harm it; it is still necessary to prove that the noble order does not enter into the social organization; that it could well be a burden for the nation, yet it doesn't know how to take part in it." Sieyes legitimizes his exclusion of the nobility through their economic and social parasitism. They "[place] their glory in remaining immobile in the middle of general movement and [consume] the best part of the product, without having in any way helped to produce it. The idleness of such a class is assuredly foreign to the nation."[14]

Thus through multiple contradictions and social antagonisms, the idea of nation was clarified in the France of the dying Ancien Régime. *Nation* took form and life in the social category that was intellectually the most mature and economically the most advanced. It is the spectacle of this France, at once one and divided, that allowed Tocqueville to write two antithetical chapters: "That France was the country where men had become the most like each other"—"How men so similar were more separated than they had even been."[15] These men "were all ready to merge together in the same mass," Tocqueville nevertheless emphasized. The Revolution was in effect going to resolve these contradictions. But by giving the rights of the nation only to property owners, by quickly identifying *patrie* and property, it would create new ones.

II

In 1789 the national question constituted only one aspect of the general problem: the revolutionary transformation of the Ancien Régime. It would not be able to dissociate in particular from the social movements and conflicts while it evolved to the same rhythm and bore their mark. The bourgeoisie called the shots. But what content did it give to the nation it was liberating and organizing? Would unity be accomplished by a compromise with the aristocracy, following the English example? Just as the aristocratic reaction had made any reform of the monarchy impossible, so its stubborn refusal of any concession in 1789 and later made all compromise solutions impossible, however sought after by certain sectors of the bourgeoisie. Indeed the aristocracy excluded itself from the nation that, as it was defined through the work of the Constituent Assembly, became a bourgeois nation.

The multiple contradictions that quickly undermined the new edifice had been expressed even before the meeting of the Estates General; the registers of grievances show them clearly. The aristocracy and the bourgeoisie were indeed in agreement about substituting the reign of law—discussed and voted on by the representatives of the nation—for royal absolutism. But this feeling of national unity was to a certain extent counterbalanced by the criticism of unitary centralization and the demand for communal and provincial autonomy. What is more, class conflict was manifested in the opposition of the three Estates. If the aristocracy accepted—not without reservation—fiscal equality, it rejected social unity by expressly demanding the preservation of orders, honorific privileges and seigniorial rights, holding on to the vote by order, a guarantee of its prerogatives. By demanding equal legal rights, the Third Estate, on the other hand, expressed its support of national unity.

For the popular classes, compiling the registers of grievances and the meeting of the Estates General was the occasion for an awakening of national consciousness. Georges Lefebvre has emphasized the essential traits of the popular mentality in 1789. The convocation of the Estates profoundly moved the people who hoped for an improvement in their condition and a rebirth of the nation. It was, according to Lefebvre, the "good news" and the "great hope." To the extent that the bourgeoisie shared that hope, the unity of the Third Estate and thus the nation was strengthened. And even more so to the extent that the whole of the Third Estate—bourgeoisie, artisans and peasants—believed in the "aristocratic plot." The conflict of the Estates, the obstinacy of the aristocracy in defending its privileges, the collusion with foreign powers admitted from the beginning and the fear of invasion felt from July 1789 on, the shortages finally described as "artificial" as a consequence of the inability to analyze the economic circumstances—all these occurrences gave form and life to the idea of an "aristocratic plot" in the collective mentality. The solidarity of the Third Estate was thus strengthened and among the people the consciousness of national unity was awakened.

What followed demonstrated the anti-aristocratic class content of this new consciousness. The belief in the aristocratic plot engendered a defensive reaction. Even before the events following the dismissal of Necker—made public in Paris on July 12, 1789—the Parisian electors had proposed to the Assembly the formation of a *bourgeois* militia described as *national*; throughout these tumultuous days, the password for the watch was, "Are you with the nation?" This defensive reaction toward the aristocracy was finally transformed into punitive determination: it was not only a question of reducing the aristocratic plot to impotency, but also of punishing the enemies of the nation, guilty of the crime of *lèse-nation* [like lèse-majesté, a crime against the sovereign]. This nationalist variation appeared at that time.[16] From July of 1789 to September of 1792, the popular massacres appear to be a national defensive reflex, in the same way as the enlistment of volunteers and the mass conscription. It cannot be denied that the Terror exhibited this same characteristic, as did the law of June 10, 1794.[17] [This law deprived suspects of the right to a trial.] From 1789 to 1794, the defensive reaction to the aristocracy and the determination to punish it had as a goal averting national peril by eliminating elements that could not be socially assimilated by the emerging nation. By emigrating, the aristocracy provided a justification for popular behavior from July 14 on; the nobles excluded themselves from the nation, proving that for them, class consciousness prevailed over national sentiment.

We cannot deny however that national unity, as it was expressed from 1789 on in the struggles of the Third Estate against the aristocracy, poorly masked the social oppositions in the very heart of the Third Estate. The bourgeoisie and popular classes could not give the same social content to the "great hope." The contradictory duality of the economic structures of the Ancien Régime opposed industrial enterprise of the new type to the traditional shop and workshop. If the capitalist bourgeoisie was demanding economic freedom, the popular classes remained supporters of regulation and controls and were demonstrating an anti-capitalist mentality. The economic crisis that appeared with the disastrous harvest of 1788, crowning the phase of "decline" that had begun ten years earlier, constituted an element of dissociation for the Third Estate, unfavorable to the formation of a unitary national consciousness. Although freedom of commerce and exportation of grain decreed in 1787 by Brienne (Necker was going to revoke it) led to progress in production, these measures seemed to profit the owners, the bourgeoisie, at the expense of the people. The people were already denouncing the feudal lord and the collectors of the tithe, accused of hoarding; now they put the blame on the grain merchant, the millers, and soon the bakers. The solidarity of the Third Estate was threatened. Throughout the Revolution the question of food distribution had profound repercussions—free trade or a controlled economy? freedom to profit or a right to survive?—that certainly affected the thinking of the various social categories about the nation. In the year II, the Parisian sans-culotterie claimed the right to survive, the recognition and application of which would permit them to be integrated into the nation on a equal basis. Hébert, however, during the popular upsurge which ended with the uprising of September 4 and 5, 1793, wrote in his *Père Duchesne*: "The homeland, f..., the merchants don't have one."[18]

Factors of dissociation, factors of unity, which one prevailed? Would the people have their place in the nation that the constituent bourgeoisie was organizing from 1789 to 1791?

By erecting the new nation on the narrow base of the propertied bourgeoisie, the Constituent Assembly doomed its work to multiple contradictions. Forced to battle the irreconcilable aristocracy, but repulsing the impatient people, it condemned the bourgeois nation to instability and soon to war.

New economic ties, which could be only bourgeois ties, cemented the new unity. The national market was unified by the radical destruction of the feudal divisions, by the freedom of interior circulation finally rid of the tollgates and multiple controls required for the collection of the salt tax, the indirect taxes and the taxes on transported goods. Thus economic relations were consolidated between different parts of the country, asserting their solidarity. The nation was defined, however, in its relations to foreign countries by "pushing back the frontiers," which assimilated the "effectively foreign" provinces of Alsace and Lorraine to the rest of the country, by aligning customs borders with political borders; and also by the protection of national production against foreign competition (even though the tariff of 1791 had been only moderately protectionist). But at the same time that the constituent bourgeoisie was accomplishing this unification, it was dissociating the Third Estate by the liberation of the economy. The abolition of trade associations and guilds and manufacturing regulations could not but arouse the irritation of the master tradesmen, stripped of their monopoly. The freedom of commerce in grains, reinstated (except for export) in August of 1789, led to general hostility among the popular classes in the towns as well as the countryside, many peasants not harvesting enough grain to survive. The hostility was no less in the countryside against the freedom of cultivation; it was thus that the bourgeois concept of property was established in its full form, in opposition to the traditional communal concepts; the collective rights that guaranteed the survival of the impoverished peasantry seemed doomed. Wouldn't the disillusion of the masses, attached to regulation and the traditional economy, risk turning them against a homeland conceived within the narrow limits of the interests of one class?

The people were excluded from the homeland by the organization of political life along property lines.[19] It is true that by the theoretical proclamation of equality, by the suppression of the trade associations ["corps"] that split up the society of the Ancien Régime, by the assertion of an individualist conception of social relations, the Constituents were laying the basis of a nation where all would meet again; they were sure enough of themselves and their future to identify the interests of their class with those of the nation. But in placing the right of property in the ranks of natural inviolable rights, they injected into their creation a contradiction that they could not overcome. The upholding of slavery, and property qualifications for suffrage, fully exposed that contradiction. Men of color were not admitted to the nation; this applied not only to slaves whose liberation would have brought an end to colonial property and exploitation, but also to free men of color left to the good will of the colonists. The *passive* citizens [those who did not meet the property qualifications] were deprived of the right of suffrage and excluded from the *national* guard. Political rights were measured out in doses according to wealth; active citizens, especially petit bourgeois and members of the liberal professions, were kept out of elective office by property qualifications; even representatives had to possess some landed property. With three million passive citizens excluded, was the nation composed of four million and more *active* who formed the primary assemblies? Or was it concentrated in the some 50,000 *electors* of the electoral assemblies, properly speaking? "The Nation, the Law, the King": the famous formula that symbolizes the constitutional work of the Assembly, under the pretense of the principle of national sovereignty, could not preserve the illusion. The nation was confined to the limits of the propertied bourgeoisie.

The federation movement could no longer mask this profound social reality. The federations, which appeared from the end of 1789 (Valence dates from November 29) and which multiplied in 1790, illustrated the unitary direction of the patriots and demonstrated the adhesion of the nation to the new order. National unity found its solemn expression in Paris during the Federation of July 14, 1790, as Merlin de Douai was to affirm in regard to the affair of the German princes who owned land in Alsace. Seeking to extract the principles of a new international law, Merlin de Douai, on October 28, 1790, put forth the concept of the nation as a voluntary association as opposed to the dynastic State. "There is no other legitimate grounds of union between you and your brothers in Alsace than the social pact formed last year between all French people, ancient and modern, in this very Assembly." This was an allusion to the decision of the Third Estate on June 17, 1789, to proclaim itself the National Assembly and that of the Assembly on the following July 9 to declare itself a Constituent Assembly. Only one question *infinitely simple* was posed: that of knowing "if it is to these diplomatic parchments that the Alsatian people owe the advantage of being French... Of what importance to the people of Alsace, of what importance to the French people, are these conventions that, in the time of despotism, had the goal of uniting the first to the second? The Alsatian people united with the French people because they wanted to; it is thus their will alone and not the treaty of Munster that legitimizes the union."[20] Alsace demonstrated this will by its participation in the Federation of July 14, 1790.

Popular enthusiasm burst forth on that day, but it could not mask the true character of the demonstration. While the theory of the voluntary nation-association was taking shape in words, a different social reality was being declared by actions. The eminent role of La Fayette in the course of the Federation underscored its meaning. Idol of the bourgeoisie, the "hero of two worlds" [having participated in both the American and French Revolutions], he intended to rally the aristocracy to the Revolution; he was the man of the compromise. The national guard that he commanded was the bourgeois guard from which the "passives" were excluded. On April 27, 1791, Robespierre rose to speak against the bourgeois privilege to bear arms. "To be armed for his personal defense is the right of every man without distinction; to be armed for the defense of the homeland is the right of every citizen. Do those who are poor thus become foreigners, slaves?"[21] In reconsidering the circumstances of the formation of the bourgeois militia in July 1789, it becomes apparent that its role was to defend all property owners not only against the excesses of the royal power and its armies, but just as much against the threat of social categories judged to be dangerous.[22] "The establishment of the bourgeois militia," the Paris deputation declared to the National Assembly on the morning of July 14, "and the measures taken yesterday have secured a quiet night for the city... a number of (armed) persons have been steadfastly disarmed and brought back to order by the bourgeois militia." At the Federation of July 14, 1790, the people, assuredly enthusiastic, were less actors than spectators. If in the act of federation the guard represented the *national* armed force, it was in opposition to the army that was only the royal armed force. It was a new order in the bourgeois sense. The guard became truly national only when the people penetrated it in force after August 10, 1792.

At that date, the war and the resulting crisis of the Revolution had burst open the too narrow frames of the bourgeois nation.

The refusal of the aristocracy to recognize the new order and to become integrated into it, much more the development of the aristocratic plot and the appeal to foreign intervention, very quickly ruined the compromise politics of La Fayette. The national consciousness of the popular masses was taking shape at the same time that the crisis of the Revolution was developing.

The decomposition of the army after 1790 demonstrated the inability of the Constituent Assembly to give a national solution to the military problem. Once the social conflict had reached the army, already disorganized by the emigration, the position of the Constituents could not leave any doubt. When the garrison at Nancy revolted in August 1790, they decreed on the 16th that "the violation by armed troops of the decrees of the National Assembly and approved by the king being a crime of *lèse-nation* exceedingly,"[23] the rebels would be pursued as guilty of this crime. The Assembly remained prisoner of its contradictions. It knew well that the two problems of national defense and revolutionary defense were indissolubly linked. But how could the royal army be shielded from aristocratic influences without nationalizing it in the real sense of the word? That would really have carried the revolution along; the Constituents kept to half measures. Robespierre denounced the peril once again on June 10, 1791. "In the middle of the ruins of all the aristocracies, what is that power that alone still raises an audacious and threatening brow? You have destroyed the nobility and the nobility still lives at the head of the army."[24]

Nevertheless the national solution had been suggested by Dubois-Crancé on December 12, 1789, to the boos of the right and the embarrassed silence of the left. "We must have a truly national conscription that would include the second head of the empire and the last active citizen, and all the passive citizens," that is to say the whole nation, except the king. Dubois-Crancé therefore proposed at the end of 1789 universal and obligatory military service and the creation of a national army.[25] In the course of the debate, the Duke of La Rochefoucauld-Liancourt declared that it would be a hundred times better to live in Morocco or Constantinople than in a State where such laws would be in force. In the *amalgame* of 1793 [fusion of military units from different classes], we find again many of the characteristics of the national system proposed by Dubois-Crancé in 1789. But the Constituent Assembly was not prepared to follow this path. It hesitated. As the crisis built up, the Assembly ordered that 100,000 men be called into the national guard at the time of Varennes. Defying the regular army, refusing more than ever to confide in the people, the Assembly left the matter up to the nation, that is, the nation as defined by the Constitution, based on property qualifications. Events were to thwart the plans of the Constituents.

The flight of the king was a decisive element in the strengthening of national consciousness among the popular masses. It showed them the collusion of the monarchy with foreign powers and aroused an intense emotion throughout the country, even in the most remote rural areas. People feared an invasion, and fortifications spontaneously arose on the borders. This social and national reflex operated as it did in 1789. When at Varennes the hussars,* who were supposed to protect the flight of the king, came over to the people, it was to the cry of "Vive la Nation!" The defensive reaction erupted. In the evening on June 22, 1791, near Sainte-Menehould, the Count of Dampierre, a feudal lord of the region who had come to greet Louis XVI on his trip to the border, was massacred by peasants. During the Great Fear of June 1791, national fervor undoubtedly constituted a resource almost as powerful as social hatred. The flight of the king appeared to prove that invasion was imminent; the popular masses mobi-

*Members of the lightly armed cavalry.

lized in the military meaning of the word.[26] The constituent bourgeoisie nevertheless kept calm, though fearing the peasant revolt and mass urban movements (the Le Chapelier law, prohibiting unions, had been passed on June 14, 1791). The Assembly created the fiction of the "abduction of the king" and Barnave shouted to the Jacobins on the evening of June 21: "The Constitution, there is our guide." In spite of the aristocratic peril, the nation did not open itself up to the people; it remained limited to the propertied bourgeoisie. At the Champ-de-Mars on July 17, 1791, the exclusively bourgeois national guard fired on the petitioners. The patriotic party found itself irremediably cut in two: behind the constitutionalists was the propertied bourgeoisie; the people were behind a minority of democratic bourgeois rallying around the Jacobins and Robespierre. The Constitution was revised and the property qualifications for suffrage were increased. "Are we going to terminate the Revolution, are we going to begin it again?" Barnave had asked on July 15 in a vehement speech. "One more step would be a disastrous and guilty act, one more step in the direction of liberty would mean the destruction of the monarchy, leading to equality and the destruction of property."[27] The nation remained a nation of property owners.

While the Constituent Assembly did its best to contain the popular upsurge, the Manifesto of Pilnitz (August 27, 1791) overexcited national sentiment. This proclamation by the sovereigns of Europe to support the king of France was taken literally by the people, accepting the meaning that the émigrés gave to it. The threat of intervention, even in the conditional ("Then and in that case..."), was considered an insult by the patriots. From that moment war seemed inevitable. Faced with this peril, the bourgeoisie was forced to appeal to the people but not without reservation. The people demanded their place in the nation, and the national problem was now posed in new terms.

III

The conflict with aristocratic Europe, carelessly set off, obliged the revolutionary bourgeoisie to appeal to the people and thus to make concessions to them. Thus the social contents of the nation was enlarged. The nation really dates from the war that was both national and revolutionary: a war of the Third Estate against the aristocracy and a war of the nation against the allied Europe of the Ancien Régime. In the face of the threat posed by the French and European aristocracy, at war inside the nation and on its borders, the fragile framework of property qualifications collapsed under popular pressure. In the year II the nation appeared in its new irresistible power.

The revolutionary bourgeoisie did not arrive at that point without hesitation and reservations, nor without a new amputation. An examination of the problem of the origins of the war and the position of the various protagonists reveals the social content that different sides intended to give to the national reality.

There can be no doubt about the position of the Court: the war was conceived as a means to restore aristocracy and absolutism. "Instead of a civil war," wrote Louis XVI to Breteuil on December 14, 1791, "it will be a political war and things will be much better. The physical and moral state of France makes it impossible to sustain a demi-campaign."

The Girondists intended to use the war to force the traitors to unmask themselves. "Let us mark in advance a place for traitors," Guadet shouted to the gallery at the legislative Assembly on January 14, 1792, "and let this place be the scaffold."[28] The Girondists believed that the war conformed to the interests of the nation. "A people who have won their liberty after ten centuries of slavery," declared Brissot to the Jacobins on December 16, 1792, "need a war: war is necessary to consolidate liberty." And this same Brissot spoke at the legislative Assembly on December 29: "The moment has finally arrived when France must display to the eyes of Europe the character of a free nation, who wishes to defend and preserve her liberty." And more specifically, in the same speech: "War is currently a national benefit, and the only calamity to fear is to not have a war... It is the sole interest of the nation to counsel war."[29] But what nation was he talking about? The clearest speech in this sense was delivered by Isnard on January 5, 1792 at the legislative Assembly. For him it was not enough to "preserve liberty," it was necessary to "consummate the revolution."[30] Isnard was giving a social content to the approaching war: "It is a question of a struggle between the patricians and equality." By patricians he meant the aristocracy; as for equality, it was only *constitutional equality* as the property qualifications for suffrage had defined it. "The most dangerous class of all," according to Isnard, "is composed of many persons who lost the revolution, but most essentially an infinite number of large landowners, rich merchants, in sum a host of opulent and proud men who cannot support equality, who regret the loss of a nobility to which they aspired... finally, who detest the new Constitution, mother of equality." He was indeed referring to the Constitution of 1791, and the equality in question "was only one of rights" as Vergniaud would soon affirm. The war desired by the Girondists conformed only to the interests of the bourgeois nation.

At this date, the Jacobins and the future Montagnards had the same concept of national reality. In his *Almanach du Père Gérard pour l'année 1792*, published with the approval of the Jacobins, Collot d'Herbois held to the concept of a nation with property qualifications and tried to justify it as he justified the absolute right to property.[31] Robespierre also remained with the property-qualified Constitution. Although violently opposed to the war, he did not have a fundamentally different position on the national problem from that of the Girondists. He also believed that it was necessary to consummate the revolution and consolidate the nation as the Constitution of 1792 had defined it; but he reversed the order of urgency. "Begin by looking at your interior position; put your own house in order before carrying freedom elsewhere," he urged the Jacobins on January 2, 1792. "Haven't you said that the seat of evil is at Coblenz? Isn't it at Paris?" Before waging war, bring the Court under control, purge the army, destroy the aristocracy. Certainly Robespierre let it be seen that it was necessary to go farther: the people are not satisfied "from the moment you give them a war"; the passive citizens must be armed, public spirit must be raised. But Robespierre did not otherwise specify his national policy.

Whatever may have been the limits of the war preached by the Girondists, it contributed to fire national sentiment and glorify its promoters with a persistent prestige that the catastrophes that followed could scarcely tarnish. They perished, not for having wanted the war that revealed the nation to herself, but for not having known how to conduct it. "Founders of the Republic," writes Michelet, "worthy of the gratitude of the world for having desired the crusade of 1792 and liberty for the whole earth, they needed to wash off their stain of 1793, to enter by expiation into immortality."[32]

On April 20, 1792, the legislative Assembly declared war on the King of Bohemia and Hungary. On April 26, at Strasbourg, Rouget de Lisle issued his *War Song for the Rhine Army*;[33] there was no doubt about the fervor, both national and revolutionary, of the one who wrote it as well as those who sung it. No distinction was made between Revolution and Nation. Tyrants and "vile despots" who contemplated returning France "to antique slavery" are denounced, but also the aristocracy, the émigrés, "this horde of slaves and traitors, these parricides, these confederates of Bouillé" [French general who organized the flight of Louis XVI]. The homeland for which "the sacred love" is glorified and to whose defense all are called ("Hear these fierce soldiers howling in the countryside...") is the homeland that since 1789 has been formed against the aristocracy.

In fact we wouldn't know how to separate what was soon to become *The Marseillaise* from its historic context, the crisis of spring 1792. National spirit and revolutionary upsurge are inseparable; class conflict underlies and exacerbates patriotism. The aristocrats opposed the king to the nation they ridiculed; those on the inside awaited the invader with impatience and the émigrés fought in the enemy ranks. For the patriots of 1792, it was a question of defending and promoting the heritage of 1789. The national crisis gave a new impetus to the popular masses, still haunted by the aristocratic plot, and widened the democratic movement. The passive citizens, counseled by the Girondists, armed themselves with pikes, donned their red bonnets and organized many fraternal societies. Were they going to break through the nation's framework of property qualifications? "The homeland," Roland writes to Louis XVI in his famous letter of June 10, 1792, "is not a word that the imagination is compelled to embellish; it is a being to which sacrifices have been made, to which one is attached more each day by the concerns it causes; it was created by great efforts which arise out of anxiety, and it is loved, as much for what it costs as for what one hopes for it."[34] The homeland was conceived for passive citizens only in equality of rights.

Now the national crisis, by overexciting revolutionary feeling, accentuated social oppositions in the very heart of the old Third Estate. Even more than in 1789 the bourgeoisie was worried; soon the Gironde faltered. The rich were taxed to arm the volunteers; the agrarian revolt broke out in Quercy, then in Bas-Languedoc, while inflation continued its ravages and subsistence [food] riots resumed. The murder of Simoneau, mayor of Étampes, on March 3, 1792, demonstrated the unmitigated conflict between popular demands and bourgeois conceptions of commerce and property. In Paris in May, Jacques Roux was already demanding the death penalty for monopolizers, while in Lyons on June 9, L'Ange, a municipal officer, was presenting his "simple and easy means to arrange for abundance and a just price for bread."[35]

A specter haunted the bourgeoisie from this time on, the specter of the "agrarian law." While Pierre Dolivier, a priest from Mauchamp, was defending the rioters of Étampes, the Gironde decreed, on May 12, 1792, in spite of Chabot's objections, a funeral ceremony in honor of Simoneau and that his mayor's sash be hung from the vaults of the Pantheon.[36] Thus the division that would soon separate the Mountain and the Gironde was clarified and we sense the profound reasons for what history has discreetly called the "national weakness" of the Girondists. Representatives of the bourgeoisie, fervently attached to economic freedom, the Girondists were afraid of the popular surge they had unleashed by their war policy; their national feeling was never strong enough to silence their class solidarity.

In June 1792, the Gironde was scarcely able to maneuver. While La Fayette and his partisans blindly clung to the conception of a nation based on property qualifications,[37] while the king awaited the arrival of the Prussians, the Girondists tried to put pressure on him by the popular demonstration of June 20. The king and his ministers were denounced as traitors by Vergniaud on July 3 and Brissot on the 10th. Brissot saw the situation clearly: "They (the tyrants) are declaring war on the revolution, the declaration of rights, the national sovereignty."[38] He proposed to declare the homeland in danger, which was done on July 11. But on the 20th, Gensonné, Guadet and Vergniaud sent the king a letter, through an intermediary, the painter Boze. By negotiating with Louis XVI after having denounced him, the Girondists condemned themselves. On the verge of taking a major step, but fearing to imperil, if not property, at least the dominance of wealth, they were scared off by the popular insurrection that they had first favored and that was going to throw down the Constitution of 1790 and the narrow framework of a nation based on property qualifications.

The revolution of August 10, 1792 was in fact national in the fullest sense of the word. Federalists from the departments of the South and Brittany played a dominant role in the preparation and unfolding of the day. Even more important, the social and political barriers that divided the nation fell. Passive citizens infiltrated, then entered in mass numbers the section assemblies and the batallions of the national guard. "A particular class of citizens," declared the Parisian section Théâtre-Français on July 30, 1792, "does not have the right to assume the exclusive right of saving the homeland." Consequently, the section called upon the citizens "aristocratically known under the name of passive citizens" to serve in the national guard, to deliberate in the general assemblies, in short to share "the exercise of that portion of the sovereignty that belongs to the section."[39] On July 30, the legislative Assembly sanctioned the current situation by decreeing the admission of passives into the national guard. "During the danger to the homeland," declared the Butte-des-Moulins section, "the sovereign should be at his post; at the head of his armies, in charge of his business; he should be everywhere."[40]

By granting universal suffrage and arming the passive citizens, the revolution of August 10 integrated the people into the nation and marked the advent of political democracy. At the same time the social character of the new national reality was accentuated. After some vain attempts, the old partisans of compromise with the aristocracy eliminated themselves. Dietrich tried to stir up Strasbourg, then fled; La Fayette, abandoned by his troops, went over to the Austrians on August 19, 1792. But even more significant, the entry of the sans-culotterie on the scene alienated from the new national reality a fraction of the bourgeoisie, whose resistance was already expressed.

The deepening revolutionary crisis in effect clarified and hardened the new traits of the nation. The massacres of September and the first Terror introduced a national aspect and a social aspect that could not be separated. The invasion (the Prussians penetrated France on August 19) was a powerful arousing factor. This period from the end of August to the beginning of September 1792, without a doubt that of the greatest danger for the Revolution, was also the time when the popular nation most strongly felt the exterior peril. But social fear was joined to national fear: fear for the Revolution, fear of the counterrevolution. "It was necessary to prevent the enemies from reaching the capital," the dragoon Marquant wrote in his *Notebook* on September 12, 1792, after the loss of the post of La Croix-aux-Bois in the Argonne, "where they would slit the throats of our legislators, give back to Louis Capet his scepter of iron, and put us back in chains."[41] As the fear and hatred of the invader grew, so did the fear and hatred of the enemy within, the aristocrats and their partisans. A social hatred, and not only among the Parisian sans-culotterie. Taine, who could not be suspected of benevolence, sketched a gripping picture of the *formidable anger* that the prospect of the reestablishment of the Ancien Régime unleashed in the breast of the peasant classes. "A formidable anger rolls from the workshop to the cottage with national songs that denounce the conspiracy of tyrants and call the people to arms."[42] At no other moment of the Revolution was there so much evidence shown of the intimate connection of national identity and social realities. "By stopping the progress of our enemies, we have halted popular revenge which ceased, one as soon as the other," wrote Azéma in his *Report* of June 16, 1793.[43] Valmy marked the end of the first Terror; it was no longer, however, the bourgeois national guard of the Federation that rallied that day to the marching order *Vive la Nation!* but an army of "tailors and cobblers."[44]

The trial and death of the king clarified even more the contours of the new nation. Saint-Just was the first to pose the problem of the judgment of Louis XVI with a national angle: "The men who are going to judge Louis have a Republic to found... We want the Republic, independence, unity... Louis XVI must be judged as a foreign enemy." (November 13, 1792). And on December 27: "The homeland is in your midst, choose between it and the king." Meanwhile Robespierre had declared on December 3: "(You have) an act of national salvation to exercise"; and he concluded by demanding that Louis XVI be declared "traitor to the French nation." The execution of the king, by dealing a decisive blow to monarchial sentiment, finally liberated the idea of nation from its royal form. But by making implacable the hatred between regicides and appellants [those who voted to appeal to the people in order to save the king], between monarchial Europe and revolutionary France, it made all compromise impossible. The new nation, identified with the Republic and founded on the strengthened solidarity of the Montagnard bourgeoisie and the people, had to conquer or die.

At the same time that they were demanding death for the king, the Montagnard leaders were trying to give a positive content to the national reality capable of rallying the popular masses. The evolution of Saint-Just is significant in this regard. In *The Spirit of the Revolution and the French Constitution* (1791), still greatly influenced by Montesquieu, Saint-Just wrote: "Where there are no laws, there is no homeland; that is why people who live under despotism have no country and only scorn or hate other nations." Going beyond this theme, banal in the 18th century, to the identification of homeland-liberty, Saint-Just, in his speech on subsistence (November 29, 1792), still without great originality, identified homeland and happiness: "A people who are not happy have no homeland." But he went farther when he emphasized the necessity, for the establishment of the Republic, "of pulling people out of a state of uncertainty and misery that corrupts them." Denouncing "the unregulated issuing of the 'signe'" [assignat—revolutionary bank notes], "you could in a moment," he said to the delegates to the Convention, "give (the French people) a homeland": by stopping the ravages of inflation, by assuring the people of subsistence and thus by connecting "closely their happiness and their liberty." Robespierre was even sharper, on December 2, 1792, in his speech on the grain riots in Eure-et-Loir; by subordinating the right of property to the right to survive, he posed the theoretical foundation of a nation enlarged to include the popular classes.[45]

But, while the necessities of war and their national meaning pushed the Montagnards toward the sans-culottes, their class spirit distanced the Girondists who were more than even entangled in their own contradictions. The Gironde declared war, but it feared that turning to the people, essential for the fight against the aristocracy and the European coalition, would result in compromising the domination of the property owners. The Gironde rejected all concessions. On December 8, 1792, Roland reestablished free trade in grains, after Barbaroux had denounced those "who wanted laws detrimental to property."[46] On March 13, Vergniaud even more strongly emphasized the class foundations of the Girondist policies, by denouncing the popular notions of liberty and equality. "Equality, for social man, is only equal rights."[47] Thus the primacy of property and wealth was preserved. Was this Girondist nostalgia for the organization of the nation by property qualifications?... At the very least, it showed contempt for the people.

The defeats of March 1793 and the resulting peril to the nation sealed the destiny of the Gironde. In this regard, the days of May 31 to June 2 constituted a national reflex as much as a revolutionary outburst, a defensive and punitive reaction against a new demonstration of the aristocratic plot. The development of the "sectional movement" in the departments made these days significant in advance; under the mask of Girondist opposition, at Bordeaux, at Marseilles, even more at Lyons, it marked a return of the aristocracy to the offensive and an attack on the national unity as expressed by the alliance of the Mountain and the sans-culotterie.

Like the nation one and indivisible, "federalism" had a social content, even more marked than its political aspect. Certainly the survival of regional particularisms is part of the explanation, but even more important is the solidarity of class interests. An extension of the civil war for which the "sectional movement" had taken the initiative in May 1793, the federalist insurrection gathered together the partisans of the Ancien Régime, the Feuillants [royalists] still attached to property qualifications, the bourgeoisie worried about property and profit. Meanwhile, the Montagnards, in order to assure the alliance of the sans-culottes, were, with some reservations, being won over to a controlled economy. On May 4, 1793, a law had established the departmental *maximum* [price] for grain and cereal. Certainly, through attachment to the principles of 1789 and concern for national independence, the Girondists rejected the [royalist] alliance of Vendée and the appeal to foreign powers, yet by their distrust of the popular masses and their extreme reluctance to integrate them into an enlarged nation, they had nonetheless played the game of the aristocracy and the coalition. In July 1793, the nation appeared on the point of disintegrating. On August 10, 1793, the holiday that celebrated the anniversary of the fall of the throne and the promulgation of the Montagnard Constitution was still one of national unity and indivisibility.

The revolutionary government, organized bit by bit in the course of the summer and fall of 1793, was set up as a symbol of this new national reality. While the Mountain in turn hesitated and discussed, the popular masses—set in motion by their needs and hatreds—pushed forward and imposed important measures; for example, mass conscription on August 23. But a strong government was nonetheless indispensable for disciplining the popular upsurge and maintaining the alliance with the bourgeoisie which alone could furnish the necessary cadres. And so it was that throughout year II the policy of the revolutionary government and the constant concern of Robespierre in particular was to preserve at any price the revolutionary unity of the old Third Estate, that is to say national unity.

It is in this sense that we can interpret certain aspects of his actions, such as the sharp check on the dechristianization movement.[48] Also in this sense, the Terror was a means of national and social defense. It still demonstrated the defensive reaction and punitive determination of the Third Estate faced with the aristocratic plot, but henceforth controlled by the government and disciplined by the law. The statistical studies of Donald Greer confirm this characteristic.[49] The Terror held sway especially where the counterrevolution was armed and treason was open: if 15% of the death sentences were pronounced in Paris, 71% came from the two principal regions of the civil war,—19% from the Southeast, 52% from the West. The reasons for sentencing correspond to this geographical division, for in 72% of the cases, rebellion was the charge. Objections will no doubt be raised about the social composition, that 85% of the condemned belonged to the Third Estate, and only 8.5% came from the nobility, with 6.5% from the clergy. "But in such a struggle," Georges Lefebvre has remarked, "renegades arouse less discretion than the original adversaries."[50]

Like the civil war, of which it is only one aspect, the Terror cut off from the nation those elements judged socially unable to be assimilated because they were aristocrats or had cast their lot with the aristocracy. The Terror contributed, in another sense, to developing the feeling of national solidarity. By giving the revolutionary government the *coactive force*, by thus restoring State power, it silenced for the moment class egoisms and imposed on all the sacrifices necessary for the salvation of the nation.

The struggle against factions fits into this same perspective: expel elements of division from the nation. Factions in fact expressed the development of social antagonism. Denouncing the factions, Saint-Just wrote of the rupture of the national front, the deals with interior and exterior enemies and the blow dealt to the unity of the Third Estate, unity essential to the victory over the aristocracy. "The foreigner will thus create as many factions as he can," he declared in his report on foreign factions on March 13, 1794. "Every party is thus criminal because it is isolated from the people and the popular societies and independent of the government. Every faction is thus criminal because it tends to divide the citizens." And in his report on law enforcement of April 15, 1794, Saint-Just declared: "You are ferocious beasts, you who divide the inhabitants of a Republic."

It is not sufficient, however, to affirm the necessity of national unity and to forge it through violence. It is still necessary to give it a content capable of rallying the masses. Profoundly marked by the social realities of their century, Montagnards and Jacobins, like the militant sans-culottes, envisioned integrating the popular masses into the bourgeois nation only through accession to property as it was defined in 1789. It is no longer a question of subordinating the right to property to the right to survival, nor of defining it as "a social institution" or a natural right. In the course of the discussion of the new Declaration of Rights that preceded the 1793 Constitution, Robespierre did not breathe a word about his proposal of April 24 ("Property is the right that every citizen has to enjoy and dispose of the portion of wealth *that is guaranteed to him by law*"). But the Mountain tried to satisfy the peasants not only by abolishing without compensation all that remained of seigniorial rights (July 17, 1793), but also by decreeing the sale of the holdings of the émigrés in small lots, payable in tewould have required the nullification of the sale of the national (June 3), and the optional distribution of communal property to each head of a family (June 10).

The culmination of this policy tending to create a nation of small landowners and to identify *patrie* with property was the issuing of the decrees of February–March, 1794. "The force of circumstances," declared Saint-Just on February 26, "is perhaps leading us to results we have not considered. Wealth is in the hands of a rather large number of enemies of the Revolution, necessities make working people dependent on their enemies. Do you think that an empire could exist if civil relations led to those that conflicted with the form of government?" This text, which might seem enigmatic, is clarified by certain precepts of *Republican Institutions*: "Give to all French people the means of obtaining the basic necessities of life, without depending on anything other than laws and without mutual dependence in the civil [social] state." And again: "Man must live independently." Here it is a question of the social and economic independence that property assures. The decrees of February–March stripped the suspected enemies of the nation of their properties in order to transfer them to the partisans of the nation, the indigent patriots. Thus these decrees did not constitute, as Albert Mathiez would have it, "the program of a new revolution," but conformed to the line of the bourgeois revolution so deeply attached to property. The confiscation of private wealth had never been more than one way to struggle against the aristocracy, once it was apparent that they would resort to treason rather than join with the new nation. When Saint-Just affirms, in his February 26 report that "the one who shows himself to be an enemy of his country cannot have property there," he is repeating an idea long held by the revolutionary bourgeoisie and already illustrated by the confiscation of the holdings of the émigrés. This was also an idea familiar to the sans-culottes and their spokesmen. In August 1793, Jacques Roux had demanded that at the end of the military campaigns, "the victorious sans-culottes and their widows be given a portion of the wealth of the émigrés, federalists and deputies who have abandoned their posts and betrayed the nation." Hanriot, the sans-culotte general of the Parisian national guard, developed similar views in a speech to the Jacobins on October 28, 1793: "It is necessary that all lost by the aristocrats be given to the patriots; houses, lands, all should be shared among those who conquer these villains."[51]

While the revolutionary government, and the Robespierrists in particular, were trying to set the nation on the foundation they considered solid—that of small property—the economic policy of year II, characterized by limits, regulations and controls, introduced an element of dissociation into the new national reality. The law of the *general maximum* [wage and price controls] of September 29, 1793 was demanded by the sans-culottes and passed under pressure from them; it was very necessary to satisfy them, because their energy was essential in the struggle against the aristocracy and for assuring the safety of the nation. But there is no doubt about the attachment of the bourgeoisie, even the Montagnards and the Jacobins, to freedom of production, nor about their hostility to controls. The artisans had demanded the *maximum* as consumers; it angered them to see it applied to them as producers. Concerned above all with maintaining the unity of the Third Estate against the aristocracy, the Committee of Public Safety, which had for a long time been loathe to impose controls, finally turned to them, essentially to aid the war effort. There was a contradiction between the interests of the revolutionary bourgeoisie and those of the sans-culotterie, and thus it was impossible for the Committee of Public Safety to have a truly effective economic policy resting on a coherent social and national base. Certainly, in the interest of national defense, the sans-culotterie had to have enough to eat, and that legitimized the *maximum*. It is still true that in the popular mentality, as in the bourgeois mentality, national and social concerns were mixed up in a contradictory manner. If the sans-culotterie demanded the *maximum*, it was much more for their economic benefit (and so that the bourgeoisie had to suffer), than out of a concern for the nation. Conversely, by using the *maximum* mostly to the advantage of national defense and the State (which historically could be only a bourgeois state), the revolutionary government deceived the popular classes. Thus the national front, on which the revolutionary government rested, split up at the end of winter 1794, and the road to Thermidor was laid.

However, in year II the war had been charged with a more specific national and social significance. "We will wage it, if we are condemned to do so, this terrible war of patriotism against tyranny," Dubois-Crancé had declared to the Jacobins on December 25, 1791.[52] The army was nationalized by the *amalgam* approved on February 24, 1793; the war in turn was nationalized. As Ferdinand Brunot remarked, the word *national* or its derivatives from that moment on appeared in all expressions referring to the army.[53] The social meaning of the war was no less clear, for one side and the other. The émigrés intended to destroy the work of 1789 and restore the domination of the aristocracy. Burke ascribed no other goal to the war that, despite all the ranting, was indeed conceived as a class war. The restoration of the Ancien Régime in the Nord department, partly occupied by the Austrian army, illustrates the social content of the war led by the European coalition: the Austrian "unity" of Valenciennes operated the counterrevolution, restored seigniorial rights and ecclesiastic tithes, returned unsold lands to resistant priests and monks; without a doubt, one the nation had been conquered, the triumphant counterrevolution, would have required the nullification of the sale of the national lands.[54] On the other side, in the ranks of the army national fervor and revolutionary spirit went hand in hand. While the coalition governments repressed the democratic spirit, refused to appeal to national feeling and to "popularize" the war, confining themselves to aristocratic prejudice ("They feared their subjects almost as much as their enemies," according to Mallet du Pan), the revolutionary government purged the leadership and dedicated itself to strengthening the public-spiritedness of the army. "It is not only from the number and discipline of the soldiers that you must expect victory," Saint-Just had declared in his speech on the reorganization of the army on February 12, 1793; "you will attain it because of the progress that the republican spirit will have made in the army."

The victory at the battle of Fleurus succeeded in breaking the national unity already shaken by social antagonisms. As long as the Revolution had been in peril, the bourgeoisie of the Convention had hesitated to compromise the national defense by getting rid of the revolutionary government. Now that victory seemed certain, feelings of class solidarity gained the upper hand. The revolutionary Third Estate, composed of antagonistic classes, split up definitively. It was a matter of ending the controlled economy and reestablishing freedom of profit, of liquidating all threat of a "popular republic"[55] and returning to liberal practice—in a word restoring the social and political domination of the bourgeoisie. The nation, for a moment enlarged to include the popular classes, once again was going to be restricted to property owners, in the narrow framework of a republic based on property qualifications. It is in this sense that 9 Thermidor [the arrest of the Robespierrists on July 27, 1794] constitutes a crucial moment in the formation of the French nation.

IV

By excluding the popular classes as well as the aristocracy, the bourgeois nation remained doomed to instability, until the day when the aristocracy showed an unexpected attachment to the land from which they had been in part dispossessed—and discovered the value of the native soil—giving them a new meaning for the word *patrie*. Then the union of all property owners—bourgeois and noble—was affirmed; patriotism became identified with love of the native land and was embodied in landed property.

The popular classes, however, did not passively accept being thrown out of the nation they had helped to found. On March 17, 1795, exhausted by hunger, the delegates of the Saint-Marcel and Saint-Jacques neighborhoods (in the Finistere and Observatoire sections) spoke to the Convention. "We lack bread; we are on the eve of regretting all the sacrifices we have made for the Revolution."[56] The spring insurrection and the repression that followed demonstrated the impossibility of stabilizing the nation on the narrow base of property and the qualified bourgeoisie. The revolutionary movement was then oriented in a new direction, not without some trial and error. Babeuf meant to assure *the common happiness* and not "the happiness of a small number;"[57] but he was only slowly freeing himself from the ideas of his century, which based the nation on property. In *Le Tribun du peuple* of January 8, 1795, he recalled the "sublime laws" of the Montagnard Convention, precisely those which permitted attainment of property. "Remember, plebeian representatives, the law by which you promised property to all the defenders of the homeland at the end of the war!... Remember the law that guaranteed plots of land to *unpropertied* sans-culottes, taken from the stores of the enemies of the homeland!" In the *Plebeian Manifesto* of November 30, 1795, doubtless moved by the sight of the misery of the times, he took the plunge, renouncing the agrarian law "which can only last a short time," advocating the elimination of inheritance and expressly stipulating the abolition of landed property. But the times were not at all ripe for a nation of the *unpropertied*!

At the same time, the white Terror, the 13 Vendémiaire [an uprising of royalists in Paris on October 5, 1795], and the émigré expedition to Quiberon demonstrated the implacable opposition of the aristocracy and mended for a moment the bonds of the union of all patriots. The persistence of the anti-aristocratic feeling in the ranks of the bourgeoisie and among the popular masses during the period of the Directory cannot be doubted. The law of October 25, 1795 prohibited relatives of émigrés from holding public office; repealed by the royalist majority of year V, it was reinstated on 18 fructidor [September 5, 1797, when Napoleon's troops occupied Paris]. Soon after, Sieyes proposed banishing those nobles who had exercised functions or enjoyed high offices under the Ancien Régime and reducing the rest to the status of foreigners; the law of November 29, 1797 was confined to the second measure. Even if this law was never applied, the intention was nonetheless quite clear.

The nation was once again defined in the narrow framework of the propertied bourgeoisie. Its principles were clearly enunciated by Boissy d'Anglas, in his preliminary address on the draft of the Constitution (June 23, 1795): "You must in the end guarantee the property of the rich... Civil equality, that's all a reasonable man can demand...[58] We must be governed by our betters: our betters are more educated and more interested in the preservation of the laws; now, with very few exceptions, you will only find such men among those who, possessing property, are attached to the country that contains it, to the laws that protect it, to the tranquillity that conserves it, and who owe to this property and the comfort it gives the education that has made them fit to discuss with wisdom and soundness the advantages and the disadvantages of the laws that decide the fate of their homeland... A country governed by property owners is in the social order; one where non-property owners govern is in the state of nature."[59] The right to property is obviously tied to freedom of the economy. "If you give some men without property political rights without reservation... they will establish or let be established disastrous controls on commerce and industry because they will not have felt nor feared nor foreseen the deplorable results." This was condemning the experience of year II and blocking all hope for the popular classes, without appeal. Thus the tradition of 1789 was revived, and through the accord of the thermidorian republicans and the constitutional monarchists, the framework was sketched for a nation of "notables," that is to say property owners who were well-off, at the least.

Access to property, once facilitated by the Montagnard legislation, was at the same time refused to the popular masses in the name of the necessities of the liberal economy. When Fayau proposed on September 13, 1794, new modes for the sale of national property that would have favored "non-propertied republicans or small property owners," Lozeau, the deputy from Charente-Inférieure, retorted that "in a Republic composed of twenty-four million persons, it is impossible for all to be farmers; ... it is impossible for the majority of the nation to be land owners, since, in that case, each one being obliged to cultivate his field or his vinyard to live, commerce, the arts and industry would soon be destroyed."[60] The Thermidorians rejected the popular ideal of a nation of small independent producers.

While the bourgeois concept of the nation was being affirmed by the Constitution of year III, the national sentiment that had up to then supported the armies took on a new significance. A certain attachment for the Republic doubtless remained, mingled with distrust of the Thermidorian government, then the Directory. Desertions were multiplying. As reinforcements had not arrived since the mass conscription, and conquests were taking the armies far from France, the soldiers were gradually being separated from the rest of the nation; this explains the appearance of the term *civvy* [*pequin* or *pekin*] that was in wide use at the beginning of the Empire.[61] Passive obedience was reinforced, soldiers became professional, and when stationed in foreign countries, their allegiance was to their commanders alone. Devotion to the nation gave way to a spirit of adventure and pillage. "Soldiers, you are naked, malnourished," declared Bonaparte in his proclamation of March 26, 1796, on the eve of the Italian campaign. "I want to lead you into the most fertile plains on earth. Rich provinces, big towns will be in your power, there you will find honor, glory and wealth." Patriotism was emptied of its republican and human content, nationalism soared; contempt for foreigners, military glory and national vanity replaced civic sentiments and revolutionary enthusiasm. Marie-Joseph Chenier, on the occasion of the death of Hoche, glorified "the Great Nation accustomed to conquering"; this expression, inspiring pride, was standard under the Directory; the Empire consecrated it.

The second coalition and the renewal of war put in doubt again the fragile equilibirum of the bourgeois nation. The national peril in June–July 1799 led to extreme measures: for one last time the Jacobins came to the fore because of their intransigence on the importance of national survival. A forced loan of 100 million was levied on the wealthy, and the law of hostages was adopted (July 12, 1799). On July 14, Jourdan gave a toast "To the resurrection of the pikes!" That was going too far, the bourgeoisie became frightened; the anti-Jacobin reaction took shape in the course of the summer; the Manege club of the Jacobins, which had been moved to Bac Street, was closed on August 13. As in year II, the danger to the homeland imposed recourse to authoritarian methods; but it was no longer in question that the social and political domination of the bourgeoisie might be balanced by the popular masses. That was the meaning of 18 brumaire [Napoleon's coup d'état of November 9, 1799]: the nation remained within the limits designated by the "notables" in year III.

The military dictatorship of Bonaparte permitted the stabilization of the bourgeois nation and at the same time its enlargement through the integration of those aristocrats and émigrés who consented to rally around. Thus the fusion of the elements of the new dominant class began to operate and one of the goals that the men of 1789 had assigned to the Revolution was attained.

This evolution was favored by a transformation of sensitivity in the ranks of the emigration. Having left France because of attachment to traditional values, a matter of honor or social egoism, having for a long time pronounced with scorn the words *nation* or *patriots*, the émigrés, through the rigors of exile, came to get to know France again, to attach themselves to a new homeland that was no longer "my religion and my king," but already "the land and the dead." Thus at the turning point from the 18th to the 19th century, the propertied bourgeoisie and the won-over aristocracy were joined together on the solid foundation of native soil and landed property, establishing a new meaning for the word *patrie*.

Through the transformation of landed property, the Revolution had tied landowners more closely to the soil. The abolition of seigniorial rights and ecclesiastical tithes had robbed the landowning peasants of all revolutionary spirit; they now felt themselves to be fully property holders, and the gulf between them and the rural non-propertied masses was widened. The sale of national lands doubtless increased the number of small landowners; even more it had reinforced the social domination of the rural bourgeoisie—the well-off husbandmen and the large farmers—as well as the urban bourgeoisie, connected to each other by the same conservative interest. From then on, for these landowning French citizens, and even more for the peasants, the homeland became a concrete notion—the soil possessed—and patriotism, stripped of all the political value it had had in 1789, became a feeling materialized in the land owned outright.

At the same time and to the extent that their exile was prolonged, the memories and regrets of the émigrés crystallized around the native land. Dispossessed of their property by the confiscation, they now discovered its sentimental value. The point of honor and the attachment to the person of the king gradually gave way to nostalgia, to tender and melancholic memories going back to childhood. "To describe this languor of the soul that one feels outside of one's homeland," Chateaubriand writes in *The Genius of Christianity* (1802), "people say: 'This man is homesick.' It is truly a sickness that can be curred only by returning home." Having left as cosmopolitans (*ubi bene, ibi patria*—wherever I feel good, there is my homeland), the émigrés discovered the perceptible reality of the absent homeland: this new theme bloomed in the volumes of poetry—*Tristes* [sadness] and *Regrets*—that multiplied during the emigration, foreshadowing the "sweet recollection" of Chateaubriand.[62]

After ten years of Revolution, aristocratic France and bourgeois France were as one. Despite all that could have separated them, they now had reached an agreement, through the secret paths of landed property, to identify the land of France and the French homeland, without caring any more about those, who not being landowners, could not concretize their patriotism in a territorial notion. The bourgeoisie and the affluent peasantry, thanks to the increased or new possession of landed property, gave to that which was only an abstract notion in 1789, richer in hope than reality, a tangible form that the social and political work of the Consulate made even firmer: the French nation was from that point on a nation of landowners. Through a completely different progression, by returning to instinctive and sentimental values stronger than their traditional prejudices, the émigrés concretized the idea of homeland and identified it with the land, thus preparing to integrate themselves in the landowning nation.

The work of Bonaparte, in this area, corresponded to the aspirations of both groups. In the *Mercure britannique* of January 25, 1799, Mallet du Pan had posed the essential condition of gathering the groups together: "adopt forms protective of individual liberty and property." For Mounier, the former Constituent, property must be the pivot of the new order he foresaw. "I no longer see but one means of salvation," he wrote to Gentz on March 4, 1798, "and that is to seek support in property." As the basis of property had changed, Mounier realized that it was bringing a new stability that was necessary to support.[63] It is on that propertied base that Bonaparte reconstructed France. When he opened the borders to the émigrés, through the *senatus consultum* of April 26, 1802, he intended "to cement peace in the interior through all that can unite the French and reassure the families"... Nothing, as much as property, was liable to reassure families and unite the French. Through their attachment to the land and landed property, Bonaparte integrated the returned émigrés into the new social hierarchy, and all the while reinforcing the principle of authority, adapted them to a social order that had been at first constructed in opposition to them. "I need a king who will be a king because I am a landowner, and who will have a crown because I have a position; it is thus necessary, in order to finish the Revolution, to create a king through the Revolution, drawing his rights from ours:"[64] proposals stated on August 21, 1801, by the émigrés to the French ambassador at Vienna, whose full value was realized only in 1830.

Only among the ranks of the old aristocracy did backward upholders of the cosmopolitan tradition or diehard supporters of divine-right monarchy refuse to return from emigration to rally around this nation of property holders. For d'Antraignes, in 1796, "the homeland is a word empty of meaning when it does not hold forth the return to the laws we lived under... The homeland limited to territory says nothing to the hearts of men... France without a king is for me only a cadaver and the dead are loved only for the memories." Likewise the viscount of Bonald justified the emigration, after the fact, by a higher concept of patriotism: "Civilized man sees the homeland only in the laws that govern society, in the order that reigns there, in the powers that govern it, in the religion professed and for him his country may not always be his homeland."[65] Was this a concept of an ideal homeland that poorly masked an obstinate attachment to aristocratic privilege? It certainly was a belated argument and one that could not excuse in the eyes of the nation, propertied or not, the war waged under foreign flags and relentlessly pursued.

*

After ten years and more of vicissitudes, national unity appeared to be strengthened: the Revolution, in this sense as in many others, precipitated its evolution. The national market was established as much as the development of communication allowed. The new State, whose institutions Bonaparate perfected, gave the clearly defined nation a solid framework with which to confront the foreigner. But the structure of the State had been transformed as had that of the society. The bourgeoisie regarded the State, constituted to respect its law and maintain its order, as the rampart of its prerogatives. This marked the limits of the nation born of the Revolution. *Nation*, *patrie*—notions all the more revolutionary in the dawn of 1789 in that they seemed to encompass all possibilities—became heavy and materialized, now that they were reduced to the limits of landed property.

The developing capitalist economy was gradually giving a new social content to national reality. Nevertheless, the land and the values it embodied demonstrated for a long time to come all their hidden prestige, deforming and obscuring in the irrational outbursts of the heart what had seemed clear in the century of the Enlightenment. Hence certain misadventures of nationalism in the 19th century and beyond, and the slow integration of personal (non-landed) wealth, tainted by its mercantile origins, into the homeland long troubled by the land and the dead. Moreover, if the capitalist economy, through the new and powerful ties it wove throughout the country and the society, in some ways integrated the popular masses into the national unity, it nonetheless created new contradictions that posed the national problem in other terms. *Nation*, *patrie*—these notions are not defined once and for all. At each stage of the historical movement, though under a mask that may appear immutable, they are expressed in new and always changing social realities.

14

Jaurès, Mathiez and the History of the French Revolution[1]

"When we contemplate the fact," wrote Albert Mathiez in 1925, "that Jaurès only took four years to raise such a monument, the four years of forced repose that the electors of Carmaux procured for him by their monumental ingratitude after the Dreyfus affair, we are filled with wonder at the power of his work, as by the steadiness of his gaze. No other history of the Revolution has penetrated reality as closely. No other has advanced knowledge so far. It is a starting point, much more than an end point. It has set in motion a movement of research and ideas which has not yet yielded, alas! all its results."[2]

End point, starting point: which is it exactly, and how is the *Socialist History of the French Revolution* to be situated in the current of revolutionary historiography at the end of the 19th and beginning of the 20th centuries? But also, more specifically here, to what extent can the work of Albert Mathiez claim to draw inspiration from that of Jaurès? To what extent is the *Socialist History* still living?

I

In the last years of the 19th century, when Jaurès undertook the writing of the *Socialist History of the French Revolution*, the first volume of which appeared in 1901, Aulard was the uncontested master of revolutionary studies, at least in the eyes of academics.

Aulard had rendered eminent service to revolutionary historiography, having discerned that historians of the French Revolution were to submit themselves to the same discipline as others, applying themselves to patient research in the archives, discovering, criticizing and publishing texts, as the Chartists had been doing for the history of the Middle Ages for a long time. This was of singular merit, if we remember that Aulard had been formed by literary studies as they were understood at the end of the Second Empire, and that he had come to the history of the Revolution through the study of its orators. Having said all that, we cannot ignore the fact that his work bears the stamp of its time. Aulard belonged to that generation who, from 1875 to 1880, had struggled to found not only the Republic, but a parliamentary and secular democracy. What interested him in the Revolution was the political history, basically the history of parties and assemblies; and this history, in his eyes, was dominated by the evolution of ideas. That is indeed how it is expressed in his *Political History of the French Revolution* (1901), whose subtitle is significant in this respect: *Origin and Development of Democracy and the Republic*; the economic and social substratum does not appear.

This is no doubt due to the Aulard's literary education; but it is difficult to believe that the conditions of political life during his years of youth and maturity had no effect. Aulard belonged to the ranks of the republican bourgeoisie; to him the bourgeoisie appeared as the natural mentor of the Third Estate; the popular masses could only support them, spurred on by need, in order to realize full political democracy. Aulard saw the Revolution *from above*, as if the popular masses had no other interests, no other needs, no other passions than those of the bourgeoisie. Finally, as religious and school questions were most important in the battles of the parties from 1880 to 1905 and beyond, the religious history of the Revolution and that of the origins of secularism were as interesting to Aulard as political history, properly speaking.

The end of the 19th century nevertheless saw the progress of capitalist economy accelerate and its domain gradually extend until it dominated all continents. Economic questions occupied a growing and finally dominant position in the policies of states and in their international relations. One of the consequences of this evolution, incontestably, was to accentuate class oppositions and to give them importance and sharpness. This led to the development of the working-class movement and the rapid expansion of socialist ideas. Such events could not fail to react upon revolutionary historiography. Research on the ideological origins of socialism in the 18th century was begun, and the first attempts to realize socialism during the Revolution were discovered.

On June 21, 1895, André Lichtenberger defended his thesis on *Socialism in the Eighteenth Century*, a work considered a classic today, even if it might seem dated on many points. Aulard reviewed it in *The French Revolution* of July 14, 1895; Jaurès gave it two and a half columns in *La Petite République* at the end of the same month. Certain historians at the turn of the century were not far from considering the political economy of the Committee of Public Safety as a first sketch of collectivism. Soon Augustin Cochin, imbued with the sociology of Durkheim, constructed an adventurous hypothesis to demonstrate that the clubs, by "socializing" thought, necessarily had to end up "socializing" the economy (*The Societies of Thought and the Revolution in Brittany*, a posthumous work, not to appear until 1925); but let's leave these exaggerations at that, though they had a long life...

A more fortunate consequence was that historians from then on took into consideration the popular masses that up to then they had been content to rank behind the bourgeoisie in the heart of the Third Estate, and began to study more closely their conditions of existence and the motives that set them in motion from 1789 to 1794-95. The study of economic and social facts gave historians a taste for the real; they suddenly realized that ideas do not propagate themselves in a void, that a great political movement presupposes, to some degree, an organization. These preoccupations were all the more essential in that socialism, in the form given to it by Marx, rests on a concept whose vigor exerted a strong intellectual attraction; that is, in the ideological climate of the period, historical materialism, or, more broadly, the economic interpretation of history. Whatever attitude one may have toward this doctrine, it is impossible to deny that it stimulated historical research and oriented that research in new directions. It is incontestable that the ideas of Marx gradually penetrated the thought of historians, that the most reticent were obliged to take into account social and economic facts and that a purely political synthesis, from the turn of the century on, was no longer acceptable. To be convinced of this, it is sufficient to refer to the works of Ph. Sagnac, who cannot be suspected of an indulgent attitude toward historical materialism and socialism; his thesis on *Civil Legislation of the Revolution* (1898) deals with the condition of the land as well as the persons involved.

It was Jaurès, however, who was the first who wanted to see in the French Revolution a social phenomenon with economic origins. The bookseller Rouff offered to publish a study on the French Revolution and socialism in June 1898. Lichtenberger had just defended his thesis, and the centennial of the birth of Michelet was about to be celebrated. On July 16, 1898, Jaurès published an article in *La Petite République* entitled "Michelet and Socialism." Michelet was not a socialist; he is "only half fair to Babeuf"; but he had a strong love for the nation combined with a broad love for humanity; his philosophy of history is "both very mystical and very realistic." And Jaurès asked himself: how can this mystical ideal be reconciled with historical materialism? "It is not possible to research it here. But there would not be a more fertile endeavor." In 1901, the introduction to the *Socialist History* answered this question.

Jaurès posed and resolved the problem before the public by publishing between 1901 and 1903 in red covers the four volumes of his *Socialist His-*

tory of the French Revolution. For the first time in revolutionary historiography, he exposed the history of the Revolution by openly giving economic and social facts as its basis. Not that Jaurès ignored the importance of the philosophical movement. It is nonetheless true, and Jaurès noted it vigorously, that the Revolution was the culmination of a long economic and social evolution that made the bourgeoisie the master of political power and the economy.

Jaurès thus subscribed to the historiographical tradition inaugurated by Barnave. We know the importance he gave to Barnave's *Introduction to the French Revolution* (written from 1791 to 1792 and published in 1843 through the efforts of his compatriot Bérenger de la Drôme). In the first volume of his *Socialist History*—the admirable description of social and economic France at the end of the Ancien Régime—Jaurès credits Barnave with being the first to formulate "most clearly the social causes and, one might say, the economic theory of the French Revolution."

The historians of the Restoration had not read Barnave, and Jaurès does not seem to have been inspired by them. But, thrown into the liberal struggle against the ultra reaction and strong in their bourgeois consciousness, they insisted on the class character of the Revolution: Thiers himself in his *History of the French Revolution* (1823), even more so Mignet in his articles in the *Courrier Français* in 1822 and 1823, and in his *History of the French Revolution* (1824), whose essential element of explanation is the class struggle. Chateaubriand characterized these works as subscribing to the "fatalist school" of thought: the Revolution was necessary, in the sense of historical necessity. As for Guizot, in the fourth of his *Essays on the History of France* (1823), he stressed that political institutions are determined by "the social condition," by the relations between various classes and by the "condition of individuals," which itself is determined in the last analysis by "the condition of lands" and the structure of property. Let us also reread the course on *The History of Civilization in France* that Guizot offered at the Sorbonne from 1818 to 1830, and particularly the 46th lesson...

The passage in the letter from Marx to Weydemeyer of March 5, 1852 is well-known: "It is not I who should receive the credit for having discovered either the existence of classes in modern society or the struggle between them. Long before me, bourgeois historians had described the historical development of this class struggle." Marx is making allusion to Guizot and also to Augustin Thierry whom, in a letter to Engels on July 25, 1854, he calls "this father of the class struggle in French historiography."

Socialist History does indeed appear as the "end point" in this historiographical tradition, that I would willingly describe as the classical social interpretation of the French Revolution, this "great drama whose essential characters are the classes."

II

End point and starting point: "I do not doubt," Albert Mathiez wrote in the *Revue critique* in 1904, "that this book will become the starting point for studies as fertile as they are varied."

We will not go over again here the novelty of the work, the new paths it opened for revolutionary historiography: farther in space, more boldly in time, more deeply into social and economic analysis, as Madeleine Rebérioux has masterfully demonstrated. Following the critique of Albert Mathiez, let us underscore two points.

Farther in space. "But even newer is this powerful tableau of political and intellectual Europe that fills the fifth volume. To see how Jaurès analyzes and criticizes the great thinkers of the period, Kant, Fichte, Godwin, etc., how he untangles the influence of events on their work and the influence of their work on events, one is lost in admiration. Pages like these will live for a long time in men's memory."[3]

More boldly in time: Jaurès researched in the French Revolution the germs of socialism that were to bloom at the dawn of the 20th century. "No one yet, even after the book of M. André Lichtenberger, had gathered as much information on the obscure social reformers, the Langes, the Doliviers, the Momoros, who were already attacking the problem of property."[4]

As for Georges Lefebvre, he was especially sensitive, as he wrote in 1932, to the deepening of the social and economic analysis; this great development represented for him what was new and original in revolutionary historiography. And he gives credit to Jaurès for the creation of the Commission "charged with researching and publishing documents from the archives relating to the economic life of the French Revolution"[5] whose consistently fertile work is well-known: publication of an imposing collection of *cahiers de doléance*, studies of the division of landed property at the end of the Ancien Régime and on the sale of national lands, on the question of communal lands and collective rights, on which Jaurès had particularly insisted in his *Socialist History.*

Renewing in these ways the perspectives of revolutionary historiography, Jaurès could not fail to exercise a decisive influence on the historians of the French Revolution, at the very least those who intended to further his classical social interpretation.

Georges Lefebvre did not wish to recognize any master other than Jaurès.[6] As for Albert Mathiez: "For me, who had the honor of attaching my name to the reprinting of his work, I humbly declare that I drew from it not only the stimulation without which my research would have been impossible, but many suggestions which served me as guidelines. Certainly, today it may happen that I reach different conclusions on more than one important point, but it is because he wrote before me that I was able to undertake such an investigation which, without him, would not have taken place. The best of his spirit lives in me, even when I contradict him."[7]

Even more explicit is the famous passage Mathiez wrote in 1922 about volume I of *Socialist History, The Constituent.* "Mingling in the feverish life of assemblies and parties, Jaurès was more capable than a professor or a scholar of reliving the emotions, the clear or obscure thoughts of the revolutionaries, he was closer to them, he understood them without their having to spell things out."[8] Reliable methodology, rich documentation, marvelous impartiality, as Aulard had already emphasized, beautiful ordering of the story—these are the characteristics that Mathiez underscores. "It was the first time that an endeavor as vast, as bold and on the whole as successfully conducted had been undertaken to join to the tableau of political events the tableau of economic events that conditioned and explained them." And again this important notation: "Today it is a common view to consider the Revolution as a conquest by the bourgeoisie. Then it was more difficult to go beyond the generalities that the historians of the Marxist school usually took pleasure in, and to carry on a precise, detailed and penetrating study of the economic power of the bourgeois class before 1789. Jaurès did it with admirable pages." And to conclude: "The spirit of the great thinker will for a long time to come quicken the hearts of citizens."

There is no reason to doubt the admiration of Albert Mathiez for Jaurès and the influence that *Socialist History* exercised on him. In fact, following in the wake of his teacher Aulard, whom he had long praised, Mathiez was first attracted to the political, and even more the religious, history of the Revolution. It was in 1898-1899 that the *Revue historique* published his "Critical Study of the Revolutionary Days of October 5 and 6, 1789"; his thesis on *The Théophilanthropie* [deist movement] *and the Revolutionary Cult* was published in 1904. When he began to separate himself from his teacher, it was over a question of political history: the personality and role of Danton. This first influence remained indelible; political history, especially parliamentary, remained until the end in the first rank of Mathiez's preoccupations. Certainly he was swayed for a time by Durkheim, whose work had recently been published—Mathiez's supplementary thesis on *The Origins of the Revolutionary Cults* (1904) is proof of Durkheim's influence.

But when he undertook to study the economic and social history of the Revolution, he did not approach it from the point of view of the people, *from below*, but *from above*, from the point of view of political parties and necessities for the conduct of the war, and thus the necessities of the revolutionary government.

We cannot, however, underestimate the influence of Jaurès on Albert Mathiez, but it is appropriate to measure it more exactly. One simple remark at the beginning: certainly Jaurès does not show hostility to Danton, but he indicates a very clear preference for Robespierre; it is at his side that he would have gone, to sit with the Jacobins. All the same, Jaurès's principal influence on Mathiez, as on many young academics of his generation, was through his socialism which reconciled the republican tradition, "democratic and social," with the Marxist interpretation of history, and through the intellectual brillance he knew how to give to his doctrine.

The First World War broke out. While still continuing his earlier research, in particular his work on Danton, Mathiez turned toward an area new for him, that of the social and economic history of the Revolution. Here again the influence of Jaurès, who had integrated the Revolution into the economic interpretation of history, is undeniable. Mathiez now begins to consider the French Revolution as a class struggle, the Third Estate against the priviliged, and becomes interested in the social and political dissociation of the Third Estate. The more he pursued his studies on Robespierre, the more he stressed the social opposition that had been gradually demonstrated between the Girondists and the Montagnards. The war succeeded in forcing the economic point of view on Mathiez's attention through the reappearance of all the social and economic difficulties faced by the Committee of Public Safety in its conduct of a great national war, obliging the governments to turn to the same procedures of control and constraint: wage and price controls, conscription, inflation, more-or-less forced loans, seizure of economic life by the State. These were the conditions behind Mathiez's *Victory in Year II* (1917) and the studies published from 1915 on in the *Annales révolutionnaires* and later collected in *The High Cost of Living and the Social Movement during the Terror* (1927).

Thus Albert Mathiez, following the example of Jaurès, contributed more than any other in bringing to light the social and economic problems of the Revolution, at least some of them. Since the publication of *Socialist History*, these concerns had not reached the educated public, not even the student milieus, as the publications of the Commission that Jaurès had created consisted of erudite works known only to specialists.

It is impossible to hide the points of disagreement [between Mathiez and Jaurès], however great the praise given. "The profound admiration that I feel for the luminous talent of Jaurès and for the rare penetration of his historical intelligence," wrote Mathiez in 1923, "has not kept me from noting from time to time the points at which I could not give my support to his theses and judgments."[9]

What Mathiez, who was not far from conceiving the profession of the historian as that of prosecutor, reproached Jaurès for first of all was his kindness and his indulgence for people. Even after his companions had found excuses for the vile deeds of a Mirabeau, the denials of a Barnave or an Adrien Duport, the suspected tricks of a Brissot... In short, he extended the practices of parliamentary camaraderie to the misfits and appeasers of the revolutionary assemblies. Jaurès felt close to Mirabeau; he admired him! Mathiez quotes Jaurès's recommendation that "one day the correspondence of Mirabeau with the Court be published. This will be, he had said, my defense and my glory. How could we accuse of treason and baseness the man who, before dying, left such a secret to posterity?" Mathiez is indignant at so much benevolence, all the more so because Aulard thought these lines were to the credit of Jaurès.[10]

Naturally the essential disagreement concerned Danton and Robespierre. Jaurès "did not want to listen to the damming accusations brought against Danton. And having covered up the faults or crimes of the great culprits, he showed a sometimes excessive severity toward the judges... Robespierre, who never sacrificed duty nor the public interest to camaraderie, was not fully understood by Jaurès." And elsewhere: "If Jaurès traced a masterful portrait of Hébertism, he showed on the other hand an excessive indulgence for Dantonism and veiled all sorts of defects... He did not know how to free himself sufficiently from a legend that has possession of the state. He was accurate in his account of Robespierre during the crisis of the summer of 1793; [but] he no longer understood him, starting with the great trials of the spring of 1794."[11]

With our more serene vision, we will not intervene in this quarrel. But we will agree with Mathiez that Jaurès lacked understanding of the terrorist mentality and that the chapters devoted to the Montagnard and the revolutionary government seem weak compared to the preceding volumes, as if Jaurès, swept along by the militant life, had lacked the inspiration to carry his great work through to a successful conclusion.[12]

Beyond these differences, Albert Mathiez, whose evolution after his brief Communist interlude became more pronounced (we are in 1923), took on the very orientation of Jaurès's work. Jaurès had learned the history of the Revolution "in the works of M. Aulard." This explains his failure to understand Robespierre. "At the period when Jaurès was on the benches at the École normale [the most prestigious liberal arts college in Paris], it was good form to scoff at the so-called mysticism of Robespierre and to exhibit a blasé and sceptical philosophy decorated with the usurped name of positivism. The generation with the dry hearts... was no longer capable of understanding the great men of the Revolution, so different from themselves." Conversely, "through a lazy and sectarian reaction, the men of the Socialist Party, under the influence of the apostle Jules Guesde, embraced with equal scorn all the men of the 1789 Revolution. They wanted to see in the revolution only a miniscule bourgeois movement, from which they had nothing to learn. Ignorant of history, these socialists were subjected in practice to the teachings of M. Aulard and his school. They shared all the anti-Robespierrist prejudices."

"Jaurès," Mathiez continues, "despite his genius, could not cut himself off from the harmful atmosphere surrounding him. Marxism had called him to socialism. He therefore embarked on his history with all the prejudices of the school." Mathiez nevertheless concedes that when Jaurès had assembled and studied the documents, when he had contact with the historical reality, "the light formed little by little in his mind." Excessive judgment marked by bias. It was not with "the prejudices of the school," and even less under the influence of the superficial Marxism of Guesde, that Jaurès embarked on and carried to a successful conclusion his *Socialist History*. If Marxism constituted the most solid leading strand, let us not forget that Jaurès also placed himself under the invocation of Michelet and Plutarch. And above all that his Marxism cannot be reduced to a vulgar economism. More important than determining whether or not he was a strict adherent to Marxism is discovering what use Jaurès made of it: "Marx himself." he recalled, "though too often belittled by narrow interpretations, never forgot that it is on men that economic forces act."

Such was the encounter of Albert Mathiez with the work of Jaurès. The influence was certain but limited. Not being a socialist, much less a Marxist, Mathiez could not put himself into the perspectives opened up by *Socialist History*; we would readily say that, aside from his Robespierrism, he remained to the end faithful to the teachings of his "master," Aulard. Accustomed from the beginning to considering revolutionary history *from above*, he was very little concerned with the popular masses, their needs, their interests, their mentality and their behavior. He was not interested in the peasants, to whom Jaurès rightly accorded such an important place in his *History*; Mathiez devoted only a few quick pages, in *The French Revolution* (1922-1927), to such basic questions as the abolition of feudal rights and the sale of national lands. Certainly it was to his credit that he finally realized that the French Revolution could be explained only by its economic and social roots. On this account, Albert Mathiez appears to us as having prepared the transition in the historical evolution between Aulard, supreme political historian, and the social historians who follow the line from Jaurès, one of the highest ranking being Georges Lefebvre.

*

It was in the light of Jaurès that Lefebvre in the first years of this century became attached to the study of the peasants of the Nord department during the French Revolution: history seen *from below*; it was *Socialist History* that decided the orientation of his research. The teaching of Georges Lefebvre inspired in its turn the following generation, in this same Jauresian line, to undertake works on the popular urban masses, particularly on the Parisian sans-culottes. The work of Jaurès still proves to be fertile: the current research on the rural community and collective rights, on agrarian egalitarianism, to which Jaurès had devoted so many pages both erudite and enthusiastic, belong to the legacy of *Socialist History.*

Not that we considered *Socialist History* as the Bible and the Prophets. A historical work remains alive only if, read and meditated, it is carried further; scholarly research and critical reflection may then lead to calling certain points into question. The problem of national wealth, that of the *assignat* and inflation—viewed by Jaurès and those that followed him as a transfer of property—could they not be considered as transfer of capital and revenue? Agrarian egalitarianism and the peasant movement—couldn't they be interpreted in a perspective other than that of Jaurès and Lefebvre? Wouldn't the peasant revolution be the expression of one of the possible variants of the bourgeois revolution? Wouldn't the negative aspects of the evolution of capitalism in French agriculture of the 19th century stem less from what the small peasantry could impose on the bourgeois revolution—namely the persistence of the village community, this "rural democracy" dear to Jaurès— than from what the peasantry could not extract from the bourgeoisie: the destruction of the great property and the end of income from land? Posing these questions shows the ever real fecundity of the work that suggested them.

Socialist History of the French Revolution has kept the force and grandeur of its first days. An act of faith, it still excites enthusiasm, it strengthens the liberating conviction. A lesson in public-spiritedness, it teaches us patriotism in the proper sense of the term, virtue according to Rousseau and Robespierre. A work of science, it teaches us the demands of scholarship, the imperative of the method, the necessity of critical reflection. The last of the vast histories of the French Revolution, the *Socialist History* of Jaurès nonetheless opened the way to contemporary scientific historiography of the Revolution, and it is far from having lost its creative spirit. It is a triple legacy of science, public-spiritedness and faith, relayed by Georges Lefebvre, that Jaurès has transmitted to us. It is this triple legacy that we intend to maintain and promote.

15

Georges Lefebvre (1874-1959): Historian of the French Revolution[1]

It would be banal to repeat here that the vision of history changes with each generation of historians. And that it is under the weight of lived experiences and real history that history is written. The history of the French Revolutioin could not escape this law. The work of Georges Lefebvre illustrates that the motivating principle of a remarkable work must be looked for in the author as a concrete individual and in real history. The real history that Georges Lefebvre lived is reflected in his work in accordance with the complex ties of the individual to history. Georges Lefebvre knew how to march with his century—that gives his work its youth and strength, despite certain zones of shadow.

I

Carried along by the general movement of history, historical studies, and more particularly revolutionary studies, have for a century now delineated a curve that could be expected.

The French Revolution was for a long time represented as an event of a political and ideological nature, representing the crowning of the century of the Enlightenment. That is certainly the way it appears in the work of Aulard, who belonged to the generation which, in the last decades of the 19th century, had struggled to establish a parliamentary, secular democracy. Like the history of Aulard, that of Mathiez kept the political dominant, though certainly the perspective was broadened between his 1904 thesis of theophilanthropy,* part of the great conflict of that period between the Church and the State, and *The High Cost of Living* (1927), a collection of articles inspired by the spectacle of high prices and their social repercussions during the World War I. Social history here joins

*A doctrine, founded during the Directory, of a good and powerful God.

political history, but Mathiez's work is still marked by his prevailing concern for the political.[2]

Soon, however, growing social and economic problems, the rapid development of the working class movement and socialist unification shaped a new generation of historians with other interests. It is to Jaurès that we owe the reversal of the historical perspective, doubtless because, as a militant of the working class movement, he quite naturally turned his attention to economic and social problems. *Socialist History of the French Revolution*, published in the first years of this century, encouraged historians to consider the Revolution as an event of a social nature and therefore with economic origins. And if since the beginning of this century, the attention of historians has more and more turned toward the study of social movements and the popular masses—history seen *from below*—would it not be because the world has entered an era of mass movements and popular revolutions?

Reflecting on these events, Georges Lefebvre arrived at a dialectical vision of historiography. There is, in his view, parallel evolution and reciprocal action between history and the concept of history. In order for there to be a transformation of the traditional concept of a narrowly political history, "the surface of things," it was necessary for there to be a certain number of events resulting from the movement of history itself. In the first rank, Georges Lefebvre placed social and economic evolution, the increasing pressure of the bourgeoisie, then that of the proletariat. "It is only in the second half of the 20th century," he writes, "that the spectacle of capitalist transformations has been one of the principal motives of the creation of economic history." And if social history has finally emerged as one of the essential elements of the historical explanation, is it not in particular "the result of the organization of the proletariat as a class"?[3] Georges Lefebvre insisted that the point of view of the historian depends on his time and his class; this point of view may make aspects of the past apparent to him that had previously remained in the shadows, or hide the reality of things from him.[4]

Georges Lefebvre often cited Tocqueville as an example for having transformed thinking about the origins of the Revolution.[5] This aristocrat, considering as one of the essential characteristics of old France the secular struggle between the monarchy and the nobility, stressed that the convocation of the Estates General was imposed on Louis XVI by the aristocracy; thus the Revolution did not begin in 1789 on the initiative of the Third Estate, but in 1787, by a first phase that Albert Mathiez termed "the nobiliary revolt" and Georges Lefebvre, in an ambiguous expression lending itself to confusion, called the "aristocratic revolution."

It is to this line of reflection on history that the work of Georges Lefebvre belongs. He has spoken about his indebtedness.

It is to Jaurès, by his own admission, that he owes the most. "I saw and heard Jaurès only two times, lost in the crowd. . . . But, no matter how carefully one searches for my master, I recognize no one but him."[6] The *Socialist History of the French Revolution*, the first volume of which appeared in 1901, decided the orientation of Lefebvre's research. Doubtless he had already been inspired by Philippe Sagnac's thesis on *The Civil Legislation of the Revolution* (1898), and by the works of the Ukranian historian Loutchisky on *Small Property in France before the Revolution and the Sale of National Lands* (1897). But the four volumes of *Socialist History* made a definitive impression on him. When in 1903, at Jaurès's instigation, the Commission and departmental committees on research and publication of documents concerning the economic life of the Revolution were created, Georges Lefebvre became one of the most active members of the committee for the Nord department.[7]

Going beyond Jaurès, but in the same line, Georges Lefebvre is recognized as having a double intellectual heritage. "It goes back," he has written, "to high school and doubtless also to my Walloon Flanders where Jules Guesde founded the French Workers Party on the base of Marxism."[8]

"My Walloon Flanders"—that of workers, of the weavers in the cellars of Lille. In the moral formation of Georges Lefebvre, his social origins play an important role. He came from the people and knew how to remain faithful to them until death. He evokes occasionally (for he indulges little in speaking about himself) his grandfather who was a carder; his father, a low-ranking commercial employee; his mother struggling to put bread on the table. From the people himself (those who frequented the small house of Boulogne-Billancourt cannot forget the modest framework of his daily existence), Georges Lefebvre espoused their cause. Until his death, he remained faithful to the teaching of Guesde and socialist unity. Until his eighties, he marked his fidelity and his debt by participating in the commemorative demonstration of the Wall of the Federations; it could be said that the memory of the 1871 Commune and its dead hung over him. Georges Lefebvre was very familiar with the works of Marx, rereading *Capital* again in his last years on the occasion of a new edition. Without adopting all its philosophical points of view, he stressed the fecundity of Marxism as a method of research. Not content with seeing in Marxism an economic interpretation of history, he insisted more and more on the dialectical aspect of the evolution of societies and sought its explanation in the analysis of the contradictions of the historical movement.[9]

This opening of the mind to social and economic realities was doubtless imposed on him by his popular origins and strengthened by his socialist options, but Georges Lefebvre wrote that he also owed it to the education he received in high school. When he left the secular elementary school, he was assigned on a municipal scholarship to the special educational program created by Victor Duruy at the end of the Second Empire. In the place of the dead classical languages, which Georges Lefebvre did not study until he entered the university, he was taught not only two living languages, a lot of mathematics and natural sciences, but also political economy and law. (These subjects were later to disappear from the high school curriculum along with the special educational programs.) As a result of this special high school education, Lefebvre later presented an image of an independent, if not self-taught, thinker in university society.

Lefebvre's first teachers, as he often said, where those of the secular school that Jules Ferry had just founded, effecting the decrees of the National Convention. In simple and moving words, he has expressed what he owes them. "Dear secular school! I cannot recall your teachers, to whom I owe so much as a man and as a citizen, without a profoundly moving feeling of gratitude and respect. They taught us the Republic with simplicity, as the natural object of support of every man worthy of the name. They taught us public spirit, this virtue that Robespierre, following Montesquieu and Rousseau, had designated as the rampart of the Republic.[10] The Republic was the ideal city where Justice and Reason reigned. Faithful to these principles, Georges Lefebvre gave his support to socialism as a united effort and a grandiose attempt to organize society on the foundations of Reason and Justice.

Finally, we could not understand Georges Lefebvre, the teacher and scholar, if we disregarded his university career. A successful candidate for the *agregation* [highest competitive examination for teachers in France] at the age of twenty-four, after having completed all his studies on scholarship, he slowly climbed the rungs of the career ladder, teaching for more than twenty-five years in high schools, first as a tutor, then as a professor.[11] In order to judge the remarkable nature of this career, we have only to compare it with that of Albert Mathiez, also born in 1874, in a family who, without being wealthy, did not expect financial aid for their son. Mathiez graduated from the École Normale Supérieure, boarded at the Thiers Foundation, and received his doctorate at the age of thirty, attaining soon thereafter a university teaching position. Georges Lefebvre taught for a long time in the provinces, with no relation to the Parisian milieus, even during his tenure at the Montaigne and Henri-IV high schools from 1920 to 1924, all his free time being devoted to his thesis, which he finished at the age of fifty.[12] "Every beautiful work," writes the poet, "is written by hand and is the result of a long wait. Every beautiful journey in life is made on foot to the rhythm of Goethe going from Weimar to Rome. But haste turns hot heads."[13]

II

Georges Lefebvre committed himself to the path opened by Jaurès before the First World War. The first result of his labors was the publication in 1914, in the collection established by Jaurès, of a volume of *Documents relating to the history of food distribution in the Bergues district during the French Revolution, 1788–year IV.*[14] From this publication in 1914 to that of forty years later, *Studies on the French Revolution*,[15] then to the posthumous two volumes, *Studies of Orleans*[16] in 1962-1963, the essential work of Lefebvre was devoted to the French Revolution. But by the breadth of his views, by the curiosity of a mind always awake, by the new perspectives he brought out, Georges Lefebvre went beyond the framework of his specialty to place himself among the ranks of the few great historians. Social historian of the Revolution, or more exactly, as Ernest Labrousse has noted, "socio-political historian of an indivisible revolutionary reality," Georges Lefebvre knew how to pose problems and clarify methods that continue to inspire French historiography of the 18th and 19th centuries. Moreover, the lines of reflection and research on history expressed in his work are paths of approach to a critical reflection capable of leading beyond the current state of historical studies.

As social historian of the French Revolution, Georges Lefebvre was naturally concerned above all with the problem of classes, as Marc Bloch wrote in his 1929 review of Lefebvre's article on the sale of national lands, published the previous year in the *Revue d'histoire moderne*. The observation is valid for the whole of his work, from the rural classes of the *Peasants of the Nord* (1924) to the *Studies of Orleans*, a contribution to the study of the class organization of urban social structures (1962-1963).

Perhaps it would be a good idea, before taking up these master works, to go back to the 1914 collection relating to the history of food distribution in the Bergues district. This is not a work of pure erudition. In a substantial introduction, Georges Lefebvre studies agricultural production and the grain trade in the northern part of maritime Flanders, which was to make up the Bergues district, then the various crises that followed one another from 1789 to 1795, the application of the *maximum* [price controls] from May 1793 to December 1794, finally the vicissitudes of regulation through August 1796.

The government was forced by political circumstances to impose the *maximum*, a measure that in no way represented an economic system adopted, after reflection, for its theoretical excellence. Lefebvre strongly underscores the contradiction between a social organization based on individual freedom and freedom of production, and the conditions under which the *maximum* was applied. In order to apply it with precision, it would have been necessary to nationalize landed property, or at least the trade in grain and the bakery trade. It was instead imposed forcibly but arbitrarily. In many villages, the *maximum* was the vehicle of the Terror and it was respected only so long as the revolutionary government lasted. After Thermidor, popular respect was lacking, and an economic terror was instituted, marked by the use of garnishing agents whose history can be followed until 1795-1976. Lefebvre moreover emphasized the social aspects of the *maximum.* In the view of many democratic republicans, it suppressed monopolizing and, to a certain extent, offset the dangers born of social inequality. But in the district of Bergues, no democrat protested its abolition. The petit bourgeoisie—artisans and shopkeepers—in favor of price controls on grain, evaded as best they could the general *maximum.* Wage earners, workers and journeymen, for whom the *maximum* on grain in year II was what the right to work would be in 1848, a legal form of the right to survival, did not intervene, either, to defend the *maximum*; still poorly differentiated from the petit bourgeoisie, they did not have a clear enough sentiment of class solidarity in opposition to the wealthy.

We only insist on this first publication of Georges Lefebvre, sometimes forgotten, in order to better emphasize his method and the scope of his views. The pages of introduction where he specifies the characteristics and importance of the *maximum* are based on two thick volumes of documents drawn from departmental and communal archives with irreproachable scholarship. Moreover, the history of economic mechanisms is not conceived as an end in itself; it leads to a study of social structures, mentalities and behaviors. The effects of inflation, price controls and requisitions are specified according to class conflicts: between peasant producers of grain and non-producer peasants, as between towns and rural areas, and in the towns, between various social categories. We find here some of the major ideas that Georges Lefebvre would pick up and develop in later works on the peasantry during the Revolution and which, applied to the study of the popular urban masses, were to prove equally fertile.

In 1924 *The Peasants of the Nord* [department] *during the French Revolution* appeared, a thesis which, by the breadth of its conclusions, went far beyond the framework of departmental monographs.[17] In the years that followed, Georges Lefebvre broadened his perspective to the national framework. In several important articles in 1928, he culminated his research on "The Division of Property and Exploitation of Land at the end of the Ancien Régime," then on "The Sale of National Land." In 1932 there appeared one after another, *Agrarian Questions at the Time of the Terror* and *The Great Fear of 1789*, then in 1933 the great article of synthesis, "The French Revolution and the Peasants."

Certainly the geographical framework of Lefebvre's great thesis may at first seem restricted, being carefully limited to the Nord department. But as H. Pirenne emphasized in his review, the importance of this region in rural France at the end of the 18th century singularly increases its range. The sureness and the scope of the documentation, the value of the statistical elaboration permit a constant discovery in this departmental monograph of incontestable facts and typical examples; as such it constitutes a contribution of the first order to the social and economic history of the end of the Ancien Régime and of the Revolution.

If we look at the causes and consequences of the Revolution, particularly in its effect on the peasants, the French Revolution appears to be a social revolution. Its impact is marked by the abolition of feudal rights and the tithe, and of the fiscal privileges of the aristocracy. It is also marked by the transfer of landed property. The property of the clergy disappeared (about 20% of the total land); the portion of land under control of the nobility fell from 22% in 1789 to about 12% in 1802, a measure of the decline of the aristocracy. Bourgeois property, however, rose in this same time period in the Nord department from 16% to more than 28%, while peasant property grew from 30% to more than 42%. These results throw a remarkable light on the situation in the Nord department characterized by irresistible demographic pressure. The Revolution was far from having distributed to the peasants all the land that it had granted to the nation. The bourgeoisie kept a considerable part of it. What is more, they imposed their concept of property. The rural masses, Georges Lefebvre emphasizes, were not hostile to individual property, but it was tightly limited by traditional notions: collective rights, common grazing land and a second planting of grass, gleaning, rights of usage in the forests and villages—amounting to a co-ownership of wealth in the eyes of the small peasantry. Through the freedom to cultivate and to enclose, the Revolution favored the rural bourgeoisie; it strengthened large property and farming concerns, with all the social consequences. Certainly the peasants of the Nord always supported the Revolution for having eradicated aristocratic domination of their villages and abolished feudalism. The agrarian Revolution nonetheless remained, in spite of appearances, moderate in its effects and "conservative"; it seems, concludes Georges Lefebvre, "like a compromise between the bourgeoisie and rural democracy."[18]

In 1933, in a forceful article, Lefebvre synthesized his essential views on "The French Revolution and the Peasants."[19] He considered what they gained more difficult to discover than what they were not able to gain. The most numerous—the farm workers, the sharecroppers and all those who were not landowners—gained nothing from the suppression of the tithe and real feudal rights. The majority obtained nothing from the national lands nor could the promise made to the indigents by the decrees of ventôse suffice. [In March, 1794, the revolutionary government decreed that the property of suspected enemies of the nation would be transferred to indigent patriots.] There were other cards to play to satisfy the peasant masses, but Lefebvre concludes, "They were not played."

A historical work remains a living force only if its significance deepens as it is read and contemplated. Concerning the agrarian work of Georges Lefebvre and the place he assigned to the peasant revolution in the heart of the French Revolution, two categories of observations seem imperative today.

First of all we will consider the problem of "feudal" exploitation in the peasant society of the Ancien Régime, more precisely that of feudal and seigniorial rights and the exact position they held among the causes of the revolutionary struggles that the peasants waged at the end of the 18th century. In short, the problem of the feudal imposition. We must remark that if Georges Lefebvre devoted a chapter of his thesis on the Nord peasants to the charges imposed on them, the tithe and feudal rights, he did not return to these problems in his great articles of synthesis in 1928 and 1933. Certainly in his study on "The French Revolution and the Peasants," he placed the problem with precision: "There was antagonism between the general progress of capitalism and the preservation of feudal rights and land taxes." But while he devoted two important articles to his research on the division of property and exploitation of land at the end of the Ancien Régime and following the sale of national lands,[20] Lefebvre did not consider it useful to write a similar clarification on the subject of feudal rights and their suppression, nor on that other essential agrarian problem: the rural community and its progressive dissociation in the revolutionary period.

The overall view of the question had been sketched, however, and the problem correctly situated by some historians of the French Revolution who, in comparison with their more illustrious successors, are sometimes unjustly discredited. Ph. Sagnac had in 1898 devoted his complementary thesis to the aggravation of feudal rights (*Quomodo jura domini aucta fuerint regnante Ludovico sexto decimo*), and the whole first part of his principal thesis deals with the abolition of the landed ancien régime. What is more, A. Aulard published in 1919 *The French Revolution and the Feudal Régime*, a work taken from a course he taught in 1912-1913, undoubtedly a simple sketch, forgotten today, but never replaced. The problem has been posed, but we cannot affirm that it has been treated in its full scope. We have sketched elsewhere some directions for research and offered some statistical findings. As an example, it would be sufficient to recall that in Haute-Auvergne the feudal imposition could carry away more than a fifth of the net product of the peasant, that in Brittany it could constitute more than a third of the revenues of the nobility. The study of the relation of feudal rights to total revenue of the seigniory, like that of the weight of the feudal tax to peasant revenue, throws, it seems to us, a clearer light on the aristocratic counterrevolution and on the antifeudal counterattack of the peasant masses.[21]

The essential theme of the work of Georges Lefebvre on the subject of agrarian history is well known: the existence, in the framework of the French Revolution, of a peasant revolution autonomous in its origins and processes, its crises and results. "But autonomous above all in its anticapitalist tendencies," and that is the point Lefebvre insists on in particular. Small landowners or small farmers and sharecroppers, day laborers or unskilled workers—each wanted to get a share of the national lands either in return for taxes or at the very least for a small price. And especially, they were profoundly attached to collective rights and to regulations—that is to say—to a precapitalist social and economic mode, because the capitalist transformation of agriculture made their living conditions worse. If, in their anti-feudal aspects, the peasant movements powerfully contributed to the progress of the bourgeois revolution from 1789 to 1792, the fact remains that the majority of peasants—through their protest actions concerning small landed property, the sharing of communal lands, the preservation of the traditional rural community—hindered the transformation of agriculture in a commercial and capitalist direction, braking the normal development of agrarian capitalism in France. "These men were turned toward the past," writes Georges Lefebvre; "they wanted to preserve it or reestablish it; or, if you prefer, it is with elements that they borrowed from the past that they constructed an ideal society. In their state of mind, there was doubtless more conservatism and routine than innovative ardor."[22] Lefebvre attributes a reactionary economic content to peasant egalitarianism.

Wouldn't a theoretical reflection supported by a broad documentary base permit the reversal of this perspective? Let us remark first of all that the problem of the revolutionary role of the small peasantry is framed by a broader question, that of the paths of passage from the old society to the new, let us say from feudalism to capitalism. In his *Studies in the Development of Capitalism* (1946, French translation in 1971*), M. Dobb has shown that the social forces that broke the fetters to the development of the capitalist mode of production came from the petit and middle bourgeoisie and the independent peasantry—a strata of merchant producers rising up against the oligrachy of big landowners and the high commercial bourgeoisie. This is "the truly revolutionary path" as Marx posed the issue in book III of *Capital* (chapter XX). Starting with the example of Japan, H.K. Takahashi, through a penetrating analysis and a comparative method, arrives at the same conclusions:[23] the prime mover of the bourgeois Revolution is found in the development of small and middle independent producers.

It is in this same line that A. Ado's reflection in the conclusion of his thesis on *The Peasant Movement during the French Revolution* (1971)[24] is situated. If the development of the capitalist economy in the 19th century presented, in French agriculture, the negative aspects that we recognize, it is not due to the efforts of very small and proletarian peasants to preserve collective rights and the traditional community, but to the insufficient results of the peasant struggles to strengthen small and middle property that would have constituted a broad base for the development of commercial production. A. Ado underscores the contradiction between the subjective character of the anti-capitalist aspirations of the peasants and the objective content, historically speaking, of their struggles. If the peasantry in its most radical sector had prevailed, it would doubtless have undermined the capitalism of the big farmers, but even more the large property of the reactionary type; it would have led to a restructuring of landed property to the advantage of small and middle producers, the starting point for rapid capitalist evolution; with competition and concentration bringing a speedy ruin to the greatest number, capitalists would have arisen in the heart of the mass of peasant producers.

Thus the specificity of "the French path" is illuminated. The rapid development of capitalism in the French countryside in the 19th century would have required a larger extension of the sector of small and middle independent production, the development of their potential, the total transformation of property relations to the detriment of the large reactionary property worked by sharecroppers or tenant farmers, as a condition of the free development of capitalism. Georges Lefebvre, knowing the persist-

*U.S. edition, International Publishers, New York, 1963.

ence of the rural community, affirms that the negative aspects of the evolution of capitalism in French agriculture in the 19th century came less from what the small peasantry could impose on the bourgeois revolution than from what they could *not* get out of it: the destruction of large property and the end of landed income. If this had happened, the autonomy of the peasant revolution in the framework of the bourgeois revolution, emphasized by Georges Lefebvre, would no longer have had a reason for existence. The peasant revolution would have been nothing but the expression of one of the possible variants of the bourgeois revolution. The subsequent delay of capitalism in rural France must be seen as due to the incomplete character of the peasant revolution, and to the impossiblity of the rural masses, given their situation, to follow to the end their "revolutionary path."

Historian of social classes, Georges Lefebvre could not fail to be interested in the history of mentality and behavior. In this field as well, he was an initiator. "Social history," he writes, "cannot be limited to describing the exterior aspects of the antagonistic classes; it must also get at the mental content of each class." And in his note "Pro domo": "As far as classes are concerned, I try hard to describe their mentality and to take into account, not only their interests, their traditions and their prejudices, but also the state of the world and the circumstances that to a certain measure permit them, in good faith, to believe themselves to be in the right."

The Great Fear of 1789 appeared in 1932.[25] The fear of July 1789 had appeared to the eyes of disconcerted contemporaries as a mystery; those who wished an explanation attributed it to a plot hatched by either the revolutionaries or the aristocrats, depending on their political leanings. Relying on earlier works that described the progression and effects of the panic, rather than its origins, supplementing these with many-sided archival research, Georges Lefebvre went back to its source, reconstituting the various currents, bringing up secondary causes along the way, finally managing to extricate the general cause: the fear of the "brigand" which is itself explained by the economic and social circumstances in the French countryside in 1789. During the Ancien Régime, begging was one of the scourges of the rural world; from 1788 on, unemployment and the high cost of grain aggravated the situation. The political crisis overexcited the imagination even more: to the fear of vagabonds, which was not a vain one, was added in 1789 that of the "aristocratic plot" to which the resistance of the nobility and the intrigues of the court gave a foundation. The fear was thus explained in depth by the play of collective forces, but also, to variable degrees, by the action of individuals. "It will certainly be thought legitimate," writes Georges Lefebvre in his preface, "that in looking for an explanation of the Great Fear, I tried to place myself among those who experienced it." This leads to this book's sharp sense of human realities and their complexity. Researching step by step the explanation of minor events, the author penetrates to the heart of the rural society of the time, in its intimate structure and the multiple currents of collective psychology. The originality of the method consists here in the study of phenomenon meriting consideration as a symptom and capable of revealing the state of the social body.

Starting with an analysis of the various components of the collective mentality, Georges Lefebvre ties it all together in his conclusion and underlines the social and political consequences of this great quivering. For the peasants, it meant a sharpened awareness of their strength and solidarity, a new taste for collective action which, once the "brigands" had gone up in smoke, naturally turned against the all too real social enemy, the feudal lord, his castle and his hated rights. The fear changed from a defensive reaction, to a class solidarity, to a punitive will. Broadening the perspective, Georges Lefebvre demonstrates the collective mental mechanism of the "revolutionary crowds" in an article that throws a particularly strong light on popular behavior in time of revolution.[26]

Beyond his positive work as social historian, Georges Lefebvre has finally pursued a general reflection on history. Conceiving history as an explicative discipline, he was ambitious enough to commit it to the path followed by the exact sciences. On the one hand, by resorting to statistical methods, he wanted to go beyond the descriptive and, by that means, introduce into historical explanation an innovative element, to bring history closer to the natural sciences. On the other hand, on these renewed scientific foundations, he wanted to search for the laws of the general movement of societies, the laws of history.[28]

Georges Lefebvre was one of the artisans of quantification in history. "It is not enough to describe," he loved to repeat, "it is also necessary to count." He had himself given an example of that in his *Peasants of the Nord*, regarding the division of property and farming interests. But he had to admit that immense sectors still needed clarification. On his initiative, the Central Commission of Economic History of the Revolution listed in the order of the day of its 1939 congress the study of social structures and the French bourgeoisie from the end of the Ancien Régime to the Restoration.[29] In his circular to researchers, Lefebvre recalled the great sources for this work: the fiscal rolls, certainly, that he had himself used, but also the notarial archives (marriage contracts, wills, inventories after death) whose use he would later insist upon. "In the economic and social domain," he wrote in his general report, "it would therefore appear that the principal progress would result from recourse to methods that statistics has elaborated and that it would thus be appropriate to introduce into the education of the historian, a course of study that would accustom him to practice these methods."[30] We know that this lesson was heard. What is not counted today?

We could however wonder if Georges Lefebvre would not have reacted against the excesses of an invasive and finally ahistorical quantitativism, data and numerical series not constituting an end in itself for the historian. Adeline Daumard and Francois Furet rashly wrote in 1959, "Scientifically speaking, there is no social history other than quantitative."[31] Georges Lefebvre had responded in advance in 1939: "This is not to say that economic and social history will cease, for all that, to be descriptive. ... Then we must not forget that history results from the interaction of a multitude of factors. ... Thus those who advocate turning to statistics do not mean to imply in any way that these will suffice to exhaust historical reality."[32] Statistical history is effective only if it is integrated into a global vision of historical evolution and opens onto social movements, the evolution of thoughts as well as institutions—and the event itself, and if it serves to support history in the deepest sense. Such is the lesson of Georges Lefebvre, and also that of Ernest Labrousse.

With his ambition to bring history, despite its special qualities, closer to the exact sciences, Georges Lefebvre intended to discover not historical laws (the word did not seem appropriate to him) but "constants" that he would consider approximate. He came to define history as "a positive discipline of the perceptible world"; he was still speaking of a "sociological history and its scientific aspirations."[33] In a comunication on "The Synthesis in History" on the occasion of the fiftieth anniversary of the Society of Modern History in 1951, Lefebvre assigned historians the ideal goal of "a superior form of synthesis." For him the perfect example was still Tocqueville's *The Ancien Régime and the Revolution*, "the most beautiful book on the French Revolution." "Tocqueville was detached from the story, and beyond the story, he tried to indicate the relations that explained precisely the facts of the story that he assumed were known." He thus determined certain general traits and shed light on a certain number of probabilities. Likewise, in comparing economic evolution and particularly the economic or social evolution of similar regions, "we can hope to succeed in detaching a certain number of general treatises from this comparison."[34] This is what Marc Bloch attempted in his two volumes devoted to *Feudal Society*, particularly admired by Georges Lefebvre.

Wouldn't we then be able to glimpse, with a certain degree of probability, the line of historical evolution? In his "Reflections on history" (1955),

Georges Lefebvre recalled Tocqueville's words in the preface to *The Ancien Régime and the Revolution*: "I have acted as doctors who, in each dead organ, try to discover the laws of life." Elsewhere, Lefebvre commented on this quotation: "He also formulates propositions that imply the determinist postulate, which are as indispensable to scientific research as they are to the work and enterprises of man." And to quote Tocqueville again: "It is not by chance that aristocracies were born and maintained; they, like all the rest, are subject to fixed laws and it is perhaps not impossible to discover them."

Georges Lefebvre, starting from the most reliable scholarship, intended to raise history to the level where it would acquire "an altogether superior intellectual value and appeal"; he joined the most legitimate ambitions of the philosophy of history, those of Saint-Simon and of Marx. It does not seem useless to us to recall this teaching in an era when some are trying to reintroduce into history—a subject that is thinkable and thus rational—the chance, the contingent, the irrational. I leave it to you to imagine what Georges Lefebvre would have thought of the theory of "the skid"... [see chapter 16].

III

Whatever updating may be necessary, Georges Lefebvre opened new paths to history—new orientations and new methods. He knew how to do that while reserving all rights to those traditional aspects of history that today are too often scorned: the story, the event, the individual.

The individual? We are familiar with the portraits sketched with a few sober and just lines. Speaking of Mirabeau and of Danton, Lefebvre notes "the animal thrust,... the muscle structure of two giants"; in sharp contrast to the physically weak—though morally "incorruptible"—Robespierre, Danton bragged of his prowess at the table and in bed. We should reread the pages on Danton's character: "Self-interested flexibility, wily prudence, venality...; but sometimes also the true realism of a statesman; then, untameable rages, careless negligence and sudden renunciations of a violent temperament that no moral or intellectual discipline tried to master; and then unpredictably, an impetuous return to conciliatory generosity and human pity also explained by temperament, too eager for pleasure to tolerate the somber reflections of mistrust and hatred."[35] We should reread several pages of the portrait of Napoleon: "above all,... a temperament."

The temperament... this preoccupation often comes up in the remarks of Georges Lefebvre in the last years of his life, particularly in explaining the behavior and the role of individuals in history by their character and temperament. There are types of human behavior discerned by characterology. But beyond the study of the character of the warrior, for example, what Georges Lefebvre proposed was "a biology of the warrior."[36] "We make a big case of the temperament of memorable characters," he wrote, "but we cannot discern with precision either its nature or its action: who will explain to us, if not the biologist, how to distinguish in this respect the ambitious from the resigned, the authoritarian from the passive, the audacious from the prudent?"[37] We grasp here one of the ambitions of Georges Lefebvre: to introduce an innovative element into the historical explanation through the study of biological factors.[38] Since history is bound up with knowledge of the perceptible world, its progress should in some way follow that of natural science.

The event? Georges Lefebvre did not feel for it that scorn so long displayed. He reconstructed it with caution and in great detail. He never ceased defending his methodical research, repeating that, "without it, there is no history," and that in order to dominate events, it is first necessary to be familiar with them.[39] This explains the attention and care he brought to publications of pure research, like the *Collection of documents relating to the sessions of the Estates General*,[40] the first volume of which (1953) did not appear without raising some objections. "Again ... a collection uniquely devoted to the minute description of events," Georges Lefebvre has an imaginary interlocutor say, "when we mean to dominate them in order to raise history above the story to a superior form, where we illuminate the characteristic traits of the life of societies, the multiplicity of its factors, the complexity of their synthetic action." And he retorts that, in order not to let himself be trapped "in this sector of history that a frightful neologism baptized 'evenementiel' [relating to the event]," it is important first of all to establish the facts as exactly as possible. "It will never be our wish to see our way cluttered with hasty generalizations constructed on the shaky foundation of imprecise notions."[41]

What better plea for 'evenementiel' history, or better yet 'historisante'—"dreadful neologisms"[42]—than the article of 1941 on "The Murder of the Count of Dampierre"?[43] The anecdotal is here elevated to the dignity of the typical. What event could be more banal at first sight—a news item among many similar news items at the time of the revolution—than the massacre by peasants of the Count of Dampierre on June 22, 1791, at about three o'clock in the afternoon, while the heavy carriage carrying the royal family moved away from Sainte-Menehould? A simple episode in the eyes of contemporaries. In actual fact, the occurrence goes beyond the anecdote: it is a question of the typical event in a situation. Georges Lefebvre's admirable analysis restores to the event all its dignity. The murder of the Count of

Dampierre was not only the result of a risky step. The peasants had long detested the Count for his relentless pursuit of the collection of his feudal rights. The episode is no doubt part of the *fear* that followed the flight of the king. But as always the essential social motivation penetrates the political event.

Finally the story. Out of necessity, Georges Lefebvre is formal and does not intend to exclude it from history. "It is not a question of renouncing the story," he wrote in his article, "Future of History" (1947). And in his "Reflections on History" (1955): "I do not associate myself with the excommunication of the story." He willingly thinks of it what La Fontaine says of "The Donkey Skin": "If the 'Donkey Skin' had been told to me, I would have taken great pleasure in it." Georges Lefebvre assigned the story both a pedagogical and civic value. It seemed to him that it was essential for its explanatory value; it was a question of finding those relations between the facts that enabled them to be understood. But for the traditional story that places politicians and conquerors downstage, he substituted a story that takes care to save from oblivion the memory of those whom Georges Lefebvre called "the light of history": the mass of workers who labor with their hands, but also "the independents who, breaking with the conformity of their world, dared to criticize its flaws and its abuses," even more the bold who ran the risk of rising up against authority ... "When I leaf through the past and their anonymous phantoms come out of the shadows, I feel that out of the mute intelligence a profound emotion, a fraternity, unites us. On the condition that the story takes pains to save their memory from oblivion, I will never abandon it; for in my eyes, these men are the light of history."[44]

If, in the work of Georges Lefebvre, critical intelligence and scientific strictness do not exclude warmth and sensitivity, it is because the historian is inseparable from the man. Georges Lefebvre has talked about and demonstrated his faithfulness to the French Revolution, to its ideas and tradition, as well as his "esteem" and "friendship" for Robespierre:[45] it is at Robespierre's side that he would have gone, to sit with the Jacobins, just like Jaurès. Faithfulness to bygone days? Ossified friendship? "Revolutionary catechism?" Georges Lefebvre remained more faithful to the spirit than the letter.

Like the men of the Enlightenment, he called his desires "the rationalization of society."[46] But as a member from the beginning of the unified socialist party founded by Jean Jaurès and Jules Guesde, he thought of this rationalization only in terms of the abolition of private ownership of the means of production. "There is a contradiction between the sovereignty of the people and universal suffrage on one hand, which put the fate of the nation in the hands of all, and the capitalist economy wherein the wage earner sees his work, his wage, and consequently his life in the hands of the one who owns the means of production."[47] It was not enough to rationalize production; it was a question of rationalizing society. When the French Revolution proclaimed equality of rights, "it was rational to hope that society would apply itself to procuring all the means to exercise these. That is why the proletariat became a revolutionary class, as the bourgeoisie had been in the past. That is why a party of rationalists, but not everyone, elaborated socialist doctrines to benefit the proletariat or, at least, advocated the intervention of the State in social relations."[48]

Let us reread, in the light of the events of these last decades, the serious pages at the end of Lefebvre's *Eighty-nine*, dictated by his concern to make the Declaration of the Rights of Man understood. The Declaration entails a risk. As the citizens are vested with the right to govern themselves, "if they abuse their power in regard to others and especially if they refuse, through selfishness, to assure the safety of the community, the community will perish and, with it, their liberty, if not their existence." Here we grasp the profound meaning of the Declaration: it presupposes that the citizens possess patriotism in the proper meaning of the term: respect for the rights of others, reasoned devotion to the community, the "virtue" of Montesquieu, Rousseau and Robespierre. Liberty requires "application, perpetual effort, rigorous self-control, possible sacrifice." It is thus more difficult to live free than to live as a slave, and that is why men so often renounce liberty; "[To live free] is in a way an invitation to live courageously and, on occasion, heroically."[49]

Liberty cannot be imagined without independence. If Georges Lefebvre retained esteem and friendship for Robespierre, it was because he was the greatest "of those who took it upon themselves to impose on all the pressing obligation of public safety."[50] As a patriot, Georges Lefebvre was deeply affected by the exemplary death of his brother, the geographer Theodore Lefebvre, professor at the Faculty of Arts of Poitiers, active in the Resistance, executed with an axe by the German Occupation. This doubtless explains the restrained emotion with which Georges Lefebvre quoted the speech of Robespierre, which he loved above all, of September 25, 1793: "What is more difficult for a patriot is that in the last two years, one hundred thousand men have had their throats cut by betrayal and weakness: it is the weakness for traitors that is ruining us. People feel sympathy for the most criminal, for those who deliver the homeland to the sword of the enemy; as for me, I can feel sympathy only for unfortunate virtue; I can feel sympathy only for oppressed innocence; I can feel sympathy only for the fate of an unhappy people whose throats are cut with so much villainy."[51]

These lines portray the historian just as accurately as the Incorruptible [Robespierre]. Lefebvre felt tied by a feeling of fraternal solidarity to all men fallen in battles for liberty. We repeat with Georges Lefebvre the vow that he expressed as a prayer: "In our daily life as simple citizens, may perseverance and courage never be lacking to us, so that we may remain worthy of those fallen heroes."[52]

16

Classical Revolutionary Historiography and Revisionist Endeavors[1]

The French Revolution has often been presented as the crowning achievement of the century of the Enlightenment and thus essentially as an ideological act. It still appears as such in the work of Aulard.[2] Jaurès was the first who wanted to see in it a social phenomenon and thus of economic origin.[3] Not that Jaurès had denied any importance to the philosophical movement. "Just as it would be vain and false," he writes in the introduction to his *Socialist History of the French Revolution*, "to deny the dependence of thought and even dreams on the economic system and the concrete forms of production, so it would be puerile and crude to summarily explain the movement of human thought solely by the evolution of economic forms." It is not solely by the force of things that the Revolution was accomplished; it is also "by the force of men, by the energy of consciousness and will." It is nevertheless true, and Jaurès notes it vigorously, that the Revolution itself was the result of a long economic and social evolution that made the bourgeoisie master of power and the economy. The historiography of the French Revolution has remained at that point: Albert Mathiez reedited the work of Jaurès in 1922; Georges Lefebvre acknowledged Jaurès as his master.[4]

Actually, the Jaurès interpretation is not new. From the period of the Restoration, historians of the liberal school, even if they were hardly interested in the economic origins of the social movement, had strongly emphasized one of the essential characteristics of our national history: the appearance, growth and final triumph of the bourgeoisie; between the people and the aristocracy, the bourgeoisie had slowly created the framework and clarified the ideas of a new society of which 1789 was the consecration. Such is Guizot's essential idea in his course on *The History of Civilization in France*.[5] Such was also the conviction of both Tocqueville[6] and Taine.[7]

From the period of the Revolution, however, Barnave had pushed the social analysis further. In his *Introduction to the French Revolution*, written in 1792, after having posited the principle that property *influences* institutions, Barnave states that the institutions created by the landed aristocracy impeded and slowed the arrival of a new era. "Once the arts and commerce succeeded in penetrating the people and created a new means to wealth to aid the laboring class, all was ready for a revolution in political laws: a new distribution of wealth produced a new distribution of power."[8] It is to this line of thought that the 1847 *Communist Manifesto* of Karl Marx, and then the first volume of *Capital* in 1867, subscribe.

Thus the social interpretation of the French Revolution plunges deeply into our historical past. From the beginning, this interpretation alone, through its scholarly demands and critical reflection, established itself as truly scientific: compare the work of Guizot–or even that of Thiers—always concerned with documents, even if they were official ones, to that of Lacretelle.[9] This interpretation was gradually perfected, in order to realize the complexity of the Revolution. Ph. Sagnac, in the last volume of *The History of France* published under the direction of Ernest Lavisse, and even more strongly A. Mathiez, have clarified what was in the 18th century the *aristocratic reaction* that culminated in 1787-1788 in the *nobiliary revolt.*[10] Yet it is not enough to distinguish between the revolt of the aristocracy and the revolution of the Third Estate. First Jaurès and then Mathiez after him have insisted on the rapid disintegration of the latter. Antagonisms were quickly manifested between the various bourgeois categories and between the bourgeoisie and the popular masses, accounting for the complexity of revolutionary history and the progression of its various stages. Following in the same spirit with his study of the peasant masses, Lefebvre demonstrated the existence, in the general framework of the Revolution, of a peasant current possessing autonomy and specificity in its origins, procedures, crises and tendencies. This same approach has been applied by several of his students to the study of the popular urban masses.[11]

Thus the social interpretation of the French Revolution was gradually perfected through a long development, secular to say the least. By its constant recourse to scholarly research ("Without scholarship there is no history," G. Lefebvre repeated), by its critical spirit, by its efforts at theoretical reflection, by its global vision of the Revolution, it alone merits to be considered truly scientific.

This deepening of the social interpretation of the Revolution has progressed to the rhythm of history itself. It would be banal to recall here that the vision of history is shaded or modified by each generation of historians: it is under the weight of lived experiences and real history that history is also written. The history of the French Revolution could not escape this law. For almost two centuries, each generation in its turn, through its hopes and dreams, studied the Revolution, matrix of our history, either to exalt it or reject it. Not without results. The movement of history has gradually revealed to each generation new aspects, more and more numerous factors and a more and more complex interaction. Thus new meanings, up to then masked by the very complexity of the phenomenon, have been brought to light. It is significant that it was in Kiev, in that Ukraine where the peasant had just been freed from serfdom, but without gaining property, that Loutchisky became that first to be attracted to the study of the agrarian question during the French Revolution; in 1897, he published *Small Property in France before the Revolution and the Sale of National Lands.* It is significant that it was during the First World War that Mathiez understood the economic necessities for conducting a great national war and the requirement of a controlled economy; he then wrote the studies that formed, in 1927, *The High Cost of Living and the Social Movement during the Terror.*

Thus the social interpretation of the French Revolution progressed at the same rhythm as history. And if, in the middle of our century, the attention of its historians is focused on the popular urban masses, wouldn't it be because the world has entered an era of mass movements? These movements don't exist without frightening the ruling classes; this leads, in the opposite direction, to those vain efforts to deny the French Revolution its historical reality or its social and national specificity, a vain precedent. Consequently, a revisionist line confronts the classical social interpretation. Thinking to discredit it, certain revisionists have baptized the classical interpretation "Jacobin historiography" of the Revolution, a description we do not challenge, understanding by that, as Georges Lefebvre has taught us, the understanding and faithfulness to the cause of the people, but without the historian abandoning any of the essential requirements of the scholarly method and critical spirit. Let us say more precisely, a progressive tradition of revolutionary historiography, from Michelet to Lefebvre, passing through Jaurès, Aulard and Mathiez, and whatever may have been the shades of difference and divergences among these men—the only tradition which, in its principled progression, has been and remains scientific.

I. Political revolution or social revolution?

The offensive against the classical interpretation of the French Revolution was expressed toward the middle of the 1950s, during the height of the Cold War. In 1964, R. R. Palmer displayed in an article entitled "The World Revolution of the West," published in the *Political Science Quar-*

terly, the conception of a "western" or "Atlantic" revolution that he was to tirelessly develop for several years. That same year, on May 6, 1954, A. Cobban, professor of French history at the University of London, gave an opening lesson entitled "The Myth of the French Revolution." Oddly enough, it was an English and an American historian who joined forces to question the experience of more than a century of French revolutionary historiography.

R. R. Palmer, at the very moment when A. Cobban was denying the anti-feudal and bourgeois nature of the French Revolution, was attempting to deny its national character. His argumentation was taken up and developed in collaboration with J. Godechot, in 1955, at the International Congress of the Historical Sciences at Rome. These ideas were taken up again and amplified by J. Godechot in *The Great Nation* (1956), and by R. Palmer in *The Age of the Democratic Revolution* (1959)—works that, it must be said, created hardly and echo among French historians and did not gain any support.[12]

According to this argument, the French Revolution would have been only "an aspect of a western or more precisely an Atlantic revolution that began in the English colonies of America soon after 1763, was prolonged by the revolutions in Switzerland, the Netherlands and Ireland, before reaching France between 1787 and 1789. From France, it rebounded to the Netherlands, overcame the German Rhineland, Switzerland, Italy, Malta, the eastern Mediterranean and Egypt." Still later, it spread to the other countries of Europe and to all of Latin America. The French Revolution would thus be integrated into "the great Atlantic revolution."[13]

Without emphasizing here how anachronistic the qualifiers *western* and *Atlantic* are in reference to their use in current international politics, let us recognize that the Atlantic Ocean has played an essential role, that cannot be underestimated, in the renovation of the economy and the exploitation of the colonial countries by the nations of western Europe. But that is not the position of our authors, who have hardly any interest in the economic and social foundations of the movement of history. In fact, they have no interest in showing that the French Revolution is but one episode in the general course of history that, after the revolutions in the Netherlands, England and America, contributed to bringing the bourgeoisie to power and liberating the development of capitalist economy. Moreover, the French Revolution did not mark the geographical limit of this transformation: capitalist economy and bourgeois power were not confined to the shores of the Atlantic Ocean. In the 19th century, the ascension of the bourgeoisie went hand in hand with the installation of capitalist economy, everywhere where that occurred. The bourgeois revolution was of universal import.

This conception of a *western* or *Atlantic* revolution, by integrating the French Revolution into a vaster uprising, by drowning it in a vague international agitation, drains it, on the other hand, of its true dimension and its national significance. Putting the French Revolution on the same plane with "the revolutions of Switzerland, the Netherlands and Ireland" strangely minimizes its depth and dimensions, the dramatic intensity of its social and political struggles and the importance of the mutation it represented in our national history. Can we really speak of the French Revolution, as R. Palmer does, as a "revolutionary upheaval common to Europe and America"?[14] If there was indeed social and political upheaval, at least in continental Europe, it was as a consequence of the revolutionary conquest and Napoleonic domination.

The western or Atlantic interpretation of the French Revolution, by draining it of all specific content—economic (anti-feudal and capitalist), social (anti-aristocratic and bourgeois) and national (one and indivisible), would nullify a half century of classical historiography from Jean Jaurès to Georges Lefebvre. Tocqueville had, however, opened the door to this idea in *The Ancien Régime and the Revolution* when he pondered: "Why have analogous principles and similar political theories led the United States to a change of government and France to a total subversion of society?"[15] Posing the problem in these terms is going beyond the surface of an institutional and political history to endeavor to reach social and economic realities in their national specificity.

Stubbornly maintained for about ten years, this theory of a western or Atlantic revolution was never able to prevail, in France at least, over the classical interpretation of the French Revolution. J. Godechot tempered it bit by bit, insisting on the anti-feudal nature of the social struggles from 1789 to 1793.[16] As for Palmer, didn't he write in one of his last works, published in 1968: "The more one stresses the idea of an expansive geographical movement, the more one sees it in the light of an essentially *bourgeois* revolution"? Farther on he states that the Revolution was "a decisive episode in the history of property and propertied classes. Everywhere where revolutionary ideas have been applied, that is to say in France and the sister republics, then in the Napoleonic empire, there was a redefinition of property. The property of the land was stripped of its feudal rights and of the aristocratic right of primogeniture."[17] An anti-feudal revolution: therefore, essentially *bourgeois* (even if the author adds: "in the sense of this confused term that is the word *bourgeoisie*").

The theory advanced by R. Palmer in 1954 belongs to the international climate of the 1950s; it was a question of exalting the ideological solidarity of the countries of the Atlantic alliance, by going back to the 18th century, to the origin of their political traditions. Once the Cold War had calmed down, people returned to a more serene vision, more consonant with reality. For R. Palmer, in his 1968 work, 1789 is also the revolution of equality, an aspect the French school has always insisted upon with vigor.

The offensive of Alfred Cobban was more dangerous. Dating from the same period, 1954, it was part of the same context as R. Palmer's endeavor. But it responded less to a conjectural incitement than to a long meditated and, so to speak, structural design consisting of rejecting all social interpretation of revolutions and finally of history. This was a defense reaction: by denying the reality of classes and class struggle, the demon of revolutions could be exorcised. "One may wonder," Georges Lefebvre wrote in 1956, "why the mythical interpretation of revolutions, or rather of certain ones, seems so in favor. It does not seem doubtful that it reflects the ideological evolution of the ruling class under the influence of democratic pressure and especially of the Russian Revolution; feeling threatened, this class repudiates the rebellion of the ancestors that assured it preeminence, because it discerns there a dangerous precedent."[18] This statement has lost none of its value if we consider the profound tendencies of American historiography or the dangerous affirmations of the group that calls itself the "Annals school."

The French Revolution would thus not be due to class conflict, as has traditionally been assumed by the French historical school since Barnave, Thiers and Guizot. Certainly there are many shades of difference among those who, following Cobban, rejected the social interpretation of the Revolution, and particularly among the American historians. But, as R. Palmer wrote, all [of them] doubt that "class analysis is the most useful instrument for understanding the French Revolution." The debate essentially turns on the significance and usefulness of certain concepts—feudalism, bourgeoisie, capitalism. Finally the question is asked: must the Revolution be considered anti-feudal and anti-aristocratic? Did it constitute the necessary transition to bourgeois and capitalist society?

A. Cobban challenges the interpretation according to which the French Revolution substituted a new social order for the Ancien Régime.[19] "If I advanced the opinion that the interpretation of the Revolution, dealing with the substitution of a bourgeois capitalist order for feudalism is a myth, that would not be suggesting that the revolution itself is mythical and nothing of significance occurred in France in that period." There *was*, then, a revolution. (A. Cobban had at first thought of entitling his lecture: "Was there a

French Revolution?"). But the concept given to it by classical French historiography is only a myth; that is, in the figurative and familiar sense of the word, it has no real basis, that it does not conform to reality.

The argumentation of A. Cobban rests on two essential points: whether the French Revolution was anti-feudal and capitalist. The Revolution suppressed feudalism: in fact, responds A. Cobban, the feudal order had long since disappeared. The Revolution allowed the establishment of capitalism: in fact, responds A. Cobban, the Revolution was the work, not of true capitalists, but of bourgeois, principally officeholders, who were already exercising all the administrative functions and who held on to them.

The first argument of A. Cobban rests on the meaning he gives to the word *feudalism.*[20] But let us first recall the adage of modern linguistics: "Words have no meaning; they have only uses." Feudalism, feudal regime, feudal rights: the use of these words, for the 18th century, could lead to controversy. The medievalists obstinately refuse this application and denounce this "abuse of language." No one contests the fact that feudalism, properly speaking, had for a long time been a system "decrepit with age and that had received extreme unction," to borrow an expression of Carlyle, while the rights pertaining to the rural seigniory still remained vigorous on the eve of the Revolution, nor that feudalism had been charged with all the rigors imposed by the seigniorial regime.

But what matters to us here is less the legal definition of feudalism than its social dimension, the sense in which it was understood not by jurists, but by peasants. As the institution declined, the meaning of the word was naturally altered and even many notaries in the 18th century, either through ignorance or in the spirit of simplification, had for a long time confused feudalism and seigniory, feudal rights and seigniorial rights. For the peasants, as for men conversant with matters of the land, *feudalism* was, in this somewhat emphatic language of the 18th century, *servitude to the land*, on which weighed the inalienable landed income, the perpetual fees, the fees received by the lord on the price of sold inherited property; also the tithes, in short the *complexum feudale* of the jurists. It is in this sense that the word was used all through the Revolution and for a long time afterwards. Merlin de Douai, specialist in this subject, explained it clearly in his report of September 4, 1789 to the Committee on Feudal Rights of the Constituent Assembly. "Although these words, *feudal rights*, in their strictest sense, designate only the rights derived from the contract of fief of which infeudation itself is the direct principle, popular usage has not refrained from extending the meaning to all rights which, most generally found in the hands of the lords, form in their whole what Dumoulin calls the *complexum feudale*. Thus, although the seigniorial income, the rights of *champart* [the lord's share of the crop], the *corvées* [statute labor], the *banalités* [exclusive rights of a lord to maintain a mill, an oven or a winepress], the obligations representing former servitude, etc., are not properly speaking feudal rights, we will not fail to concern ourselves with them."[21]

Even more important than the still living reality of the word is its social weight. The problem may be envisioned from a double point of view. It would be necessary in the first place to measure the imposition that feudal rights represented on total production, and then the burden that they laid on the peasants; in the second place, we must calculate the portion of these rights in the total revenue of the seigniory. It cannot be a question here of entering into the details of the methodology of this research. Let us simply recall, for sake of example, that the feudal imposition could take away up to a fifth (20%) of the net product (that is after deducting from the gross product the cost of seed, cultivation and maintenance) of the peasant of Haute-Auvergne. And that in this same province, feudal rights constituted a third of the seigniorial revenue.[22] More generally, J. Meyer estimates that the French nobility took a third of the agricultural revenue of the country.[23] The relation of feudal rights to peasant revenues accounts for the behavior of the peasant masses at the end of the Ancien Régime and during the Revolution. The relation of feudal rights to the total revenue of the seigniory sheds light on the behavior of the nobility, being one of the motivations of the counterrevolution. The Auvergne nobility had good reason to resist the abolition of feudalism, going as far as counterrevolution and emigration. And there was good reason for the peasant revolt to hold sway in Haute-Auvergne from 1789 to 1792. For the peasants as well as the lords, feudalism, like the Revolution, was far from being a myth.

A. Cobban's second argument concerns the composition of the revolutionary assemblies. In Great Britain, the growth of the capitalist bourgeoisie was that of a class engaged in commerce and industry, and thus composed of merchants and bankers, of manufacturers and entrepreneurs. Now, in the Constituent Assembly, this category made up only 13%; two-thirds of the deputies of the Third Estate belonged to the liberal professions. Is it possible to attribute to these men the will to substitute the capitalist order for the old order? What is more, continues A. Cobban, out of the 1,539 members of the Constituent Assembly and the Convention, 629 held public office before the Revolution, of which 289 held tenured offices.[24]

This personnel is found again under the Consulate and the Empire, not only in subordinate functions, as under the Ancien Régime, but even in managerial posts held before 1789 by the nobiliary oligarchy. The Revolution is thus reduced to an institutional aspect: neither bourgeois nor capitalist, it simply would have resulted in placing the administration and the government between the hands of these professional bureaucrats to whom the monarchial State already owed its effectiveness.

This second aspect of the critical argumentation of A. Cobban was taken up, at a more recent date and with various nuances, by some American historians. Without going into the complexity of the discussions and the polemics, let us recall the stands taken by Elizabeth L. Eisenstein in regard to the bourgeoisie and of George V. Taylor in regard to capitalism.[25]

E. L. Eisenstein, in an article published in 1965, picked out the occurrences of the word *bourgeoisie* in G. Lefebvre's *Eighty-Nine*; she considered the usage excessive. According to Eisenstein, Lefebvre did not offer sufficient proof for assertions such as "The bourgeoisie demonstrated a keen political sense" and "The bourgeoisie set the nation in motion," and thus he quite simply evaded reality and attributed to the bourgeoisie alone a revolutionary action whose protagonists in fact belonged to diverse social categories. Eisenstein asserts that the revolutionary initiative went back to a group of partisan intellectuals with new ideas and who, though of diverse social origins, pursued common political goals. The men that G. Lefebvre encompasses in the abstract category of bourgeoisie would have constituted only a tiny minority of the activists. "The bourgeoisie was not the originator of the strong protest movement of 1788 and did not play an important role in the events and reforms of 1789." This revolutionary role is attributed to "a group of agitators of various orders and social classes." Elizabeth Eisenstein implicity calls into question the definition of the bourgeoisie and thus the bourgeois character of the Revolution.

G. V. Taylor challenges the concept of capitalism. By capitalism, this author essentially means the investment of private capital in order to profit; by capitalists, essentially the class of entrepreneurs as Adam Smith defined them: the initiators of new forms of economy, having a taste for risk in their concern for the maximum profit. Taylor opposes to them the rich who were not capitalists, concerned with stable investments even if the profit is mediocre. This "non-capitalist" wealth, "proprietary wealth" according to the author, consisted essentially of landed wealth, urban buildings, venal charges and diverse private income; it would have constituted 80% of the total wealth of France. Most of the wealth belonging to the upper strata of the Third Estate came from the "proprietary wealth," while numerous nobles were already involved in capitalist enterprises. The Revolution, despite the suppression of venal charges, would have scarcely changed the relations between capitalist wealth and proprietary wealth. "The fundamental question", Taylor writes, "is to know if the bourgeoisie of 1789, however it is defined, was economically opposed to other classes enjoying a different source of revenue." Taylor's response is negative. Between a large part of the nobility and the proprietary sector of the middle classes, there was "identity of forms of investment and socio-economic ideas, so that in the last analysis these two classes, economically speaking, formed one and the same group." Like Cobban, Taylor concludes that the French Revolution could not have been a struggle between classes opposed by different forms of wealth and distinct economic interests. The opposition was purely legal, not economic. The French Revolution was "an essentially political revolution leading to social reforms, and not a social revolution having political consequences."

As for the problem of the bourgeoisie, the importance of the role of the intellectuals and officials in the maturation and conduct of the Revolution cannot be denied. Among the various bourgeois categories, they no doubt counted as the most progressive elements. We cannot inordinately minimize the role of the ideological movement in preparing for the Revolution. The tenured officeholders in particular, having reached a level of comfort, if not wealth, strengthened in their independence by the venality of their office, constituted a cultivated milieu where criticism of the existing order was given free rein. In this sense, both officals and intellectuals contributed to the formation of the ideology that incited the awakening and then the class consciousness of all the bourgeois categories—a phenomenon without which the Revolution would be inconceivable.

Bourgeois categories, we said; it is indeed necessary to state that, concerning the society of the Ancien Régime, the word *bourgeoisie* is most often used in the plural, even by French historians. Would that not indicate a desire, more or less explicit, to deny, if not social realities, at least class realities? The bourgeoisie was, without a doubt, diverse and multiple; rarely is a social class homogenous. But the bourgeoisie was also *one*. In the 18th century, as in every period of history, class distinctions were numerous, varied, often hardly perceptible: birth and income, education and language, dress and dwelling, life style... none of these criteria, taken in isolation, alone constitute the distinctive characteristic of the class. In the first rank of bourgeois criteria was doubtless fortune, not so much its size but its origin, the form and manner in which it was managed and spent—to live "bourgeoisement." There is no doubt that a Frenchman of the 18th century discerned without difficulty if so and so belonged to the aristocracy or came from the bourgeoisie: "That smells bourgeois."

It is necessary to go further and attempt a definition implying a minimum of systematization—a simple approach that will allow us to grasp the unity of social types whose appearance is sometimes contradictory. The discussion on the "New paths toward a history of the western bourgeoisie in the 18th and 19th centuries," during the Congress of Historical Sciences in Rome in 1955, many furnish the elements of this approach.[26]

In the view of E. Labrousse: "In good standing, the group of officers, clerks, bureaucrats carrying out administrative tasks, from which will be kept whatever is not consolidated in the nobility. In good standing, the proprietor, the *rentier*, living *bourgeoisement*.... Bourgeois also, naturally, the liberal professions, in the sense we still mean today. All these varieties came from the vast family of heads of enterprises who constitute numerically the bulk of the class: proprietors or administrators of independent means of production served by wage labor, from whom they drew their principal income and took for themselves, notably, the commercial and industrial profit. This was a multiple family, from the financier, the shipowner, the manufacturer, the *negociant*, the merchant, down to the last ranks of the small categories—the owner of the shop and workshop, the independent artisan."

P. Vilar was more systematic in his clarifying remarks in the discussion that followed: "Well then, when it's a question of grasping the origin and statistical mass of the bourgeois, E. Labrousse has done just that in Marxist terms: 'proprietor or administrator of independent means of production.' There we have some criteria in front of us: 1) Having the free use of the means of production. 2) Applying to those means of production, by free contract, a labor force that has only its labor power at its disposal. 3) Taking for one's own use the difference between the value realized by the merchandise and the remuneration of the applied labor force. There is no bourgeois who does not live, directly or indirectly, from the social imposition thus defined." This outline of a definition would seem to permit us to better situate the position and the role of the bourgeoisie in the French Revolution.

As for the problem of capitalism, there is again no doubt that the intellectuals and officials, like the members of the liberal professions, would care little about promoting its development. It would however be necessary to clarify if, as members of the Constituent Assembly, these men came under the influence of economic groups concerned with ridding themselves of all regulations. Moreover, 13% of the Constituent were *negociants* and manufactures, two pressure groups that dominated the debates in a very active manner; the "extraordinary deputies of manufacture and commerce" who represented the interests of the ports and the Massiac Club, defender of the interests of the planters of Santo Domingo, the shipowners and refiners intervened each time that the colonial regime was called into question.[27] Let us remark that on the other hand, as partisans of individual liberty and the freedom to think, the Constituents were themselves, implicitly, for economic freedom. If the Constituent Assembly did not explicitly proclaim this economic freedom, it at least established and stubbornly maintained free trade in grain, abolished the corporations and suppressed the monopoly of the great commercial companies—all reforms favorable to the development of free enterprise and free profit.

Even though many revolutionaries were partisans of the extension of small property and did not suspect the possibilities of capitalist concentration, even though the most democratic had as their ideal a society of small, independent producers, the results of the Revolution were nevertheless completely different; it is impossible to measure them against the intentions of the revolutionary partisans. As Elizabeth Eisenstein has suggested, the initiators of a social movement are not necessarily the beneficiaries; we cannot argue with the fact that several leaders of the bourgeois revolution were not bourgeois. History, on the other hand, is not only the actions of the actors on stage; that would be "in total contradiction with the very idea of social history," as G. Shapiro has stressed in his polemic with E. Eisenstein.[28] As for the French Revolution, the essential fact is that the old system of production was destroyed and that the Revolution established freedom of enterprise and profit with no restrictions, thus opening the way to capitalism.

The victory over feudalism and the Ancien Régime did not signify, however, the simultaneous appearance of new social relations and new economic structures. It is patently obvious that after ten years of revolution, society would not yet be essentially bourgeois nor the economy specifically capitalist. The passage to capitalism is not a simple process by which the capitalist elements develop in the bosom of the old society until the moment when they are strong enough to break its bounds. It would still be a long time before capitalism affirmed itself definitively; its progress was slow during the revolutionary period; the size of the enterprises often remained modest, with commercial capital prevailing. The ruin of the feudal landed property and of the corporative and regulated system, assuring the autonomy of the system of capitalist production, uncompromisingly paved the way to a new organization of production and exchange—revolutionary transformation par excellence. The history of the 19th century, that of the working class in particular, proved that this was no myth.

II. Revolution: necessary or contingent?

At the moment when Elizabeth Eisenstein's article was reviving the discussion among American historians of the bourgeois nature of the French Revolution, in France itself in 1965 a revisionist undertaking on a completely different scale was begun and has since been stubbornly pursued. Here the historical context is no longer that of the Cold War, but it would not be possible to abstract this endeavor from the social conditions and political struggles of the France of 1965. The goal is still the same: while denying the reality of classes, find an alternative explanation for the revolutionary upsurge. Thus we have this effort to modernize and reassert the value of the liberal theme of the duality of the French Revolution, but without the rationality and necessity that characterized the analysis of a Thiers or a Guizot. What is proposed is an aristocratic and bourgeois revolution of the Enlightenment, followed, with no necessary connection, by a popular revolution, violent and reactionary. Thus a reformist way and a revolutionary way would confront each other.

This interpretation was first expressed in the work of Edgar Faure, *Turgot's Disgrace (May 12, 1776)*, published in 1961.[29] But could the liberal reform then undertaken succeed with the persistence of the feudal structures and aristocratic privilege that this minister, however enlightened, never intended to touch?... In a similar vein is the work *The Revolution* by F. Furet and D. Richet.[30] Of the various themes developed and tirelessly taken up again, two are worth retaining: that of the "revolution of elites" and that of the "skid" of the revolutionary movement, both implying the contingent nature of the Revolution. "Was the Revolution inevitable?" No, without a doubt, for our authors: "All still depends on the ability of the King of France to arbitrate and reform."

"Revolution of elites": revolution of the Enlightenment, revolution of 1789.[31] All during the 18th century, a community of ideas and states, a common society life doubtless brought together the aristocratic and bourgeois elites still characterized by an equal aspiration to political freedom, as well as an equal revulsion to the popular masses and democracy. The revolution was made in these enlightened minds before being transposed into law and order. The men of '89 had been won over to the spirit of reform, generally widespread, whether it was that of aristocratic liberalism or that of bourgeois thought. There would thus have been "a tactical convergence against absolutism," a provisional alliance of the diverse leading social forces of the pre-Revolutionary period. Thus, 1789 would have been the outcome of this awakening of consciousness of the elites, a revolution of the Enlightenment, and ideology would constitute the driving element of history. "The 1789 Revolution resulted from a double awakening of consciousness of the elites effected through a long progression. Consciousness of their autonomy, first, in relation to the political order, of their necessary control, then of power. Unanimous consciousness where the nobility played the role of initiator and educator, but that broadened out to include wealth, property and talent. That was the Revolution of the Enlightenment."[32]

We cannot but underscore the simplifying nature of these views. And first of all did the Enlightenment really have a unifying function? It does not seem so, if we follow the ambiguous "fortune" of such-and-such a philosopher. L. Althusser has stressed in his *Montesquieu* (1959) "the paradox of posterity" for this theoretician of the aristocratic reaction, claimed not only by the Constituents of 1789, but even by Marat and Saint-Just.[33] As for Rousseau, who as we know so nourished Jacobinism, he was also one of the doctrinal sources of the counterrevolution. The pragmatism of the Enlightenment—it is deformed as it is refracted into the various social milieus following diverse ends.[34]

As for the elites, D. Richet concedes that, despite their common will, they were divided on the problem of privilege—that's putting it mildly. In fact, there was no unified French elite. J. Meyer, the most recent historian of the nobility strongly affirms: "The French nobility neither knew how nor wanted to integrate the intelligentsia and the new social forces. ... The State did not know how to conduct a policy acceptable to the most dynamic elements of the bourgeoisies."[35] There is the heart of the problem. The revolution of the Enlightenment, that is, the reform, stumbled against privilege. Neither the nobility nor the monarchy could accept, without repudiating themselves, the suppression of privilege; on the other hand, the bourgeois elites could not accept its preservation. An internal necessity impelled the confrontation of the two categories. As for the "ability of the King of France to arbitrate and reform," an in-depth analysis, not of the government of Louis XVI, but of the monarchial State at the end of the Ancien Régime, would show that it could in fact only swing "to one side." Well before the Revolution, the monarchy had proved that it was the State of the aristocracy, a position that the speech and Declaration of Louis XVI on June 23, 1789 was to illustrate again.[36]

"Skid of the Revolution": this theory is even more dangerous than that of the so-called "revolution of elites." Our authors in fact distinguish three revolutions in 1789: that of the Constituent Assembly that bears the mark of the "triumphant" 18th century as the *cahiers de doléance* allow us to define it; that of the Parisians who "did not rise to safeguard the National Assembly and its conquests; that was only an objective consequence of their desire to save themselves"; finally that of the peasants who "knocked loudly at the door of the bourgeois Revolution reluctant to open up to them."[37]

Certainly we no longer conceive of the French Revolution as that of the Third Estate, unrolling without contradiction its majestic course, as it is represented to a certain extent by J. Jaurès in his *Socialist History*. G. Lefebvre has shown the existence of an autonomous and specific peasant current within the revolution of the Third Estate; his disciples, of a popular urban current, called sans-culotte, also autonomous and specific. The general course of the bourgeois revolution cannot, however, be altered. Would there not be, therefore, any organic link between these various currents?

Our authors are astonished by the alliance between this opulent bourgeoisie of the 18th century and the people of the cities and countryside. They judge it "unexpected," for lack of having given sufficient attention to the structures of the society of the Ancien Régime characterized by privilege and remnants of feudalism. It is in view of this meeting—contingent, in their eyes—between the bourgeoisie and the popular urban and rural masses that the root of their hypothesis lies, that of the "three revolutions of 1789," a notion indispensable to the following hypothesis, without a doubt the most astonishing and the most dangerous, that of the "skid" of the revolution from 1792 to 9 Thermidor [July 27, 1794: the fall of Robespierre].

The reformist revolution of 1789, defined by the program of its enlightened leaders and by a compromise *from above*, having thus failed through the inability "of the monarchy to arbitrate and to reform," was definitively turned from its initial course in 1792 by popular intervention. "A skid" implies that this intervention was neither indispensable to the success of the bourgeois revolution nor fundamentally motivated by it. Just as the meeting of the three revolutions of 1789 had been purely fortuitous, so the revolution of 1792-1794 would be merely contingent, an accident. "Let us dare to say it: as a consequence of such accidents, didn't the liberal revolution born of the 18th century, and that the French bourgeoisie would effect decades later, fail for the time being?" Our authors don't ask themselves if it is not precisely in this period, which they call "a skid," that the bourgeoisie was able to exterminate all the forms of counterrevolution and thus render possible, in the long run, the liberal system that prevailed definitively after 1794. Nor do they ask about the profound causes of the intervention of the popular masses; for them, it depended only on the myth of the aristocratic plot. As for the war, it would be due in the last analysis to the "passionate expansionism of France."[38] Thus everything is reduced to mental determinations. There is no question of daily bread, the essential motivation of the popular masses from 1789 to 1795. "The Revolution was led by the war and the pressure of the Parisian crowd off the great path traced by the intelligence and wealth of the 18th century."[39] The popular masses would be moved only by myths and fantasies; the war would be only an accident.

Thus these authors reintroduced the chance and the irrational into history which is, however, a thinkable and thus rational subject. The theory of the "skid," by making the revolution a contingent phenomenon ("the limited and contingent events of 1789-1793," writes D. Richet elsewhere, without fear of ridicule),[40] without internal historical necessity, breaks with the line of classical revolutionary historiography, from Barnave to Thiers and Tocqueville, from Jaurès to Lefebvre.

Barnave, in his *Introduction to the French Revolution* (1792), had already indicated with prophetic lucidity the rooting of the Revolution in the deep structures of the French society of the Ancien Régime.[41] In the Restoration period, this historians of the liberal school in turn insisted on the internal logic of the revolutionary movement from 1789 to November 1799—Guizot, certainly, but also Thiers and Mignet, each publishing a *History of the French Revolution* in 1823 and 1824.[42] This was a "fatalist" school, to use Chateaubriand's expression, in the sense that they saw in the Revolution the logical development of given cause and in the Terror an evil necessary to the salvation of the nation. The idea of necessity presides over their work, giving them methodological unity and clarity. "The interior resistance," according to Mignet, "led to the sovereignty of the multitude, and the aggression from outside led to military domination." And again: "Three years of the dictatorship of [the Committee of] public safety, if they were lost for liberty, they were not lost for the Revolution." We see the same point of view in the work of Thiers, and the same idea of a "fatal force" that stimulated the course of the Revolution and surmounted all obstacles until the goal was reached. This is a concept of a global and necessary revolution, although historical necessity does not exclude free will, for man retains full responsibility for his acts. Certainly we must here acknowledge the role of circumstances: it was a question of justifying the hopes and assuring the positions of the liberal party against the ultra reaction. These historians had not, however, subordinated historical truth to their political position. They had determined one of the constants of classical revolutionary historiography.

Tocqueville, in turn, with his customary perception, had indicated the necessity of the Revolution. "The Revolution was least of all," he writes in *The Ancien Régime and the Revolution* (1856), "a fortuitous event. It is true that it took the world by surprise, and yet it was only the complement of a much longer work, the sudden and violent termination of an undertaking on which ten generations of men had worked."[43] Jaurès and his introduction to *Socialist History* must be read again. Lefebvre must be read again...

But let us conclude. There were not three revolutions in 1789, but a single one, bourgeois and liberal, with popular support, particularly among the peasants. There was not a skid of the Revolution in 1792, but a will of the revolutionary bourgeoisie to maintain the cohesion of the Third Estate through an alliance with the popular masses, without whose support the gains of 1789 would have been forever compromised. Year II was not a "time of distress,"[44] but a moment of radicalization necessary to assure victory over the counterrevolution and the coalition, and thus the salvation of the bourgeois revolution.

We cannot leave the current estate of historiography of the French Revolution and the critics of the classical social interpretation without some reflections on methodology.

The history of the Revolution, like any historical subject, is structured and thus thinkable, scientifically knowable, like any other reality. The goal of the historian is to achieve, if not certitudes, at least probabilities or networks of probabilities, or even better, as Georges Lefebvre said, tendential laws. Tocqueville wrote in *The Ancien Régime and the Revolution:* "It is not by chance that aristocracies were born and maintained; like all the rest, they are subject to fixed laws and it is perhaps not impossible to discover them."[45] Abandoning this constant line of our classical historiography, departing from this requirement of rationality, reintroducing into history the contingent and the irrational does not seem to constitute progress in the profession of historian, but indeed retreat and almost a surrender.

In his concern for rationality, the historian must ceaselessly go from scholarly research to critical reflection. He advances between two pitfalls: on one hand, an all-purpose schematization that impoverishes and dessicates the rich historical subject; on the other hand, a cursory empiricism that, in the name of the complexity of the real, considers and treats only one particular case. As for the French Revolution, if the historian intends to understand and arrive at some explanation of causes and effects, it is essential to have recourse to some theory connecting ideas to the needs and pressures of society.

This explains the necessity of definitions and the requirement of conceptualization; let us think about the discussions concerning the word *bourgeoisie*. History can progress only if it is supported by basic concepts, clearly elaborated. Rejecting this necessity has the effect of challenging history and particularly social history as an explicative discipline. Again it's a matter of reaching an understanding on necessary concepts and their definitions; modifiable, certainly, and always perfectible. Theory ceaselessly solicits every reflection of the historian, and it is through the expedient of conceptualization and theorization that he can hope to draw the anatomy and physiology of societies and revolutions.[46]

We are a long way from accepting the criticism of the classical social interpretation of the French Revolution. The historians who reject this interpretation are no longer capable of a global vision of the revolutionary phenomenon nor of giving it a total explanation. The polemic basically turns on the nature and role of the aristocracy and the bourgeoisie,[47] and on the nature and role of the urban masses. The peasantry is not brought into play, yet it accounts for at least 22 million souls out of a total of 28 million in the whole country. Scholarly research since Loutchisky and Lefebvre and critical reflection have stressed the importance of the agrarian question and affirmed that it occupies an "axial position" in the French Revolution. This fundamental problem is perfectly concealed by revisionist criticism.

We are forced to state that there is no longer any total history of the Revolution; there are only partial histories that carve out particular areas and thus break the links that unite them to other aspects of this living and rich subject that is history.[48] It is certainly not a question of saying everything about everything, but of emphasizing how the particular depends on the whole (and reciprocally). Far be it from us to deny the necessity of partial histories; they can also give us the historic specificity of their object of study, but on the condition that they are joined in a necessary manner to the heart of the historic totality. Too often, however, we see these partial histories confining themselves to their limited object, and no longer emerging with anything but remarks for internal use; they have therefore missed their goal of true historical reflection. How can historians write about the nobility in the society of the Ancien Régime, without at the same time posing the peasant question in all its breadth? Every particular problem must be thought about historically; it cannot be detached from its historic context in order to abstract from it certain ideal aspects for stranger and stranger extraneous ends. The practice of partial history, without a global vision, contains the germ of true adulteration; in the end it is destined to sterile abstraction. The revisionist designs on the classical social interpretation of the French Revolution seem indeed to have arrived at that point. What scientific global interpretation have Cobban and his emulators offered as a substitute? Obeying fads, transitory by definition, criticizing without constructing, denying all rationality in the historical movement, they have made only a partial history, purely circumstantial, old before its time and already outdated.

"In order to discover the historical life," writes Michelet, "it would be necessary to patiently follow it in all its paths, all its forms, all its elements. But it would also be necessary, with a still greater passion, to remake, reestablish the play of all that, the reciprocal action of these various forces in a powerful movement that would become life itself."

17

The French Revolution in the History of the Contemporary World[1]

The Revolution of 1789–1794 marked the advent of modern society—bourgeois and capitalist—in the history of France. Its essential characteristic is to have effected the national unity of the country on the base of the destruction of the seigniorial regime and the privileged feudal orders; according to Tocqueville in *The Ancien Régime and the Revolution*, its "particular object was to abolish everywhere the remnants of the institutions of the Middle Ages."[2] Its historical significance is further clarified by the fact that the French Revolution in the end succeeded in establishing a liberal democracy. From this double point of view, and the perspective of world history which concerns us here, it deserves to be considered as a classical model of a bourgeois revolution.

The comparative study of the French Revolution thus poses two series of problems.

Problems of a general nature: those concerning the historical law of the transition from feudalism to modern capitalism. To take up again the question posed by Marx in book III of *Capital*, this transition is carried out in two ways: by the total destruction of the old economic and social system—that is, the "really revolutionary way"—or by the preservation of large sectors of the old mode of production in the heart of the new capitalist society—that is, the way of compromise.[3]

Problems of a special nature: those that bear on the specific structure of French society at the end of the Ancien Régime and that take into account the particular characteristics of the French Revolution in regard to the various types of bourgeois revolutions.[4]

From this double point of view, the history of the French Revolution cannot be isolated from that of Europe. In all the European countries, the formation of modern society is drafted in the very heart of the old economic and social system with its vestiges of feudalism, then forged at their expense. In all the European countries, this evolution was made with varying degrees to the advantage of the bourgeoisie. The French Revolution was not the first to benefit the bourgeoisie; before it, the revolution in Holland in the 16th century, the two revolutions of England in the 17th century, the American Revolution in the 18th century paved the way for this revolution. Once again it is a question of recognizing the specific traits of the French Revolution.

I

At the end of the 18th century, France and the major part of Europe were subject to what has been called the Ancien Régime.[5] This was characterized on the social plane by aristocratic privilege, on that of the State by monarchial absolutism of divine right.

The aristocracy, whose role had not ceased to diminish since the Middle Ages, nevertheless remained in the first ranks of the hierarchy.[6] The social structure of France was always essentially aristocratic; it conserved the character of its origin in the period when land constituted the only form of social wealth, and thus conferred on those who possessed it power over those who cultivated it. The Capetian monarchy had indeed, with great effort, stripped the feudal lords of their royal rights and the nobles and high clergy of all political influence. Having become subjects, the nobles and clerics had nonetheless remained the privileged; the feudal lords had kept their social and economic privileges, the seigniorial rights always underscoring the subjection of the peasants.

Socially privileged, but politically diminished, the aristocracy did not pardon the absolute monarch for having stripped it of all political authority; it denounced despotism and demanded liberty; it intended to have a share in the power. Its ideal of a *tempered* monarchy fit into the framework of the theory of historic right. It had been expressed from the end of the reign of Louis XIV, particularly by Fénelon, whose political ideas were not only conveyed in the allegories of the *Adventures of Télémaque* (1699), but were more explicitly clarified in *The Projects of Government . . . to be proposed to the Duke of Burgundy*, published in 1711 under the title *Tables of Chaulnes*.[7] This anti-absolute aristocratic reaction was diversified, from the first half of the century on, in two currents: one of feudal reaction corresponding to the interests of the nobility of the sword, whose principal representative was the count of Boulainvillers;[8] the other of parlementary reaction corresponding to the nobility of the robe, declaring itself by the publication in 1732 of the *Judicium Francorum*.[9] The theories of the parlementary and feudal reaction were taken up again in the middle of the century, no longer by obscure pamphleteers, but by Montesquieu, with the publication in 1748 of *The Spirit of the Laws*.[10] This aristocratic demand for liberty, in the face of monarchial absolutism, was only, as Georges Lefebvre remarked, a "relic of the past."

However, the rebirth of commerce and the development of craft production since the 10th and 11th centuries had created a new form of wealth, personal and moveable, and thus given birth to a new class, the bourgeoisie, whose importance was established by admission to the Estates General in the 14th century. In the framework of the feudal society, the bourgeoisie had continued to expand to the very rhythm of the development of capitalism, stimulated by the great discoveries of the 15th and 16th centuries and the exploitation of the colonial worlds, as well as the financial dealings of a monarchy always short of money. In the 18th century, the bourgeoisie were leaders in finance, commerce and industry; they provided the monarchy with administrative cadres as well as the resources necessary to operate the State. Thus even while the aristocracy was becoming ossified in its caste, the bourgeoisie was expanding in number, in economic power, in culture and in consciousness. The progress of the Enlightenment had undermined the ideological foundations of the established order, at the same time that it was expressing the class consciousness of the bourgeoisie, and its good conscience. As a rising class, believing in progress, it was convinced that it was representing the general interest and assuming responsibility for the nation; as a progressive class, it offered a decisive attraction for the popular masses as well as for dissident sectors of the aristocracy. But bourgeois ambition, prompted by the social and economic reality, collided with the aristocratic order of laws and institutions.[11]

The bourgeoisie, like the aristocracy, hoped to have a share of the power and demanded liberty from the monarch. But rather than justifying this demand by historic right, as the aristocracy did, the bourgeoisie proclaimed natural right: society is founded on the free contract between its members. Government, on the free contract between that one who governs and those who are governed, such that power is conceived only to benefit the community and to guarante the rights of the citizens.[12] In 1724 the French translation of Locke's *Treatise on Civil Government* (1690) appeared, a work that inspired the whole century. Theoretician of the English Revolution of 1688-89, Locke expressed the ideal of the bourgeoisie, transforming (one might say)"an historical accident into an event dictated by human reason." His political ideal—and this explains his profound influence—coincided with that of a bourgeoisie in full expansion, presenting a complex mixture of empiricism and rationalism: defend the established social order and property, but appeal to morality; concern with effective power, but necessity of consent; individualism, but recognition of majority rule.

Political freedom was certainly important, but even more so was economic freedom, that of enterprise and profit. Capitalism required freedom because freedom was necessary to assure its development, freedom in all its forms: freedom of the person, a condition for hiring labor; freedom of property, a condition for its mobility; freedom of thought, a condition for research and scientific and technical discoveries.

Unlike the aristocracy, the bourgeoisie did not demand only power and freedom; it meant to suppress privilege and acquire equal rights. In the second half of the 18th century, the bourgeoisie in effect found itself battling against the aristocracy. For centuries, the bourgeoisie had dreamed of becoming noble; the venality of offices had provided the means to this end. From the 16th century on, the French monarchy had put bourgeois wealth to good use by putting some public offices up for sale along with the added attraction of accompanying privileges and personal or hereditary nobility. Thus, while many bourgeois families were directly infiltrating the nobility, a nobility of the robe was being established, which, although sustaining ever closer relations with the aristocracy, nevertheless remained bourgeois, especially in the administration of its wealth. But in the 18th century, the nobility of the robe was tending to close its ranks, even while the bourgeoisie remained too numerous to be able to hope to be admitted.[13] "In one way or another," Sieyes wrote in his brochure *What is the Third Estate?* "all the branches of executive power have fallen to the caste that supplies the Church, the robe and the sword. A sort of spirit of co-fraternity makes the nobility prefer themselves to the rest of the nation. The usurpation is complete; they truly reign."[14] The bourgeoisie demanded the suppression of privilege, and equal rights.

In France, therefore, in the second half of the 18th century, the development of the capitalist economy, on the base of which the power of the bourgeoisie was erected, was checked by the feudal framework of society, by the traditional and regulated organization of property, production and trade. "It was necessary to break these chains," the authors of the *Communist Manifesto* wrote—"they were broken." In this way the problem is posed of the passage from feudalism to capitalism. It did not escape the most perceptive men of the period. Far from being inspired by an abstract individualism, as Taine would have it, the revolutionary bourgeoisie had a clear understanding of the economic reality that produced its strength and determined its victory. Barnave was the first to formulate, more than half a century before Marx, the theory of the bourgeois revolution. In his *Introduction to the French Revolution*, written in 1792, Barnave set down the principle that property *influences* institutions. "The reign of the aristocracy lasts so long as the farm population continues to ignore or neglect the arts, and landed property continues to be the only wealth. ... Once the arts and commerce succeed in penetrating the people and create a new means to wealth to aid the laboring class, all is ready for a revolution in political laws: a new distribution of wealth produces a new distribution of power. Just as the possession of land elevates the aristocracy, industrial property elevates the power of the people; they obtain their freedom." When Barnave writes "people," he means the bourgeoisie.[15]

The Dutch and English revolutions had already shown that the deep causes of the bourgeois revolution are to be sought in the feudal vestiges and contradictions of the old society. But this aspect does not explain all the characteristics of the French Revolution. The reasons why it constituted, by its very violence, the most resounding episode in the class struggles that carried the bourgeoisie to power must be sought in certain specific traits of the French society of the Ancien Régime.

Without a doubt, the bourgeoisie would have been content with a compromise that would have given it a share of the power, similar to the English oligarchy of the 18th century. The aristocracy stubbornly refused, since all compromise stumbled against feudalism. The peasant masses could not tolerate the preservation of this system; the nobility as a whole could not envisage its suppression, which would mean their decline. On the basis of the economic and social compromise represented by the repurchase of feudal rights decreed in principle on the night of August 4 [1789] and systematized by the law of March 15, 1790, the Constituent bourgeoisie for a long time tried desperately to reach a political compromise with the aristocracy.[16] The obstinate resistance of the bulk of the small nobility that lived for the most part from landed income, the stubborn and aggressive will of the peasants to end all vestiges of feudalism, were reason enough for this policy of compromise and conciliation. In order to triumph, the bourgeoisie had to resolve to form an alliance with the popular masses.

The popular masses bore all the weight of the Ancien Régime; they could no longer tolerate it.

The popular urban masses, artisans and shopkeepers, journeymen and apprentices, service workers, to a lesser degree manufacturing workers, were pushed to revolt by the worsening of their living conditions. These have been exposed by the works of C.-E. Labrousse.[17] From 1726–1741 to 1785–1789, the long-term rise in prices brought about a 62% increase in the cost of living. On the average, bread accounted for about half of the popular budget; the seasonal variations in the price of grain raised the price of bread by 88% in 1789. This price increase forced the wealthy categories to economize; it overwhelmed the poor. The nominal increase in wages, 22% on the average, did not come close to compensating the increase in prices. As usual, wages followed prices, but without catching up; more precisely, real wages were lowered by about 25%. This worsening of living conditions of the popular masses did not escape the better observers of the period: as early as 1766, Turgot first formulated the "iron law" of wages, in his *Reflections on the Formation and Distribution of Wealth*. More than to the demands for liberty, the popular urban masses were sensitive to the demand for daily bread; they placed up front the question of subsistence. They countered the demand for economic freedom with the right of survival, very specifically price controls and regulation. They countered the equal rights that the bourgeoisie claimed from the aristocracy with "equal enjoyment."[18]

The popular urban masses, soon to be designated by the term sans-culotterie, properly speaking, lacked class consciousness. Scattered in numerous workshops, neither specialized—as a result of limited technological development—nor concentrated in large enterprises or industrial districts, often poorly differentiated from the peasantry, the wage-earners were no more capable than the peasants of conceiving effective solutions to their misery; the weakness of the guilds vouched for that. Hatred of the aristocracy and unmitigated opposition to the "fat" and the rich provided the ferment of unity for the laboring masses. When the poor harvests and the resulting economic crisis set them in motion, they lined up, not as a distinct class, but as part of the craft industry, behind the bourgeoisie; in this way, the most effective blows were struck against the old society. But this victory of the popular masses could be only a "bourgeois victory"; the bourgeoisie accepted the popular alliance against the aristocracy only because the masses remained subordinate. In the opposite case, the bourgeoisie would have renounced, as in Germany in the 19th century and to a lesser degree in Italy, the support of allies deemed too dangerous.

The peasant masses constituted the bulk of the French population, doubtless 22 to 23 million out of about 28 million.[19] In 1789, the great majority of the peasants had been free for a long time, serfdom surviving in only a few regions, Nivernais and Franche-Comté in particular. The feudal relations of production nonetheless dominated the countryside, as is evidenced by the seigniorial fees and ecclesiastical tithes. Certain historians tend to minimize the weight of feudalism at the end of the Ancien Régime. Tocqueville had already answered them in a chapter of *The Ancien Régime and the Revolution*: "Why feudal rights had become more odious to the people in France than anywhere else." If the French peasant had not possessed the land, he would have been less sensitive to the burdens that the feudal system placed on landed property.[20] It would even be appropriate, in order to better define the problem, to specify quantitatively the feudal imposition; for the three subdivisions of Aurillac, Mauriac and Saint-Flour, according to fiscal documents, it would be about 10% of the taxed product (that is, the average net product), not taking into account the *lods et ventes* [fees received by the lord on the price of sold inherited property], the *banalités* [exclusive rights of lord to maintain a mill, an oven or a winepress] and the *dîme* [ecclesiastical tithe].[21] Yet it is the total weight that tenure supported in relation to production that we would have to determine in order to have an idea of the relative burden imposed by the whole of the *feudal complex.* In these same subdivisions of Haute-Auvergne, a third of the revenues of the seigniory, in round numbers, came from feudal rights. This percentage would in a large measure account for the resistance of the Auvergne nobility to the abolition of feudalism, for their refusal of all compromise, and in the last analysis for the agrarian troubles as counterrevolutionary endeavors from 1789 to 1792 and 1793. "Imagine," writes Tocqueville regarding the French peasant of the 18th century, "the condi tion, the needs, the character, the passions of this man, and calculate, if you can, the store of hate and desire amassed in his heart."[22]

To the hatred of feudalism, let us add the hunger for land that tormented the peasant, made still sharper by the demographic upsurge that characterized the 18th century. While about 130,000 members of the clergy shared 10% of the land among themselves, very unequally moreover, the nobility (about 350,000 persons) held about 20%; while the bourgeoisie held for themselves about 30%, the portion for the 22 to 23 million peasants was only 35%.[23] We cannot stress enough the importance of the peasant question in the heart of the bourgeois revolution. For Gramsci, Jacobinism, the very essence of the French Revolution, is characterized by the alliance of the revolutionary bourgeoisie and the peasant masses.

The popular masses, peasant or urban, had a social ideal corresponding to the economic conditions of the times: conception of a limited right to property, protest actions against concentration of farming and industrial concerns. In order to freely dispose of their persons and their labor, peasants and artisans first had to break their enforced allegiance, whether attached to the land or prisoners of the corporation. These conditions explain their hatred of the aristocracy and the Ancien Régime and the fact that the popular classes were the driving force of the bourgeois revolution. But, whether they were immediate producers or dreaming of attaining that state, peasants and artisans understood property to be based on individual work and dreamed of a society of small independent producers; in a confused way, they intended to prevent the establishment of a monopoly of wealth along with a dependent proletariat.[24] These profound aspirations account for the social and political struggles during the Revolution, of their turns and progression; from 1789 to 1793, we saw a deepening of the struggle of the bourgeoisie against the aristocracy, marked by the growing role of the middle layers and the popular masses, not by a change in the nature of the social struggles. In this sense, it is possible to speak of a "change in the front" of the bourgeoisie after the fall of Robespierre: before and after 9 Thermidor, since that aristocracy had not been disarmed, they remained the basic enemy. This was proved by the law of November 29, 1797, inspired by Sieyes, that reduced the former nobles to the state of foreigners. The French Revolution is indeed "a bloc": antifeudal and bourgeois throughout its various ups and downs.

This rooting of the Revolution in French society, this continuity and unity, were underscored by Tocqueville with his customary lucidity, while noting their necessity. "What the Revolution was least of all was an accidental event. It is true that it took the world by surprise, and yet it was only the complement of a much longer work, the sudden and violent termination of an undertaking on which ten generations of men had worked."[25]

II

At the end of the 18th century, the traits that we have just sketched and that characterized the Ancien Régime did not isolate France from the rest of Europe. Everywhere the ascent of the bourgeoisie operated to the detriment of the aristocracy and within the very framework of feudal society. But since the development of the capitalist economy was unequal in the various European countries, these traits affected them to varying degrees.

In the countries of central and eastern Europe, the bourgeoisie was small in number and its influence was weak. The great discoveries of the 15th and 16th centuries, the exploitation of colonial worlds, displacing the new maritime routes toward the west, had further retarded their economic and social development. The aristocracy dominated and prevailed over the monarchs. In Poland, the nobility constituted "the republic" by itself; it had annihilated the elective royalty. In Hungary, the nobility held the reforms of Joseph II in check. In Prussia and Russia, if monarchial power was strengthened, the monarch had in return abandoned the peasants to the discretion of the nobles, and the conditions of serfdom were aggravated.

The evolution of the maritime states was completely different. Holland and England had been the great beneficiaries of economic development since the 16th century and had already completed their bourgeois revolutions, followed in the second half of the 18th century by the United States.

The comparison that can be established between the conditions and aspects of mutation in these three countries allows us to underscore the ways the French Revolution modified these perspectives and to restore to it its irreducible character.

The Dutch Revolution was completed at the end of the 16th century in the framework of the war for independence, even though revolution and national struggles do not exactly overlap. The war, properly speaking, continued a long time after the bourgeoisie had seized power. In this regard, the years 1568–1572 had been decisive. The Dutch bourgeoisie had already been so well settled at the turn of the century that it founded in 1602 the famous India Company, while opening the Amsterdam Stock Exchange in 1613. Basing its power on the great maritime commerce and colonial exploitation, the bourgeoisie was master of the republic for almost a century. After the assassination of the Witt brothers in 1672, the bourgeoisie had to consent to share power with the nobility and the house of Orange. This social and political compromise nevertheless safeguarded the constitutional regime and bourgeois freedoms.

The English Revolution of the 17th century had much greater repercussions than that in Holland which had preceded it. For a long time it was considered a "Puritan revolution," more precisely, since the great work of Gardiner published in the second half of the last century; there it appeared as a conflict both between the Puritans and partisans of the Archbishop Laud over religious problems, and between the Crown and the House of Commons over constitutional problems. After Gardiner, much research has drawn attention to the important economic changes preceding the civil war and that contributed to its outbreak, while works on the relation between Calvinism and capitalist development no longer allow us to speak of a "Puritan revolution" without at the same time posing the problem of the social implications of Puritanism. Let us remark, however, that if the historian tries by analyses to clarify the relations between the economic, the political and the religious, in reality these relations remain inextricably mingled.[26]

The English Revolution, sticking to its general results, played a role in the history of England equivalent to that of the French Revolution in French history. It not only replaced an absolute monarchy in power by a representative government, and put an end to the exclusive domination of a persecuting State Church, but also largely cleared the way for the development of capitalism. According to one of its more recent historians "it brought the Middle Ages to an end."[27] The last vestiges of feudalism were swept away, feudal tenure abolished, assuring the class of landholders absolute possession of their property. The confiscation and sale of the lands of the Church, the Crown and the partisans of the king broke the traditional feudal relations in the countryside and accelerated the accumulation of capital. The guilds lost all economic importance; the commercial, financial and industrial monopolies were abolished. This was the end of the paternalistic intervention of an incompetent government; the control of economic life passed to the Parliament which favored a much greater freedom for internal commerce. "The Ancien Régime had to be reversed," writes Ch. Hill, "so that England might know this freer economic development, necessary to maximize national wealth and to gain a leading position in the world; so that policy, including foreign policy, might pass under the control of those who had importance in the nation; so that the society might be freed from the obligation of conforming to outdated rules imposed by a persecuting Church State. The Court of High Commission, the Star Chamber and the monopolies symbolized the three enemies; religion, liberty and property the three causes that the Long Parliament defended."[28]

The English Revolution was, however, much less radical than the French; to repeat Jaurès's expression in his *Socialist History*, the English Revolution remained "narrowly bourgeois and conservative," while the French Revolution was "broadly bourgeois and democratic." Certainly the English Revolution had its Levellers, but that didn't assure the peasants any hold on the land; moreover, they disappeared in the following century. The reason for this conservatism would have to be sought in the rural nature of English capitalism that made the *gentry* a divided class: numerous gentlemen before 1640 were actively engaged in the raising of sheep, the garment industry or mining. If, on the other hand, the English Revolution saw, with the Levellers, the appearance of political theories founded on the rights of man which, through Locke, were transmitted to the revolutionaries of America and France, it kept itself in the end from proclaiming the universality and equality of rights, as the French Revolution was to do—and with what brilliance!

The English Revolution, in fact, following its "respectable" new development in 1688, ended up with a social and political compromise that made the bourgeoisie and the aristocracy partners in power; this episode would be comparable to the French revolutionary days of July 1830, keeping in mind that any return to the Ancien Régime was impossible. The origins of the English compromise must be sought in the specific characteristics of that society and in the precedents of English history. In England, the aristocracy displayed characteristics completely different from those on the continent. It had few privileges, even paying taxes like everybody else; only the *lords* formed a legally distinct order, with their dignity passing to the eldest sons, the younger ones being *commoners*, like the *gentry* and the *squires*. The military character of this aristocracy had been greatly attenuated, all the more so after being decimated by the massacres of the War of the Roses and reconstituted by the Tudors when its bourgeois origin was at hand. Let us add that the prejudice [of the aristocracy] against demeaning itself did not exist in England, as neither the law nor custom prevented the noble from getting involved in business, and that nothing held up social ascent, money being in the end the principal criterion of social distinction. The maritime and colonial expansion, the struggle against Spain and France had also reinforced this solidarity between the landed aristocracy and the capitalist bourgeoisie. Once royal despotism was eliminated, they quite naturally shared power, and the bourgeoisie had no need to invoke equality of rights. The political compromise of 1688–89 established a constitutional government of king, lords and the House of Commons where the small nobility sat beside the bourgeoisie, for the electoral system based on property qualifications was so disorganized and corrupt that the power of money was absolute. The establishment of political liberty had not struck a single blow at the social heirarchy.

Locke justified the revolution of 1688 by natural right: society, founded to safeguard individual liberty, rested on the free contract between citizens; likewise, the governmental authority rested on a contract between the sovereign people and their proxy, who must use its power only to enforce the imprescriptible rights conferred on the individual by the Supreme Being. We cannot stress enough the influence of Locke's works on the philosphers of the continent during the 18th century. Once the Whig oligarchy was installed, however, all search for the justification for power ceased, for the theory of the contract could serve as an argument for the democratic movement that threatened its domination. It is through history that English liberties were justified; indeed ever since the Magna Carta, history provided plenty of precedents against royal despotism. Custom and tradition thus constituted the foundation of English liberties, not philosophical speculation. "You have remarked," Burke wrote in his *Reflections on the French Revolution* (1790), "that from the time of the Magna Carta until the Declaration of Right [of 1689], it has always been the policy of our Constitution to claim and demand our liberties as a *heritage*, a *legacy*, that we have derived from our ancestors and that we must transmit to our posterity; like property belonging exclusively to the people of this kingdom—without any kind of reference to any other right more general or more ancient... We have an hereditary Crown, and hereditary Peerage, a House of Commons and a people holding their privileges, their franchises and their liberties through inheritance from a long line of ancestors."[29] The British Constitution recognized the rights of Englishmen, not the rights of men: universalism was missing from English liberties.

The American Revolution, like its precursor, but to a lesser degree, was marked by empiricism. Also a bourgeois revolution, in the framework of a war for independence, it invoked natural right in solemn Declarations. This right had remained strong among the Puritan communities that had fled England during the reign of the first two Stuarts in order to escape monarchial despotism and Anglican intolerance. Thus when the American colonies broke with the mother country, it was in the name of the theory of free contract that they justified their secession, and their Declarations proclaimed the rights of man, not just those of Americans—universalism of the natural right appeared in public law. It is not possible, however, to conceal the flagrant contradictions that marked the application of the principles so solemnly proclaimed. Neither liberty nor equality were completely recognized. The Blacks remained slaves. And, if equality of rights was admitted between whites, the social hierarchy founded on wealth did not suffer any blows; even more, the States remained in control of their electoral systems and their first Constitutions maintained property qualifications. The names of Washington and Franklin symbolize the social and political compromise that dominated the life of the Union during the first decades of its history: an aristocracy of landowners, issuing from the British gentry, in particular the great planters of the Southern states; upper bourgeoisie of financiers, merchants, shipbuilders and manufacturers of the New England states.[30] Certainly Franklin, a former typographer, was of modest extraction, but he did not disdain gain, and through commerce he climbed the social ladder. In this society, even more clearly than in the Old World, wealth constituted the criterion of hierarchy, money the factor of mobility. Equality of rights was not invoked, the leaders deeming that equality would come by itself in a country that did not know legal privileges, but also because this principle could serve as a justification for the demands of the popular masses. Liberty thus remained the essential principle of the Constitution of the United States, "not the aristocratic liberty of their mother country," Tocqueville specified, "but the bourgeois and democratic liberty for which world history has not yet presented a complete model."[31] That was *democracy in America*: the government of the nation by itself, certainly, but according to modalities that nonetheless favored the wealthy few.

The revolutions of Holland, England and America have the value of example: bourgeois revolutions, but leading to a conservative compromise which, under the cover of "bourgeois liberty," safeguarded the dominance of wealth. With the aristocracy accepting the new order, equality of rights was not demanded. The French Revolution followed a completely different course.

III

If the French Revolution was the most dazzling of the bourgeois revolutions, eclipsing by the dramatic character of its class struggles the revolutions that preceded it, this was due to the obstinacy of the aristocracy rooted in its feudal privileges, refusing all concessions, and to the opposing determination of the popular masses. The bourgeoisie had not sought the ruin of the aristocracy, but the refusal of compromise and the counterrevolution obliged them to pursue the destructioin of the old order. But they only achieved that by forming an alliance with the rural and urban masses, to whom they were forced to give satisfaction: the popular revolution and the terror made a clean sweep; feudalism was irremediably destroyed and democracy established.

The French Revolution took the "truly revolutionary path" from feudalism to capitalism. By wiping the slate clean of all feudal vestiges, by liberating the peasants of seigniorial rights and ecclesiastical tithes, and to a certain degree from community constraints, by destroying the trade monopolies and unifying the national market, the French Revolution marked a decisive stage on the path to capitalism. Suppressing feudal landed property, it even freed small direct producers, making possible the differentiation of the peasant mass and its polarization between capital and wage labor. This led to entirely new relations of production; capital, once under feudal domination, was able to make the value of work mercenary. In this way, the autonomy of capitalist production was finally assured in the agricultural domain as well as the industrial sector. Two conditions appeared necessary in this passage to capitalist society, in the light of the French Revolution: the breaking up of feudal landed property and the emancipation of the peasants. The agrarian question indeed occupies "an axial position" in the bourgeois revolution.

The active element of this revolution was less the commercial bourgeoisie (to the extent that they remained solely commercial and intermediary, they accommodated themselves to the old society—from 1789 to 1793, from the "Monarchiens" to the "Feuillants," then the Girondists, they generally supported compromise) than the mass of small direct producers from whom the feudal aristocracy exacted overwork and overproduction with the support of the judicial apparatus and the means of constraint provided by the State of the Ancien Régime. The political instrument of change was the Jacobin dictatorship of the small and middle bourgeoisie, supported by the popular masses, social categories whose ideal was a democracy of small autonomous producers, independent peasants and artisans, freely working and trading. The peasant and popular revolution was at the heart of the bourgeois revolution and pushed it forward.[32].

The victory over feudalism and the Ancien Régime did not, however, mean the simultaneous appearance of new social relations. The passage to capitalism is not a simple process, by which the capitalist elements develop in the womb of the old society until the moment when they are strong enough to break through its framework. A long time would still be needed before capitalism would assert itself definitively in France; its progress was slow during the revolutionary period, the dimension of enterprises often remaining modest, with commercial capital dominating.[33] The ruin of feudal landed property, and the corporative, regulated system, by assuring the autonomy of the capitalist mode of production, also uncompromisingly paved the way for bourgeois relations of production and trade—revolutionary transformation par excellence.

Overturning economic and social structures, the French Revolution at the same time shattered the state apparatus of the Ancien Régime, sweeping away the vestiges of old autonomies, destroying local privileges and provincial particularisms. It thus made possible, from the Directory to the Empire, the establishment of a modern State responding to the interests and requirements of the new bourgeoisie.

The French Revolution holds a singular place in the history of the contemporary world.

As a revolution for liberty, it invoked natural right, as did the American Revolution, and conferred upon its work a universal character that the English Revolution had ignored. But who could deny that the Declaration of 1789 affirmed this universality with much more force than the American Declarations? Let us add that the French Declaration went much further on the road to freedom, affirming freedom of conscience and admitting Protestants and Jews into the "city"; but by creating the civil state, on September 20, 1792, it also recognized the right of the citizen to adhere to no religion. It liberated the white man; but by the law of February 4, 1794, it also abolished "Negro slavery in all the colonies."

As a Revolution for equality, the French Revolution went far beyond the revolutions that preceded it. Neither in England nor in the United States was emphasis placed on equality, as the aristocracy and the bourgeoisie were partners in power. The resistance of the aristocracy, the counterrevolution and the war forced the French bourgeoisie to push the struggle for equal rights to the first rank. In this way it could rally the people and win. But what was drafted in 1793-1794 was a regime of social democracy characterized by a compromise between bourgeois conceptions and popular aspirations. The popular masses realized what fate awaited them: that's why they demonstrated hostility to the economic freedom that opened the way to concentration and capitalism. At the end of the 18th century, the ideal of the people was that each peasant would be a landowner, each artisan independent and each wage earner protected against the all-powerful rich.

After August 10, 1792, when the throne was overturned, and the revolutionary bourgeoisie had instituted universal suffrage and sealed its alliance with the sans-culottes, it was indeed necessary to go beyond theoretical equality of rights and move toward that "equality of enjoyment" that the people demanded. This led to the management of the economy to set prices in harmony with wages and assure daily bread for all: price controls and regulation were instituted by the law of the "general maximum" on September 29, 1793, and war manufacturing and foreign commerce were nationalized. There was also the endeavor to establish public education accessible to all by the law of December 19, 1793. In addition, there were also the beginnings of social security with the law of national charity of May 11, 1794. This egalitarian republic filled the propertied bourgeoisie with indignation and dread; after 9 Thermidor, it was banned forever. But the conviction remained in the consciousness of the people that freedom without equality meant only privilege for some, that liberty and equality are inseparable, that political equality by itself can be only a facade when social inequality asserts itself. "Liberty is but a vain phantom when a class of men can starve others with impunity," the *enragé* Jacques Roux had declared to the gallery of the Convention on June 25, 1793. "Equality is but a vain phantom when the rich, through their monopolies, exercise the right of life and death on their fellow men."[34]

Finally as a revolution for unity, the French Revolution made the nation one and indivisible.[35] Certainly the Capetian monarchy had established the territorial and administrative framework of the nation, but without completing this task; in 1789, national unity remained imperfect. The nation was still divided territorially by the incoherence of administrative divisions and the persistence of the "feudal parcelling"; the diversity of weights and measures and interior customs posed obstacles to the formation of a national market. Moreover, the nation was socially divided, for the Ancien Régime was organized into a hierarchy and partly into guilds. (As Georges Lefebvre remarked, whoever says "guild" implies "privileges.") Everywhere inequality reigned in a nation created by a unitary government, whose cohesion had been reinforced in the 18th century through the multiple bonds woven by material progress, the expansion of the French language, the development of culture and the brilliance of the Enlightenment.

Once the orders, states, and guilds were abolished, the French people were free and equal under the law, constituting a nation, one and indivisible. The rationalization of institutions by the Constituent Assembly, the return to centralization by the revolutionary government, the administrative exertions of the Directory, the reconstruction of the State by Napoleon—all completed the work of the monarchy of the Ancien Régime, destroying autonomies and particularisms, putting in place the institutional framework of a unified State. At the same time, the consciousness of a unified nation was awakened and strengthened by civil equality, the 1790 federations movement, the development of the network of Jacobin societies, and the antifederalism and the congresses or *central meetings* of the popular societies in 1793. The advances of the French language went in the same direction. New economic ties reinforced the national consciousness. Once the feudal parcelling was destroyed, and the tolls and interior customs abolished, the "withdrawal of barriers" to the political frontier tended to unify the national market, which was, moreover, protected from foreign competition by a protectionist tariff. The French Revolution gave a strength and effectiveness to the national sovereignty that up till then it had not had.

A new public international law was expressed. Seeking to define its principles, during the affair of the German princes who owned land in Alsace, Merlin de Douai in effect posited the nation conceived as a voluntary association against the dynastic State. Speaking on October 28, 1790, he said, "There is between you and your Alsacian brothers no other legitimate title of union than the social pact formed last year between all old and modern French people in this Assembly"—an allusion to the decision of the Third Estate on June 17, 1789, to proclaim itself a National Assembly, and to that of the Assembly on the following July 9 to declare itself a Constituent Assembly, and to the *federative pact* of July 14, 1790. One sole question, "infinitely simple," remained: that of knowing "if it is to these diplomatic parchments that the Alsacian people owe the advantage of being French . . . What do these conventions matter to the people of Alsace or the people of France, when in the times of despotism, they had as their object to unite the first to the second? The Alsatian people joined the French people because they wanted to; it is their will alone, and not the treaty of Münster, that legitimized the union."[35] This will had been demonstrated by participation in the Federation of July 14, 1790. The international public law was revolutionized as the interior public law was—nations now had the right to self-determination.

After ten years of revolution, the French reality appeared to be radically transformed. The aristocracy of the Ancien Régime was ruined, its privileges and social domination stripped away with the abolition of feudalism. We should not stretch this point, however; many nobles did not emigrate and succeeded in safeguarding their landed patrimony; the Napoleonic consolidation restored their social prestige; the squire replaced the feudal lord. The fusion of this landed aristocracy and the upper bourgeoisie constituted the dominant class in the new society.

At the other extreme of the social scale, the popular urban classes had not drawn any positive advantage from the Revolution. In fact, by proclaiming economic freedom, and by prohibiting unions and strikes by the Le Chapelier law of June 14, 1791—a truly constituent law of free-trade capitalism (the prohibition persisted until 1864 for the right to strike and until 1884 for the right to unionize), the bourgeois revolution left the popular urban classes defenseless in the new economy. Liberalism, founded on the ideal of an abstract social individualism, profited the most. Economic freedom accelerated the concentration of industrial enterprises, transforming the material conditions of social life, but at the same time altering the structure of traditional popular classes: how many artisans, working their way up in industry, were reduced by capitalist concentration to the rank of proletarians?

The peasantry were split up, in the end. The abolition of the ecclesiastical tithe and real feudal rights profited only the landowning peasants; farmworkers and sharecroppers gained only from the abolition of serfdom and personal feudal rights. The national lands were sold in such a way that peasant property was increased to the advantage of those who already owned land: the *laboureurs*, or big farmers from the regions with large areas of cultivation. In the Nord department from 1789 to 1802, their share of the land rose from 30 to 42% (that of the bourgeoisie rose from 16 to 28%, while the percentage held by the nobility decreased from 22% to 12%, that of the clergy from 20% to 0). From that time on, a powerful minority of proprietary peasants, attached to the new order, rallied around the bourgeoisie in its conservative proposals. In this way is the social work of the French Revolution measured in the countryside, an accomplishment further clarified by comparative study. While the French peasant increased his share of the land, the English peasant, freed from serfdom and feudal obligations from the beginning of modern times, was expropriated in the course of the vast movement of regrouping and enclosure of lands, and was reduced to the ranks of a wage-earning day laborer—free, certainly—but without land. In Central and Eastern Europe, serfdom persisted; the great landowning nobles exploited their lands by means of statute labor owed to them by the peasants. Serfdom was not abolished until 1807 in Prussia, 1848 in Bohemia and Hungary, and 1861 in Russia. And the liberated peasant did not receive any land; the aristocracy maintained its landed privilege until the revolutions of the 20th century. By comparison, as far as the society resulting from the French Revolution goes, Jaurès was able to speak of "rural democracy."

Upon seizing power in November 1799, Bonaparte declared, "the Revolution is over." He thus assigned an end point to the task of demolishing the Ancien Régime. But it was not in the power of a single man, no matter how brilliant, to change the characteristics of the new society that had already been clearly sketched. The actions of the First Consul, then the Emperor, whatever his evolution may have been, essentially belonged to the line of the revolutionary heritage. The desire for order on the part of both old and new property owners facilitated the stabilization efforts of the Consulate. The social hierarchy was reestablished, with the administration reorganized according to the wishes of the "notables"; but control of the government eluded them. In 1814, the Charter allowed them to believe that they would see themselves in power: the aristocratic reaction, once again, contested their claim. In this sense, the Restoration represents the epilogue of the drama. The Revolution in 1789 did not really end until 1830 when, having brought a king to power who accepted their principles, the bourgeoisie took definitive possession of France.[37]

The characteristics that we have just sketched account for the repercussions of the French Revolution and its value as an example in the evolution of the contemporary world. Without a doubt, the armies of the Republic and then of Napoleon knocked down the Ancien Régime in the European countries they occupied, more by force than by ideas. By abolishing serfdom, by freeing the peasants of seigniorial fees and ecclesiastical tithes, by putting in circulation the wealth of *mainmorte*, the French conquest cleared the path for the development of capitalism. If nothing remained of the continental empire that Napoleon had had the ambition to found, it nevertheless destroyed the Ancien Régime everywhere it had time to do so. In this sense, his reign prolonged the Revolution, and he was indeed its soldier, a fact for which the sovereigns of the Ancien Régime never ceased reproaching him.[38]

After Napoleon, the prestige of the Revolution did not vanish. With the passage of time, it appeared both as the daughter of reason and the daughter of enthusiasm. Its memory evoked a powerful emotion, the storming of the Bastille remaining the symbol of popular insurrection and *La Marseillaise* the battle song for liberty and independence. In this sense, the French Revolution indeed has mythical value, in the sense Georges Sorel intended:

it seduced the imagination and the heart; announcer of better times, it incited people to action. Beyond this revolutionary romanticism, its ideological attraction was no less powerful; the French Revolution affirms itself as an immense effort to set society on a rational foundation.

IV.—THE FRENCH REVOLUTION AND EQUALITY[39]

It is trite to write that the vision of history changes with each generation of historians, that it is under the weight of real history and lived experiences that history is written. That of the French Revolution could not escape this law. For almost two centuries, each generation has questioned itself about the Revolution, through its enthusiasms or hatreds, as through its dreams and hopes. As there is no disinterested interrogation, we have never investigated the French Revolution except as ourselves. For the historians of the Restoration, Mignet as well as Thiers, it was, in their liberal struggle against the ultrareaction, the realization of the idea of Liberty. As for Michelet, during the July monarchy when the working class consciousness was awakening and a new social ideal was being expressed, he defined the Revolution as the coming of the Law, the resurrection of the Right, the realization of Justice."

It is thus in the light of our times, the second half of the 20th century, that we again question the Revolution under the weight of the problems imposed on us, and what problem is more pressing in our day than that of Equality, equality between citizens, equality between nations? The spirit of the Revolution, "the inextinguishable spark," to borrow Michelet's expression, would it not be that of Equality? Wouldn't the French Revolution have been, throughout its many turns and successive forms, the realization of the idea of Equality?

As a necessary stage in the transition from feudalism to capitalism, the French Revolution still imposes itself on contemporary history by the solutions that it has successively brought to the problem of equality of rights. The capitalist transformation of the economy, by concentrating industrial enterprises, multiplying and gathering together the workers, awakening and clarifying their class consciousness, placed the principle of equality of rights in the forefront of humanity's concerns. So much so that this essential principle, which the bourgeoisie of 1789 had posited with brilliance to justify the abolition of nobiliary privilege based on birth, manifested consequences that the Constituents had not foreseen, despite the malevolent warnings of certain perceptive adversaries. "The Negroes in our colonies and the domestics in our houses," wrote Rivarol in the *Journal politique national*, "can, with the Declaration of Rights in their hands, chase us off our inheritance. How did it happen that an assembly of legislators did not know that natural right cannot exist for an instant beside property?"[40] That posed the problem of the content of rights: theoretical equality or real equality? Even more precisely, equality of rights and of means.

This problem was clearly enunciated by a certain Athenas, "notable" of Nantes, in a letter to the legislative assembly on June 2, 1792. "All men are equal in rights and unequal in means; but, if this civil inequality is inevitable, its excesses are dangerous and harmful. The rights of men have never been so misunderstood as when the disproportion of means has been extreme between them. The ways of a good administration should tend unceasingly to bring together civil equality and natural equality, and equality of means and equality of rights, to attenuate the causes that favor the enormous accumulation of wealth in the hands of a few, to the prejudice of the multitude that remains stripped of all: the individuals of this last class are the ones I am particularly looking at. The Revolution made them free men; what remains is to make them citizens by binding them to the fatherland by the benefits it offers them."

The problem could not be better stated. It remained to be solved. The French Revolution opened three paths leading to the future. To Verginaud who stated on March 13, 1793, "Equality for social man is only that of rights." Felix Lepeletier responded on the following August 20, "Cause the inequality of enjoyment to disappear," while in year IV, Babeuf advocated "the community of goods and of work" to finally reach "perfect equality." The French Revolution opened three paths which the history of the contemporary world successively followed.

1) For bourgeois liberalism, that of the Constituents of '89 like that of the Anglo-Saxons, equality is only equality of rights. All citizens are free to partake of it, but not all have the means to do so. If liberty was associated with equality in the Declaration [of the Rights of Man], it was a question of an affirmation of principle that legitimized pulling down the aristocracy and the abolition of nobiliary privilege, more than authorizing popular hopes. By placing property in the ranks of natural imprescriptible rights, the Constituents introduced into their creation a contradiction that they could not surmount; the maintenance of slavery and property qualifications for suffrage fully exposed the contradiction. The right to vote was meted out following the payment of a contribution based on the degree of wealth. Thus the rights that the constituent bourgeoisie had recognized for people and citizens were only those of the bourgeois man; for the mass of "passive" citizens, these rights remained abstract and theoretical.

The revolutionary bourgeoisie always held the line there, clearly affirming its principles each time that the popular movement threatened the new edifice. "The Revolution is over," stated Duport on May 17, 1791. "It is necessary to end it and preserve it by combatting excess; it is necessary to restrain equality, reduce liberty and set public opinion; the government must be strong, solid, stable."[41] "Are we going to end the Revolution, are we going to start it up again?" Barnave asked in a vehement speech, after the flight of the king to Varennes on July 15, 1791: "You have made all men equal before the law; you have consecrated civil and political equality ... One step more would be a disastrous and blameworthy act, one step more in the direction of liberty would be the destruction of royalty; [one step more] in the direction of equality, the destruction of property. If you still wanted to destroy, when all it was necessary to destroy no longer exists; if you believed you had not done everything for equality, when equality of all men is assured, would you find another aristocracy to annihilate, other than that of property?"[42]

In this same line is Vergniaud's speech to the Convention on March 13, 1793, at the moment when the Parisian sectional uprising was expressing itself: "Equality for social man is only that of rights. It is no more equality of fortune than equality of height, strength, wit, activity, industry and work."[43]

After Thermidor, the bourgeoisie hardened. They no longer concealed their view that the rights of men were for property owners. "You must in the end guarantee the property of the rich," Boissy d'Anglas declared in his preliminary discourse for the draft of the Constitution. "Civil equality, that is all that a reasonable man can demand ... We need to be governed by our betters who are more educated and more interested in the maintenance of laws; now, with very few exceptions, you will only find such men among those who, possessing property, are attached to the country that contains it, to the laws that protect it, to the tranquility that conserves it, and who are indebted to that property and to the comfort it gives, etc. ... A country governed by property owners is in the social order, the one governed by non-property owners is in the state of nature."[44] Hereditary property in a certain sense survives the privilege of birth.

The path of bourgeois liberalism was brilliantly affirmed in the 19th century. Reassuring in its conservative compromise, it lost none of its value.

2) For the supporters of social democracy, as it was sketched in year II, the right to survival took precedence over the right to property, and equality had to be that of "enjoyment." In his speech on December 2, 1792, on the wheat riots of the Eure-et-Loir department, Robespierre, subordinating the right to property to the right of survival, posited the theoretical foundation of an egalitarian nation. "The authors of the theory [of property as a right] have considered the most necessary elements of life as only ordinary merchandise; they have made no distinction between the wheat trade and indigo trade; they have written more about trade in grains than the subsistence of the people ... they have put great store in the profits of the merchants or landowners, while the lives of men count for almost nothing ... The first of rights is the right to exist; all others are subordinated to that one."[45]

In his discourse of April 24, 1793, Robespierre arrived at a new formulation of the right to property. The passage is famous: "Ask the merchant of human flesh what property is; he will tell you, by showing you that long coffin that he calls a shop where he has packed and chained up men who appear to be alive: 'There is my property; I bought them for so much a head'. ... In the eyes of people like that property bears no moral principle. Why does your Declaration of Rights seem to introduce the same error? By defining liberty as the first of man's goods, the most sacred of the rights of nature, you have said, and justly so, that it is limited by the rights of the other; why have you not applied this principle to property which is a social institution, as if the eternal laws of nature were less inviolable than the conventions of men? You have multiplied the articles to assure the greatest liberty in the exercise of property and you have not said a single word to determine its legitimacy." Robespierre consequently proposed the following article: "Property is the right that each citizen has to enjoy and dispose of that portion of wealth that is guaranteed to him by law."[46] Property was thus no longer a natural right, prior to all social organization, as the Declaration of 1789 had affirmed; it was now inscribed in a social and historical framework, defined by law.

Property was also certainly understood in this way by the popular masses. They had always shown hostility to the economic freedom that opened the way to capitalism and concentration of industry, thus to their proletarianization; not only did the rights of man and citizen remain illusory for them, private ownership of the land and workshops placed them in a position of dependency to those who, in fact, alone had the privilege of enjoying this property. They thus invoked the right to survival and advanced the demand, counter to the proprietary bourgeoisie, of "equality of enjoyment."[47] After August 10, 1792, the revolutionary bourgeoisie was determined to gain the upper hand in the popular alliance. Universal suffrage was instituted, a democratic and social republic drafted. The national community, invested with the right of control over private property, intervened to maintain a relative equality by reconstituting small property, as economic evolution was tending to destroy it, in order to prevent the reestablishment of the monopoly of wealth and the formation of a dependent proletariat.[48] This led to the Montagnard laws allowing the proliferation of small property owners, the controlled economy to harmonize prices and wages, a public educational system open to all, and finally "the national charity." Thus the goal of "the common happiness" assigned to society by the Declaration of Rights of June 24, 1793 was realized. That ideal of an egalitarian society as defined by Saint-Just in his *Republican Institutions* was made fact: "Give to all Frenchmen the means of obtaining the first necessities of life, without depending on anything but the law and without mutual dependence in the civil state." Or again: "Man must live independently."

The attempt to establish social democracy in year II, if it filled the bourgeoisie with dread, nonetheless served as an example after 1830, when the republican party reappeared, and especially after 1848, when the reinstituted universal suffrage conferred an increased strength to its principles. The attempt of year II nourished social thought in the 19th century, and its memory carried great weight in political struggles. The Montagnard drafts were slowly elaborated during the Third Republic—first of all the public education open to all, demanded in vain by the sans-culottes as one of the necessary conditions of social democracy.

But at the same time economic freedom and capitalist concentration widened social disparities and reinforced antagonisms; the "equality of enjoyment" slipped farther and farther away, out of reach. Cramped by their situation, artisans and shopkeepers, descendants of the sans-culottes of '93, still attached to small property based on individual work, oscillated from utopia to revolt. The same contradiction between the demands for equal rights proclaimed in principle and the consequences of the right to property and economic freedom, and the same impotence, weighed on the attempts at social democracy. The tragedy of June 1848 bears witness to this, as does that of May 1871, without even mentioning the ups and downs of the Third Republic.

"Time of anticipation," E. Labrousse said of year II. Wouldn't it be the time of utopias? In the fourth fragment of *Republican Institutions*, Saint-Just wrote: "We must have neither rich nor poor." But he noted at the same time in his diary: "Don't permit the sharing of property." The egalitarian republic of year II indeed remained in the realm of anticipation: Icaria never attained, but always pursued. Equality was truly the rock of Sisyphus that the legislator rolled tirelessly up the slope.

Rousseau wrote in chapter 16 of book V of *The Social Contract:* "In regard to equality, we must not mean by this word that the degrees of power and wealth are absolutely the same; but that power never reaches a level of violence and is only exercised by virtue of rank and law; and as for wealth, no citizen would be opulent enough to be able to buy another, nor poor enough to be forced to sell himself.... If you want to give the State solidity, bring extreme degrees as close together as possible; do not allow people to be either opulent or beggars.... It is precisely because the force of circumstances always tends to destroy equality that the force of legislation must always be to maintain it." The force of circumstances: that is, the free play of economic laws in a system where property, certainly limited, was nevertheless maintained with all the consequences harmful to equality.

3) Babeuf, however, from the time of the Revolution, untangled the contradiction, opening a third path to the future, thus conferring an extension of extraordinary breadth and strength to the principle of equality of rights.[49]

In his first letter to Coupé de l'Oise, on August 20, 1791,[50] Babeuf criticized the Declaration of Rights of 1789. "Who can support a nominal equality? There is really no motivation to expose oneself in order to preserve it; it is not worthwhile for the people to be stirred for it. Equality must not be the baptism of an insignificant transaction; it must manifest itself through immense and positive results, through easily appreciable efforts and not by illusory abstractions. It cannot be an academic question of grammar and legislation. We can no longer evoke a question of equality except as a question of numbers. All must be brought down to weights and measures."

Like the sans-culottes and the Jacobins, Babeuf proclaimed that the goal of society is "the common happiness." The Revolution must assure all citizens "equality of enjoyment." But private property, necessarily introducing inequality, and the "agrarian law"—that is, the equal sharing of property—only "lasting one day" ("on the day following its establishment, inequality would rise again"), the only means of arriving at "equality in fact" and to "assure to each and his posterity, however numerous, sufficiency, and nothing more," is "to establish a communal administration, suppress private property, attach each man to the industry he knows, according to his talent, oblige him to dispose of the fruits of his work in communal stores, and establish a simple system of distribution, an administration of subsistences that, keeping records of all individuals and all things, will divide subsistences in the most scrupulous equality."

This program, set forth in the *Manifesto of Plebians* and published by the *Tribun du peuple* on November 30, 1795, represented a profound renewal, or more precisely an abrupt change of the sans-culotte and Jacobin ideologies, both characterized by attachment to private property founded on individual work. "The community of goods and work" advocated by Babeuf was the first form of revolutionary ideology of the new society issuing from the Revolution itself. In other words, Babeuf presented the abolition of private ownership of the means of production and the establishment of a communist democracy as alone capable of fully realizing equality of rights. Through Babouvism, communism, until then a utopian daydream, was set forth in a coherent ideological system. Through the Conspiracy of Equals, communism entered into the history of social and political struggles.

The importance of the Conspiracy and of Babouvism can be measured only on the scale of the 19th century. In the history of the Revolution and the Directory, they constituted only a simple episode that doubtless changed the political equilibrium of the moment, but that had no profound resonance. In his letter of July 14, 1796, a true political testament, Babeuf recommended to Félix Lepeletier that he gather all his "drafts, notes and sketches of democratic and revolutionary writings, all of importance to our mighty goal"; that is, perfect equality, common happiness. "When people come to dream again of the means of procuring for humanity the happiness that we proposed, you will be able to search through these notes and present to all the disciples of Equality... what the corrupt men of today call my dreams."[51]

Responding to this wish, Buonarroti published in Brussels in 1828 the history of the *Conspiracy for Equality, called of Babeuf.*[52] This work had a profound effect on the generation of 1830; thanks to this work, Babouvism was joined like a link in the chain of communist thought. In this way ideas were born of the French Revolution that led, to use the words of Marx, "beyond the ideas of the old state of things": ideas of a new social order that would not be the bourgeois order.

*

The French Revolution is consequently situated in the very heart of the history of the contemporary world, at the crossroad of the diverse social and political currents that divided nations and still divides them. A classical bourgeois revolution, it represented—by the uncompromising abolition of feudalism and the seigniorial regime—the starting point for capitalist society and a liberal representative system in the history of

France. A peasant and popular revolution, it tried twice to go beyond its bourgeois limits: in year II an attempt that, despite the inevitable failure, still served for a long time as a prophetic example; and, at the time of the Conspiracy for Equality, an episode that stands at the fertile origin of contemporary revolutionary thought and action. This explains these vain but dangerous efforts to deny the French Revolution its historic reality or its social and national specificity. But this also explains the shaking felt throughout the world and the way the French Revolution still stirs the consciousness of the people of our century.

Tocqueville, in *The Ancien Régime and the Revolution*, recalls the "two principal passions" of the French at the end of the 18th century: "one, deeper and coming from farther back, is the violent and inextinguishable hatred of inequality"; "the other, more recent and not so deeply rooted, led them to wish to live not only as equals, but free." That was 1789: "a time of inexperience, without a doubt, but also of generosity, enthusiasm, virility and grandeur, a time of immortal memory, which men will turn to regard with admiration and respect. . . . Thus the French were proud enough of their cause and themselves to believe they could be equal in liberty."

Equality in freedom: an ideal never attained, but always pursued, that never ceases to inflame men's hearts.

CALENDAR of the French Revolution

The year was divided into 12 months of 30 days each, with the last 5 days in the year declared holidays.

Year I: Sept. 22, 1792 through Sept. 16, 1793 + 5 days (Sept. 17-21) as holidays
Year II: Sept. 22, 1793 through Sept. 16, 1794, etc.*

Year I		**New Calendar**	
Sept.	22, 1792	1 vendémiaire	
Oct.	1	10 "	
Oct.	22	1 brumaire	autumn
Nov.	1	11 "	
Nov.	21	1 frimaire	
Dec.	1	11 "	
Dec.	21	1 nivôse	
Jan.	1, 1793	12 "	
Jan.	20	1 pluviôse	winter
Feb.	1	13 "	
Feb.	19	1 ventôse	
March	1	11 "	
March	21	1 germinal	
April	1	12 "	
April	20	1 floréal	spring
May	1	12 "	
May	20	1 prairial	
June	1	13 "	
June	19	1 messidor	
July	1	13 "	
July	19	1 thermidor	
Aug.	1	14 "	summer
Aug.	18	1 fructidor	
Sept.	1	15 "	
Sept.	16	30 "	
Sept.	17-21	5-day holiday	
Year II			
Sept.	22, 1793	1 vendémiaire, etc.	

* Year IV was a leap year.

Glossary

amalgame: fusion of troops of different origins; specifically, the union of the troops of the former royal army and volunteers from year II.
appellants: those who appeal a judicial decision; specifically, those who tried to save the King's life.
Ami du peuple: (The People's Friend)—newspaper founded by Marat.
assignat: paper money created by the revolutionary government.
Babouvism: doctrine of Babeuf and his followers that projected the establishment of an egalitarian society.
cahiers de doléance: the list of grievances drawn up by each of the three orders—the aristocracy, the Church and the Third Estate—for presentation at the convening of the Estates General on May 1, 1789.
citoyens actifs: those who had the vote, based on property qualifications and taxes paid. **citoyens passifs:** those who did not meet the qualifications for suffrage. **citoyenne:** woman active in revolutionary activity; women voted and took part in the governance of the sections for a brief time during the revolution.
comitats: administrative subdivision in Hungary.
Commune de Paris: municipal government of Paris from 1789 to 1795. [**La Commune de Paris** is also the name of the revolutionary government that controlled Paris from March 18 to May 27, 1871.]
Cordeliers: Taking their name from their meeting place, a former monastery of the religous order of followers of St. Francis of Assisi, the Cordeliers Club was an egalitarian popular society that made no distinction between members and whose deliberations were always open. Many of the most influential revolutionary leaders took part in the debates of the club: Danton, Marat, Desmoulins, Hébert, Chaumette. The club opposed the disarming of the citizens and the distinction between active and passive citizens. From the beginning, the Cordeliers pushed for the establishment of a Republic.
département: principal administrative division of France.
devoir: association of skilled workers and jouneymen.
Enragés: extremist revolutionaries, led by Jacques Roux (see chapter 10), who were a powerful force in Paris in 1793, mobilizing the citizens against hoarders and speculators.
ex voto: painting, plaque or object bearing an inscription of gratitude, placed in a church or chapel to give thanks for a favor granted or to honor a vow.

Fédération: celebration of the first anniversary of the storming of the Bastille on July 14, 1790: La Fayette swore an oath to defend the Constitution, followed by the King, then the crowds of people representing the different sections of Paris and many of the departments of France. The **fédérés** were citizen soldiers from the provinces who came to Paris for the occasion.

fermiers généraux: a group of financiers who paid large sums for the privilege of collecting the indirect taxes and the income from the royal domains.

Feuillants: constitutional monarchists who resigned from the Jacobins.

généralité: financial division of France under the Ancien Régime.

Girondists: political group sitting on the right during the Convention, their most famous leaders were from the Gironde department—Vergniaud, Guadet. They came to power in 1792 and lost power in May, 1793.

Grenelle Affair: August 28, 1796. An attempt by followers of Babeuf (who was in prison awaiting trial) and other rebels to seize an army camp at Grenelle, a small town on the Seine, later annexed by Paris. Many insurgents were killed on the spot; the rest, 132, were arrested and some were executed in the next two months.

Hébertists: partisans of Jacques Hébert, ultrarevolutionary who exercized great power in the Commune of Paris and had a large following among the sans-culottes.

Indulgents: those who favored a policy of clemency during the first Terror, largely followers of Danton.

Intendant: administrator of a **généralité**.

Jacobins: members of a republian club who exerted great influence during the revolution. They were of the middle bourgeoisie and though moderate at first, became increasingly revolutionary. The club was closed by the government in 1795.

journalier: day-laborer

laboureur: a wealthy farmer, usually a figure of some importance in the village community.

lèse-nation: crime against the nation; cf. **lèse-majesté:** crime against the sovereign.

livre: unit of weight and monetary value. There were 20 **sous** in a **livre**, 3 **livres** in an **écu**, and 8 **écus** in a **louis**.

mainmorte: state of serfs deprived of the right to dispose of their goods through a will.

Montagnards: collectively known as the Mountain, these deputies occupied the higher seats in the Convention. Both Danton and Robespierre were in this group of the upper bourgeoisie.

négociant: wholesale merchant and distributor.

parlement: court of law under the Ancien Régime; these judicial bodies, controlled by the aristocracy, were often at odds with the Church and the royal court.

particularism: tendency of former French provinces to conserve their traditional culture and language and to resist the centralized revolutionary nation.

pays: subdivisions of the départements.

Père Duchesne: newspaper founded by Hébert, the title refers to a stock character in the theaters of the market festivals.

rentier: person whose income comes from investments and property.

roturier: commoner; i.e., all who were not aristocrats; the Third Estate.

sans-culotte: literally, without breeches—the dress of aristocrats. The sans-culottes were the active force of the revolution, particularly in year II, when they controlled the sectional assemblies and participated in many demonstrations and marches. They were largely artisans, skilled workers and shopkeepers; often they employed apprentices and journeymen in their workshops. The class lines were blurred in this bourgeois revolution against the feudal monarchy. The sans-culottes were defined more by their income and their living conditions than by their relation to the means of production. The exploitation of labor did not become the major issue until the revolution of 1848.

section: a neighborhood of Paris. Paris was divided into about fifty sections; each section had an assembly that debated the Constitution and elected representatives to the Constituent Assembly and the Commune of Paris.

Tribun du peuple: (People's Tribune)—newspaper founded by Babeuf.

venality: under the Ancien Régime, the **vénalité des offices** meant the sale of State offices. Those who bought offices owned them and controlled the funds collected.

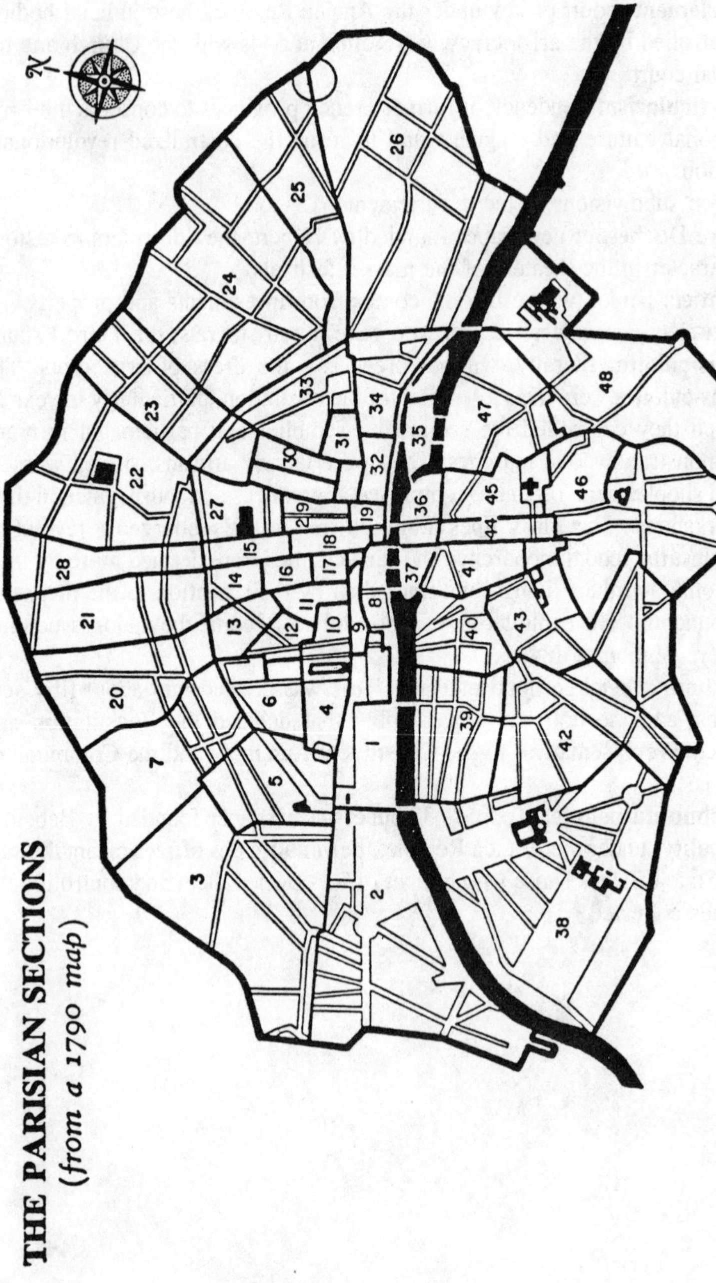

THE PARISIAN SECTIONS
(from a 1790 map)

Historical Table of the Parisian Sections
May 21, 1790–19 Vendémiaire, year IV

1. *Tuileries* section (1790–year IV)
2. *Champs-Elysées* section (1790–year IV)
3. *Roule* section; renamed *République* (October 1792–30 Prairial, year III); restored to *Roule* (30 Prairial, year III–year IV)
4. *Palais-Royal* section; renamed *Butte-des-Moulins* (August 1792–August 1793); becomes *Montagne* section (August 1793–21 Frimaire, year III); restored to *Butte-des-Moulins* (21 Frimaire, year III–year IV)
5. *Place-Vendôme* section; renamed *Piques* (September 1792–5 Prairial, year III); restored to *Place-Vendôme* (5 Prairial, year III–year IV)
6. *Bibliothèque* section; renamed *Quatre-Vingt-Douze* (September 1792–October 1793); renamed *Lepeletier* (October 1793–year IV)
7. *Grange-Batelière* section; renamed *Mirabeau* (August–December 1792); renamed *Mont Blanc* (December 1792–year IV)
8. *Louvre* section; renamed *Muséum* (May 6, 1793–year IV)
9. *Oratoire* section; renamed *Gardes-Françaises* (September 1792–year IV)
10. *Halle-au-Blé* section.
11. *Postes* section; renamed *Contrat-Social* (August 18, 1792–year IV)
12. *Place Louis XIV* section; renamed *Mail* (August 1792–September 1793); became *Guillaume-Tell* section (September 1793–Messidor, year III); restored to *Mail* (Messidor, year III–year IV)
13. *Fontaine-Montmorency* section; renamed *Molière-et-Lafontaine* (October 1792–September 12, 1793); became *Brutus* section (September 12, 1793–year IV)
14. *Bonne-Nouvelle* section
15. *Ponceau* section; renamed *Amis-de-la-Patrie* (September 1792–year IV)
16. *Mauconseil* section; renamed *Bon-Conseil* (August 1792–year IV)
17. *Marché-des-Innocents*; renamed *Halles* (September 1792–May 1793); became *Marchés* (May 1793–year IV)
18. *Lombards* section
19. *Arcis* section
20. *Faubourg-Montmartre* section
21. *Poissonnière* section
22. *Bondy* section
23. *Temple* section
24. *Popincourt* section
25. *Montreuil* section
26. *Quinze-Vingts* section.
27. *Gravilliers* section
28. *Faubourg-Saint-Denis*; renamed *Faubourg-du-Nord* (January 1793–year IV)
29. *Beaubourg* section; renamed *Réunion* (September 1792–year IV)
30. *Enfants-Rouges*; renamed *Marais* (September 1792–June 1793); became *l'Homme-Armé* section (June 1793–year IV)
31. *Roi-de-Sicile* section; renamed *Droits-de-l'Homme* (August 1792–year IV)

32. *L'Hôtel-de-Ville* section; renamed *Maison-Commune* (August 21, 1792–Fructidor, year II); became *Fidélité* (Fructidor, year II–year IV)
33. *Place-Royale*; renamed *Fédérés* (August 1792–July 4, 1793); became *Indivisibilité* (July 4, 1793–year IV)
34. *Arsenal* section
35. *l'Ile Saint-Louis* section; renamed *Fraternité* (November 1792–year IV)
36. *Notre Dame* section; renamed *Cité* (August 1792–21 Brumaire, year II); became *Raison* section (21–25 Brumaire, year II); restored to *Cité* (25 Brumaire, year II–year IV)
37. *Henri IV* section; *Pont-Neuf* (August 14, 1792–September 7, 1793); became *Révolutionnaire* section (September 7, 1793–1 Frimaire, year III); restored to *Pont-Neuf* (10 Frimaire, year III–year IV)
38. *Invalides* section.
39. *Fontaine-de-Grenelle* section.
40. *Quatre-Nations* section; renamed *Unité* (April 1793–year IV)
41. *Théâtre-Français* section; renamed *Marseille* (August 1792–August 1793); became *Marseille-et-Marat* (August 1793–Pluviôse, year II); became *Marat* section (Pluviôse, year II–22 Pluviôse, year III); restored to *Théâtre-Français* (22 Pluviôse, year III–year IV)
42. *Croix-Rouge* section; renamed *Bonnet-Rouge* (October 3, 1793–Germinal, year III); renamed *Bonnet-de-la-Liberté* (Germinal–Prairial, year III); became *Ouest* section (Prairial, year III–year IV)
43. *Luxembourg* section; renamed *Mucius-Scaevola* (Brumaire, year II–Prairial, year III); restored to *Luxembourg* (Prairial, year III–year IV)
44. *Thermes-de-Julien*; renamed *Beaurepaire* (September 8, 1792–20 Pluviôse, year II); *Chalier* (20 Pluviôse, year II–Pluviôse, year III); restored to *Thermes-de-Julien* (Pluviôse, year III–year IV).
45. *Sainte-Geneviève*; renamed *Panthéon-Français* (August 1792–year IV)
46. *Observatoire* section
47. *Jardin-des-Plantes*; renamed *Sans-Culottes* (August 1792–10 Ventôse, year III); restored to *Jardin-des-Plantes* (10 Ventôse, year III–year IV)
48. *Gobelins* section; renamed *Finistère* (August 1792–year IV)

HISTORIC PROVINCES of FRANCE

(before 1790)

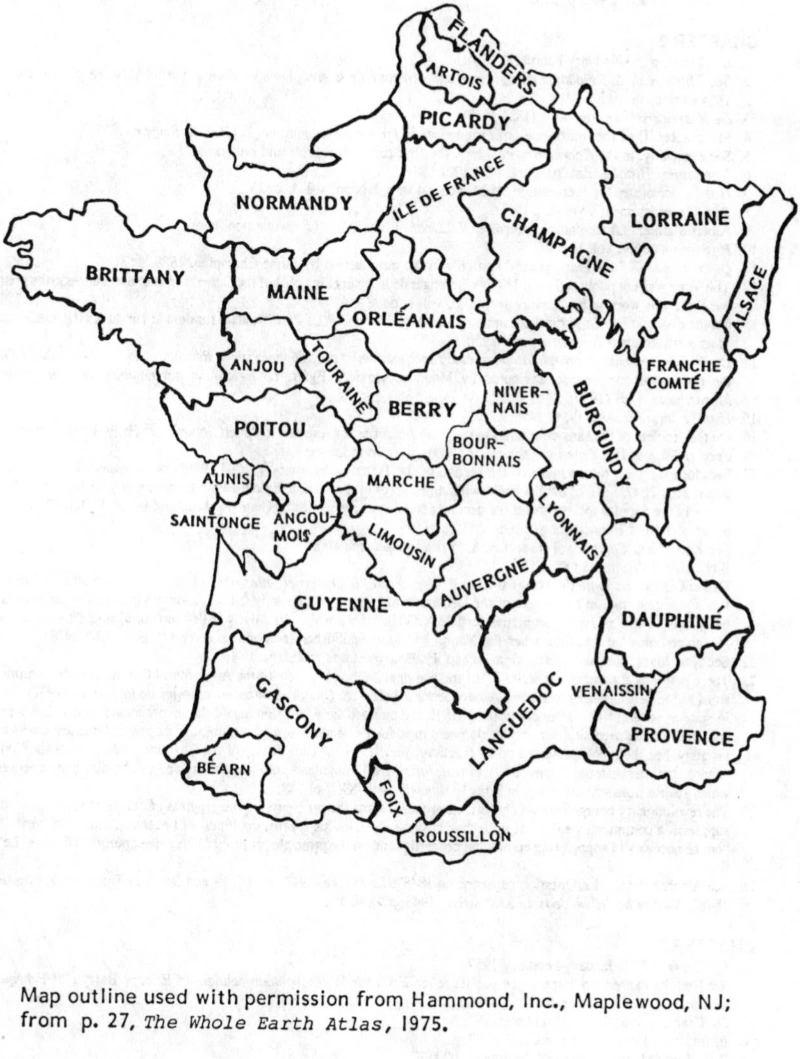

Map outline used with permission from Hammond, Inc., Maplewood, NJ; from p. 27, *The Whole Earth Atlas*, 1975.

Reference Notes

CHAPTER 1

1. Report of synthesis presented to the second session of the international colloquium organized in Paris from July 3-7, 1978, for the bicentennial of the death of Voltaire and Rousseau, published in the *Annales historiques de la Révolution française*, 1979, n° 4, p. 519.
2. J. Pappas, "Le Roi philosophe d'après Voltaire et Rousseau," *A.H.R.F.*, 1979, n° 4
3. A. Ado, "Catherine II et la Russie," *A.H.R.F.*, 1979, n° 4
4. E. Balazs, "Joseph II et la Hongrie," *A.H.R.F.*, 1979, n° 4
5. P. Vilar, "L'Espagne de Charles III," *A.H.R.F.*, 1979, n° 4
6. F. Diaz, "L'Italie des princes éclairés," *A.H.R.F.*, 1979, n° 4
7. K. Tonnesson, "Le Cas danois," *A.H.R.F.*, 1979, n° 4
8. E. Faure, *La Disgrace de Turgot, 12 mai 1776*, Paris, 1961
9. *Receuil de documents relatifs aux séances des États Généraux*... sous la direction de G. Lefebvre, t. 1er (II), *La Séance du 23 Juin*, Paris, 1962, p. 275.

CHAPTER 2

1. *La Pensée*, n° 53, January-February, 1954.
2. See *l'Histoire de la Révolution d'Angleterre and l'Histoire de la civilisation en France*, particularly the preface to the 1855 edition.
3. *De la démocratie en Amerique* (1836-1839)
4. See chapter III of the fourth book of *Origines de la France contemporaine*, I. *L'Ancien Régime* (1875)
5. See especially, in the *Communist Manifesto*, the first part, "Bourgeois and proletariat"
6. Jean Jaurès, *Histoire socialiste*, vol. I-IV, 1901-1904
7. *Histoire socialiste*, Mathiez edition, 1922, general introduction, vol. I, p. 23
8. *Ibid.*, "avertissement", vol. I, p. 5
9. Albert Mathiez, *La Révolution française*, 1922, vol. I, chap. II, "La revolte nobiliaire"
10. *Histoire socialiste*, vol. I, p. 40
11. *Qu'est-ce que le Tiers État?*, critical edition with an introduction by Edme Champion, 1888, p. 31
12. This work was not published until 1843 by Bérenger de la Drôme, in vol. I of the *Oeuvres* of Barnave. Jaurès gives great weight to this work in his *Histoire socialiste*, vol. I, p. 98
13. On the dissociation of the rural community, see Albert Soboul, "La Communauté rurale à la fin du XVIIIe siècle" *Le Mois d'ethnographie française*, April 1950
14. *De l'influence attribuée aux philosophes, aux francs-maçons et aux illuminés sur la Révolution de France*... (1801). On the politics of compromise attempted by Mounier, see Jean Egret, *La Révolution des notables, Mounier et les Monarchiens, 1789* (1950)
15. *Histoire socialiste*, vol. IV, p. 1458
16. On the problem of the sans-culotterie, see several directions for research in Albert Soboul, *Les Papiers des sections de Paris (1790-Year IV), Repertoire sommaire* (1950), p. 6, introduction
17. See, for examples, the petitions of the section of the Tuileries, February 4, 1793 (*Bibliothèque nationale*, ms. F. fr., Nouv. acq., 2647, f. 7), of the Société des Hommes libres of the section of Pont-Neuf, 1st month of year II (*ibid.*, 2713, f. 46), of the popular society and of the general assembly of the section of Unité (*Archives nationales*, D. III, 225, d. 2), of the section of Bonnet-Rouge (ibid., 253^{3}, d. 1).
18. See Karl Marx, *Capital*, vol. I, section 8, "Primitive accumulation"
19. B.N., Lb^{40}, 2140, imp. in-8°, p. 6
20. Daniel Guérin, *La Lutte de classes sous la Ire République, Bourgeois et "bras nus" (1793-1797)*, 2 volumes, 1946
21. It is significant that, in his project of the Declaration of Rights of September, 1792, Momoro guarantees the inviolability only of the industrial properties (article XXVII); "those which are falsely called territorial properties" will be guaranteed only "at that time when the Nation will have established laws on that subject." (B.N., Lb^{41} 2978).
22. See Karl Marx, *Communist Manifesto* , chap. I, "Bourgeois and prolelariat"
23. These petitions abound in the series F^{10} of the National Archives (papers of the Agricultural Committees or Commissions of the revolutionary assemblies). See Georges Lefebvre, *Questions agraires au temps de la Terreur* (1932).
24. In spite of several timid attempts in the year II, the bourgeoisie which dominated the revolutionary assemblies were conscious of the necessity, for the development of industrial enterprises, of prohibiting the peasant masses access to property. See the report presented on 27 fructidor, year II, by Lozeau, deputy of the Charente-Inférieure, at the Convention, "on the material impossibility of transforming all Frenchmen into landowners and on the dire consequences which such a transformation would bring" (*Moniteur*, vol. XXI, p. 748).
25. The revolutionary bourgeoisie was nevertheless conscious of the necessity, for the progress of capitalist agriculture, of suppressing communal wealth and collective customs. See, in this regard, the report of Lozeau, in messidor, year II, "on the neccisity of suppressing communal properties and on the principles of property in a free country" (B.N., 8° Le^{38} 841).
26. See Albert Soboul, "La Question paysanne en 1848", *La Pensée*, 1948, n°s 18, 19 and 20; "Les Troubles agraires de 1848", *1848 et les Révolutions du XIXe siècle*, 1948, n°s 180 et 181.

CHAPTER 3

1. *La Pensée*, n° 71, January-February 1957
2. We find the expression "republique populaire" in *Essai sur la dénonciation politique* of Etienne Barry (*Bibliothèque nationale*, Lc2 809, imp in-8°).
3. *Du Contrat social*, book III, chapter XV
4. *Bibliotheque Victor-Cousin*, ms 118, f. 97
5. B.N., Lb^{40} 461, imp. s.d. in-8°, Tourneux, n° 8917

6. *Archives de la préfecture de police*, A A/266, p. 250
7. B.N., Lb^{41} 2064, imp. in-8°; Tourneux, n° 8664. The piece is signed *Robespierre*, president
8. *Archives nationales*, B I 15
9. B.N., Lb^{41} 1154 g., imp. in-folio plano; Tourneux, n° 6162
10. A.N., B I 14
11. A.N., B I 14
12. A.N., F^{7} 4718, dossier Gaudet
13. *Archives départementales de la Seine*, D 1017
14. A.D.S., D 771, Address of the General Council of the Commune to the forty-eight sections
15. B.V.C., ms. 118, f. 13
16. B.N., Lb^{41} 10842, imp. in-4°
17. B.N., Lb^{41} 2098, imp. in-8°; Tourneux, n° 7892
18. B.N., Lb^{41} 2068, imp. in-8°; Tourneux, n° 8708
19. B.N., Lb^{41} 3166, imp. in-8°
20. A.D.P., 4 AZ 698
21. B.V.C., ms 120
22. B.N., Lb^{41} 2098, imp. in-8°; Tourneux, n° 7892
23. B.N., Lb^{41} 1964 (1), imp. in-8°; Tourneux, n° 7932
24. A.D.S., D 783, imp. in-8°; *Moniteur*, vol. XV, p. 8
25. *Moniteur*, vol. XV, p. 702; cited by Vergniaud in his speech to the Convention, 13 March 1793.
26. A.D.P., A A/266, p. 248, true copy signed *Varlet*
27. B.V.C., ms 118, F. 104
28. A.N., C 255, d. 480, p. 14
29. *Moniteur*, vol. XVI, p. 537
30. *Moniteur*, vol. XVI, p. 543
31. A.N., C 255, d. 483, p. 15
32. A.N., C 258, d. 529, p. 31; *Moniteur*, vol. XVI, p. 689
33. *Moniteur*, vol. XVI, p. 739. "Our intention," declared Herault, "has been to give to the section of the people who elected a deputy the responsibility of judging his conduct, and we have added that a deputy was not eligible to run again until after his conduct had been approved by his nominators."
34. *Affiches de la Commune*, 5 August 1793
35. B.N., Lb^{41} 1875, imp. in-4°; Tourneux, n° 8241
36. A.D.S., D 933
37. A.P.P., AA/266, pp. 306-309
38. B.N., ms. Nouv. acq. fr. 2707, f. 33
39. B.N., Lb^{41} 2064; Tourneux, n° 8664
40. A.N., B I 15
41. B.N., Lb^{41} 1154 g, imp. in-8°; Tourneux, n° 6162
42. A.D.S., D 833
43. B.N., Lb^{41} 1769, imp. in-folio plano; Tourneux, n° 7986
44. B.N., ms., Nouv. acq. fr. 2647, f. 29
45. *Moniteur*, vol. XIV, p. 281
46. B.V.C., ms 120
47. A.D.S., D 686
48. A.N., F I, CIII, Seine 1
49. Lb^{41} 3038, imp. in-8°; Tourneux, n° 8749
50. A.N., C 355, pl. 1864, p. 49
51. A.N., W 138
52. B.N., Lb^{41} 530, imp. in-4°; Tourneux, n° 8784
53. B.N., ms. Nouv. acq. fr. 2713, f. 29
54. A.N., F^{7} 4589, pl. 2, p. 21
55. A.N., FI 4774^{41}
56. A.D.S., D 1001; F. Braesch, *Procès-verbaux de l'assemblée generale de la section des Postes*, p. 154
57. A.N., AD I 49, imp. in-4°; Tourneux, n° 21824
58. B.N., Lb^{41} 1760, imp. in-8°; Tourneux, n° 8615
59. *Journal de la Montagne*, 4 ventôse year II
60. A.N., D III, 251-252, d. 1
61. A.N., W 112
62. A.N., F^{7}* 2510
63. A.N., F^{7} 4595, pl. 1, p. 10

CHAPTER 4

1. *La Pensée*, n° 65, January-February 1956
2. See what I wrote on the sans-culottes, in "Classes and Class Struggles during the French Revolution," *La Pensée*, n° 53, January-February 1954, pp. 39-62.
3. *Of the Influence attributed to Philosophers, Free-Masons and Visionaries on the French Revolution*... 1801
4. *Archives nationales*, F^{7} 4747, "Bases and Circulations which served as a rule to set the indemnities claimed by the people's representative Isnard," 30 germinal year II.
5. See chapter 20, "Historical Information on Commercial Capital" of volume III of *Capital*
6. *Histoire socialiste*, IV, 1848. Duplay was a purchaser of national wealth in the year IV (1796) (*ibid.*, V, 460).

7. A.N., F^{7} 4577 a 4775^{51}
8. A.N., F^{7} 4774^{35}, Maron dossier
9. A.N., F^{7} 4774^{40}
10. "The Moralizing Critic or the Critical Moral", *Oeuvres philosophiques*, Éditions Costes, vol. III, p. 130
11. A.N., C 355, pl. 1860, p. 19
12. *Moniteur*, reprint, vol. XVI, p. 759
13. *Archives départementales de la Seine*, 4 AZ 698, no date
14. *Moniteur*, reprint, vol. XVII, p. 484, t. XX, p. 233
15. *Bibliothèque nationale*, Mss. New French Acquisitions 2647, f. 7
16. A.N., F^{7} * 2517, minutes of the revolutionary committee of the section of Finistère
17. A.N., F^{7} * 2510, minutes of the general assemblies of the section of the Invalides
18. *Moniteur*, reprint, vol. XVIII, p. 16
19. A.N., D III, 255-256^{1}, d. 2, p. 2 and 4
20. A.N., D III, 253^{1}, d. 1, p. 13
21. B.N., Mss. New French Acquisitions, 2652

CHAPTER 5

1. Text of a communication presented to the Colloquium on the Commune held at Varsovie, April 20-23 1971. (*La Pensée*, July-August 1971.)
2. K. Marx, *Civil War in France*, Collected Works, Vol. 22, (New York: International Publishers, 1986), p. 334.
3. Lenin, "The State and Revolution," *Selected Works*, (New York: International Publishers, 1971), p. 303.
4. G. Lefebvre, *Le Directoire*, 2nd Edition, p. 35. See also the preface of Georges Lefebvre to Buonarroti, *Conspiration pour l'Égalité dite de Babeuf*, (Éditions sociales, 1957). "One can wonder if Buonarroti's book was not a subject of meditation for Lenin as it was for Blanqui." (p. 11)
5. "What is a political revolution in general? What in particular is the French Revolution? A war declared between the patricians and the plebeians, between the rich and the poor." (Babeuf, *Le Tribun du peuple* n° 34, 15 brumaire Year IV).
6. See A. Mathiez, "La Révolution française et la théorie de la dictature. La Constituante", *Revue historique*, n° 32, July-August 1929, p. 304. See also p. Bastid, *Sieyes et sa pensée*, 2nd ed. (Paris, 1970), p. 391, "Pouvoir constituant et pouvoir constitué."
7. A. Mathiez, *ibid*. Quite rightly, he takes the opposite view to A. Aulard who, in his speech of April 6, 1923 entitled "La théorie de la violence et la Révolution française" (Paris, 1923), tried to refute "the legend which shows the men of the French Revolution as theoreticians of violence and this Revolution as an example of productive violence."
8. On the campaign of Marat's newspaper in 1789, see in particular , n° 5, September 15, *Observations importantes sur les droits des Constituants et les devoirs des Constitues;* , n° 6, September 16, that carries the first attacks against the Committee of Subsistances of the Hotel-de-Ville; n° 7, September 17, that denounces the slowness and false steps of the National Assembly. See J. Jaurès, *Histoire socialiste de la Révolution française*, edition A. Soboul, vol. I, p. 518.
9. "In September and October 1789, the policies of Marat would have probably led to the dictatorship of a moderate Committee nominated by the National Assembly." (J. Jaurès, *Histoire socialiste*, edition A. Soboul, vol. I, p. 518.) See J. Massin, *Marat*, p. 98.
10. We find the expression *république populaire* in a text from July, 1793. On all these aspects, see A. Soboul, *Les Sans-culottes parisiens en l'an II. Mouvement populaire et Gouvernement révolutionnaire. 2 juin 1793—9 thermidor an II*, (Paris, 1958), p. 505, a chapter devoted to the political tendencies of the Parisian sans-culotterie.
11. Quoted without reference by F. Braesch, *La Commune du 10 aout 1792*, (Paris, 1911), p. 1092.
12. *Archives nationales*, AD XVI, p. 37; Buchez and Roux, chap. XXV, p. 104.
13. A.N., F^{7} 4774^{45}, denunciation, n.d. (Year III). B.N., Lb^{40} 1781; Tourneux, n° 8755
14. B.N., Mss. Nouv. acq. fr. 2663, f. 178
15. A. Soboul, *op. cit.*, p. 549, publicity, "safeguard of the people"; p. 561, unity, "guarantee of victory"
16. B.N., Lb^{40} 1831, imp. s.l., 16°, 8 p.; Tourneux, n° 8107
17. B.N., Mss. Nouv. acq. fr., 2713, f. 29
18. A.N., F^{7} 4774^{41}, Mardin dossier, locksmith
19. A. Soboul, *op. cit.*, p. 655. See also A. Aulard, "Le tutoiement pendant la Révolution", *La Révolution française*, Vol. XXXIV, p. 481
20. *Archives du département de la Seine* , 4 AZ 269 *ter*, 8°, 4 p.
21. *Journal de la Montagne*, 22 brumaire Year II; *Moniteur*, Vol. XVIII, p. 402
22. *Journal de la Montagne*, 9 brumaire Year II; *Moniteur*, Vol. XVIII, p. 290
23. *Bibliothèque Victor-Cousin*, ms 118, f. 11
24. G. Tridon, *op. cit.*, 2nd ed., p. 13-14. See below, note 26
25. Michelet, *Histoire de la Révolution française*, book IX, chap. IV
26. G. Tridon, *Les Hébertistes. Plainte contre une calomnie de l'histoire*, (Paris, 1864). This brochure offers no interest except from the point of view of the history of ideas in the 19th century; it was reprinted during the Commune.
27. *Les Origines de la France contemporaine. L'Ancien Régime*, book III, "L'esprit et la doctrine," chap. IV, 3
28. "It was a very exclusive society, concentrated on itself. They knew each other and that's all they knew; all that was not Jacobin was for them suspect." (Michelet, *Histoire de la Révolution française*, book IX, chap. III.)
29. See A. Cochin, *Les Sociétés de pensée et la Révolution en Bretagne*, (Paris, 1925); L. de Cardenal, *La province pendant la Révolution*..., (Paris, 1929), in particular book IV, "Les moyens d'action". More cursory, but more objective, Gaston-Martin, *Les Jacobins*, (Paris, 1945), p. 89, "La méthode"
30. A.D.S., 4 AZ 590
31. *Moniteur*, Vol. XVIII, p. 110. "Your Committee of Public Safety, placed in the center of all achievements, has calculated the causes of public misfortunes, finding them in the weakness with which decrees are executed..., in the instability of the attitudes of the State, in the vicissitude of the passions which influence the government."

32. *Moniteur*, vol XVIII, p. 584, 590, 610
33. Robespierre presented the theory of the revolutionary government, but after the event, in his *Rapport sur les principes du Gouvernement révolutionnaire* (5 nivoise Year II – December 25, 1793) and in his *Rapport sur les principes de morale politique qui doivent guider la Convention* (18 pluviôse Year II – February 5, 1794). His theory is essentially based on the distinction between the constitutional government whose aim is to "conserve the Republic," and the revolutionary government whose aim is to "found the Republic." "If the force behind the popular government in peace is virtue, the force behind the popular government in revolution is virtue combined with terror..." These themes are well known. Actually neither Robespierre nor any Jacobin had a real theory of the revolutionary state. With his spiritualist education and his belief in the omnipotence of ideas and appeals to virtue, Robespierre was incapable of a precise social analysis. The Jacobins did not constitute a class, even less a class party. The Jacobin revolutionary state, in the final account, was based on a spiritualist conception of social relations: the consequences of this proved fatal to their state.
34. A.N., AF II 66, pl. 488, p. 11. No mention of the piece is found in the *Recueil des Actes du Comité de salut public*.
35. Saint-Just, *Moniteur*, Vol. XIX, p. 688. Collot d'Herbois, *Journal de la Montagne*, 24 germinal year II; *Moniteur*, vol. XX, p. 203; *Jacobins*, vol. VI, p. 61
36. *Journal de la Montagne*, 28 and 29 floreal year II; *Moniteur*, Vol. XX, p. 489; *Jacobins*, Vol. VI, p. 125. Couthon: "Division is harmful and unity of opinion cannot be broken without great danger. If you conserve all these societies...., the public mind will be tremendously divided... government operations will be hampered."
37. The Robespierrist line of revolutionary historiography had been asserted as early as 1828 with the *Conspiration pour l'égalité dite de Babeuf*. After Lapponneraye who published a *Histoire de la Révolution française* in 1838, let us signal Tissot, *Histoire de Robespierre* (1844). In this same line, see Cabet, *l'Histoire populaire de la Révolution* (1845) and Louis Blanc, *l'Histoire de la Révolution*, which began to appear in 1847 with a complete edition in 1862, and Esquiros, *l'Histoire des Montagnards* (1848).
38. "Notes inédites de Blanqui sur Robespierre", published by A. Mathiez, *Annales historiques de la Révolution française*, 1928, p. 305
39. A. Bougeart, *Marat, l'Ami du peuple* (Paris: 1862), 2 vol., vol. II, p. 260 and p. 340
40. See V. M. Daline, *Gracchus Babeuf avant et pendant la Révolution française, 1785-1794* (Moscow: 1963), in Russian; review by A. Soboul, *Revue d'histoire moderne et contemporaine*, 1966, p. 166.
41. See M. Dommanget, "La structure et les méthodes de la Conjuration des Egaux", *Annales révolutionnaires*, 1922, p. 177 and 281; reprinted in *Babeuf et la Conjuration des Égaux* (Paris: 1970), p. 145
42. See especially Buonarroti, *Conspiration pour l'Egalité dite de Babeuf* (Brussels: 1928). We are using the 1957 edition (Paris: Éditions sociales), with a preface by G. Lefebvre.
43. Buonarroti, *ed. cit.*, vol. I, p. 84, "Points de ralliement offerts aux républicains"
44. Buonarroti, *ed. cit.*, vol. II, p. 84, Sixth evidence, "Première instruction du Directoire secret, adressée à chacun des agents révolutionnaires principaux." "At the same time that we are arming ourselves with all suitable precautions to render us elusive and our measures impossible to confound, we want you to be shielded from any surprise.... The secret directory has carried prudence to the point of isolating from each other the twelve principal agents... the same precautions of isolation are taken for the intermediate agents... In general, the secret Directory has adopted an overall system of isolating everyone, of cutting all communications, and it will subordinate the whole organization to this order, such that each individual employed directly or indirectly by the Directory will not be able to betray anyone, and his ruin will take only him from the revolutionnaries."
    We must not exaggerate the strictness of the clandestine nature of the Conspiracy of Equals. Grisel's denunciation was enough to bring about the arrest of the leaders: they had not foreseen this situation nor designated any deputies. There was the same lack of precaution concerning the names and addresses of the revolutionary agents which were seized by the police in the place Babeuf was staying when he was arrested, along with numerous pieces which aided the prosecution in the trial of Vendome. See the remarks of Dommanget, *art. cit.*, p. 166.
45. Buonarroti, *ed. cit.*, vol. II, p. 82, Fifth evidence, "Organisation des agents principaux au nombre de douze et des agents intermédiaires. Premières fonctions de chacun d'eux." Let us add to the agents of the "arrondissements" the military agents charged with the same functions by the batallions stationed in Paris and the surrounding areas.
46. *Ibid*, Vol. II, p. 192, Twenty-fifth evidence, "The Directory of the agents."
47. M. Dommanget, *art. cit.*, p. 166
48. Buonarroti, *ed. cit.*, Vol. I, p. 84, "Autorité à substituer au gouvernement de l'an III", and p. 109, "Autorité à substituer à l'autorité existante"
49. See also this note of Buonarroti: "The experience of the French Revolution, and most particularly the troubles and changes of the national Convention, have seemingly sufficiently demonstrated that a people, whose opinions have been formed under a regime of inequality and despotism, are ill suited, at the beginning of a regenerating revolution, to designate by their votes the men charged with directing and consummating that revolution... Perhaps the real sovereignty of the people requires that at the birth of a political revolution less attention be given to collecting the votes of the nation and more to causing the supreme authority to fall, in the least arbitrary manner posible, into wise and strong revolutionary hands." (Buonarroti, *ed. cit.*, p. 111, n. 1)
50. Buonarroti, *ed. cit.*, vol. I, p. 85, "Autorité à substituer au gouvernement de l'an III"
51. *Ibid.*, vol. I, p. 109, "Autorité à substituer à l'autorité existante"
52. *Ibid.*, vol. I, p. 115, "Corps composé d'un démocrate par département, à proposer au peuple de Paris en insurrection"

CHAPTER 6

1. *Annales historiques de la Révolution française*, 1956, n° 3, p. 236-254
2. Buchez and Roux, *Histoire parlementaire de la Révolution française*, vol. XXV, p. 325
3. *Histoire socialiste*, vol. IV, p. 1448
4. *Archives nationales*, F[7] 4774[46]
5. F. Braesch, "Essai de statistique de la population ouvrière de Paris vers 1791", *La Révolution française*, vol. LXIII, 1912, p. 288

6. A. N., C 271, pl. 666, p. 37
7. A. N., W 345, d. 676, p. 7, affaire Chardin
8. A. N., C 295, pl. 994, p. 27. Address to all good sans-culottes, signed Servant. No indication of the source of this pure popular document.
9. See Ferdinand Brunot, *Histoire de la langue française*, vol. IX, p. 711. He finds the expression *honnêtes gens* for the first time in Babeuf's *Tribun du peuple* (, n° 35, II, 93). Actually it can be found in manuscript documents from June of 1793 on.
10. On September 25, 1793, the carpenter Bertout (doubtless meaning an employer carpenter) was arrested on the order of the Piques section for having desired "another government to oppress 'la canaille', because the 'honnêtes gens' were lost." (A.N., F 4596, pl. 11, p. 3.) Here "la canaille" obviously designates the lower classes: the notion of work does not appear in this expression. See also the remarks of a certain Appert, arrested as a suspect on 25 brumaire year II (November 15, 1793) for having accused the patriots "of using tactics to have the 'honnêtes gens' rejected in order to put 'la canaille' in their place." (A.N., F 4580, pl. 6.)
11. A.N., D III 256, p. 128
12. A.N., F 4699
13. A.N., F 4765
14. A.N., F 4592, pl. 4, p. 58. According to the testimony of his section, Becquerel was nevertheless a good patriot.
15. *Le Tribun du peuple*, n° 34, 15 brumaire, year IV (November 6, 1795)
16. A.N., F 4709
17. A.N., F 4727
18. A.N., F 4775
19. *Le Père Duchesne*, n° 283, no date. See also n° 339: here Hébert defines the sans-culottes as "the poor devil who lives from day to day and who sweats blood and water to feed his family."
20. A.N., C 272, pl. 675, p. 8
21. A.N., F 4645. The social position of the three suspended commissioners confirms that it is indeed a question of class conflict: one was an apothecary, another a former hat manufacturer and the third a construction entrepreneur. As an aggravating circumstance, they had refused "the allowances that their colleagues, true sans-culottes, could not do without: and taking this as a pretext for believing themselves obliged to render public service, they took it upon themselves to give orders to men who knew more about public matters than they did."
22. A.N., F 4775. The word *ouvrier* [worker] implied poverty in this period. Ferdinand Brunot emphasizes that under the Consulate and the Empire as economic and social conditions worsened, 'ouvrier' becomes a synonym for indigent (*op. cit.*, vol. IX, p. 1198).
23. A. N., F 4774
24. N° 339, no date (pluviôse year II, January-February 1794)
25. A. N., F 4736, dossier Guin
26. *Bibliothèque nationale*, Lb 1733
27. *Archives départementales de la Seine*, D* 9 989
28. Sans-Culottes Section. Address to the National Convention, September 2, 1793, Imp. Renaudière, no date, in-8°, 6 p. (B.N., Lb 2140). This petition is analyzed by A. Lichtenberger, *Le Socialisme et la Révolution française*, p. 170 and by G. Lefebvre, *Questions agraires au temps de la Terreur*, p. 78. On the basis of this text we note that the limitation of farming concerns, or the division of the big farms, a demand familiar to the sans-culottes of the country which would have assured them all independent work was not unknown to the Parisian sans-culottes. It was however rarely specified. Hébert makes mention of it in number 345 of his *Père Duchesne* (pluviôse year II): "In order to kill with one blow the farmer and merchant aristocracy, all the big farms should be divided into smallholdings." This demand also figures among the *XVI commandements patriotiques* of Palloy: "...never have more than one farm to cultivate." A.N., AD I 65.) This would have limited free enterprise; even the Montagnard Convention never consented to it.
29. B.N., Lb 2383, Paris, year I, imp. in-8°, 132 p.
30. Albert Soboul, "Les Institutions républicaines de Saint-Just, d'après les manuscrits de la Bibliothèque nationale", *A.H.R.F.*, 1948, p. 193
31. "Discours sur Robespierre", *A.H.R.F.*, 1933, p. 492
32. *Bibliothèque historique de la Ville de Paris*, 109 586. See article XXVII.
33. *Idées sur l'espèce de gouvernement populaire qui pourrait convenir à un pays de l'étendue et de la population présumée de la France. Essai présenté à la Convention nationale par un citoyen*, 1792, Imp. in-8°, 62 p. (A.N., AD I 65). The author also fixes an upper limit to dowries consisting "of rural property or other real estate", but in money, effects of commerce.... they will be able to be carried "to indeterminate values". These ideas obviously betray a certain social position.
34. B.N., Ms. Nouv. acq. fr. 2647, f. 7. The General Assembly of the Tuileries section to its citizens, February 4, 1793.
35. *Moniteur*, vol. XVII, p. 281
36. *Moniteur*, vol. XVIII, p. 16
37. A.N., D III 255-256, d-2, p. 2. This petition was printed (*ibid.*, p. 4, imp. in-8°, 4 p.). It appears in the *Moniteur*, vol. XIX, p. 554.
38. A.N., F* 2510
39. A.N., D III 253, d. I, p. 13
40. B.N., Ms. Nouv. acq. fr. 2652
41. Cited by Georges Lefebvre, *Questions agraires au temps de la Terreur*, 2nd ed., 1954, p. 41.
42. *Ibid.*
43. *Moniteur*, vol. XXI, p. 750

CHAPTER 7

1. *Annales historiques de la Révolution française*, 1954, n° 1, p. 1-22. Study prepared in collaboration with George Rudé.

2. "Le maximum des salaires et le 9 thermidor", 1927, p. 149. Quotation given in a note by Michel Eude, *Études sur la Commune robespierriste*, p. 137, n. 3.
3. Leon Biollay, *Études économiques sur le XVIIIe siecle. Les prix en 1790* (Bibliothèque nationale, Lb^{41} 11364, in-8°). See chapter I, "Les salaires". The author makes vague reference to AD II B 1 in the National Archives; since the Rondonneau collection has since been reclassified, this classification mark no longer exists. Let us recall that neither the *Journal de la Montagne* nor *Le Moniteur* report the decree of 21 messidor nor the publication of 5 thermidor.
4. This file is reported in *Etat sommaire des versements faits aux Archives nationales par les ministres...*, vol. II, part 1, 1927: F^{12} 1516 to 1544", Maximum: tableaux dressés en l'an II, correspondence (departmental classification); 1544bis and ^{ter}, Paris.
5. This file is mentionned under the heading "maximum", subdivision XI (Commerce and Industry) of the manuscript inventory of the Rondonneau collection (section subsequent to 1789) filed in the offices of the National Archives.
6. This document is noted by Tourneux under n° 14736 of his *Bibliographie de l'histoire de Paris pendant la Révolution française*, 1900, vol. III, 2nd division, chap. XIII, par. 2, E, "Fixation des prix et salaires".
7. "VIII. The maximum, or the highest price respective to salaries, wages, labor and day work in each place, will be set beginning with the publication of this law, until next September, by the general councils of the communes, at the same rate as in 1790, to which will be added half of that price over and above." (*Moniteur*, vol. XVIII, p. 6)
8. See chapter X, 3rd part, "Le maximum des salaires", in Albert Mathiez, *La Vie chère et le Mouvement social sous la Terreur*.
9. In his petition of June 25, 1793, which in more ways than one should be considered as the manifesto not of the "Enragés" (Albert Mathiez, *Annales révolutionnaires*, 1914, vol. VII, p. 547), but of the sans-culotterie, Jacques Roux does not mention the "maximum" of wages. On the other hand, it is demanded by the Sans-Culottes section in its petition of September 2, 1793, but at the same time there must be limits on "the profits of industry" and "the advantages of commerce" (B.N., Lb^{40} 2140, in-8°).
10. It is understood that here it is a question of the general table of the "maximum" that Article VIII of the September 29, 1793 law required the general councils of the communes to post, not of specific rates fixed by the law for a specific group of occupations, especially for those who were working in enterprises controlled by the government.
11. Reports by Grivel, 13-14 and 28 nivôse, by Siret, 3 pluviôse year II (A.N., F^{7} 36883, F^{11} 201). See Albert Mathiez, *La Vie Chère...*, p. 586.
12. See Leon Biollay, *op. cit.*
13. The new economic policy was marked from the beginning of germinal by the dismissal of the Revolutionary Army, the removal of the commissioners for monopolies, and the recasting of the laws and monopolies. On the new orientation of foreign trade, see Georges Lefebvre, "Le Commerce extérieur en l'an II", *La Révolution française*, 1925, vol. LXXVIII, p. 132 and 214.
14. A.N., F^{1} III Seine 13. See Michel Eude, *Etudes sur la Commune robespierriste*, p. 115. See also the reports of the observer Bacon (A.N., W 174). On 7 germinal, some workers declared "that the basic foodstuffs, especially meat, were brought up to a very high price and that in all that there would only be the rich who would find an advantage". On 8 germinal, a worker in an arms factory lamented, "It's damned awful, we are more unfortunate than before, for with our money, we can't have anything; we must die of hunger, they fool us with beautiful words."
15. "What we want to do is to cure the commerce that is usurious, monarchic and counter-revolutionary; but we must treat it, not kill it." (*Moniteur*, vol. XIX, p. 631).
16. *Moniteur*, vol. XX, p. 91
17. *Moniteur*, vol. XXI, p. 44
18. On worker agitation after germinal year II, see Albert Mathiez, *La Vie chère...*, p. 585, Arne Ording, *Le Bureau de police du Comité de salut public*, p. 74, Michel Eude, *Etudes sur la Commune robespierriste*, p. 132. We bring to this subject a certain number of new documents drawn in particular from the alphabetical series of the collection of the Committee of General Security.
19. A.N., W 124, report of police surveillance, public attitude, 3 floréal year II; *Moniteur*, vol. XX, p. 302. We have found the dossiers for two arrests: those of Francois Bertrand, Gardes-Françaises section, and of Guy, Bonne-Nouvelle section (A.N., F^{7} 4597, pl. 1, p. 2, and F^{7} 4737). The grounds for arrest are entered as: "for having taken part in a gathering of tobacco grinders, maison Longueville, and for having presented a petition to the General Council of the Commune demanding a wage increase."
20. A.N., F^{7} 4437. Arne Ording (*op. cit.*, p. 78) only cites the first part of this note, thus giving a poor account of the true thought of Saint-Just. On this matter, see also the brief account of Albert Matthiez (*op. cit.*, p. 590).
21. A.N., W 124, report of police surveillance, public attitude, 5 floréal year II. We have discovered no other mention of this endeavor.
22. A.N., W 124, and 170, reports of police surveillance, public attitude, 12 and 15 floréal year II; *Moniteur*, vol. XX, p. 378.
23. *Moniteur*, vol. XX, p. 421
24. A.N., W 124 and 170, reports of police surveillance, public attitude, 14 and 15 floréal year II.
25. *Moniteur*, vol. XX, p. 382
26. *Journal de la Montagne*, 18 floréal year II; cited by Albert Mathiez (*op. cit*, p. 591) and Michel Eude (*op. cit.*, p. 136); no mention in the *Moniteur*. On 14 floréal, the General Council of the Commune addressed the bureau of the general assemblies of the sections, to invite them "to enlighten our brothers the workers about the maneuvers of traitors who are trying all means to shatter the harmony that must exist between us"; the authorities do not want to be forced to "use the means of repression that the law prescribes for making wandering brothers return to their duty." (B.N., Ms., Anc. suppl. fr., 8606, f. 165, extract of the register of deliberations; no mention in the *Moniteur*.)
27. *Archives de la Préfecture de police*, A A/19, pp. 204 and 215
28. *Moniteur* vol. XX, p. 699

29. A.N., H 2121. Bureau of the Municipal Corps. The Municipal Corps gave way on one point: the decree of 19 prairial was applied from the 1st messidor, and retroactively from 11 prairial as it was first stipulated. Let us note, by way of comparison, that in 1790 the grocers' assistants received 2 *livres* 5 *sols* a day.
30. A.N., H 2121, f 19
31. A.N., F^{7} 4585, pl. 2., p. 32. Declaration by different carpenters and entrepreneurs of works for the Republic, n.d., p. 34. Declaration of Louis Ballu and Pierre Quantinet, carpenters, before the justice of the peace, 29 prairial and 5 messidor year II.
32. A.N., F^{7} 4437; cited by Arne Ording, *op. cit.*, p. 78
33. A.N., F^{11} 451; cited by Albert Mathiez, *op. cit.*, p. 593
34. A.N., F^{7} 3821; cited by Arne Ording, *op. cit.*, p. 78-79
35. A.N., F^{7} 4437; cited by Arne Ording, *op. cit.*, p. 78. See a note of Albert Mathiez, "L'Agitation ouvrière à la veille du 9 thermidor", *Annales historiques de la Révolution française*, 1928, p. 271.
36. A.N., F^{7} 3821
37. A.N., F^{7} 4435; cited by Arne Ording, *op. cit.*, p. 79
38. Let us simply mention the dissolution of sectional societies, imposed by the governmental authorities. From germinal to prairial, 35 societies were dissolved (see their addresses to the Convention in the series C of the National Archives).
39. A.N., F^{7} 3821, n. d.; cited by Arne Ording, *op. cit.*, p. 78
40. A.N., AF II 47, pl. 368, p. 38
41. A.N., AF II 48, pl. 374, p. 10
42. A.N., F^{7}* 2507, f. 316; cited by Albert Mathiez, "Le Maximum des salaires et le 9 thermidor", *A.H.R.F.*, 1927, p. 149.
43. A.N., F^{7} 4432; mentioned by Albert Mathiez, *art. cité*. On this gathering, see also the accounts of the events of 9-10 thermidor by the revolutionary committees of the sections of Homme armé, Popincourt, Marchés, Fraternité, Cité (A.N., AF II 47, pl. 364-366).
44. Mentioned by Albert Mathiez, *art. cité*, according to the Second Justificatory Memoir of Fouquier-Tinville, published by H. Fleischmann, *Les Réquisitoires de Fouquier-Tinville*, p. 205.
45. A.N., F^{7} 4432, pl. 1, fol. 40
46. Aulard, *Paris sous la Réaction thermidorienne*, vol. I; mentioned by Albert Mathiez, art. cité.
47. A.P.P., A A/163, Lombards section, f. 297. See R. Cobb, "Une coalition de garçons brossiers de la section des Lombards", *A.H.R.F.*, 1953, p. 67.
48. B.N., ms. F. fr., nouv. acq. 2716, f. 8, imp. in-folio plano
49. Cited by Leon Biollay, *op. cit.*
50. A.N. F^{12} 1544^{w}. Tarif du maximum des salaires, façons, gages, mains-d'oeuvre, journées de travail dans l'étendue de la Commune de Paris, présenté par la Commission du Commerce et des approvisionnements de la République au Comité de salut public le 22 thermidor l'an deuxième, manuscript 36 cm x 24 cm, 24 pages of which two are blank, signed *Les commissaires*, Jouenneault, Picquet.
51. A.N., F^{12} 1544^{w}, printed in-folio plano. This document contains, besides the table of the maximum, a decree in eight articles of the Committee of Public Safety, 28 thermidor year II, setting down the publication of the maximum and penalties for infractions. This decree has been published by Aulard in his *Actes du Comité de salut public*, XVI, 114, according to an unrecorded minute of Lindet (A.N., AF II 80; the table is not attached). This table and the decree of 28 thermidor have been published, under the same title as the document above, in the form of a brochure in-4°, of 16 pages (A.N., F^{12} 1544^{w}).
52. All these documents are contained in a dossier of file F^{12} 1544^{w} of the National Archives.
53. *Op. cit.*, p. 606

CHAPTER 8

1. *Annales historiques de la Révolution française*, 1960, n° 4, p. 436-457
2. *Archives nationales*, W 561, dossier 1, Indication of persons appropriate to command the artillerie or command the service in various sections; dossier 2, Lists of individuals in the state to command; dossier 8, Addresses of the subscribers to the *Tribun de peuple*. The register of these subscribers is found in W 563, dossier 42, p. 1. The file F^{7} 4277 contains a copy of these lists of men appropriate to command; the file F^{7} 4278, the list of subscribers. The lists of men appropriate to command and those of gunners have been printed without changes in the two volumes in-8°: "Copie des pièces saisies dans le local que Baboeuf [sic] occupait lors de son arrestation" (Paris, National Printshop, frimaire and nivôse year V; *Bibliothèque nationale*, Lb^{42} 232), in particular in the second volume ("Suite de la copie"...). No reproduction of these items in Victor Advielle, *Histoire de Gracchus Babeuf et du babouvisme d'après de nombreux documents inédits*, Paris, printed by the author, 1884, 2 vol. in-8°; B.N., Ln^{27} 35677.
3. A.N., F^{7} 4278, p. 53. See also the printed: *Acte d'accusation dressé par le jury d'accusation du département de la Seine contre Gracchus Babeuf et les cinquante-neuf [59] prévenus de la conspiration du 22 floréal*..., Paris, fructidor year IV; in-8°, 71 p.; B.N., Lb^{42} 2708; Tourneux, n° 4637. The printed list in fact includes 54 names, the manuscript list 56 (the same, plus Felix Lepeletier and General Rossignol).
4. A.N., F^{7} 4278. This manuscript list can be compared with several printed lists (see Tourneux, n° 4706 to n° 4709), in particular: "Official list of 132 prisoners made at the camp of Grenelle, their names, first names, occupations, the name of their various sections and streets... the various jobs they had during the Revolution", Imp., n.d., in-8°, 8 p.; B.N., Lb^{42} 1123; Tourneux, n° 4707.)
5. On the subscribers to the *Tribun du peuple*, see Albert Mathiez, *Le Directoire*, Paris, 1934, p. 191-197. Mathiez, holding to the numeration of the register of subscribes, counts 642 subscribers: this does not distinguish departmental subscribers and Parisian subscribers, a distinction that seemed important to us. Mathiez, to demonstrate his theory (that these subscribers, are victims of the thermidorian reaction, "that they are thirsty for vengeance", p. 195, that they simply see in Babeuf "a man who would avenge them", p. 192) insists on the bourgeois character of the subscribers to the *Tribun du peuple*, passing very rapidly over subscribers coming from the sans-culotterie and the popular categories.

6. The important source of the minutes of the police commissioners at the Archives of the Prefecture of Police (A A/48 to A A/265) has not really been used for the period of the Directory. On the conditions of reading in the popular milieux in year II, see several quick references in my thesis, *Les sans-culottes parisiens en l'an II*, p. 670-673.
7. Let us note in this regard the collective subscription n° 492 taken by the "Citizens Together, Café of the Friends of the Country", Quinze-Vingts section.
8. Let us note one subscriber in Switzerland, a doctor in Zurich (Usteri, correspondant of Rousseau, who will play an important role in the Swiss revolution of 1798); another in Genoa (occupation not indicated). Moreover 5 subscribers are in the army: 2 at Sambre-et-Meuse (one leader of a batallion, one of a demi-brigade), 1 at Rhin-et-Moselle (health officer), 2 in Italy. In a Belgium departmentalized on 9 vendemiaire year IV, 4 subscribers: 2 at Brussels (one of which is employed by the army of the Nord), one at Anvers (public prosecutor), one at Jemappes (occupation not indicated).
9. 4 subscribers: Drôme, Jura, Hautes-Pyrénées, Sein-Inférieure. 3 subscribers: Ain, Ardèche, Aveyron, Charente, Côte-d'Or, Gers, Ille-et-Vilaine, Isère, Meurthe. 2 subscribers: Aisne, Aude, Calvados, Corrèze, Doubs, Indre-et-Loire, Loir, Loiret, Lot, Manche, Haute-Marne, Puy-de-Dôme, Rhône-et-Loire, Haute-Saône, Seine, Somme. 1 subscriber: Basses-Alpes, Ardennes, Ariège, Aube, Charente-Inférieure, Eure, Eure-et-Loir, Finistère, Indre, Loir-et-Cher, Haute-Loire, Mainte-et-Loire, Mont-Terrible, Nièvre, Oise, Basses-Pyrénées, Haut-Rhin, Sarthe, Vienne et Haute-Vienne.
10. Among these 5 subscribers: Bouchotte and a bookseller; for 3 subscribers, the occupation is not indicated. The sixth subscriber of the Moselle is the president of the municipal administration of Bouzonville. That the influence of Bouchotte on his compatriots was undeniable, we have the proof of his election as municipal officer of Metz 13 germinal year IV, (April 2, 1798); see General Herlaut, *Le Colonel Bouchotte*, vol. II, p. 353.
11. Pas-de-Calais: 20 subscribers, 10 at Arras (5 merchants or "négociants", 1 printer, 1 surgeon, 3 whose occupation is not indicated), 3 at Saint-Pol (1 innkeeper), 2 at Saint-Omer (one apothecary), 1 at Hesdin ("négociant"). We cannot specify if the "citoyenne" Lebas in question here is the wife or the mother of the member of the Convention. Likewise, is the "citoyenne" Darthé the wife or the mother of Babeuf's companion? Among the subscribers of Arras, we point out Léandre Lebon, the brother of the member of the Convention. On these subscribers of Pas-de-Calais, see Albert Mathiez, *op. cit.*, p. 192.
12. Nord: 18 subscribers, 10 at Valenciennes, 4 at Lille, 2 at Avesnes, 1 at Cambrai.
13. Plus a notary and a "négociant"; for 4 subscribers, the occupation is not indicated.
14. Var: let us add one subscriber for each of the three towns of Brignoles, Grasse and Vidauban; only 4 subscribers live in villages, 2 of these at Cotignac.
15. The president of the municipal administration and 3 municipal officers, one police officer, 2 café-owners and 1 innkeeper, 1 "négociant"' no indication for one subscriber. Among them is Viala, doubtless the father of the young "martyr of liberty".
16. At Lorient: 1 employee of the Navy, 1 painter, 1 merchant-watchmaker, 1 notary; at Vannes: 1 captain of the army of Côtes-de-Brest, 1 whose occupation is not indicated. Ille-et-Vilaine: 2 subscribers at Rennes (1 man of law, 1 chief of the police brigade); 1 subscriber at Port-Malo (occupation not indicated).
17. Hérault: only one farmer, residing at Lodève; 1 notary and 1 man of law, 1 "négociant" and 1 cloth merchant, 1 secretary of municipal administration and 1 clerk of the court, 1 captain and 1 medical student.
18. Saône-et-Loire: 2 "négociants", 1 stationer and 1 bookseller, 1 municipal officer and 1 secretary-clerk of the municipal administration of Mâcon, 1 health officer.
19. At Valenciennes.
20. The socio-occupational description is imprecise, with 6 subscribers listed as "cultivateurs" [farmers]: 1 at Lodève (Hérault), 1 in the Rhône department (commune not identified), 2 in Pas-de-Calais (1 at Bouret near Frévent), 1 at Union-sur-Sarthe (Saint-Léger-sur-Sarthe, Orne), 1 at Curçay (Vienne). Two subscribers are described as "agriculteurs" (doubtless indicating a higher social level than that of the "cultivateurs"): one near Condom (Gers), the other at Puget-près-Solliès (Var). Two "propriétaires" [landowners]: one at Rieupeyroux (Aveyron), the other at Chateaurenard (Loiret). Let us also mention a "proprietaire" at Toulon, no indication as to whether or not the property is developed.
21. Among the 7 subscribers: 1 construction entrepreneur, 2 factory directors, 4 manufacturers (1 manufacturer-tanner at Cottignac, Var, 1 cloth finisher at Valenciennes, 1 sheet manufacturer at Lodève, 1 manufacturer—no other description—at Lille).
22. Legal professions: 6 notaries, 6 men of law, 1 juror-vendor. Medical professions: 3 doctors and 1 medical student, 2 health officers, 1 surgeon, 2 pharmacists. Let us add 1 man of letters and 1 dramatic artist.
23. Commissioners of executive power: those of Lure and Chartre. Presidents of municipal administration: those of Avignon, Bouzonville (Moselle), of Périgueux, of Pont-sur-Allier (Pont-du-Château, Puy-de-Dome), of Valenciennes.
24. Among the 16 merchants, 6 are called "marchands" with no other qualification. For 10, the nature of the commerce is specified: wine merchants (2), brewer, grocer, candle merchant, watchmaker, wool merchant, draper, saddler, stationer.
25. Plus 2 gunsmiths, 2 apothecaries, 1 carpenter, 1 glazier, 1 painter, 1 tailor, 1 tanner, 1 earthenware potter, 1 jeweller, 1 goldsmith, 1 watchmaker, 1 baker.
26. Booksellers: at Autun and at Metz. Printers: at Arras, Nancy, Coutances, Périgueux, Tarbes, Foix and Marseille.
27. For comparison with the Parisian sectional personnel of year II, we refer once and for all to Albert Soboul, *Les Sans-culottes parisiens en l'an II*, p. 439-451.
28. Former deputies to the Convention: Alard, Amar, Bassal, Bayle, Brisson, Choudieu, David, Drouet, Fouché, Frécine, Grosse-Durocher, Javogues, Lacoste, Lecointre de Versailles, Mallarmé, Massieu, Pelletier, Ricord, Roux-Fazillas. Deputies to the "Anciens" (all former members of the Convention): Charlier, Derenty, Vernerey. Deputies to the "Cinq-Cents" (all former members of the Convention): Brival, Deville, Grégoire, Guyardin, Ingrand, Méaulle, Plazanet. Let us add Faitpoul, minister of Finances, and General Fyon who will be ordered arrested as an accomplice of Babeuf, and Laronde.
29. Two construction entrepreneurs 1 clog manufacturer. Here we find again Jean-Pierre Larue, former revolutionary commissioner of the Lombards section, journeyman mason in 1789, construction entrepreneur in year II, "having made

his fortune," according to his accusers in year III, "through work furnished to him by the former Commune", detained at Plessis from 17 germinal to 21 thermidor year III.

30. Including Souberbielle, Honoré Street, Robespierre's doctor, and Laboureau, health officer, Théâtre-Français section, former revolutionary commissioner, the informer at the trial of the Hébertists.
31. Let us add Claude Fiquet, architect, Temple section, former police administrator.
32. Merchants: 3 wine merchants, 2 merchant-jewellers, 1 carpenter, 1 sadler, 1 button merchant, 1 haberdasher, 1 grocer, 1 merchant of paintings.
33. Including Chrétien, Lepeletier section, already cited above, and Leclerc, Pont-Neuf section, former member of the Electoral Club.
34. Among the painters, Camus of the Poissonnière section, former juror of the revolutionary Tribunal, civil commissioner until germinal year III, detained from 5 prairial to 30 thermidor, and Michel, of the Bonne-Nouvelle section, detained from 5 prairial to 25 fructidor year III. Among the carpenters: entrepreneur in carpentry (cf. A. Soboul, *op. cit.*, p. 440) or a simple carpenter? It would be necessary to be acquainted with the exact state of affairs of the Duplays in year II and in year IV. Among the shoemakers, Humblet, former revolutionary commissioner of the Quinze-Vingts section, detained from 4 messidor to 25 fructidor year III.
35. Let us add: 3 tailors, 2 secondhand clothes dealers, 2 jewellers, 1 engraver, 1 watchmaker, 1 mirror cutter, 1 porcelain manufacturer, 1 locksmith, 1 cutler, 1 tinsmith, 1 caster, 1 glazier, 1 dealer in carvings, 1 tapestry-maker, 1 currier, 1 saddler (Cochery, of the Quinze-Vingts section, detained from 29 germinal year III to 26 vendémiaire year IV), 1 cartwright, 1 saltpetre dealer, 1 hosier, 1 hatter, 1 booter, 1 printer. Among the shopkeepers properly speaking: 1 grocer, 1 confectioner, 1 apothecary, 1 herbalist, 1 seed merchant, 1 bookseller, 1 stationer.
36. 2 jewellers, 1 watchmaker, 1 engraver and 1 mirror cutter. Let us note here two Bodson, of the Pont-Neuf section, one a mirror cutter, one an engraver. The latter, Joseph Bodson, member of the August 10 Commune, former revolutionary commissioner, member of the Electoral Club, detained from 22 fructidor year II to 7 vendémiaire year III, then from 14 prairial to 15 fructidor year III, will take part in the Conspiracy of Equals. One peculiar case, that of the watchmaker François Bachelard, Contrat Social section, subscriber to the *Tribun du peuple* in year IV, but moderate in 1793, detained from September 19, 1793 to 6 floreal year II, anti-terrorist in year III.
37. Revolutionary commissioners: Bodson (Pont-Neuf section), Chalendon (Homme-Armé), Chrétien (Lepeletier), Humblet (Quinze-Vingts), Laboureau (Théâtre-Français), Larue (Lombards), Legray (Muséum), Sandoz (Unité), Vacret (Montreuil), Vergne (Lepeletier). Civil commissioners: Camus (Poissonnière), Lacroix (Mont-Blanc), Reis (Place-Vendôme), Saint-Omer (Muséum). Let us also note Hu, justice of the peace (Panthéon) and militants like Damour (Arcis), Gros de Luzerne (Butte-des-Moulins)... For the identification of sectional personnel with Babouvist personnel, we refer once and for all to Albert Soboul, *Les Sans-culottes parisiens en l'an II*, 1958, index of names of persons; Kare D. Tönnesson, *La Défaite des sans-culottes*, 1959, index of names of persons with bibliographic annotations. "The presence on the list of numerous widows of guillotined revolutionaries expresses this sentiment of vengeance," writes Albert Mathiez (*op. cit.*, p. 195). And regarding the "numerous agents of the committees of the Terror" that are found among the subscribers: "What these men liked in Babeuf's newspaper were the attacks on their persecutors, the glorification of the role they played in the Terror, the promise of revenge" (p. 196). Without a doubt. But why not also assume fidelity to a political ideal which, whether a case of "large landowners", "wealthy bourgeois" (A. Mathiez, *op. cit.*, p. 196) or of sans-culottes, could be the same? The campaign of the *Tribun du peuple* consolidated the left opposition against the Directory, an opposition not only made up of former Robespierrists, nor even of former terrorists, as Albert Mathiez would have it. On the renewal of sans-culotte revolutionary personnel in the year IV, see below.
38. Lombards section: 1 jeweller, 1 embroiderer, 1 shoemaker, 1 wigmaker, 1 confecti0oner, 1 apothecary, 1 painter of buildings. The teacher was Valentin Hauy. Gravilliers section: 1 carpenter, 1 carver, 2 fanmakers, 1 naturalist, 1 secondhand clothes dealer, 1 wine merchant, 1 stallholder, 1 haberdasher and 1 former haberdasher. Temple section: 2 wigmakers or coiffeurs, 1 enameler, 1 gardener, 1 café-owner. Liberal professions: 1 engineer and 1 architect. For the Amis-de-la-Patrie section, the indications are too fragmentary.
39. To attach to the list of these 62 democrats, there is a single list of 20 "patriots democrats" of l'Homme-Armé section "who were in the Pantheon society"; actually, with the exception of 7 names, the two lists match up.
40. For the whole of the VIIth arrondissement, 115 artisans or shopkeepers: 21 shoemakers, 9 tailors, 7 hatmakers, 5 painters, 5 golsdmiths, 4 wigmakers, 4 locksmiths, 3 gilders, 3 glaziers, 3 makers of height gauges, 3 café-owners, 3 hosiers, 2 carpenters, 2 tapestry makers, 2 casters, 2 enamelers, 2 perfurmers, 2 haberdahers, 2 fanmakers, 2 blacksmiths, 2 grocers, 2 holders of a furnished house [to let], 1 beltmaker, 1 saddler, 1 currier, 1 cutler, 1 scissors-grinder, 1 plumber, 1 potmaker, 1 boilermaker, 1 furbisher, 1 jeweller, 1 gem-setter, 1 ribbon maker, 1 dyemaker, 1 mason, 1 secondhand furniture dealer, 1 cook, 1 butcher, 1 fruiterer, 1 public writer, 4 shopkeepers rightfully called merchants: 1 fruiterer, 1 tapestry dealer, 1 coal merchant, 1 merchant with no other qualification. Let us underline the importance of the shoemakers; on the other hand, there are few bar owners here.
41. 3 surgeons and 1 dentist, 1 teacher, 1 bailiff, 1 architect, 1 manufacturer of razor strops and 1 entrepreneur in masonry.
42. For example, in the XIIth arrondissement, the Jardin-des-Plantes and Finistère sections. For the Piques section (Ist arrondissement), the Faubourg-Montmartre section (IInd), the Gardes-Françaises and the Marchés sections (IVth), the documents contain lists of gunners: determining element of the revolutionary days of struggle and true active element of the Parisian sans-culotterie in year II.
43. Lombards section: Blandin, justice of the peace; Cordas, embroiderer, revolutionary commissioner, commissioner of monopolizing. Gravilliers section: Boursault, teacher; Bruyas, silk worker; Cazenave, health officer; Égasse, wine merchant; Lepage, fanmaker; Planson, carver—all revolutionary commissionners; Chicot, blacksmith, civil commissioner; Camelin, former hosiery merchant; Petit, fanmaker—former militants. No former partisan of Jacques Roux figures on this list (cf. Walter Markov, "Les Jacquesroutins", *A.H.R.F.*, 1960, p. 163).Temple section: Duthill; Louis, gardener; Mallais, coiffeur until 1789, then shoemaker; Prinet, engineer—all former revolutionary commissioners; Charles, employee; Dreux, café-owner—former militants. Amis-de-la-Patrie section: Genois, member of the Committee of Public Safety of the department of Paris; Sellier, carver; Simon, engraver—revolutionary commissioners.

44. Réunion section: 7 revolutionary commissioners (Dolizy, shoemaker; Favereau, employee; Guy-Damour, holder of a furnished house; Mansuy, teacher; Moutardier, boilermaker; Pages, scissors-grinder; Tard, hatter); 2 civil commissioners (Petit, fanmaker; Simon, stationery merchant); 1 second commander (Davranche, shoemaker). All together 10 former members of the sectional personnel out of 43 democrats indicated. L'Homme-Armé section: 8 revolutionary commissioners (Biot, tailor; Broucotte, painter; Cazenave, sculptor; Chalandon, shoemaker; Kruber, hosier; Peteil, saddler; Polin, carpenter; Savart, "rentier", in fact a former domestic worker); 4 civil commissioners (Desmarests, employee; Dufour, grocer; Gauche, gem cutter; Noury, surgeon); 1 justice of the peace (Trescon, grocer); 1 militant (Bernard, glazier). Or 14 out of 62. Arcis section: 4 revolutionary commissioners (Camus; Champon, ribbon maker; Mercier, hosier; Poignon, wigmaker); 1 president of the popular society (Monnier, tailor); 4 militants (Courtois, shoemaker; Henry, furbisher; Joly, dyemaker; Leclerc, secondhand furniture dealer). Or 9 out of 32. Droits-de-l'Homme section: 5 revolutionary commisionners (Douzel; Gervais, maker of height gauges; Houdaille, jeweller; Mazin, tapestry maker; Tamponnet, construction entrepreneur); 2 civil commissioners (Millet, bailiff; Roger, carpenter); 1 second commander (Fayolle); 2 militants (Fougue, fruiterer; Robert, tailor). Or 10 out of 36.
45. On 2 vendémiaire year IV (September 24, 1795), Varlet was still writing to the Committee of General Security to demand his freedom. See J. Zacker, "Varlet pendant la réaction thermidorienne", communication to the Babouvist Colloquium of Stockholm, August 21, 1960 *A.H.R.F.*, 1961, p. 19-34.
46. Bodson, engraver (Pont-Neuf section); Chrétien, café-owner (Lepeletier); Cordas, embroiderer (Lombards); Dufour, carpenter (Faubourg-Montmartre); Goulard, printer (Observatoire); Vacret, merchant stocking maker (Montreuil); Vergne, employee (Lepeletier). On Cordas, see Henri Calvet, *L'Accaparement à Paris sous la Terreur*, p. 65 and 94. Reis, saddler, former civil commissioner of the Place-Vendômes section, is given as resident of the Mont-Blanc section. The printed bill of indictment (B.N., Lb[42] 2708) gives Claude Fiquet, architect, as former member of the revolutionary committee of the Temple section; in fact, we have found no document permitting the inscription of Claude Fiquet, former police administrator, on the list of sectional personnel.
47. Monnier, beltmaker, and Mugnier, tailor.
48. Here we find again the usual range of crafts and small businesses. Let us note two printers. The proletarian element is represented by a stocking worker (Boudin, already cited) and a wood turner.
49. Bodson, Chrétien, Dufour, Vacret, Vergne — all former revolutionary commissioners; Reis, civil commissioner (see note 46); Breton, wine merchant (Amis-de-la-Patrie), Clerez, tailor (Halle-au-Blé), Monnard, hatter (Bon-Conseil).
50. Let us mention as a matter of interest Rose Adelaïde Fournier, "girl of joy, slept under the tent with the soldiers". Or a total of 132 persons arrested.
51. Butte-des-Moulins and Roule sections: 8 arrests each. Faubourg-Montmartre and Fidélité (Maison-Commune): 7 each. Place-Vendôme: 6. Contrat-Social: 5. Finaly 4 arrests in each of the following sections: Tuileries, Halle-au-Blé, Bonne-Nouvelle, Amis-de-la-Patrie, Bon-Conseil, Arcis, Gravilliers, Invalides, Unité, Thermes, Panthéon.
52. Let us add 7 hatmakers, 6 tailors, 3 painters, 3 wigmakers, 3 gardeners and the usual span of diverse crafts. The arts crafts are poorly represented (2 engravers, 1 jeweller, 1 watchmaker). No café owner or innkeeper (only 1 wine merchant, 1 caterer, 1 renter of furnished rooms) whereas this occupational category was relatively well represented among the subscribers. Few shopkeepers properly speaking: 1 grocer, 1 fruiterer, 1 stationer; 3 merchants, with no other qualification. In addition, 4 militants, including General Fyon, already noted among the subscribers to the *Tribun du peuple*.
53. Roule section: Deschamps, vinegar-maker, army captain; Auvray, gardener, elector of 1792, juror at the revolutionary Tribunal. Butte-des-Moulins section: Bonbon, shoemaker, revolutionary commissioner; Bruchet, carver, elector of 1792, "'boutefeu' [spark that lit the cannon] of the general assembly and the popular society". Bonne-Nouvelle section: Dudouyt, tailor, revolutionary commissioner, moved from the Place-Vendôme section; Réaume, carver, former captain of the revolutionary army, detachment at Lyon. Amis-de-la-Patrie section: Cailleux, ribbon maker, member of the Commune of August 10, elector of 1792, member of the central revolutionary committee of May 31.
Arcis section: Joly, caterer.
Gravilliers section: Houdemart, clog maker, and Lepage, fanmaker, elector of 1792, both revolutionary commissioners.
Droits-de-l'Homme section: Douzel, public writer, Houdaille, jeweller, revolutionary commissioner.
Unité section: Sandoz, watchmaker, elector of 1792, revolutionary commissioner; Paulin, coiffeur.
54. Besides General Fyon, Bruchet, Dudouyt and Sandoz, cited in the preceding note, Legras, shoemaker (Contrat-Social section) and Salignac, currier (Faubourg-Montmartre).
55. Man having our confidence in the case where the responsible leader of the VIIth arrondissement would be arrested: Moutardier, boilermaker, former revolutionary commissioner. Municipal [representative] for the VIIth arrondissement: Mulot d'Angers, "rentier". Representatives of the section to the General Council of the Commune: Pelletier, hatter; to the Department of Paris: Cassel, goldsmith. All these men naturally figure on the broad lists of "patriots appropriate to command".
56. Kare D. Tönnesson, *La Défaite des sans-culottes*, p. 379.
57. We cannot agree with Albert Mathiez when he makes the subscribers to the *Tribun du peuple* solely bourgeois, former Robespierrists or former terrorists animated with a desire for revenge. "Why did these bourgeois subscribe to Babeuf's newspaper? Because they had been worried, because they had been disarmed in year III. They saw in Babeuf a man who would avenge them." (*op. cit.*, p. 192). And he adds: "Let us have no doubt that they were indifferent to the communist doctrines; most were large landowners, wealthy bourgeois who had absolutely no intention of sharing their wealth." (p. 196) Without a doubt. But that's short changing all the representatives of the sans-culotterie who were subscribers to the *Tribun du peuple*, who, if they had not accepted the community of wealth, nonetheless had a conception of property different from that of the "large landowners" and the "wealthy bourgeois". What is there in common on this point between Groslevin, subscriber n° 350 *bis*, of Dompierre by way of Avesnes, patriot of '89, but speculator on national wealth (Georges Lefebvre, *Les Paysans du Nord*, p. 484 f.) and the café owner Chrétien of the Lepeletier section (subscriber n° 62) or the shoemaker Legras of the Contrat-Social section (subscriber n° 613)?
58. *The Holy Family*, Marx-Engels *Collected Works*, Vol. 4, p. 119

CHAPTER 9

1. *Annales historiques de la Révolution française*, 1957, n° 3, pp. 193-213
2. A. Mathiez *Les Origines des cultes révolutionnaires (1789-1792)*, p. 11
3. *Histoire des sectes religieuses... depuis le commencement du siècle jusqu'à l'époque actuelle...*, 1810
4. *À la recherche d'une religion civile*, 1895
5. *Histoire de la Révolution française*, "De la religion nouvelle", book III, chap. XI and XII
6. *Histoire de la Révolution française*, book XIV, chap. I. This chapter has the significant title: "The Revolution was nothing without the religious revolution."
7. *Le Culte de la Raison et le Culte de l'Être suprême*, 1892, p. vii and viii
8. *Les Origines des cultes révolutionnaires (1789-1792)*, 1904
9. Especially on his article, "De la définition des phénomènes religieux", *Année sociologique*, 1899
10. *Op. cit.*, p. 13
11. *Op. cit.*, p. 62
12. Abbé Augustin Ceuneau, *Un culte étrange pendant la Révolution. Perrine Dugué, la sainte aux ailes tricolores, 1777-1796*, Laval, 1947. See G. Lefebvre, "Perrine Dugué, la sainte patriote", *A.H.R.F.*, 1949, p. 337.
13. Roger Joxe, "Encore une sainte patriote: sainte Pataude", *A.H.R.F.*, 1952, p. 91. Adapted from *Le Journal de Chateaubriand*, n° 4, May–July, 1950, under the title "La fosse à la fille". Sainte Pataude, that is to say Saint Republican. We could note that Sainte Pataude and Sainte Tricolore both appeared in the West. This emerges from the population of this religion; even when they adhered to the Revolution, they conserved their attachment to traditional religion just as well as the royalists. Even better, perhaps, because to our knowledge no *chouan* has been spontaneously promoted to sainthood by popular sentiment.
14. We cannot conceal the insufficiency of this analysis. But we can only ask questions for which the documents permit no response. In the case of Perrine Dugué: does a commentary exist that explains the meaning of her ascension? What did people do at her chapel? were the ceremonies there sporadic or regular? at what date? what did they consist of? how is the memory of Perrine preserved? In the case of Marie Martin: are there sources earlier than the 1950 account? when did the cult begin? what do we know about past ceremonies on her tomb? What do people do there now at Easter, Pentecost and Saint-John's Day? why do people go there on Mondays? is there syncretism—Sundays being reserved for traditional religion, Mondays for the new cult? And more general questions: if there is a cult, what are the elements: ceremonies, rites, prayers, symbols? who participates in these rites? What population categories? what age groups? how many? were the followers good Catholics or lukewarm Christians? what was the position of the Church? what exactly was the political portion of the content of the beliefs and dogma?
15. *Archives nationales*, C262, d. 580, p. 2
16. A.N., C 259, d. 540; *Moniteur*, vol. XVII, p. 243
17. *Journal de la Montagne*, August 3, 1793
18. *Bibliothèque nationale*, LB^{41} 1994; Tourneux, n° 8417
19. Ferdinand Brunot, *Histoire de la langue française*, vol. IX: *La Révolution et l'Empire*, Paris, 1937, p. 625 ("Transposition des mots religieux")
20. *Affiches de la Commune, August 3 and 6, 1793; Journal de la Montagne*, August 4, 1793; *Moniteur*, vol. XVII, p. 300
21. A.N., C 266, pl. 629, p. 17; *Affiches de la Commune*, August 6, 1793; *Journal de la Montagne*, August 7, 1793; *Moniteur*, vol. XVII, p. 323, 331
    See also the Funeral Oration of Marat delivered by Guiraut, in this same Contrat-Social section, on August 9, 1793 (imp. in-8°, 15p., noted by Tourneux, n° 8751)
22. *Affiches de la Commune*, August 15, 1793; *Journal de la Montagne*, August 16, 1793
23. *Bibliothèque Victor-Cousin*, ms. 117
24. *Affiches de la Commune*, September 1, 1793; *Moniteur*, vol. XVII, p. 545. On September 2, a delegation from Fontaine-de-Grenelle announced to the Jacobins that the first child to be born in the section would receive the name Marat; on the 4th, a child was thus baptised (B.V.C., ms 120).
25. B.N., LB^{41} 1752 and 1979; Tourneux n°s 8131 and 8132; *Moniteur*, vol. XVII, p. 659
26. A.N., C 275, pl. 710, p. 29; *Journal de la Montagne*, September 16, 1793. In the course of this ceremony, the speeches were interrupted, for the first time, it seems, by choirs.
27. B.N., LB^{41} 2036; Tourneux, n° 8872; *Journal de la Montagne*, September 23, 1793; *Moniteur*, vol. XVII, p. 721
28. *Archives de la Prefecture de police*, A A/266; B.N., LB^{41} 1879; Tourneux, n° 8242; *Journal de la Montagne*, October 5, 1793; *Moniteur*, vol. XVIII, p. 34
29. B.N., LB^{41} 2053 and LB^{41} 489 bis; Tourneux, n°s 8695 and 8696; *Moniteur*, vol. XVIII, p. 76
30. A.P.P., A A/266; B.N., LB^{41} 2102; Tourneux, n° 8268; *Journal de la Montagne*, 23 of the first month year II; *Moniteur*, vol. XVIII, p. 114. "Ceremony remarkable for the order that reigned and the attentiveness of all the citizens," declared the commissioners of the General Council of the Commune.
31. B.N., LB^{41} 1996; Tourneux, n° 8420. See, on this procession in honor of Marat, David's request to the Convention, October 14, 1793 (A.N., C 276, pl. 714, p. 17; *Moniteur*, vol. XVIII, p. 125). The painter announced that he had just finished the painting representing the last breath of Marat; he asked permission to lend it, along with the painting of the assassinated Lepeletier, to his fellow citizens of the Museum section (David section). Art was no longer reserved for a privileged minority.
32. A.N., C 280, pl. 761, p. 9; B.N., mss. nouv. acq. fr., 2173, f° 52
33. A.N., C 279, pl. 760, p. 20; *Journal de la Montagne*, 7 brumaire year II
34. *Archives départementales de la Seine*, D 976. Tourneux, n° 7996; *Journal de la Montagne*, 10 brumaire year II
35. B.N., LB^{41} 1154 m; *Affiches de la Commune*, 10, 11 and 12 brumaire year II. A funeral ceremony in honor of Chalier was celebrated on 30 frimaire year II (December 20, 1793). The organizers took care to not only recall the great deeds of Chalier, but also to make "his prophecies" known: a procedure borrowed from hagiography. Three groups in the cortege marched under banners bearing the "prophecies" of Chalier. Here is the third, which refers to the repression which

followed the capture of Lyon by the troops of the Convention: "Aristocrats, royalists, 'rollandins', egoists, moderates, stragglers, tremble. At the first attack against freedom, the bloodied waves of the Saône and the Rhône will wash your bodies away into the terrifying seas." (B.N., LB[41] 1337; Tourneux, n° 6452). If the tone is apocalyptic, the allusion remains purely political.

36. See for example: *Pratique du bon Français, lue dans le temple de la Raison, section des Tuileries*, 10 brumaire year II (october 31, 1793) (B.N., LB[40] 2181; Tourneux, n° 9028û. This brochure contains: "Invocation républicaine, Salutation républicainre, Credo républicain, Commandements républicains." See also: *Prières républicaines du matin et du soir, lues à la section des Tuileries (B.N., LB[40] 2199; Tourneux, n° 9029)*. Here, by way of example, are the first two o' the ten republican commandments, edited by the popular society of the Friends of Liberty, Bonnet-Rouge section:
    I. Frenchman, you will defend your country
       In order to live freely.
    II. You will pursue all tyrants
       As far as Indostan and beyond.
37. A.N. W 112
38. A.N., F' 4774[81], dossier André Prieur
39. *Journal de la Montaigne*, 10 frimaire year II; *Moniteur*, vol. XVIII, p. 549.
40. *Moniteur*, vol. XVIII, p. 575
41. A.N., t., W 112, report of Prevost; W 174, report of Monic
42. B.N., LB[41] 1154; *Moniteur*, Vol. XX, p. 88
43. A.P.P., A A/266

CHAPTER 10

1. *Annales historiques de la Révolution française*, 1981, n° 2
2. *Moniteur*, vol. IV, p. 560
3. *Moniteur*, vol. IV, p. 560
4. *Moniteur*, vol. VII, p. 356. Issy-l'Évêque, Autun district, Saône-et-Loire department
5. *Moniteur*, vol. VII, p. 651. On this matter, see P. Montarlot, *Un essai de commune autonome et un procès de lèse-nation. Issy-l'Évêque, 1789-1794*, Autun, 1898. The case is simply mentioned in A. Lichtenberger, *Le Socialisme et la Révolution française. Étude sur les idées socialistes en France de 1789 à 1796*, Paris, 1899, p. 158. See also *Cahiers des paroisses et communautés du bailliage d'Autun pour les États Généraux de 1789*, published by A. de Charmoyse, Autun, 1895. The *cahier de doéances* [register of grievances] of the parish and community of Issy-l'Évêque (p. 109 and 111) demands in particular the suppression of the salt tax and forced labor, and the repurchase of the rights of *mainmorte* and *banalités* [communal property]; "that necessary deductions from the *dime* [tithe] be made to sustain a vicar, a school master and to maintain the sacristy of the church and for the relief of the poor of the parish." Article 4 (p. 110): "The poor devastate the countryside and often force workers to make contributions by their threats; that each parish be ordered to feed the poor."
6. Duvergier, vol. I, p. 52
7. See M. Dommanget, *Histoire du drapeau rouge*, Paris, n.d., p. 30
8. *Jacobins*, vol. III, p. 443; *Moniteur*, vol. XI, p. 693. See A. Soboul, *Les Sans-culottes parisiens en l'an II*, Paris, 1958, p. 650.
9. G. Brégail, *Les Curés rouges et la Société montagnarde d'Auch*, Auch, 1901, in-8°, 16 p. (B.N., Lk' 33035)
10. Éd. Campagnac, "Un prêtre communiste: le curé Petit-Jean", *La Révolution française*, November, 1903, p. 425; "U. curé rouge: Métier, delegate of the people's representative Du Bouchet", *Annales révolutionnaires*, 1913, p. 47. Éd. Campagnac uses the expression [red priest] again in 1922: "Une chanson patoise contre un curé rouge", *Annales revolutionnaires*, 1922, p. 430.
11. Vol. IX, *La Révolution et l'Empire*, part II, p. 628
12. M. Dommanget, *Jacques Roux, le curé rouge. Les Enragés contre la vie chère sous la Révolution*, Paris, Spartacus, Cahiers mensuels, December, 1948; "Curés rouges et Prêtres ouvriers", *L'École libératrice*, June, 1955, n° 37.
13. F. Bridoux, *Histoire religieuse du département de Seine-et-Marne pendant la Révolution*, Melun, n.d., 2 vol.
14. Abbé J. Gallerand, *Les Cultes sous la Terreur en Loir-et-Cher (1792-1795)*, Blois, 1928
15. L. Guilleaut, *Histoire de la Révolution dans le Louhannais*, Louhans, 1899-1903, 2 vol.
16. Éd. Campagnac, "Un curé rouge: Métier", *art. cité*.
17. S. Bianchi, "La Déchristianisation de l'an II. Essai d'interprétation", *Annales historiques de la Révolution française*, 1978, n° 3, p. 354
18. Here we follow for Petit-Jean, Éd. Campagnac, *art. cité*; for Dolivier, J. Martin, thesis for higher studies, Institut d'historie de la Révolution française, Paris, 1968 (typed manuscript); for Jacques Roux, M. Dommanget, brochure cited above, note 12, and the series of works by W. Markow, *Jacques Roux oder vom Elend der Biographie*, Berlin, 1966, *Die Frieheiten des Priesters Roux*, Berlin, 1967, *Jacques Roux, Scripta et Acta*, 1969, *Excurse zu Jacques Roux*, Berlin, 1970; for Croissy, G. Lefebvre, "où il est question de Babeuf", *Annales d'Histoire sociale*, t. VII, p. 52, reprinted in *Études sur la Révolution française*, 2nd ed., Paris, 1963, p. 406.
19. *Discours à ses paroissiens pour leur annoncer son mariage*, Bibliothèque nationale, 8° Ln 27 6141, imp. in-8°, 22 p.
20. See Jean Meslier, *Oeuvres complètes*, vol. I, Paris, 1970, p. ci, A. Soboul, "Le Critique social devant son temps"
21. *Le Vœu national ou Système politique propre à organiser la nation dans toutes ses parties et à assurer à l'homme l'exercice de ses droits sociaux*, B.N., 8° Lb 39 8241, imp. in-8°, 78 p. followed by *Première suite...*, B.N., 8° Lb 39 4448, and *Seconde suite...*, B.N., 8° Lb 39 4448 bis.
22. On this political context of direct democracy, see A. Soboul, *Les Sans-culottes...*, pp. 56-58

CHAPTER 11

1. On this fundamental distinction, see L. Devance, "Le Féminisme pendant la Révolution française", *Annales historiques de la Révolution française*, 1977, n° 3, p. 341.

2. Laintullier, *Les Femmes célèbres de 1789 à 1795*, Paris, 1840. For a more complete bibliography, see the article cited by L. Devance.
3. Marie Cérati, *Le Club des Citoyennes républicaines révolutionnaires*, Paris, 1966. By way of comparison, see, Mlle. H. Perrin, "Les clubs de femmes de Besançon", *Annales révolutionnaires*, 1917, p. 629.
4. *Archives nationales*, F7 4585, pl. 5, p. 73
5. A.N., F7.4610
6. A.N., C 261, a. 572, p. 29; *Archives parlementaires*, vol. LXVIII, p. 139
7. A.N., F7 4586, pl. 3; D III 240-242, d. 4. The sisters Barbot, keeping a haberdasher's shop, were arrested on 5 prairial year III for their participation in "the revolt of women" of the preceding days. Notorious terrorists, they were said to have declared on 1 prairial that, "if the Jacobins have control, guillotines will be placed on the corner of every street to render justice to all the aristocrats, moderates and merchants."
8. *Archives parlementaires*, vol. LXVIII, p. 254, 255, 283, 286, 314, 381
9. A.N., C 261, d. 573, p. 62
10. A.N., C 262, d. 574, p. 5
11. A.N., C 263, d. 574, p. 1
12. *Archives parlementaires*, vol. LXVIII, p. 254
13. *Bibliothèque nationale*, Lb^{40} 2411; imp. s.l.n.d., in-8°, 4p.; Tourneux, n° 10059
14. See Isabelle Bourdin, *Les Sociétés populaires à Paris pendant la Révolution*, Paris, 1937, chap. I, p. 15
15. A.N., DIII 240-242, d. 1, p. 21, Buchez and Roux, vol. XIII, p. 452
16. B.N., Mss. Nouv. acq. fr. 2713, f. 40, 53
17. B.N., Lb^{40} 2449, imp. in-8°, 16p.; Tourneux, n° 9911
18. P. Caron, *Paris pendant la Terreur — Rapports des agents secrets du ministère de l'Intérieur*, 4 vol. in-8°
19. A.N., F^7 36883; P. Caron, *Paris...*, vol. II, p. 398
20. A.N., W. 112; P. Caron, *Paris...*, vol. IV, p. 222, 265, 339, 361, 381
21. A.N., F^7 4774^{64}, dossier Paulin; 4774^{80}, dossier Potel
22. A.N., F^7 4774^{42}, dossier Mercereau
23. B.N., Lb^{40} 485, imp. in-8°, 4 p.; Tourneux, n° 8882
24. On the soap riots of June, 1793, *Moniteur*, vol. XVI, p. 754, 761, 759, XVII, p. 1, 2; *Archives parlementaires*, vol. LXVII, p. 543, A. Mathiez, *La Vie chère et le Mouvement social sous la Terreur*, Paris, 1927, p. 235; A. Soboul, *Les Sans-culottes parisiens en l'an II*, La Roche-sur-Yon, 1958. The *Moniteur* of July 1, 1793 published the names and addresses of 15 women arrested on June 28 and imprisoned at the Force [prison in Paris] "on charges of rioting and pillaging soap"; all the popular quarters of Paris are represented. We have not been able to find the dossiers of these arrests.
25. *Archives de la préfecture de police*, A A/240, f. 156-157
26. A.N., W77, pl. 1, 3 pieces; Tuetey, vol. XI, n°s 60, 61 and 62. The agitation in the cotton workshops stopped, according to the administrators, with the arrest of Hébert.
27. A.N., F^7 4748, dossier Jannisson; W 385, d. 2523, case Benoite Tribel, wife Jannisson; Wallon, vol. IV, p. 493
28. A.N., c 262, d. 574, p. 32; B.N., Lb^{40} 1729, imp. in-8°, 2 p. Tourneux, n° 8495; *Archives parlementaries*, vol. LXVIII, p. 381 (29); A.N., C 261, d. 573, p. 12
29. A.N., C 261, d. 573, p. 12
30. A.N., F^7 4775^{20}, dossier Six
31. A.N., F^7 4637. The *citoyenne* Chalandon was released on 25 vendémiaire year IV.
32. A.N., intervention of Fabre d'Églantine at the Convention, 8 brumaire year II (October 29, 1793), against the feminine clubs composed not of mothers, but "of adventurers, wandering knights, emancipated girls, female grenadiers" (*Moniteur*, vol. XVII, p. 290).
33. A.N., F^7 4384, pl. 5, p. 39

CHAPTER 12

1. *Régions et régionalisme en France du XVIIIe siècle à nos jours*, Paris, P.U.F., 1977, p. 25
2. The edict is not dated: "in the month of June" the text says; but it was sent to the Parlement on the 17th, and registered on June 22, 1787; measures for implementing the law were passed on June 23 and August 5. The *provincial* assembly had the *généralité* as a framework; this administrative reform did not affect the *pays d'États* [more important regional divisions]. In the speech that he gave at the closing of the Assembly of notables, Loménie de Brienne defended his conception of the plan to unify France under the common system of the new administration. "The uniformity of principles does not always lead to the uniformity of means and the king will not regard as unworthy of his attention whatever considerations may be demanded by the costumes and usages to which people of certain provinces may attach their happiness." See P. Renouvin, *Les Assemblées provinciales de 1787. Origines, développement, résultats*, Paris, 1921; J. Egret, *La Pré-Révolution française, 1787-1789*, Paris, 1962, p. 109.
3. *Dictionnaire de l'Académie*, 4th ed., 1762
4. See A. Brette, *Les Limites et les Divisions territoriales de la France en 1789*, Paris, 1907, chap. III, "Le mot 'province'"
5. This discussion follows the analysis of G. Dupont-Ferrier, "De quelques synonymes du terme 'province' dans le langue administratif de l'ancienne France", *Revue historique*, 1929, vol. CLX, p. 241 and vol. CLXI, p. 278.
6. Quoted by F. Brunot, *Histoire de la langue française des origines à 1900*, vol. IX: *La Révolution et l'Empire*, part II, Paris, 1937, p. 1015
7. Alice Marcet, "Le Roussillon, une province à la fin de l'Ancien Régime"
8. Arthur Young, *Voyages en France en 1787, 1788 et 1789*, ed. H. Sée, Paris, 1931, vol. I, p. 123
9. See Ph. Torreilles, *La Diffusion du français à Perpignan, 1600-1700, 1914.*

10. P. Vilar, *La Catalogne dans l'Espagne moderne. Recherches sur les fondements économiques des structures nationales*, Paris. 1962. 3 vol.
11. M. Bordes. "La Gascogne à la fin de l'Ancien Régime: une province?"
12. M. Bordes. *D'Etigny et l'Administation de l'intendance d'Auch. 1751-1767*. Paris-Auch. 1957. 2 vol.; by the same author. "Une grande circonscription administrative du XVIIIe siecle: l'intendance d'Auch". *L'Information historique*. 1962. p. 1
13. L. Trénard. "Des Pays-Bas français aux départements du Nord et du Pas-de-Calais"
14. A. Gamblin. "Les régions du nord de la France". *Hommes et Terres du Nord*. 1968. p. 3
15. F.-X. Emmanuelli. "De la conscience politique à la naissance du *provençalisme* dans la généralité d'Aix à la fin du XVIIIe siècle"
16. On the cultural particularism of Provence. see. among the most recent works. M. Agulhon. *Pénitents et francs-maçons de l'ancienne Provence*. Paris. 1968. M. Vovelle. *Piété baroque et Déchristianisation en Provence au XVIIIe siecle*. Paris. 1973.
17. Abbé Papon. *Histoire générale de Provence*. Paris. 1777-1786: Ch.-F. Bouche. *Essai sur l'histoire de la Provence*. Marseille. 1785: M. Achard. *Dictionnaire de la Provence et du Comtat Venaissin*. Marseille. 1785: by the same author. *Description... de la Provence*. Aix. 1787-1788. and *Droit constitutif du pays de Provence*. 1788.
18. M. Gresset. "Les Francs-Comtois entre la France et l'Empire"
19. O. Karmin. "Appel d'un noble franc-comtois à l'empereur Léopold en 1791". *Annales révolutionnaires*. 1924. p. 371
20. B. Grosperrin. *L'Influence française et le Sentiment national français en Franche-Comté de la conquête à la Révolution, 1674-1789*. Paris. 1967.
21. M. Lambert. *Les Fédérations en Franche-Comté et la fête du 14 juillet 1790*. Paris. 1890.
22. Article 10 of the decrees of August 5-11. 1789. leading to the abolition of the feudal regime. "A national constitution and public liberty being more advantageous to the provinces than the privileges that some enjoy. and that must be sacrificed to achieve the close unity of all parts of the empire. it is declared that all the particular privileges of the provinces. principalities. *pays*. cantons. towns and communities of inhabitants. whether financial. or of another nature. are abolished irrevocably and will remain joined to the natural right of all the French people."
23. Buchez and Roux. *Histoire parlementaire*..., vol. III. p. 260
24. See J. Godechot. "Des provinces aux départements". *La Provincia*, Barcelona. 1966: cf. *Annales historiques de la Révolution francaise*, 1968. p. 279.
25. Consequently. the Committee drew up two tables. eminently instructive. that it had posted and that served as the basis of discussion for the deputies of the various provinces. These tables have been published by A. Aulard. "Départements et Régionalisne". *Études et Leçons sur la Révolution française*, 7th series. Paris. 1913. p. 49.
26. J. Bourdon. "Pinteville de Cernon. ses chiffres de population et sa critique des départements". *Annales historiques de la Révolution française*, 1954. p. 346
27. *Opinion de M. Target sur la division du royaume à la séance du 10 novembre 1789* (Archives nationales. AD XVIIIe 3)
28. *Rapport sommaire de la nouvelle division du royaume*... (B.N.. 8° Le^{29} 416)
29. For a recent bibliography on the formation of the departments. see J. Godechot. *Les Institutions de la France sous la Révolution et l'Empire*, 2nd ed.. 1968. p. 91.
30. *Courrier de Provence*, n° XCIII. January 12-15. 1790. vol. V. p. 10
31. The essential texts are F. Brunot. *Histoire de la langue française*, vol. IX: *La Révolution et l'Empire*, part I. "Le français langue nationale". Paris. 1927: M. de Certeau. D. Julia. J. Revel. *Une politique de la langue. La Révolution française et les patois: l'enquête de Grégoire*, Paris. 1975.
32. A.N.. F^{17} 1309. d. 2 (cited by F. Brunot. *op. cit.*, p. 28).
33. *Compte rendu à la Convention nationale... 6 janvier 1793* (B.N.. 4° Lf^{132} 3). p. 234
34. Cited by F. Brunot. *op. cit.*, p. 176
35. *Ibid.*
36. *Recueil des actes du Comité de salut public*, vol. X. p. 135
37. *Ibid.*, vol. IX. p. 104
38. *Rapport sur l'ouverture d'un concours pour les livres élémentaires de la première éducation... 3 pluviôse an II* (B.N.. 8° Le^{38} 662. imp. in-8°. 12 p.).
39. *Rapport et Projet de décret... sur les idiomes étrangers et l'enseignement de la langue française... 8 pluviôse an II* (B.N.. 8° Le^{38} 673. imp. in-8°. 14 p.)
40. *Moniteur*, vol. XVI. p. 392
41. F. Brunot. *op. cit.*, part II. "Les événements. les institutions et la langue". Paris. 1937. p. 860
42. *Oeuvres de Maximilien Robespierre*, vol. IX: *Discours*. part IV. Paris. 1958. p. 13. At the end of this stormy session. the Convention declared the French Republic to be one and indivisible.
43. There is no recent comprehensive work on federalism. See H. Wallon. *La Révolution du 31 mai et le Fédéralisme en 1793, ou la France vaincue par la Commune de Paris*, Paris. 1886. 2 volumes. vol. II. The local studies are of a higher quality. but the author publishes numerous texts emanating from departmental assemblies and Girondist deputies. We are grateful to Mlle J. Chaumié. honorary conservateur of the National Archives. specialist in the history of the Gironde. for the valuable information she was gracious enough to give us.
44. Almost all the depositories of the Departmental Archives contain documents on the Girondist federalism in the series L.
45. *Archives départementales Eure*, 12 L 23. dossier Gironde. With some variations. the various Girondist commissions of the departments ascribed to similar oaths. See also the correspondance of the Girondist deputies with their leaders and their accounts of the uprisings of May 31 and June 2. 1793. numerous copies of which were distributed in the departments. For example: Bergoeing. ... *A ses commettants et à tous les citoyens de la République*, Caen. 1793 (B.N.. 8° Lb^{41} 715); Brissot. ... *A ses commettants sur la situation de la Convention nationale, sur l'influence des anarchistes et les maux qu'elle a causés*..., Paris. n.d. [1793] (B.N.. 8° Lb^{41} 652); Buzot. *Lettres à ses commettants publiées à la suite de ses Mémoires sur la Revolution*..., Paris. 1828; Lanjuinais. *Fragment historique sur le 31 mai*, Paris. 1825; Saladin. *Compte*

rendu et déclaration... sur les journées des 27 et 31 mai, 1er et 2 juin 1793, Paris, n.d. [1793] (B.N., 8° Lb41 3040): Barbaroux, *A ses commettants*, Lyon, n.d. [1793] (B.N., Fol. Lb41 687).

46. *Examen critique de la Constitution...*, no place of publication indicated, 1793 (B.N., 8° Lb41 705)
47. *A.D. Eure*, 12 L 23, dossier Gironde
48. *Ibid.*, dossier Bouches-du-Rhône. Paris, "this city too long imperious."
49. *Ibid.*, dossier Pyrénées-Orientales
50. *Aux citoyens français sur la nouvelle constitution*, n.p., 1793 (B.N., 8° Lb41 703)
51. *A.D. Eure*, 12 L 23, dossier Rhône-et-Loire
52. Fr. Rouvière, *Histoire de la Révolution française dans le département du Gard...*, Nîmes 1887-1889, 4 vol., vol. III, pl. 288. "When the French people created a National Convention and placed their trust in the meeting of its representatives, they did not understand that their power... would pass, even momentarily, into the hands of a few individuals and that sheltered by their inviolability they could exercise with impunity a sovereign and arbitrary authority. Representatives, you were sent uniquely to put together some laws, to give us collectively a republican Constitution, and not to in turn command the armies nor reign over the departments."
53. The Declaration of Rights of June 24, 1793 is, in this sense, more precise than that of August 26, 1789. "The right of property belongs to every citizen to enjoy and to dispose according to his pleasure of his wealth and his revenues, of the fruit of his labor and his industry." (Article 16). "No type of work, of culture, of commerce may be forbidden to the industry of the citizens" (Article 17).
54. See the remarks of L.S. Gordon, "The federalist insurrection of the summer of 1793", *Annuaire d'Études françaises, 1967*, Moscow, 1968; in Russian, summary in French.
55. The best work is still that of A. Duchatelier, *Histoire de la Révolution dans les départements de l'ancienne Bretagne*, Paris, 1836. See also B.-A. Pocquet du Haut-Jussé, *Terreur et Terroristes à Rennes, 1792-1795*, Mayenne, 1974; D. Stone, "La Révolte fédéraliste à Rennes", *Annales historiques de la Révolution française*, 1971, p. 36. Here we would like to thank R. Dupuy, of the University of Haute-Bretagne, specialist in the history of the Revolution in the Breton departments.
56. *Rapport sur la situation politique des cinq départements de la ci-devant Bretagne*, National Convention, session of June 23, 1793 (B.N., 8° Le38 19, imp. in-8°, 10 p.)
57. A. Duchatelier, *op. cit.*, p. 399
58. See for example the anonymous *Adresse aux Bretons*, January 30, 1790 (A.N., 8° Lb39 2874, imp. in-8°, 34 p.). "This assembly, that one would rather take for a horde of savages than for civilized men, executes a general upheaval... And it is in this moment of delirium that, for the first time, we will identify ourselves with the French! Shouldn't we rather, profiting from the physical and moral impotency of this ungrateful nation, all of whose efforts have tended to destroy our contract! should we not break all ties with it, or at least rigorously revive all our conditions?" See also de Botherel, former public prosecutor of the Estates of Brittany, *Protestations adressées au roi et au public...*, Nantes, 1790 (B.N., 8° Lb39 2971).
59. *Recueil des Actes du Comité de salut public*, vol. VI, p. 311
60. M. Garden, *Lyon et les Lyonnais au XVIIIe siècle*, Paris, 1970, p. 593, conclusion
61. See M. Garden, *op. cit.*, part III, chap. IV, "Du corps de métier à la lutte des classes"
62. M. Wahl, *Les Premières Années de la Révolution à Lyon, 1788-1792*, Paris, 1894, p. 7
63. M. Garden, *op. cit.*, p. 593
64. [Anonymous], *Histoire de Commune-Affranchie recueillie dans les conversations d'un soldat du siège*, Lyon, 1843, p. 7
65. The violence of class conflicts is expressed in the vocabulary. Significantly, it was in Lyons that the word *muscadin* [fop] appeared. The history of this word has been traced by C. Riffaterre, *La Révolution française*, vol. LVI, 1909, p. 385. From Lyons, the word reached Paris in 1793.
66. B.N., 8° Lb39 6133, imp. in-8°, 16 p.
67. See the important unpublished thesis of Ta Koï, *Les "Chalier" et les sans-culottes lyonnais*, University of Lyon-II, 1975.
68. *Histoire de Lyon...*, vol. II, p. 297
69. On the federalist movement of Lyon, C. Riffaterre, *Le Mouvement antijacobin et antiparisien à Lyon et dans le Rhône-et-Loire en 1793*, Lyon-Paris, 1912 and 1928, 2 vol. See also E. Herriot, *Lyon n'est plus*, Paris, 1937-1940, 4 vol.
70. B.N., 8° Lb41 2728, imp. in-8°, 16 p.
71. By way of comparison, it will be interesting to read the pages that P. Vilar dedicated to the theme, "Histoire et Sociologie devant le phénomène *nation*" in the preface to *La Catalogne dans l'Espagne moderne, Recherches sur les fondements économiques des structures nationales*, Paris, 1962, 3 vol., vol. I, p. 29
72. The marketplace is the first school where the bourgeoisie learns nationalism."
73. *Marxism and the National Question* appeared for the first time in 1913 under the signature Stalin in numbers 3-5 of the bolshevik review *Prosvechténié*, under the title *La Question nationale et la Social-démocratie*.

CHAPTER 13

1. *L'information historique*, 1960, n° 3 and n° 4
2. Of Ferdinand Brunot, to be precise; along the same lines, see: "Le Mysticisme dans le langage de la Révolution", *Les Cahiers rationalistes*, n° 38, February 1935.
3. Quoted by Ferdinand Brunot, *Histoire de la langue francaise*, vol. VI, *Le XVIIIe siecle*, p. 137.
4. Quoted by F. Brunot, *op. cit.*, vol. VI, p. 134
5. *Op. cit.*, vol. VI, p. 138
6. *Op. cit.*, vol. VI, p. 135
7. In Voltaire's *Dictionnaire philosophique* published in 1764, the word *nation* does not appear and neither does the passage we are quoting. The editors of Kehl recast in the *Dictionnaire philosophique* the *Questions sur l'Encyclopédie* (1770-1772). Voltaire had already written in his *Pensées sur le gouvernement* (1752): "A republican is always more attached to his homeland than a subject to his, for the reason that one loves his own possession more than that of his master."

8. Quoted by F. Brunot, *op. cit.*, vol. VI, p. 134
9. Vol. III, p. 184
10. Sebastien Mercier continues: "The military laughs at the blows falling on the lawyer; the lawyer watches with indifference as the priest is degraded; the priest believes he can exist independently of the other estates; and pride no less than interest has divided adjoining professions that have the closest relations to each other; so that the prosecutor and the bailiff look at each other as two different castes. The notary and the clerk—each considers himself above the other" (*Tableau de Paris*, vol. II, p. 195).
11. *Le Point du jour*, October 6, 1789, III, p. 214; quoted by F. Brunot, *op. cit.*, vol. IX, p. 636.
12. *L'Ancien Régime et la Révolution*, 1952 edition, p. 244
13. *Ibid.*, p. 139
14. *Qu'est-ce que le Tiers Etat?* Champion edition, 1888, p. 30. Sieyes gives his first chapter the title: "The Third [Estate] is a complete nation." And he concludes: "The third [estate] thus embraces all who belong to the nation; and all who are not the third cannot see themselves as being of the nation."
15. *L'Ancien Régime et la Révolution*, *op. cit.*, p. 143 and 147
16. Ferdinand Brunot, *op. cit.*, vol. IX, *La Révolution et l'Empire*, p. 637
17. See Georges Lefebvre, "Sur la loi du 22 prairial an II", *Études sur la Révolution française*, 1954, p. 67.
18. Hébert continues: "As long as they [the merchands] believed that the Revolution would be useful to them, they supported it, they lent a hand to the sans-culottes to destroy the nobility and the parlements, but that was in order to put themselves in the place of the aristocrats. Now since [the classification] active citizen no longer exists, since the unfortunate sans-culotte enjoys the same rights as the rich tax collector, all these j...-f... have changed sides and they use all possible means to destroy the Republic." (N° 279, "The great anger of Père Duchesne when he sees that the fat continue to eat the little people.")
19. Let us underscore, from the point of view of the national problem, the contradiction of the administrative work of the Constituent Assembly. By suppressing the privileges of individuals, trade associations, provinces and towns on the night of August 4, the Assembly realized in principle the legal unity of the nation; but the French will henceforth administer themselves. On the one hand, the new territorial division into departments, districts and cantons broke the traditional framework of provincial life and completed the work of national unification begun by the monarchy. On the other hand, the new administrative organization, through decentralization and departmental and communal autonomy, was running counter to national unity and, as the crisis deepened, risked tending toward federalism and putting the very existence of the nation in danger. The events that followed June 2, 1793, and the fall of the Gironde were to demonstrate this contradiction.
20. *Moniteur*, vol. VI, p. 239
21. Robespierre, *Discours*, Bouloiseau-Lefebvre-Soboul edition, vol. II, 1952, p. 261. Robespierre concluded that the State must arm all citizens, "that it must, like Switzerland, pay them when they leave their homes to defend it."
22. Along these lines, see L. Girard, "Reflections on the national guard", *Bulletin de la Société d'histoire moderne*, May, 1955, p. 25. See also the deliberations and decisions of the various Parisian districts mentioned by Alexandre Tuetey, *Répertoire général des sources manuscrites de l'histoire de Paris pendant la Révolution française*, vol. I, 1890, p. 17. Finally see the observations of Jules Flammermont, *La Journée du 14 juillet 1789*, 1892, p. CLXXXI for example. After the clashes between the demonstrators and the Royal German Guard of the Prince of Lambesc on July 12, the royal troops withdrew behind the Seine, to the Military School and the Champ-de-Mars; Paris was left to itself, as the police inspectors had gone into hiding at the beginning of the riots. It was also in anticipation of the excesses of the *dangerous* classes that the bourgeois militia was formed.
23. *Moniteur*, vol. V, pl. 410
24. Robespierre, *Discours*, *op. cit.*, vol. II, p. 468
25. In the armed nation, Dubois-Crancé distinguishes three forces corresponding to what have since been termed active, reserve and territorial. Jean Jaurès rightly insists on the originality and import of Dubois-Crancé's ideas in his work *L'Armée nouvelle*, 1910, p. 209.
26. See Georges Lefebvre, "Le Meurtre du comte de Dampierre (June 22, 1791)", *Études sur la Révolution française*, 1954, p. 288.
27. *Moniteur*, vol. IX, p. 143
28. *Moniteur*, vol. XI, p. 119
29. *Moniteur*, vol. X, p. 753, 759
30. *Moniteur*, vol. XI, p. 45. "A war is ready to be ignited, a war essential to the consummation of the revolution."
31. *Bibliothèque nationale*, 8° Le[39] 36 A. According to Père Gérard ("Deuxième entretien. De la nation", p. 55), "the nation is the totality of citizens; it is in this totality that sovereign power resides. From that power flow all others, by the means of different elections, and no power can be legitimate if it is not conferred by the nation." To a peasant who asked him then why one must have a property qualification to be an elector, Père Gérard replied: "Because it was thought that the one with wealth or land would inspire more confidence." A very poor explanation, that did not satisfy the author, as Collot d'Herbois added: "Moreover, the nation is not only composed of active citizens; it is composed of all French people, whatever their religion, their condition or their color." Same embarrassed explanation concerning the definition of property as a natural and absolute right ("Cinquième entretien", p. 57). "Even those who have nothing have an interest in property being respected; for it is not only material possessions such as money, furniture, lands, houses, animals that constitute property; industry, love of work are also resources whose product forms property, perhaps the most precious of all." Père Gérard moves on to a eulogy of work. We are not far from the "enrichissez-vous" [get rich] of the propertied bourgeoisie.
32. *Histoire de la Révolution française*, édition de la Pléiade, vol. II, p. 776. The Girondists going to their death singing *La Marseillaise*. *Le Chant des Girondins* ("To die for the homeland is the most beautiful fate..."), that contributed its part to creating the Girondist legend, dates from 1847 (music by Varney, words by Alexandre Dumas, the father, in his play *Le Chevalier de Maison-Rouge*).

33. It was Dietrich, mayor of Strasbourg and supporter of La Fayette, who sung le *Chant de guerre pour l'armée du Rhin* for the first time in his wife's salon. The well-known painting by Pils, *Rouget de Lisle singing la Marseillaise* (1849), is inaccuarate on this point. Let us recall here that Rouget de Lisle, who lived until 1836 and left important musical works, composed *Roland à Ronceveau* in which we find the refrain: "To die for the homeland is the most beautiful fate...", that Alexandre Dumas reproduced in his play of 1847.
34. Buchez and Roux, vol. XV, p. 42.
35. See Félix Duhem, "François-Joseph L'Ange, 1743-1793", *Annales historiques de la Révolution française*, 1951, p. 38. The author sees in L'Ange's system, "the prototype if not the archetype of Fourier's"; it is at the least an important effort, before Babeuf, to design a nation of equals.
36. *Moniteur*, vol. XII, p. 368. The petition of Dolivier was presented to the Jacobins on April 27 and to the legislative Assembly on May 1, 1792 (*Jacobins*, III, p. 540; *Moniteur*, vol. XII, p. 274); it was printed B.N. 8° Lb^{39} 5805, imp. in-8°, 20 p.).
37. La Fayette, "seeing the French Constitution threatened by inside seditionaries as much as by enemies from the outside" called on the Assembly, on June 18, 1792, to break the popular movement (*Moniteur*, vol. XII, p. 692). He denounced all those who "detest the national guard": that is, the bourgeois, property-qualified guard. At the end of July, rather than confronting the enemy, La Fayette brought his troops close to Compiègne.
38. *Moniteur*, vol. XII, p. 83
39. B.N., Mss., Nouv. acq. fr. 2684, f. 125. Imp. in-8°, 4 p., signed *Danton*, president, *Anaxagoras Chaumette*, *Momoro*, secretaries. Hanriot expressed the same views, but more simply, when he spoke to the Finistère section on May 31, 1793 on the proper place of arms: "For a long time the rich made the laws, it must now be time for the poor to have their turn and for equality to reign between rich and poor." (A.N. F7 4774^{38}).
40. A.N., AD I 69. Imp. n.d., in-8°, 8 p.
41. Quoted by Pierre Caron, *Les Massacres de septembre*, 1935, p. 415, n. 3. There is in these lines, writes Pierre Caron, the "echo of a collective feeling."
42. H. Taine, *La Conquête jacobine*, edition in-16°, 1911, I, p. 176. "It is not a question of choosing between order and disorder, but between the new regine and the old, for behind the foreigners, we perceive the émigrés at the border. The shock is terrible, especially in that deep layer that alone bore almost all the weight of the old edifice, among the millions of men who live with difficulty from the work of their arms, ... who, taxed, stripped, treated harshly for centuries, enduring, from father to son, misery, oppression and disdain. They know, through their own experience, the difference between their recent condition and their present condition. They only have to remember to see again in their imagination the enormity of royal, ecclesiastical and seigniorial taxes." The social order established by the Constituent was to suffer the repercussions of popular pressure: on August 25, 1792, seignorial taxes were abolished without compensation, unless the original title subsisted.
43. Report presented to the Convention "on the fate of prisoners released following the events of the first days of last September". Cited by Pierre Caron, *op. cit.*, p. 470.
44. See what Michelet has written on this subject in *Histoire de la Révolution française*, édition de la Pléiade, vol. I, p. 1130.
45. "The authors of the theory did not consider food products as the most necessary to life but only ordinary merchandise; they made no distinction between the commerce of wheat and that of indigo; they have held forth more on the commerce of grains than on the subsistence of the people.... For them profits of the merchants and landowners count a lot, the life of men count for almost nothing.... The first right is that of survival. The first social law is therefore that of guaranteeing to all members of society the means of survival; all others are subordinated to that one." (*Moniteur*, vol. XIV, p. 694)
46. *Moniteur*, vol. XIV, p. 694
47. *Moniteur*, vol. XV, p. 705. Vergniaud continues: "It [equality] is no longer that of fortune, but that of ability, strength, spirit, activity, industry and work." He criticizes on the other hand "the abuse that [the anarchists] have done to the word sovereignty. They came very close to overturning the Republic, by making each section believe that sovereignty resided in its bosom."
48. On December 6, 1793, the Convention repealed by a solemn decree the principle of freedom of cults. In conclusion, it invited "all good citizens, in the name of the homeland, to abstain from all arguments theological or foreign to the greater interests of the French people, in order to cooperate to their fullest in the triumph of the Republic and the ruin of its enemies." See Robespierre's speech to the Jacobins on November 21, 1793: in the critical situation where France finds herself, it is dangerous to incite new divisions.
49. Donald Greer, *The Incidence of the Terror during the French Revolution. A statistical interpretation*, Cambridge, U.S.A., 1935.
50. *La Révolution française*, p. 405
51. On this interpretation of the decrees of ventôse, see my work, *Les sans-culottes parisiens en l'an II*, p. 708.
52. Speech on the present state of affairs (B.N., Lb^{41} 662, imp. in-8°, n.d., 31 p.)
53. *Histoire de la langue française*, vol. IX, p. 922
54. Georges Lefebvre, *Les Paysans du Nord pendant la Révolution française*, p. 548, "La contre-révolution autrichienne (1793-1794)"
55. We find the expression "popular republic" in the *Essai sur la dénonciation politique* of Étienne Barry, 1793 (B.N. 8° LC^{2} 809)
56. *Moniteur*, vol. XXIII, p. 717
57. *Le Tribun du peuple, n° 34, 15 brumaire year IV*
58. "Absolute equality is an illusion; in order for it to exist, it would be necessary to have complete equality of mind, virtue, physical strength, education and fortune among all men." Vergniaud had offered the same argument on March 13, 1793. See above, note 47.
59. *Moniteur*, vol. XXV, p. 92. "Man without property, on the contrary, needs a constant virtuous effort to be interested in the order that conserves nothing for him, and to oppose movements that give him some hope." Along the same lines, see the interventions of Mailhe and Lanjuinais on August 13, 1795. (*Moniteur*, vol. XXV, p. 497)

60. *Moniteur*, vol. XXI, p. 748
61. See Ferdinand Brunot, *op. cit.*, vol. X, p. 999
62. See the examples given by Fernand Baldensperger in *Le Mouvement des idées et l'émigration française (1789-1815)*, vol. I, p. 308.
63. See F. Baldensperger, *op. cit.*, p. 279 and 289. See also, p. 283, the analysis of the work of Mounier, *Adolphe ou Principes élémentaires de politique et Résultats de la plus cruelle des expériences* (1795). "Most of the French people," writes Mounier in his next-to-the-last chapter, "now yearn for order, repose, personal security and respect of property."
64. *Ibid.*, vol. II, p. 293
65. "Emigration, forced for some," writes Bonald, "was legitimate for all. The soil is not the *patrie* of the civilized man; it is not even that of the savage, who believes himself always in his *patrie* when he carries with him the bones of his fathers." *(De l'émigration)* See F. Baldensperger, *op. cit.*, vol. I, p. 299.

CHAPTER 14

1. *Annales historiques de la Révolution française*, n° 3, p. 443
2. Review of volumes VII, *La Montagne*, and VII *Le Gouvernement révolutionnaire* of *l'Histoire socialiste de la Révolution française*, 2nd edition (A. Mathiez ed.) *A.H.R.F.*, 1925, p. 75.
3. Review of volumes III, *La Législation*, IV, *La République*, and V, *La Révolution et l'Europe*, of *Histoire socialiste*, 2nd edition (A. Mathiez, ed.), *Annales révolutionnaires*, 1923, p. 417.
4. *Ibid.*
5. Cf. the draft legislation presented by Jaurès to the Chamber of Deputies, November 27, 1903. "The basis of history does not consist in the exterior development of political forms. It is indeed certain that it is the play of economic interests, of social forces that determines the movement of history. Now, while for the history of the French Revolution, that is to say for the history of the very origins of the modern world... the publication of documents of a political nature has multiplied, ... for the documents concerning the social and economic life of the French Revolution, there is no collection."
6. We will not insist here on the influence that the *Histoire socialiste de la Révolution française* exerted on Georges Lefebvre, contenting ourselves with referring to the study of J.-R. Suratteau. "It is to Jaurès that I owe the most... No matter how carefully one searches for my master, I recognize no one but him." ("Pro domo", *A.H.R.F.*, 1947, p. 188.)
7. Cf. above, note 2
8. Review of volume I, *La Constituante*, of *Histoire socialiste*, 2nd edition, (A. Mathiez, ed.), *Annales révolutionnaires*, 1929, p. 255.
9. Cf. above, note 3
10. "He," writes Aulard, "whose socialism should have shut out Mirabeau, he felt Mirabeau more than anyone before him, he saw in him the only man of the Revolution who truly had genius and, with a sure hand, he placed that mind above all others."
11. Cf. above, note 2
12. Regarding volumes VII, *La Montagne*, and VIII, *Le Gouvernement révolutionnaire*, of his edition, Mathiez writes: "Jaurès, philosopher that he remained, was above all interested in ideas (123 pages are devoted to the analysis of the social ideas of the principal delegates to the Convention, and, as a consequence, Jaurès returns again to the ideas of Condorcet and Robespierre). He did not have the time, in these conditions, to study closely the institutions of the Terror and their functioning... He says almost nothing about the Revolutionary Tribunal which he considered wrongly, following the tradition, as a pure machine of political repression. He neglected the work accomplished by the representatives on assignment."
13. Cf. above, note 3

CHAPTER 15

1. *A.H.R.F.*, 1975, n° 1
2. See E. Labrousse, "Georges Lefebvre dans l'évolution de l'historiographie française," *A.H.R.F.*, 1969, p. 459. *A.H.R.F.*, 1969, p. 459.
3. That is one of the principal ideas of Georges Lefebvre's course, *Notions d'historiographie moderne*, taught at the Sorbonne in 1945-1946 and published under the title *La Naissance de l'historiographie moderne* (Paris 1971). Georges Lefebvre rose up against the assertion of Fénelon that "the historian belongs to no time, to no country". See also "Réflexions sur l'histoire", *La Pensée*, May-June, 1955 p. 27.
4. Georges Lefebvre has stressed on several occasions that the historian writes for the ruling classes. Consequently, "historiographie must necessarily reflect the general movement of history, for as the ruling classes change, so does their mentality". ("La Synthèse en histoire", *Bulletin de la Société d'histoire moderne*, October-November 1951, p. 7)
5. On Tocqueville, whose influence on Georges Lefebvre was decisive, see the introduction that Lefebvre wrote to *L'Ancien Régime et la Révolution*, vol. II of Oeuvres complètes, Paris, 1952. See also the article "A propos de Tocqueville", *A.H.R.F.*, 1955, p. 313
6. "Pro domo", *A.H.R.F.*, 1947, p. 788
7. See the introduction to *Paysans du Nord*, p. v.
8. "Pro domo", *art. cit.*, p. 189. Biographical notations on Georges Lefebvre, furnished by himself, will be found in *A.H.R.F.*, 1946, p. 185 and 1947, p. 188 ("Pro domo"). See also the brief biographical notice published in the front of *Etudes sur la Révolution française*, Paris, 1954, in-8°, 328 p. A list of the principal publications of Georges Lefebvre will be found in this work (p. vii), which, on the occasion of his eightieth birthday, reprints his most important articles.
9. See what Georges Lefebvre writes in *La Naissance de l'historiographie moderne*, *op. cit.*, p. 308.
10. "Le 24 février 1848", speech delivered on February 24, 1946, *1848 et les Révolutions du XIXe siecle*, 1946, n° 172, p. 7.
11. First a tutor at the Tourcoing high school, Georges Lefebvre was name professor at the Boulogne-sur-Mer high school. Passing the teachers' examinations in history and geography, he began at the Cherbourg high school, then returned to

his native Nord, teaching successively at the high schools of Tourcoing, Saint-Omer, and Lille. The war and invasion made it necessary for him to withdraw to Orleans. Once peace came, he finally arrived at the great Parisian high schools: Pasteur, Montaigne, then Henri-IV.

12. At the University of Lille, Georges Lefebvre had been the student and disciple of the medievalist Charles Petit-Dutaillis. A few years later, and although he had already turned toward revolutionary studies, Georges Lefebvre accepted his teacher's proposal to translate into French the *Constitutional History of England* of W. Stubbs. The first two volumes of this translation were published in 1907 and 1923, the third in 1927. At this date, with the historiography of medieval England progressing, Georges Lefebvre, again on the request of Petit-Dutaillis, consented to write an original study on the English Parliament in the 13th and 14th centuries, which was inserted in the translation of Stubbs. Georges Lefebvre liked to recall that he had thus paid in part for the printing of his thesis. This work offered enough interest to be translated into English (Charles Petit-Dutaillis and Georges Lefebvre, *Studies and Notes Supplementary to Stubbs's Constitutional History*, vol. III, Manchester, 1929); in 1930, the three volumes were published in a single volume, with pages 345-505 representing the contribution of Georges Lefebvre.

    Receiving his doctorate in 1924, Georges Lefebvre began teaching at the university level at the Faculty of Arts of Clermont-Ferrand. In 1928 he was name to that of Strasbourg, where Marc Bloch, the author of *Caractères originaux de l'histoire rurale française* (1931), was teaching. Georges Lefebvre always acknowledged his intellectual debt to Bloch. Called to the Sorbonne in 1935, he was appointed two years later to the chair of the History of the French Revolution, a position he held until 1945. Editor of the Bulletin devoted to the Revolution and the Empire in the *Revue historique* since 1928, Lefebvre was invited in 1932, on the death of Albert Mathiez, to assume the presidency of the Society of Robespierrist Studies and to take the editorship of the *A.H.R.F.*, a task he carried out until his death. He did it, as he wrote, "through friendship to the memory of Maximilien Robespierre" (*Études sur la Révolution française, op. cit.*, notice biographique, p. v.).

13. Jean Cocteau, *Discours aux étudiants d'Oxford*.
14. Lille, 1914, in-8°, CXXIV-670 p. The second volume appeared in 1921 (Lille, 1921, in-8s2o, 704 p.) This study was completed by an article "La Réquisition de l'an IV dans le ci-devant district des Bergues", *Revue du Nord*, February 1920, p. 26. This is a collection of documents preceded by an introduction.
15. Paris, 1954; 2nd ed., 1963, with an introduction by A. Soboul, in-8°, 446 p.
16. Paris, 1962-1963, 2 vol. in-8°, vol. I, *Contribution à l'étude des structures sociales à la fin du XVIIIe siècle* (276 p.); vol. II, *Subsistances et maximum, 1789 – an IV* (474 p.)
17. Lille, 1924, in-8°, XXV—1020 p.; 2nd ed. Paris, 1972 (reprint). An edition was obtained by the Italian editor Laterza (Bari, 1959, in-8°, XXVII—923 p.; preface by A. Saitta and A. Soboul; the infrapaginal notes and statistical tables were not reproduced). See the report of the oral defense by A. Aulard, *La Révolution française*, vol. LXXVII, 1924, p. 218; the reviews of A. Matthiez, *A.H.R.F.*, 1924, p. 470, of H. See, *Revue historique*, vol. CXLVII, 1924, p. 90, of H. Pirenne, *Revue belge de philologie et d'histoire*, 1926, p. 198.

    In this review, Pirenne spoke of the book as "a model of conscientiousness or, to put it better, of scientific abnegation". The word is not too strong for whoever knows the thankless nature of the perusal of landed property documents and their statistical elaboration. Eleven hundred registers studies in a single series of registration! "The greatest difficulty," Pirenne continued, "consisted in criticizing and combining the data furnished by the administrative lists, filling in the gaps, calculating the errors, and extracting by combination, comparison and interpretation every sort of precision. We imagine what such work demands in terms of both prudence and ingenuity and what a mass of precise knowledge it requires about all that concerns men and things: morals and customs, rights and institutions, agricultural technique, weights, measures and currencies." Albert Matthiez, in *A.H.R.F.*, stresses the importance of the subjects treated. "There was enough material there for several different theses: feudal rights, taxes, national lands, *maximum*, terror, religious question, etc. Never has the social history of the Revolution been searched with this depth and breadth. The 200 pages of statistical tables that end the volume, the critical notes that accompany each chapter bear witness to the conscientiousness of the worker, who belongs to the race of Benedictins."

18. Conclusion, p. 882
19. Lectures at the Center for Studies of the French Revolution, at the Sorbonne, December 12 and 14, 1932; text published in *A.H.R.F.*, 1933, p. 97, and in *Cahiers de la Révolution française*, 1934, n° 1, p. 7; reprinted in 1954 in *Études sur la Révolution française*, p. 247.

    Let us note here *Questions agraires au temps de la Terreur* (Strasbourg, 1932, in-8°, 256 p., enlarged 2nd ed., La Roche-sur-Yon, 1954, 274 p.; Russian translation, Moscow, 1936). In this work, a collection of documents, Georges Lefebvre presents the results of his research on problems that inflamed the peasants from the beginning of the Revolution and consequently could command the attention of the government of year II: alienation from the national lands, seen from the angle of the decrees of ventôse, division of the large farms, condition of sharecropping, regulation of cultivation. Despite the sometimes technical aspect of the questions studied, we encounter the great problems first raised in the framework of the Nord department. After the *dîme* and feudal rights had disappeared, the Montagnard Party could only keep the revolutionary spirit of the rural masses alive and profit from it by formulating a new agrarian program. Sensitive to the desires expressed by the peasants in the documents published here, a faction of the Montagnards and especially the Robespierrists tried to get a part of the national lands reserved for the impoverished peasants: that was the object of the decrees of ventôse year II. In accordance with the wishes of the peasant masses, all heads of family would have become landowners due to the division of national and communal lands; the great property, intact and uncontested, would have been inevitably subdivided into small plots, as all concentration was forbidden; the right to property would remain carved up by the traditional rights to fallow lands and meadows, forests and wasteland. Thus the capitalist tansformation of agriculture that could profit only a minority of affluent peasants would have been slowed down, if not stopped. There was a great distance between this potential program and the measure proposed by Saint-Just on 8 ventôse that constituted the whole agrarian program of the Robespierrists. Saint-Just wanted to create a certain number of small landowners, continuing and enlarging the work of the Constituent. He certainly did not ignore the petitions that poured in from the countryside, but he remained mute on all the other demands of the impoverished peasantry. Here the agrarian history of France meets up with the political history of the Revolution.

20. These two articles have been published in the *Revue d'histoire moderne*, 1928, and reprinted in *Études sur la Révolution française, op. cit.*, p. 202 and 223.
21. On these problems, see A. Soboul, "La Révolution française et la 'féodalité' — Notes sur le prélèvement féodal," *Revue historique*, 1968, n° 487, p. 33; by the same author, "La Révolution française et la féodalité," *A.H.R.F.*, 1968, p. 289.
22. "La Révolution française et les paysans," *Études sur la Révolution française, op. cit.*, 2nd ed., p. 249.
23. H. K. Takahashi, "La Place de la révolution de Meiji dans l'histoire agraire du Japon," *Revue historique*, October-December 1953, p. 229.
24. A. Ado, *Le Mouvement paysan pendant la Révolution française*, Moscow, 1971, in-8°, 454 p., in Russian. Cf. A. Soboul, "Sur le mouvement paysan dans la République française," *A.H.R.F.*, 1973, p. 85.
25. *La Grande Peur de 1789*, Paris, 1932, in-8°, 272 p.; 2nd ed., Paris, n.d. [1956], in-8°, 272 p., with an addendum paginated 1 to 6 that gives a critical bibliography of works published from 1932 to 1935; Italian translation, Turin, 1953. See the review by M. Bloch, *Annales d'histoire économique et sociale*, 1933, p. 302.
26. Communication presented to the Center of Synthesis, on the occasion of the Week of Synthesis of 1932, dedicated to the crowd ["foule"]. The text was published, with the other papers, in a volume entitled *La Foule* (Paris, 1933), under the title "Foules historiques, les Foules révolutionnaires" (p. 79; see the discussion, p. 108), then in *A.H.R.F.* (1934, p. 1). It was reprinted in 1954 in *Études sur la Révolution française*, p. 271.
Georges Lefebvre gave a beautiful example of analysis of an act of punitive will in his article "Le Meurtre du comte de Dampierre (22 juin 1791)," *Revue historique*, 1941; reprinted in *Études sur la Révolution française*, p. 288. This murder was not just the consequence of an imprudent action of the count going to greet the king at Sainte-Menehould, on the way back from Varennes... See below, note 43.
27. It is necessary to cite here the general works of Georges Lefebvre where he focuses his work and our knowledge. Published by Armand Colin, *Les Thermidoriens*, Paris, 1937, in-16°, 220 p., and *Le Directoire*, Paris, 1946, in-16°, 198 p. Completing the brilliant synthesis of Albert Mathiez on the period 1789-1794, these works denote a rare mastery of judgment of men and events. More extensive are the two volumes of the collection "Peuples et civilisations": *La Révolution française*, Paris, 1930, in collaboration with Ph. Sagnac and R. Guyot; new edition in 1951, in-8°, 674 p.; 2nd ed., enlarged, 1957, 686 p., with bibliographical additions; 3rd ed., revised and enlarged by A. Soboul, 1963, 698 p.; *Napoleon*, Paris, 1936; 4th ed. enlarged, 1953, in-8°, 610 p.; 5th ed. revised and enlarged by A. Soboul, 1954 626 p.
Georges Lefebvre's mastery of the art of synthesis seems to us best proved in the fluent and brilliant work, with clear contours, *Quatre-vingt-neuf* [Eighty-nine] (Paris, 1939, in-8°, 308 p.; translations: English, 1947; Italian, 1949; Japanese, 1952). Devoid of notes or references, written for the general public, this book is understandable without sacrificing events to an arbitrary simplification. The reciprocal action of the economy and social factors on political life is always analyzed with precision. The various protagonists appear in succession. First the aristocracy who, profiting from the crisis of the monarchy, thought they could get their revenge and regain the political authority that the Capetian dynasty had stripped them of. Then, advancing in the path opened to them, the bourgeoisie and behind them the popular urban masses and finally the peasants. The class conflicts could not hide the action of men that Georges Lefebvre brings back to life. La Fayette, symbol more than leader, Mirabeau, Sieyes, "the soul of the legal revolution"; but not one could impose himself to the point of symbolizing the revolution of 89 that remains "the collective work of the Third Estate". There is a beautiful example of method and expostion, simple and clear, a great historical lesson.
28. We will cite the following articles: "Avenir de l'histoire," *Revue historique*, January-March 1947, p. 55; "Recherche et Congrès," *ibid.*, July-September 1951, p. 1; review of the book of Marc Bloch, *Apologie pour l'histoire ou Métier d'historien, ibid.*, July-September 1953, p. 89; "La Synthèse en histoire," *Bulletin de la Société d'histoire moderne*, October-November 1951, p. 7; "Quelques réflexions sur l'histoire des civilisations," *A.H.R.F.*, April-June 1955, p. 97; "Réflexions sur l'histoire," *La Pensée*, May-June 1955, p. 27.
29. See the circular sent on this subject of great methodological interest (*A.H.R.F.*, 1939, p. 86). Always preoccupied with these problems, Georges Lefebvre, in a communication to the Society of Modern History in 1955, signalled the importance of mortgage archives for social history ("Archives hypothécaires," *Bulletin de la Société d'histoire moderne*, November-December 1955, p. 9). Lefebvre stressed the double interest of the mortgage loan for social history: for the bourgeoisie, it was always a convenient and fruitful investment procedure; the indebtedness of the landowning peasantry and the expropriation it could entail play a not inconsiderable role in the concentration of landed property. The importance of this problem, underscored by Marx and Tocqueville, is recognized in the failure of the Second Republic.
30. "Extrait du rapport general... 1er juin 1939," *Assemblée générale de la Commission centrale et des Comités départementaux*, 1939, Commission of research and publication of documents relative to the economic life of the Revolution, Besançon, 1942, vol. I, in-8°, 452 p., p. 27.
31. A. Daumard and F. Furet, "Méthodes de l'histoire sociale. Les archives notariales et la mécanographie", *Annales E.S.C.*, 1959, p. 676
32. "Extrait du rapport général...", p. 27 (cited above, n. 30)
33. "Réflexions sur l'histoire", *art. cit.*, p. 32 and 33
34. "La Synthèse en histoire", *art. cit.*, p. 12
35. "Sur Danton", *A.H.R.F.*, 1932, reprinted in *Études sur la Révolution française*, 2nd ed., p. 92
36. "La Synthèse en histoire", *art. cit.*, p. 11
37. "Réflexions sur l'histoire", *art. cit.*, p. 31
38. Georges Lefebvre had been particularly struck by certain aspects of the works of George Rudé on the composition and behavior of the revolutionary crowd. See in *A.H.R.F.*, 1959, p. 174, his review of G. Rudé, *The Crowd in the French Revolution*, Oxford, 1958. The book of Louis Chevalier, *Classes laborieuses et Classes dangereuses à Paris, pendant la première moitié du XIXe siècle*, Paris, 1958, had seemed to him to constitute an important milestone in this line of research. He stressed, in his review (*A.H.R.F.*, 1959, p. 173), the deplorable biological consequences of the conditions of popular existence: epidemics and death, certainly, but also "the deterioration of health, morals and behavior which tend toward violence," so that the bourgeoisie suffered an awareness of living beside a population who, in the main

hardworking, harbored categories that the conditions of living rendered "distinct by their physical aspect, their biological traits, as much as by their intellectual and moral characteristics."

39. "Réflexions sur l'histoire", *art. cit.*, p. 32
40. *Recueil de documents relatifs aux séances des États Généraux. Mai-Juin 1789*, under the direction of G. Lefebvre, vol. I, *Les préliminaires. La séance du 5 mai*, Paris, 1953, in-8°, XXXII-380 p.; II, *La séance du 23 juin*, Paris, 1962, in-8°, XXXIV-362 p.
41. "Le recueil de documents sur les États Généraux," *A.H.R.F.*, 1954, p. 296
42. "La Synthèse en histoire", *art. cit.*, p. 9 and 10
43. "Le meurtre du comte de Dampierre, 22 juin 1791," *Revue historique*, 1941, reprinted in *Études sur la Révolution française*, p. 288; 2nd ed., p. 393.
44. This very beautiful page concludes the "Réflexions sur l'histoire," *art. cit.*, p. 34. On man as a factor in history, see the same article, p. 32: "subject, of course, to the influence of other factors," it is he who makes history. "Marx found it amusing that, history being the deed of man, it could be questioned that man participated in it." See also "Quelques réflexions sur l'histoire des civilisations," *art. cit.*, p. 102; Georges Lefebvre rises up against "an imperfect idea" that many hold of the Marxist method. "Man makes history," he writes, "and consequently, Marx has noted, his nature is inscribed among the original factors."
45. See the two speeches delivered by Georges Lefebvre at the unveiling of the bust of Robespierre at Arras, October 15, 1933 (*A.H.R.F.*, 1933, p. 484 and p. 492).
46. "Le 24 février 1848," *art. cit.*, p. 16
47. *Qu'est-ce que le capitalisme?* Union française universitaire, Paris, 1946, in-8°, 18 p., p. 17, lecture delivered by Georges Lefebvre on February 16, 1946.
48. *Ibid.*, p. 18
49. *Quatre-vingt-neuf*, p. 245. See the review of this book by Lucien Febvre in *Annales d'histoire sociale*, 1940, p. 147. "Virile words," Febvre concludes: "they deserve to be contemplated and followed."
50. "Discours sur Rosbespierre," *art. cit.*, p. 510.
51. "Pro domo", *art. cit.*, p. 190. "In our sad days," Georges Lefebvre adds, "I cannot reread this page without a trembling emotion."
52. "Le 24 février 1848," *art. cit.*, p. 17.

CHAPTER 16

1. *La Pensée*, n° 177, September-October 1974, pp. 40-58.
2. See especially A. Aulard, *Histoire de la Révolution française. Origine et développement de la démocratie et de la République, 1789-1804*, (Paris, 1901).
3. *Histoire socialiste (1789-1900)* under the direction of J. Jaurès, who edited the first four volumes dedicated to the French Revolution up to 9 Thermidor (Paris 1901-1904). New edition revised and annotated by A. Soboul (Paris, 1968-1972, 6 vol.)
4. "But, no matter how carefully one searches for my master, I recognize no one but him." ("Pro domo," *A.H.R.F.*, 1947, p. 188).
5. *Histoire de la civilisation en France depuis la chute de l'Empire romain* (1828-1830; 4 vol.). "Considered from the social point of view and in its relations with the various classes that coexisted on our territory, the one that is called the Third Estate has been progressively extended, raised and has first powerfully modified, then surmounted and finally absorbed, or almost so, all the others." (46th lesson). When Guizot writes "Third Estate," he means the bourgeoisie.
6. See the introduction to *De la démocratie en Amérique* (1836). Tocqueville asks himself: "Would it be wise to believe that a social movement that has come so far will be suspended by the efforts of a generation? Do people think that after having destroyed feudalism and kings, democracy will retreat before the bourgeois and the rich?"
7. *Les Origines de la France contemporaine. L'Ancien Régime* (1876). See chapter III on book IV.
8. *Introduction à la Révolution française*, part I, chap. III. Written in 1792, this work was published in 1843 in volume I of the *Oeuvres* of Barnave edited by Bérenger de la Drôme. Jaurès places great emphasis on this work in his *Histoire socialiste* (I, 98).
9. Lacretelle, dit le Jeune, *Histoire de la Révolution française*, Paris, 1821-1826, 8 vol.
10. A. Mathiez, *La Révolution française*, 1922, vol. I, chap. II, "La révolte nobiliaire."
11. *Les Paysans du Nord pendant la Révolution française* (1924); *Questions agraires au temps de la Terreur* (1932); *La Grande Peur de 1789* (1932). A. Soboul, *Les sans-culottes parisiens en l'an II. Mouvement populaire et Gouvernement révolutionnaire. 2 juin 1793-9 thermidor an II* (1958); G. Rudé, *The Crowd in the French Revolution* (1959). For various reasons, R. Cobb cannot be considered a disciple of G. Lefebvre.
12. R.R. Palmer, "The World Revolution of the West," *Political Science Quarterly*, 1954; J. Godechot and R.R. Palmer, "Le Problème de l'Atlantique du XVIIIe siècle au XXe siècle," *X Congresso internazionale de Scienze storiche. Relazioni*, Florence, 1955, vol. V, p. 175; J. Godechot, *La Grande Nation. L'expansion révolutionnaire de la France dans le monde. 1789-1799*, Paris, 1956, 2 vol.; R.R. Palmer, *The Age of the Democratic Revolution. A political history of Europe and America. 1760-1800*, Princeton, 1959; J. Godechot, "Révolution française or Révolution occidentale," *L'information historique*, 1960, p. 6 (with a bibliography on the question); J. Godechot and R.R. Palmer, "Révolution française, occidentale ou atlantique," *Bulletin de la Société d'histoire moderne*, 1960; J. Godechot, *Les Révolutions, 1770-1799*, Paris, 1960, coll. "Nouvelle Clio." On J. Godechot's *La Grande Nation*, see G. Lefebvre's review, *A.H.R.F.*, 1957, p. 272; on R. R. Palmer's *The Age of the Democratic Revolution*, see M. Reinhard's review, *ibid.*, 1960, p. 220.
13. J. Godechot, *La Grande Nation...*, vol. I, p. ii.
14. R.R. Palmer, *1789, Les Révolutions de la liberté et de l'égalité*, Paris, 1968, p. 305.
15. And again, still from Tocqueville: "But why did this revolution, prepared for everywhere, threatening everywhere, break out in France rather than elsewhere? Why did it have certain characteristics in France that were not found anywhere else or only partly appeared?" (*L'Ancien Régime et la Révolution*, new edition, Paris, 1952, with an introduction by G. Lefebvre, p. 96.)

16. Let us recall here that J. Godechot organized an international colloquium at Toulouse, November 12-16, 1968, on *L'Abolition de la féodalité dans le monde occidental*, Paris, 1971, 2 vol.
17. R.R. Palmer, *1789*..., p. 307
18. G. Lefebvre, "Le Mythe de la Révolution française", *A.H.R.F.*, 1956, p. 337
19. Cobban, *The Myth of the French Revolution*, London, 1955; see G. Lefebvre, "Le Mythe de la Révolution française," *art. cit.* From the same point of view, A. Cobban, *The Social Interpretation of the French Revolution*, Cambridge, 1964. The essential points of these articles were taken up again in A. Cobban, *Aspects of the French Revolution*, New York, 1968: "The State of Revolutionary History," p. 9; "Historians and the Causes of the French Revolution," p. 29; "The Myth of the French Revolution," p. 264; "The French Revolution: Orthodox and Unorthodox Interpretations," p. 275. For interesting reading on this controversy, see, G.J. Cavanaugh, "The Present State of French Revolutionary Historiography: Alfred Cobban and beyond," *French Historical Studies*, 1972, n° 4, p. 587.
20. For all that follows, *see* A. Soboul, "La Révolution française et la 'féodalité.' Notes sur le prélèvement féodal," *Revue historique*, fascicule 487, July-September 1968, p. 33; by the same author, "Survivances féodales dans la société rurale française au XIXe siècle," *Annales E.S.C.*, 1968, p. 965. For a regional example, illustrating our remarks, see M. Leymarie, "Les Redevances foncières seigneuriales en Haute-Avergne," *A.H.R.F.*, 1968, p. 299.
21. *Rapport fait au nom du Comité des droits féodaux le 4 septembre 1789, sur l'objet et l'ordre du travail dont il est charge...* (B.N., 8° Le 29 193, imp. in-8°, 30 p.).
22. M. Leymarie, "Les Redevances seigneuriales en Haute-Avergne"
23. J. Meyer, *Noblesses et Pouvoirs dans l'Europe d'Ancien Régime*, Paris, 1973, p. 251. For a very enlightening regional example, see, by the same author, *La Noblesse bretonne au XVIIIe siècle*, Paris, 1966, 2 vol., p. 651, "Les composantes du revenu foncier de la noblesse."
24. "Let us first of all praise Mr. Cobban," writes G. Lefebvre in the article cited above (note 18), "for the care he has taken in listing the members of the Constituent and the Convention according to their social background, following the example of research of this type that Anglo-Saxon historians, through the impetus given by Namier, have undertaken for the House of Commons. These investigations could go deeper and are recommended to French scholars."
25. Elizabeth L. Eisenstein, "Who intervened in 1788?" A Commentary on *The Coming of the French Revolution,*" *American Historical Review*, LXXI, October, 1956, p. 77; George V. Taylor, "Non-Capitalist Wealth and the Origins of the French Revolution," *ibid.*, *LXXII*, January, 1967, p. 469. See R.R. Palmer, *"Polémique américaine sur le rôle de la bourgeoisie dans la Révolution française,"* *A.H.R.F.*, 1967, p. 368.
26. E. Labrousse, "Voies nouvelles vers une histoire de la bourgeoisie occidentale aux XVIIIe et XIXe siècles," *X Congresso internazionale di scienze storiche, Relazioni*, Florence, 1955, vol. IV, p. 365. Of particular documentary interest are the studies relative to the bourgeoisie in the *Assemblée générale de la Commission centrale... 1939* Commission d'histoire économique et sociale de la Révolution, Besançon, 1942, 2 vol.), vol. I, p. 33; P. Léon, "Recherches sur la bourgeoisie française de province au XVIIIe siècle," *L'Information historique*, 1958, p. 101.
27. See essentially J. Letaconnoux, "Le Comité des députés extraordinaires des manufactures et du commerce et l'oeuvre de la Constituante," *Annales révolutionnaires*, 1913, p. 149; G. Debien, *Les Colons de Saint-Domingue et la Révolution. Essai sur le club Massiac. Août 1789-août 1972*, Paris, 1953.
28. G. Shapiro, "The Many Lives of Georges Lefebvre," *American Historical Review*, LXXII, January, 1967, p. 502.
29. E. Faure, *La Disgrâce de Turgot. 12 mai 1776*, Paris, 1961, coll. "Trente journées qui ont fait la France." See the review of this work by J. Godechot, *A.H.R.F.*, 1962, p. 105.
30. F. Furet and D. Richet, *La Révolution*, vol. I *Des États Généraux au 9 thermidor*, Paris, 1965, vol. II, *Du 9 thermidor au 18 brumaire*, Paris, 1966; new edition in one volume, *La Révolution française*, Paris, 1972. On this work see Cl. Mazauric, "Réflexions sur une nouvelle conception de la Révolution française," *A.H.R.F.*, 1967, p. 339. From the same point of view, see D. Richet, *La France moderne: l'esprit des institutions*, Paris, 1973.
31. D. Richet, "Autour des origines idéologiques lointaines de la Révolution française: élites et despotisme," *Annales E.S.C.*, 1969, p. 1.
32. *Ibid.*, p. 23
33. L. Althusser, *Montesquieu. La politique et l'histoire*, Paris, 1959. "This feudal enemy of despotism became the hero of all the adversaries of the established order. By a strange turn of history, the one who was looking toward the past appeared to open the doors of the future."
34. See *Utopie et Institutions au XVIIIe siècle. Le pragmatisme des Lumières*, textes recueillis par P. Francastel, Paris-La Haye, 1963.
35. J. Meyer, *Nobles et Pouvoirs*..., p. 253
36. "The king wishes that the ancient distinction of the three orders of the State be conserved in its entirety, as essentially connected to the constitution of his kingdom" (Art. I of the Declaration of the king). Cf. *Recueil de documents relatifs aux séances des États Généraux...* under the direction of G. Lefebvre, vol. 1, 2, *La Séance du 23 juin*, Paris, 1962, p. 275.
37. F. Furet and D. Richet, *La Révolution*, p. 106 and p. 120
38. *Ibid.*, p. 270
39. *Ibid.*, p. 358
40. D. Richet, *La France moderne*..., p. 7. "Everything happens as if the events, limited and contingent, of 1789-1793 had imposed a decisive break between a *before* and an*after* ." For the idea of revolution, this author tends to substitute in a significant manner that of transition. See the article quoted above (note 31), "Autours des origines idéologiques de la Révolution française." "On the broad level of economic forces, a slow but revolutionary mutation was operating from the 16th to the 19th century, that is the very history of capitalism, one of the major events of modern times. It can be baptised, if you wish, a bourgeois revolution, but it was a multisecular movement whose decisive stage took place in the second half of the 19th century." (p. 22).
41. See above, note 8
42. On these liberal historians of the Restoration, founders of classical revolutionary historiography and intiators of the social interpretation of the Revolution, see the excellent introduction of C. Jullian to his *Extraits des historiens français du XIXe siècle*, Paris, 1898; G. Lefebvre, *La Naissance de l'historiographie moderne*, Paris, 1971, chap. XI; B. Réizov, *L'Historiographie romantique française. 1815-1830*, Moscow, n.d., chap. VII.

43. *L'Ancien Régime et la Révolution*, edition cited above (note 15). Tocqueville adds: "If it had not taken place, the old social edifice would have notheless fallen everywhere, sooner here, later there; only it would have continued to fall bit by bit instead of collapsing all at once. The Revolution achieved suddenly, by a convulsive and painful effort, without transition, without precaution, without regard, what would have been achieved slowly by itself, in the long run. That was its work." (p. 96.)
44. F. Furet and D. Richet, *La Révolution*, p. 294
45. Quoted by G. Lefebvre, "Réflexions sur l'histoire", *La Pensée*, May-June 1955.
46. See A. Soboul, "Description et Mesure en histoire sociale," *L'Histoire sociale. Sources et méthodes*, Paris, 1967, p. 9.
47. The most recent to date: C. Lucas, "Nobles, Bourgeois and the Origins of the French Revolution," *Past and Present*, n° 60, August 1973.
48. We refer here to the reflections of Hegel on general history and special history (course of 1822 on historiography, *Introduction à la philosophie de l'histoire)*.

CHAPTER 17

1. *Studien über die Revolution*, Berlin, Akademie-Verlag, 1969, p. 62
2. *L'Ancien Régime et la Révolution*, book II, chap. I, ed. 1952, with an introduction by G. Lefebvre, p. 99.
3. *Capital*, vol. III, chap. XX, "Historical view of merchant capital." On the problem of the transition from feudalism to capitalism, cf. *The Transition from Feudalism to Capitalism, A Symposium* by P. M. Sweezy, M. Dobb, H. K. Takahashi, R. Hilton, C. Hill, London, 1954; R. Hilton, "Y eut-il une crise générale de la féodalite?," *Annales, E.S.C.*, 1951, n° 1; G. Procacci, G. Lefebvre and A. Soboul, "Une discussion historique: du feudalisme au capitalisme," *La Pensée*, 1956, n° 65.
4. These are problems posed in particular by G. Lefebvre, "La Révolution française dans l'histoire du monde," *Annales, E.S.C.*, 1948, reprinted in *Études sur la Révolution française*, 1954, 2nd edition, 1963, p. 431.
5. The expression *Ancien Régime* appeared at the end of the year 1789; naturally it is charged with emotional content: there is almost a repudiation in this alliance of words (F. Brunot, *Histoire de la Langue française*, vol. IX, *La Révolution et l'Empire*, p. 621). The expression, consecrated by its use, is historically valid; we understand poorly the obscure reasons why certain historians currently are tending to reject it.
6. On the problems of the French nobility in the 18th century, we will content ourselves with citing one old article: M. Bloch, "Sur le passé de la noblesse française: quelques jalons de recherche," *Annales d'histoire économique et sociale*, 1936, p. 336; and a recent article: A. Goodwin, "The Social Structure and Economic and Political Attitudes of the French Nobility in the Eighteenth Century," International Committee of Historical Sciences, XII Congress, Vienna, 1965, *Rapports, I. Grands thèmes*, p. 356; by the same author, "General Problems and the Diversity of European Nobilities in the Modern Period," *ibid.*, p. 345. We refer to the critical bibliography of J. Meyer, *La Noblesse bretonne au XVIIIe siècle*, Paris, 1966, vol. I, P. XXI.
7. See B. Mousnier, "Les Idées politiques de Fénelon," *XVIIe siecle*, 1951-1952.
8. Boulainvilliers (1658-1722), *Histoire de l'ancien gouvernement de la France, avec XIV lettres historiques sur les parlements ou États généraux* (1722), *Essai sur la noblesse de France contenant une dissertation sur son origine et son abaissement* (1732).
9. *Le Judicium Francorum* reprints an anti-absolutist pamphlet from the time of the Fronde, *Les vertiables maximes du gouvernement de la France justifiées par l'ordre des temps depuis l'établissement de la monarchie jusqu'aux temps présents* (1652). See also, in the same line, a writing circulated in manuscript copies, *Essai historique concernant les droits et prérogatives de la Cour des pairs de France*.
10. See basically book XXX. Cf. L. Althusser, *Montesquieu. La politique et l'histoire*, 1959.
11. We can only refer here to general works: J. Aynard, *La bourgeoisie française*, 1934; B. Groethuysen, *Origines de l'esprit bourgeois en France*, vol. I: *L'Église et la Bourgeoisie*, 1927; F. Borkenau, *Der Uebergang vom feudalen zum burgerlichen Weltbild. Studien zur Geschichte der Philosophie der Manufakturperiode*, 1934; see the remarks of L. Febvre, "Fondations économiques, Superstructure philosophique: une synthèse," *Annales d'histoire économique et sociale*, 1934, p. 369. Of precise documentary interest are the studies relating to the bourgeoisie in *Assemblée générale de la Commission centrale…*, 1939, Commission d'histoire économique et sociale de la Révolution, 1942, vol. I, p. 33; P. Léon, "Recherches sur la bourgeoisie française de province au XVIIIe siecle," *L'Information historique*, 1958, n° 3, p. 101. On the current orientation of research, E. Labrousse, "Voies nouvelles vers une histoire de la bourgeoisie occidentale aux XVIIIe et XIXe siècles," *X Congresso internazionale di scienze storiche… 1955. Relazioni*, Florence, 1955, vol. IV, p. 365.
12. On natural right, an ample bibliography will be found in R. Derathé, *Jean-Jacques Rousseau et la Science politique de son temps*, Paris, 1950. Natural right was developped in the 17th century by Protestant authors, principally jurists—Grotius, Althusius, Hobbes, Pufendorf—certain of whom were then translated and commented on by Barbeyrac et Burlamaqui. The authors of the 17th century were criticized by Rousseau who drew the logical consequences from natural right, by formulating the theory of inalienable and indivisible popular sovereignty.
13. See J. Egret, "L'Aristocratie parlementaire à la fin de l'Ancien Régime," *Revue historique*, July-September 1952, p. 1. Essential are the works of J.-Fr. Bluche, *L'Origine des magistrats du Parlement de Paris au XVIIIe siecle*, 1956, *Les magistrats du Parlement de Paris au XVIIIe siècle. 1715-1771*, 1960.
14. *Qu'est-ce que le Tiers État?* by Em. Sieyes, critical edition by Ed. Champion, Paris, 1888, p. 35.
15. *Oeuvres de Barnave*, published by M. Bérenger de la Drôme, 1843, vol. I, p. 12 and p. 13. The *Introduction à la Révolution française* has been republished by F. Rude, Paris, 1960. In fact, this important text is still awaiting a critical edition.

    Having forcefully affirmed the necessary connection between political institutions and the movement of the economy, Barnave attaches to it the educational movement. "To the degree that the arts, industry and commerce enrich the laboring class of people, impoverish the great landowners and bring the classes closer together by fortune, the progress in education brings them closer by custom and recalls, after a long oblivion, the primitive ideas of equality."

16. The important problem of repurchase of feudal rights and of their abolition has been definitively tackled by Ph. Sagnac, *La Législation civile de la Révolution française*, 1898; in a still valuable sketch, A. Aulard, *La Révolution française et le Régime féodal*, 1919; M. Garaud, *La Révolution et la Propriété foncière*, 1959. But only local or regional monographs would permit the drawing up of a true and complete picture of the partial survival, the vicissitudes and the final disappearance of the feudal regime during the Revolution; let us indicate two classical works, A. Ferradou, *Le Rachat des droits féodaux dans la Gironde. 1790-1793*, 1928; J. Millot, *L'Abolition des droits seigneuriaux dans le département du Doubs et la région comtoise*, 1941. Likewise, on the agrarian riots and the jacqueries which, from the Great Fear to the definitive abolition of feudal rights (July 17, 1793), marked the revolutionary history of the peasantry, we have only fragmentary local studies at our disposal. This history remains to be written.
17. C.-E. Labrousse, *Esquisse du mouvement des prix et des revenus en France au XVIIIe siecle*, Paris, 1933, 2 vol.; *La Crise de l'économie française à la fin de l'Ancien Régime et au début de la Révolution*, Paris, 1944.
18. On the social aspirations of the popular masses, see A. Soboul, *Les sans-culottes parisiens en l'an II*, Paris, 1958, part II, chap. II.
19. On the peasant question, the works of Georges Lefebvre are essential: *Les Paysans du Nord pendant la Révolution française*, 1924, *Questions agraires au temps de la Terreur*, 1932, *La Grande Peur de 1789*, 1932, and the articles appearing and regroupes in *Études sur la Révolution française*, 1954; 2nd edition, 1967: "Répartition de la propriété et de l'exploitation foncières à la fin de l'Ancien Régime," 1928, p. 279; "La Vente des biens nationaux," 1928, p. 307; "La Révolution française et les Paysans", 1932, p. 338.
20. *Op. cit.*, p. 99. "The effect of the Revolution has not been to divide the soil but to liberate it for a moment. All the small landowners were, in effect, severely hampered in the exploitation of their lands and endured many constraints that they were not allowed to deliver themselves from." (p. 102) "If the peasant had not owned the soil, he would have been insensitive to several of the burdens that the feudal system laid on landed property. Of what importance was the tithe to one who was not a farmer? It was imposed on the product of cultivation" (p. 105).
21. M. Leymarie, "Les Redevances foncières seigneuriales en Haute-Auvergne," *Annales historiques de la Révolution francaise*, 1968, n° 3.
22. *L'Ancien Régime et la Révolution*, p. 106
23. G. Lefebvre, "Répartition de la propriété et de l'exploitation foncières à la fin de l'Ancien Régime"
24. The petition of the Parisian section of Sans-Culottes of September 2, 1793 intended to not only limit "the profits of industry and commerce" by general price controls, and limit the extent of agricultural exploitations ("Let no one be able to hold more land to rent than what is needed for a determined quantity of plows"), but to also impose a maximum on wealth. What would it be? The petition does not specify, but makes it clear that it would correspond to the small artisan and shopkeeper property: "Let no one have more than one workshop, or one shop." These radical measures, concludes the Sans-Culottes section, "would make the too great inequality of wealth disappear gradually and increase the number of property owners" (*Bibliothèque nationale*, Lb 40 2140, imp. in-8°, 6 p.).
25. *L'Ancien Régime et la Révolution*, p. 96
26. From the point of view that concerns us here, the essential works are those of Ch. Hill, the true leader of the school: with M. James and E. Rickwoord, *The English Revolution, 1640*, London, 1940, partial reediting, 1949; with E. Dell, *The Good Old Cause*, London, 1949; *The Century of Revolution, 1603-1714*, London, 1961; finally *Society and Puritanism in Pre-Revolutionary England*, London, 1964. For an overview of the problems currently under debate: M.-L. Agostini, *L'Historiographie contemporaine de la Révolution anglaise de 1640*, Diplôme d'études supérieures, Faculté des lettres de Clermont-Ferrand, 1967.
27. Ch. Hill, "La Révolution anglaise du XVIIe siecle. Essai d'interprétation", *Revue historique*, n° 449, 1959, pp. 5-32
28. *Ibid.*, p. 32
29. *Réflexions sur la Révolution française*, translated by J. D'Anglejean, Paris, 1912, p. 52. This work became the gospel of the counter-revolution. Burke set an ending point for social evolution, declaring that the hierarchy of classes was divinely ordained; the French Revolution, by destroying the aristocracy, was destructive of all social order. In this way Burke discerned, as early as 1790, the essential work of the Revolution.
30. From the point of view that concerns us here, see Ch. A. Beard, *Economic Interpretation of the Constitution*, New York, 1913; 2nd ed., 1923; F. Jameson, *The American Revolution considered as a Social Movement*, 1926; 2nd ed., 1940.
31. *De la démocratie en Amérique*, 1836-1839
32. On the theoretical aspects of these problems, see M. Dobb, *Studies in the Development of Capitalism*, London, 1946; H. K. Takahashi, *Shimin Kakumei-no kozô* [Structure of the bourgeois revolution], Tokyo, 1951, reviewed by Ch. Haguenauer, *Revue historique*, n° 434, 1955, p. 345.
33. We must however stress the progress of the economy in the course of the Napoleonic period which was tightly bound to the revolutionary period. See E. Labrousse, "Le Bilan du monde en 1815. Éléments d'un bilan économique: la croissance dans la guerre," Comité international des sciences historiques, XIIth Congress, Vienna, 1965, *Rapports, I. Grands thèmes*, p. 473.
34. *Adresse présentée à la Convention nationale au nom de la section des Gravilliers*, by J. Roux (Archives nationales, W 20, d. 1073, imp. in-8°, p. 12).
35. On this problem in its totality, see A. Soboul, "De l'Ancien Régime à l'empire: problème national et réalités sociales," *L'Information historique*, 1960, pp. 59-64 and 96-104. [This article appears as chapter 13 of this book.]
36. *Moniteur*, vol. VI, p. 239
37. See above for the comparison that must be established between the French Revolution of 1830 and the "respectable" English Revolution of 1688. Both ended up replacing one king with another, without attacking the social structure in any way. In July, 1830, it was a matter of a sort of legal insurrection punishing the violation of the Charter. But the fundamental difference to which the Anglo-Saxons are especially sensitive, is that the Revolution of 1688 was "respectable" because it was provoked by the leaders of the social hierarchy and carried out without the intervention of the popular masses; in France, Charles X was expelled not by a William of Orange, but by the people of Paris, armed behind

barricades. See in this line the review by G. Lefebvre, in the *Annales historiques de la Révolution française*, 1955, p. 176, of the book by L. Pinkham, *William III and the Respectable Revolution*, Cambridge, Mass., 1954.

38. *Lendemains*, n° 12, November, 1978
39. See A. Soboul, "Le Bilan du monde en 1815. Esquisse d'un bilan social," Comité intrnational des sciences historiques, XIIth Congress, Vienna, 1965, *Rapports. I. Grands thèmes*, p. 517.
40. *Journal politique national*, n° 19, end of August 1789. The Constituents "thus declared, to the whole universe, that all men are born and remain free, that one man could not be more than another man, and 100 other discoveries of this nature, that they congratulate themselves for having been the first to reveal to the world, indeed ridiculing England philosophically for not having known how to begin their Constitution in 1688."
41. *Moniteur*, vol. VIII, p. 426
42. *Moniteur*, vol. IX, p. 143
43. *Moniteur*, vol. XV, p. 705
44. *Moniteur*, vol. XXV, p. 92. "Absolute equality is an illusion." Boissy d'Anglass continued: "in order for it to exist, it would be necessary to have complete equality of mind, virtue, physical strength, education, and fortune among all men." Singular continuity of views from the Girondins to the Thermidoriens.
45. *Moniteur*, vol. XIV, p. 637. See G. Lefebvre, "Sur la pensée politique de Robespierre," *Études sur la Révolution française*, 2nd ed., p. 144, excerpts of two speeches delivered on October 15, 1933, on the occasion of the unveiling of the bust of Robespierre in the town hall of Arras, published in *Annales historiques de la Révolution française*, 1933, p. 484 and 492.
46. *Oeuvres* de Maximilien Robespierre, vol. IX, Discours, Part 4, p. 459.
47. Speaking in the name of the commissioners of the primary assemblies, Félix Lepeletier declared to the Convention on August 20, 1793: "It is not enough for the French Republic to be founded on equality; it is still necessary that the laws and customs of its citizens tend, in perfect harmony, to eliminate the inequality of enjoyment; it is necessary that a happy existence be assured to all French people" (*Journal de la Montagne*, August 21, 1793).
48. On this subject, see J. Belin, *La Logique d'une idée-force. L'idée d'utilité sociale pendant la Révolution française 1789-1792*, Paris, 1939, and the observations of G. Lefebvre, *A.H.R.F.*, 1947, p. 381.
49. The stage of Babouvist studies can be seen in *Babeuf (1760-1797), Buonarroti (1760-1837), Pour le deuxième centenaire de leur naissance*, publication of the Société des Etudes robespierristes, Nancy, 1961; Cl. Mazauric, *Babeuf et la Conspiration pour l'Égalité*, Paris, 1962; *Babeuf et les problèmes du babouvisme*, collection of articles under the direction of A. Soboul, Paris, 1963; V. M. Daline, *Gracchus Babeuf before and during the French Revolution. 1785-1794*, Moscow, 1963, in Russian; reviewed by A. Soboul, *Revue d'histoire moderne*, 1966; V. M. Daline, A. Saita, A. Soboul, *Inventaire des manuscrits et imprimés de Babeuf*, Paris, 1966.
50. M. Dommanget, *Pages choisies de Babeuf*, Paris, 1935, p. 103
51. *Ibid.*, p. 313
52. Last edition, Paris, 1957, preface by G. Lefebvre

Albert Soboul, the man and the historian

Albert Soboul was an eminent scholar whose work heightened and deepened France's and the world's understanding of the great French Revolution which, as he loved to say, "ushered in the contemporary world." Born on April 27, 1914, in Ammi-Moussa in Oranie (Algeria) into a colonist family of small farmers originally from the Ardèche region in France, Albert Soboul became an orphan during the First World War and ward of the state from early childhood. He and his sister were raised in Nîmes by their aunt, the famous teacher Marie Soboul, who was the director of the Normal School for young girls and in whose memory a school was founded in Revolution Square in Nîmes. In these secular and exemplarily republican surroundings, Albert Soboul received an education dominated by the highest virtues of the democratic spirit and civic devotion, a Rousseauist formation also marked by a respect for books that forge a soul, notably those by the great historians, Michelet and Mathiez.

After studying at the lycée in Nîmes, then at the famous Louis-le-Grand school in Paris, A. Soboul was admitted to advanced work in history in 1938; he immediately received a scholarship for a year's research that allowed him to begin his exploration of the French Revolution after a short disappointing association with the grat medievalist Marc Bloch. Called up as a simple soldier in 1939, he served in the horse-drawn artillery; in 1940, with a battery and six horses, he was led on a long retreat from northern to southwestern France, never engaging in battle. This humiliating experience had a lasting effect upon him. After his discharge, he became professor at the Joffre lycée in Montpelier. A member of the Communist Party since 1932, Soboul was arrested during a patriotic demonstration on July 14, 1942 and immediately fired by the "pseudo-government of Vichy" as he called it. For two years, while participating in clandestine activities, he made a living from various odd jobs. With the Liberation, he was reappointed professor in Paris, teaching first at the Marcellin-Berthelot lycée, then at the Henri-IV lycée. After two years of unpaid leave, from 1946-1948, he was again appointed professor at Henri-IV. From October 1950 to October 1953, he held a post at the National Center of Scientific Research, then received an appointment as professor at the Jeanson de Sailly lycée, then again at Henri-IV where he stayed through the defense of his doctoral dissertation (November 29, 1958) until he was named as director of teaching at the Humanities Department at Clermont-Ferrand University on September 28, 1960. He became a tenured professor at this university on November 1, 1962, and in 1967 was named to the chair of the History of the French Revolution at the Sorbonne, replacing Marcel Reinhard in this prestigious position held over the years by Aulard, Stignac, Mathiez and Lefebvre. Albert Soboul devoted himself to his work as teacher, historian and director of research until his death. He hoped to continue teaching two more years after his retirement in 1982, in order to finish directing the theses of several of his students; he had a right to ask for this extension as compensation for the withdrawal of his teaching contract by the Vichy Government, thus finishing his career with the two years that a traitorous government had stolen from him. But death prevented him from winning back those lost years.

A scholar known throughout the world, Albert Soboul taught and gave lectures in Latin America as well as the United States, in Great Britain and Australia, in the People's

Republic of China as well as Japan, in the Soviet Union and Germany, throughout Europe, Africa and the Middle East.

He was a corresponding member of the Academy of Sciences in Budapest and in Berlin, and an honorary doctor at Karl Marx University in Leipzig, Lomonosov University in Moscow and at several others in Australia and America. For more than a quarter of a century, the name of Albert Soboul honored French science and historiography. Such were the work and the man.

Claude Mazauric, Historian
Director of Éditions sociales.

Adapted for this edition by International Publishers